Team-Based Learning in the
Social Sciences and Humanities

Team-Based Learning in the Social Sciences and Humanities

Group Work That Works to Generate Critical Thinking and Engagement

Edited by
Michael Sweet
and
Larry K. Michaelsen

Sty/us

STERLING, VIRGINIA

Published by Stylus Publishing, LLC
22883 Quicksilver Drive
Sterling, Virginia 20166-2102

Library of Congress Cataloging-in-Publication-Data
Team-based learning in the social sciences and humanities :
group work that works to generate critical thinking and
engagement / edited by Michael Sweet and Larry K.
Michaelsen.—1st ed.
   p. cm.
Includes bibliographical references and index.
ISBN 978-1-57922-609-1 (cloth : alk. paper)
ISBN 978-1-57922-610-7 (pbk. : alk. paper)
ISBN 978-1-57922-611-4 (library networkable e-edition)
ISBN 978-1-57922-612-1 (consumer e-edition)
1. Social sciences—Study and teaching (Higher)
2. Humanities—Study and teaching (Higher)   3. Team
learning approach in education.   4. Critical thinking—Study
and teaching (Higher)   I. Sweet, Michael, 1970–
II. Michaelsen, Larry K., 1943–
H62.T288   2012
300.71′1—dc23   2011033146

13-digit ISBN: 978-1-57922-609-1 (cloth)
13-digit ISBN: 978-1-57922-610-7 (paper)
13-digit ISBN: 978-1-57922-611-4 (library networkable
e-edition)
13-digit ISBN: 978-1-57922-612-1 (consumer e-edition)

Printed in the United States of America

All first editions printed on acid free paper
that meets the American National Standards Institute
Z39-48 Standard.

Bulk Purchases

Quantity discounts are available for use in workshops and
for staff development.
Call 1-800-232-0223

First Edition, 2012

10   9   8   7   6   5   4   3

We would like to thank the contributors to this volume for their patience and flexibility, but mostly for their passion and commitment to make the world a better place one classroom at a time. For all the team-based learners in the social sciences and humanities who do not appear in this book, we know you are unsung heroes and we want to support you however we can. We would also like to thank our wives, Laura and Chris, for their graceful acceptance of the demands put upon us and them by what we feel is a calling to share Team-Based Learning with the world. Finally, we'd like to thank Lucas Horton and Joseph Rodriguez for their input on backward design and Michelita Matthews for her editorial support at the 11th hour.

Contents

Introduction

Many of us in the social sciences and humanities began our careers by sitting in large classrooms and listening to lectures. Fortunately, these sips of exposure inspired us, and we hung on through introductory courses, finding our way into smaller and more engaging upper-division and graduate seminars. In these courses, we were asked to make sense of the material on our own terms, to use what we were learning to make decisions relevant to the practices of the discipline, to mix our ideas with those of our teachers and peers. In those classes, we connected—to new abilities within ourselves, to our disciplines, to our fellow students, and to the teachers who created these opportunities for growth.

Now we stand on the other side of the classroom and look out at increasingly large collections of students and wonder if it is possible to bring the creative—even fiery—learning experience of the small class to the large lecture setting. Is it possible to put our students into the material in ways that most nourished us in our upper-division and graduate seminars? Is it possible that we don't have to settle for "exposing" students to material and hoping that a handful in each class hangs on, like we did, to finally wash up on the shores of our more engaging upper-division seminars?

In the face of these virtuous desires, we get understandably frustrated by how many students won't participate, come unprepared, or even skip class entirely except when there are tests. "We are smart people"—we say to ourselves—"and we are teaching smart students." Surely there has got to be a better way.

Perhaps we experiment with new approaches to teaching, exploring our way through active learning techniques including various forms of group work. When trying group work for the first time, we wade among the groups in class hoping to listen in on clusters of engaged critical thinkers, only to discover a whole new bouquet of problems. Group conversations quickly turn to football and parties. Hard-working students must suffer while freeloaders are happy to let others do the heavy lifting. Groups are unbalanced and at the end of the semester produce work little better than the best students in the group could have done individually.

In group-work experiences like this, students may engage with each other but not with the content and certainly not with any kind of critical thinking. It can feel like an exercise in futility. We can be tempted to throw up our hands and conclude that group work doesn't work.

But the longing persists. When asked what they want more of in their classrooms, teachers in the social sciences and humanities are quick to say critical thinking and engagement. These teachers want a classroom full of motivated students who not only apply their mental faculties to the discipline but do so with a focused, respectful, and energetic dialogue.

Creating that classroom experience is what this book is about.

PART ONE

Foundations

CHAPTER 1

Critical Thinking and Engagement

Creating Cognitive Apprenticeships
With Team-Based Learning

Michael Sweet and Larry K. Michaelsen

The circumstances in which Larry Michaelsen began experimenting with Team-Based Learning may feel familiar to you. On the one hand, our classes keep getting larger. On the other hand, we want to see more critical thinking and student engagement. But beyond a we-know-it-when-we-see-it intuitive sense of critical thinking and engagement, what do we mean when we use those words? In this chapter, we explore these ideas and describe in practical terms how the four components of Team-Based Learning provide a frame in which the artistry of your instruction can cultivate a classroom full of engaged critical thinkers.

In 1979 Larry Michaelsen taught business management courses of about 40 students each, and he used class time mostly for in-depth discussions about case studies. The classes were small enough that he could count on a sufficient number of students to come prepared and be motivated by the lively give-and-take discussions about significant problems. In this format, he could hear his students thinking critically about the material, and he felt it was really helping them learn to think like business management scholars.

In a single stroke of policy change, however, his course enrollments jumped from 40 to 120, and large classes present an array of challenges to a mostly discussion-based class. Students can feel intimidated by a sea of strangers, anxious about appearing overeager (the "gunner" or teacher's pet), and anonymous enough to feel comfortable coming to class with little or no preclass preparation. Faced with a situation where discussion seems to be out of the question, many teachers in large classrooms simply resort to lecturing. But Michaelsen was unwilling to give up the engaged critical thinking he had found so satisfying in his smaller classes. By experimenting and adding elements over time, he began developing an instructional strategy to which many teachers have since contributed and that we now know as Team-Based Learning (TBL). TBL consists of basic elements, each of which emerged as relevant for practical reasons.

First, in a moment of desperation, Michaelsen tried an experiment to help motivate students to read assigned materials before coming to class. Students always read right before a test, he thought, so why not begin the unit with a small test? Furthermore, because his academic discipline stresses the importance of group communication skills, he thought that perhaps letting students take a test on their own and then take the same test again in groups could give them insight into differences between the individual experience and the group experience of the same task.

He assigned the readings for the first unit, gave the individual test, collected the answer sheets, and held his breath as he listened in during the group test. Much to his relief and delight, he heard students giving each other the very lectures he had hoped to avoid giving himself. They were deeply engaged in the content, thinking critically about evidence from various perspectives, distinguishing among shades of meaning, consequences, and implications. They were sharing the answers they had given as individuals and comparing their rationales for choosing one answer over another. Importantly, they were also developing into cohesive social units in the process—transforming from groups into teams. Having borne unexpected fruit, this experiment in motivating students to prepare grew over time into a practice we now call the Readiness Assurance Process (RAP): an individual Readiness Assurance Test (iRAT) followed immediately by a team Readiness Assurance Test (tRAT). With a little extra tweaking, readiness assurance became the first of the four practical components of TBL.

Knowing from the scholarship in his own discipline that relationships in groups develop and become richer over time, Michaelsen decided to keep students in the *same* teams all semester so these relationships could continue deepening and becoming more effective for learning. Indeed, as they got to know each other, the students became better able to argue their way to the right answers on the tRATs. This practice of forming students into permanent teams also underwent some important fine-tuning over time, ultimately growing into a second pillar of how we practice TBL today.

To address the perennial problem of freeloaders in these permanent groups, Larry decided to add a mechanism that allowed students to actually weigh in on the performance of their teammates and do so in a way that had a real impact on their final grades. This practice, generally known as peer evaluation, fit into the evolving system and grew into the third major component of TBL.

Michaelsen's teaching practice had always included assignments that forced students to make the kinds of decisions they would face in the future when applying the material in a job setting. He felt that grappling with the specifics of a situation in which one's course material is useful gives students critically important experience applying that material in real contexts. Over the years, he and many others learned a great deal about how to effectively design application-based assignments, and these methods became the fourth principle component of TBL. These four elements—readiness assurance, properly used (permanent) teams, peer evaluation, and application exercises—have developed over time into a synergistic system that has exploded out of the business management classroom and found implementation in virtually every discipline around the world.

In this chapter, we describe the four elements of TBL working together as a frame. We chose the metaphor of a frame for two reasons. First, TBL is like the frame around a piece of artwork because the purpose of that frame is not to draw attention to itself but rather to provide structure and focus to what it surrounds. Second, the frame of a house consists of several mutually supporting elements that combine to create a structure that none of them could create alone. Each of the four pieces of TBL is essential, but within the frame they create, you bring your art to the nature of the experience. In fact, if you switch to TBL, there's no reason you can't keep using many of the materials you already use. Every teacher is different, and every implementation of TBL is a creative act. The diversity and size of the community of teachers using TBL today is a testament to that fact.

But before we get into the practical mechanics of how TBL works, let's step back for a minute and consider two laudable goals: critical thinking and engagement. These words arise again and again in conversation with teachers about what they want for their students. But what do those enticing words really mean?

CRITICAL THINKING: WHAT IS IT?

It's safe to say we all want our students to become better critical thinkers. Most of us have an intuitive sense for critical thinking—we know it when we see it, like Michaelsen did as he listened to his students taking their first team tests. But beyond that general intuitive sense, what constitutes critical thinking? What elements do we seek to cultivate if we want to develop our students' critical thinking abilities?

The literature on critical thinking goes all the way back to Socrates, though much contemporary scholarship on critical thinking in education builds on a study by Glaser (1941) in which he identified three aspects of critical thinking: a thoughtful attitude or disposition, a range of reasoning skills, and the ability to apply those skills. Later scholars, such as Paul (1995) and Halpern (2003), added a fourth element: a habit of reflecting upon one's own thinking to continually improve it. Halpern is a former president of the American Psychology Association, and her book *Thought and Knowledge* brings a great deal of empirical evidence to bear in validation of this four-part framework. As a result, the critical thinking framework we have found the most useful consists of four major elements:

1. A critical thinking attitude
2. The ability to use specific critical thinking skills
3. The ability to apply those skills in new contexts
4. Habits of reflection upon one's own thinking

To lay the foundation for later discussions about how TBL cultivates these four elements of critical thinking, let's unpack each of them briefly.

Critical Thinking Attitude

According to Halpern (2003), a critical thinking attitude is a habitual willingness or commitment to engage in purposeful deliberation about claims or ideas rather than simply accepting them at face value. It is the foundation of critical thinking behavior and consists of the willingness to (a) engage in and persist at a complex task, (b) use plans and suppress impulsive activity, (c) remain flexible or open minded, (d) abandon nonproductive strategies, and (e) remain aware of social realities (such as the need to seek consensus or compromise) so that thoughts can become actions. Once these pieces are in place—once students are motivated to think critically—then they are ready to acquire specific thinking skills.

Ability to Use Specific Critical Thinking Skills

Most authors agree that critical thinking is an umbrella concept comprising many specific skills, but ideas about which skills belong under the umbrella vary from author to author. Paul and Elder (2008) described the critical thinker as one who raises vital questions and problems, formulates them clearly and precisely, gathers and assesses relevant information, then uses abstract ideas to interpret that information and draw well-reasoned conclusions. The critical thinker then tests those conclusions against relevant criteria, thinks open-mindedly within alternative systems of thought, recognizes assumptions as well as implications and consequences, and communicates effectively with others. In contrast, Halpern (2003) used somewhat more technical language. In her view, critical thinking includes deductive inference, argument analysis, hypothesis testing, understanding probability, decision making, problem solving, and creative thinking. Clearly, there is a great deal of overlap between these taxonomies, but to the classroom teacher, teasing out differences at this level can feel like nit-picking. The point here is to identify precisely the intellectual skills we want our students to acquire in our classrooms and to use our content as the landscape where these skills will be learned and used.

The good news is that we do not need to neglect our content and start teaching classes exclusively about how to think critically. In fact, not only can we teach critical thinking skills in the contexts of our disciplines, but it works best when we do. A meta-analysis of the research on critical thinking instruction found that critical thinking skills are actually best taught alongside or in combination with concrete disciplinary subject matter (Abrami et al., 2008). Across the 117 studies included in this analysis, subject matter courses with explicitly stated critical thinking learning goals had greater pre/post–critical thinking effect sizes than critical thinking courses whose only goal was to teach critical thinking with no specific disciplinary subject matter.

Ability to Apply Critical Thinking Skills in New Contexts

What originally was referred to as the ability to apply critical thinking skills in new contexts, cognitive psychologists now call *transfer*. Regardless of the label used, as teachers we clearly want to avoid filling our students' heads with inert knowledge, that is, knowledge that one has no sense of when or how to use. Alfred North Whitehead first described inert knowledge in 1929, and it stands in marked contrast to knowledge that is easily retrieved and used to guide one's actions in the moment. To learn to do this, Halpern (2003) argues that students require *structure training* where they learn the important cues in a situation in which a given thinking skill is appropriate. This way, they'll be able to recognize those features in new contexts and be prompted to use the right thinking skill at the right time. As you'll see in later pages, TBL is built from the ground up with the goal of application and transfer in mind.

Habits of Reflection Upon One's Own Thinking

Finally, having acquired a critical thinking attitude, learned some critical thinking skills, and applied those in new contexts, good critical thinkers are "brave enough to risk being wrong, and wise enough to realize that much can be learned from errors and failed solutions" (Nelson, 2005, p. xiv). Simply put, good critical thinkers will think about their own thinking, which educational research calls *metacognition*. In TBL, team experiences are designed not only to push students into moments of metacognitive reflection but to do so in conversation with their teammates as the team pursues consensus on a specific question, thereby making various kinds of thinking explicit and open to exploration by the members of the team. As these kinds of thinking increasingly approximate the kinds of thinking common to your discipline, your students can more accurately be considered *cognitive apprentices* to your field—a notion we explore in the following section.

To an experienced teacher, this four-part framework of critical thinking feels comprehensive; it includes motivation, specific thinking skills, the ability to transfer those skills, and habits of reflection to keep the process in constant evolution. As teachers we are powerless to help our students learn to think more effectively unless we are able to see and hear their thinking. Once we know whether and how they are actively engaged with the content, we can more fully diagnose and participate in their development as thinkers.

How then can we use classroom time to best stimulate that engagement? How can we organize classroom activities to give students the kind of intellectual participation in our fields that will not only reveal their thinking to us, but also help them firmly grasp—and make use of—the intellectual tools vital to our disciplines?

ENGAGEMENT AS COGNITIVE APPRENTICESHIP

Barkely (2010) explores engagement as a process that begins at the intersection of motivation and active learning:

> Motivation and active learning work together synergistically, and as they interact, they contribute to incrementally increase student engagement. Rather than a Venn diagram where engagement is the area of overlap between active learning and motivation,

thereby limiting the influence of each, engagement may be better described as a double helix in which active learning and motivation are spirals working together synergistically, building in intensity, and creating a fluid and dynamic phenomenon that is greater than the sum of their individual effects. (p. 7)

This description is not only precise but poetic, and we agree completely with it as far as it goes. However, we believe much of what is nourishing for the teacher when students are engaged is what the students are actually engaged in. In other words, it is not engagement on its own we are after; it is engagement in the practice of our disciplines. When students are engaged in exploring the intellectual and emotional terrain that has so shaped our own lives, then the experience is transformative for everyone involved.

For this reason, we believe a more robust way to think about engagement is in terms of apprenticeship. For centuries, apprenticeship has been understood as an early step in mastering a trade. For example, a traditional blacksmith's apprentice may have started out sweeping the shop and stoking the furnace but worked up to handling a hammer and tongs and eventually making his or her own unique contributions to the blacksmithing world.

Today the idea of cognitive apprenticeship has taken hold to describe instructional practices that involve students in learning by doing, when the doing involves learning how to think in certain ways (Collins, Brown, & Newman, 1989). Lave and Wenger (1991) described apprenticeship activities as "legitimate peripheral participation" in a community of practice (p. 29), and characterized learning as an increase in the level of that participation. In our cases, the communities of practice are our disciplines, and our challenge is to build courses in which class time can mostly consist of giving students legitimate participation (however peripheral) in the intellectual practices of our disciplines. In TBL this means equipping students to make the kinds of decisions we make in our disciplines and letting them practice doing so.

Covering content is a fundamentally different instructional act from requiring students to use that content. This is illustrated in Figure 1.1 and Figure 1.2, which provide an example of what the difference between covering and using content might look like in a sociology class.

In one classroom students are listening to lectures and taking end-of-unit tests, while in the other students are applying course concepts to make and justify discipline-based decisions. Critiquing policies to determine their theoretical perspectives can much more clearly be considered legitimate peripheral participation in the field of sociology than the acts of passively listening to lectures and taking tests. Lecturing exposes students to sociology, but application activities get them *thinking like a sociologist*.

For many of us, this is a new way of thinking about how we use class time. As students, we were exposed to content mostly by reading, listening to lectures, taking tests, and writing papers. Of those four activities, we probably learned the most from writing papers because it required us to engage our own thinking and start making decisions based upon our understanding of the field. But not every class is a writing class, and as class sizes grow, paper assignments become increasingly unrealistic.

FIGURE 1.1
Covering Course Content in a Sociology Class

Teacher covers the fundamental differences between structuralist and critical schools of thought.

1. Students hear a lecture on the evolution of the structuralist school of sociological thought.
2. Students next hear a lecture on the evolution of the critical school of sociological thought.
3. Students then hear a lecture that compares/contrasts the two schools of thought in terms of *structure* and *agency*. This lecture gives examples of how the two perspectives might describe the problem of homelessness in America and go about addressing it in terms of funding and measurement.
4. At the end of the unit, students are tested on their understanding of the histories of and difference between the two schools of thought.

FIGURE 1.2
Using Course Content in a Sociology Class

Students evaluate media coverage and public policy using structuralist and critical schools of thought.

1. Given a *Newsweek* article on homelessness in America, students must attribute to the author a primarily structuralist or critical point of view by evaluating how the article describes structure and agency in the experience of America's homeless.
2. Given three proposed homelessness intervention programs, students critique each program by analyzing their funding sources and performance measures to decide which program the *Newsweek* author would most likely support.
3. In each case, students turn in short (half-page) written rationales for their choice and are graded on their use of supporting evidence from course readings: relevance, specificity, fidelity (i.e., not an out-of-context sound bite), and clarity.

It can be a new and surprisingly humbling experience to realize you do not have a clear idea of how you want students to actually use the material you expect them to master in your courses. In fact, many of us have become so focused on covering the content it can be very hard to even start thinking about how we want students to use it. Fortunately, there are some very practical ideas for breaking out of the content rut and defining much deeper learning goals.

First, A Useful Menu of Verbs

Bloom's (1956) taxonomy of instructional objectives is one of the most practical pieces of educational scholarship around. It breaks down into six levels the kinds of thinking we want our students to be able to do, and offers specific verbs we can use to start writing instructional objectives toward these ends. The term *instructional objectives* is a bit too jargony for us, so from here on out, let's just call them *learning goals*. The taxonomy has since been revised by Anderson and Krathwohl (2001) and is roughly hierarchical, proceeding from the simplest and most basic learning goal (remember) to the most complex and sophisticated form (create).

Figure 1.3 is a summary of these levels and verbs. Go ahead and skim over it from top to bottom to get a sense of verb-based instructional objectives and maybe get some ideas for what learning goals in your own class could look like. Think of this as a menu you can pick and choose items from that feel right to you.

When planning a TBL course, one generates clusters of these learning goals to form between five and seven units that unfold sequentially over the course of a term. For example, the sociology activity described in Figure 1.2 requires students to attribute and critique the writing in a *Newsweek* article, using their knowledge of differences between structuralist and critical schools of thought, so this activity may be one of several that contain a unit on structuralism versus critical theory. That unit could be one of, say, six units in the overall length of the course.

Zooming Out: The Language of Backward Design

After reviewing the menu of practical, useful verbs to use when designing your learning goals, let's zoom out a bit and survey a useful way to organize those verbs and goals.

Understanding by Design by Wiggins and McTighe (2005) has contributed greatly to the thinking and tool sets of teachers around the world. The book describes a system for mapping out the journey that students can take as cognitive apprentices, going deeper into a discipline, step by step. We briefly summarize their system here and highly recommend their book as well as their *Understanding by Design Professional Development Workbook* (McTighe & Wiggins, 2004).

Wiggins and McTighe (1998) coined the term *backward design* to describe the process of deciding from the outset specifically what we want our students to be able to do with course material, and the process of designing backward from learning goals instead of forward from teaching goals. The authors offer a practical system for developing one's learning goals using the following six increasingly specific prompts, shown in Figure 1.4 on page 15, which we summarize and then explore through example:

1. What are the *big ideas* in your course?
2. What specifically do you want students to *understand* about those ideas?
3. What could count as *evidence* of that understanding?
4. What *performance tasks* can produce that evidence?
5. What *criteria* can you use to judge the quality of that evidence?
6. What do students need to *know* to perform those tasks which produce that evidence?

FIGURE 1.3
The Cognitive Process Dimension of Bloom's Revised Taxonomy of Learning Objectives

---

1. Remember: Retrieve relevant knowledge from long-term memory.

Recognize—Locate knowledge in long-term memory that is consistent with presented material (e.g., recognize the dates of important events in U.S. history)

Recall—Retrieve relevant knowledge from long-term memory (e.g., recall the dates of important events in U.S. history)

2. Understand: Construct meaning from instructional messages, including oral, written, and graphic communication.

Interpret—Change from one form of representation to another (e.g., paraphrase important speeches or documents)

Exemplify—Find a specific example or illustration of a concept or principle (e.g., give examples of various artistic painting styles)

Classify—Determine that something belongs to a category (e.g., classify observed or described cases of mental disorders)

Summarize—Abstract a general theme or major point(s) (e.g., write a short summary of events portrayed in a video)

Infer—Draw a logical conclusion from presented information (e.g., infer grammatical rules from examples in a foreign language)

Compare—Detect correspondences between two ideas, objects, and the like (e.g., compare historical events to contemporary situations)

Explain—Construct a cause-and-effect model of a system (e.g., explain the causes of important 18th-century events in France)

3. Apply: Carry out or use a procedure in a given situation.

Execute—Apply a procedure to a familiar task (e.g., divide one whole number by another whole number, each with multiple digits)

Implement—Apply a procedure to an unfamiliar task (e.g., determine which statistical test is appropriate for a given data set)

4. Analyze: Break material into its constituent parts and detect how the parts relate to one another and to an overall structure or purpose.

Differentiate—Distinguish relevant from irrelevant parts or important from unimportant parts of presented material (e.g., distinguish between relevant and irrelevant data in a case-based word problem)

Organize—Determine how elements fit or function within a structure (e.g., structure evidence in a historical description into evidence for or against a particular historical explanation)

Attribute—Determine a point of view, bias, values, or intent underlying presented material (e.g., determine the author's political point of view for a given essay)

FIGURE 1.3 (Continued)

---

5. Evaluate: Make judgments based on criteria and standards.

Check—Detect inconsistencies or fallacies within a process or product, determine whether a process or product has internal consistency, detect the effectiveness of a procedure as it is being implemented (e.g., determine whether a given conclusion follows from the supporting evidence)

Critique—Detect inconsistencies between a product and external criteria, determine whether a product has external consistency, detect the appropriateness of a procedure for a given problem (e.g., decide which of two methods is the best way to solve a problem)

6. Create: Put elements together to form a new, coherent whole.

Generate—Come up with alternative hypotheses based on criteria (e.g., generate hypotheses to account for a given set of observations)

Plan—Devise a procedure for accomplishing some task (e.g., outline a research paper on a given topic)

Produce—Invent a product (e.g., complete a research paper on a given topic)

Note: Adapted from *A Taxonomy for Learning, Teaching and Assessing: A Revision of Bloom's Taxonomy of Educational Objectives* (pp. 63–91), by L. W. Anderson & D. R. Krathwohl (Eds.), 2001, Boston, MA: Allyn & Bacon.

Now let's look at each of these six steps a bit more closely.

What are the big ideas in your course? Big ideas are abstract and transferable concepts, themes, or processes at the heart of a subject or topic, for example, confidence, error, validity, reliability, and deception. These ideas are abstract enough to be useful across disciplines from statistics to biology to literature. A handful of big ideas for your course can serve as organizers for the more concrete aspects of the course and can help you prioritize what and what not to teach (since we can't teach everything).

What specifically do you want students to understand about those ideas? Understandings are where you import the big ideas into your specific context. For example, some understandings in a statistics course might be

- Type I and Type II errors can lead to inaccurate conclusions,
- statistics can be presented in ways that are misleading,
- sampling procedures can affect validity, and
- a confidence interval indicates the reliability of a significant finding.

What could count as evidence of that understanding? How can students demonstrate they have grasped these understandings? This is where you use the verbs in Bloom's taxonomy (Anderson & Krathwohl, 2001; Bloom, 1956) to operationalize the construct of learning as you want it to occur in your classroom. A teacher might decide evidence from the students would count as their truly having grasped the understandings in the list in the second step. To continue with our statistics example, examples of this evidence would include:

- Appropriately selecting a statistical test for a set of data,
- Correctly interpreting a statistical analysis,
- Accurately evaluating the skew and kurtosis of a distribution, and
- Defensibly arguing whether a given statistical interpretation is misleading.

What performance tasks can produce that evidence? Performance tasks require students to put the intellectual tools of your discipline to use. Ideally, they consist of some scenario describing a kind of problem your discipline addresses in the real

FIGURE 1.4
The Iterative Process of Backward Design

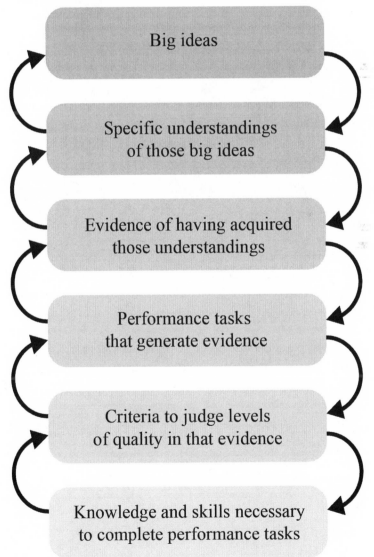

world. Continuing with our statistics example, a teacher might give the students the following problem:

> A newspaper article suggests that elementary students who have Internet access at home receive lower standardized test scores than students who do not. Read the article and the accompanying figures. Describe how the statistical information presented in the article may be used to mislead the reader. Explain any potential problems you see with the statistical procedures used.

What criteria are useful to judge the quality of the evidence students produce? To really evaluate whether students are using course concepts well, one must put forethought into how to evaluate what the students produce. For example, a simple scoring guide like Figure 1.5 (also called a *rubric*) might help make that determination.

What do students need to know to perform those tasks? Finally we come to the last step in backward design, which is where traditional design begins: What specifically do students need to read, hear, see, or experience for them to produce evidence of their having grasped the discipline's understandings? In other words, what do they need to know first? Having decided precisely what you want students to make of the material, you may find yourself assigning only selective page ranges in the textbook or assembling a more robust reading packet than before because now your reading assignments are customized and targeted at the specific learning goals you have developed for your students.

We have found the backward design process to be iterative. Though we may begin designing a course with some big ideas and understandings in mind, as we identify what would count as evidence of understanding and design performance tasks to produce that evidence, the big ideas and understandings evolve. It is best for us to allow ourselves the freedom to move back and forth through the steps of backward design, as the overall design of the course comes into focus.

Even with Bloom's taxonomy (Anderson & Krathwohl, 2001; Bloom, 1956) and the backward design process (Wiggins and McTighe, 2005) in hand, identifying the

FIGURE 1.5
Sample Scoring Guide for a Performance Task

Criteria	Very good	Acceptable	Poor
Describe misleading information	Accurately identifies all misleading information presented and misleading absences of information.	Accurately identifies either misleading information or misleading absences of information.	Accurately identifies neither misleading information nor misleading absences of information.
Describe problems with procedures used	Correctly identifies incorrect test for data type used and sampling issues.	Correctly identifies incorrect test for data type used or sampling issues.	Correctly identifies neither incorrect test for data type used nor sampling issues.

clusters of things you want your students to do with your course content can be hard to do by yourself. Models of learning goals written by others are often helpful, and Sunay Palsole (Chapter 14) and Ronnie Chamberlain (Chapter 17) offer excellent examples of learning goals they use in their classes. Further, designing learning goals can be a great opportunity to brainstorm with a colleague or fellow teacher—in fact, working together on something like this can make it quite fun, turning a potentially daunting task into a creative challenge you enjoy together.

If you do not have easy access to someone you'd enjoy working with on this kind of thing, the Team-Based Learning Collaborative (TBLC) is full of energetic and creative teachers in every discipline.[1] We know how hard it can be to make this shift to TBL, and we are eager to support new folks in any way we can. Post a message on the TBL Listserv, and you will find you are most decidedly not alone.

As we conclude this section on engagement, it is useful to return to the notion of cognitive apprenticeship as legitimate peripheral participation in one's discipline. The learning objectives you identify and organize into clusters to form the units of your course are the forms of legitimate peripheral participation you are providing your students. It would be ideal if an archeologist could bring an excavation into every classroom, or a political scientist could bring members of a political resistance group into every classroom for students to interview. These experiences would give students opportunities to learn the many motor and social skills involved in professional fieldwork in these disciplines. Of course, these kinds of activities are impossible for countless practical reasons. However, we can give students practice in making the kinds of decisions that professionals in our disciplines make when confronted with meaningful and challenging problems. In the classroom, we are training cognitive apprentices.

We add one final note about apprenticeship to reassure those who might resist thinking of their undergraduate students as apprentices. For many, the archetypal "master-apprentice" relationship can imply a great deal of individualized time and attention from the master. As class sizes continue to grow, this perceived ingredient of apprenticeship can be increasingly off putting. We just don't have the time to personally mentor each and every student as individual apprentices.

However, Lave and Wenger's (1991) cross-cultural study of different kinds of apprenticeship (midwives, tailors, quartermasters, butchers, and recovering alcoholics) reveal the opposite to be true:

> In apprenticeship opportunities for learning are, more often than not, given structure by work practices instead of by strongly asymmetrical master–apprentice relations. Under these circumstances learners may have a space of "benign community neglect" in which to configure their own learning relations with other apprentices. . . . It seems typical of apprenticeship that apprentices learn mostly in relation with other apprentices. (p. 93)

Most of us need only to think about the strong bonds we formed with our peers in graduate school to realize how powerful apprentice-to-apprentice relations can be.

Therefore, if we take seriously the apprenticeship model, we must put our students in a meaningful relationship to one another while they do together the work of apprentices, which is legitimate peripheral participation. This kind of coapprenticeship relationship is the social foundation of TBL and the key to TBL's scalability into classes of 200 students and more.

Having made our case for the importance of critical thinkers' working together as cognitive apprentices in your discipline, let us make no bones about the fact that not all group work is created equal. Some forms of group work, in fact, damage student learning as the blind lead the blind into instructional regression. For this reason we take great pains in the next section to be very detailed about how TBL works best, and we emphasize repeatedly that all four pieces of the frame must be in place to achieve the best possible experience for engaged critical thinkers in your classroom.

THE PRACTICAL FRAMEWORK OF TBL

TBL is not just group work of any kind. It involves a specific sequence of activities and feedback designed to quickly change groups of individual students into high-performance learning teams in which participants know each other, need each other, and hold each other accountable for preparation and contribution. TBL is also a lot of fun.

Articles and book chapters elsewhere have described TBL using the principles of accountability, groups, feedback, and assignment design (e.g., Michaelsen, Knight, & Fink, 2004; Michaelsen & Sweet, 2008). This section takes a new look at TBL from a slightly different perspective, focusing on what we call the four practical pieces that make up the frame of TBL (see Figure 1.6):

FIGURE 1.6
The Frame of Team-Based Learning

- Proper teams (strategically formed and permanent)
- RAP at the beginning of each unit
- Application activities in 4-S format
- Student-to-student peer evaluation

Proper Teams (Strategically Formed and Permanent)

When forming students into teams, our experience strongly agrees with research that has found it is critical for teachers to strategically arrange students into balanced teams (e.g., Oakley, Felder, Brent, & Elhajj, 2004).

To organize balanced teams, consider what characteristics will make it easier or more difficult for a student to do well in your course, for example, previous course-work in the discipline, professional experience in the field, a high level of anxiety about the subject matter, or growing up far from the geographic location where the course is being taught. The goal is to distribute students with assets and liabilities in relation to your specific course evenly across teams. On the first day of class, many teachers have a tradition of collecting some information about their students, and this is a natural time to gather the information you need to organize your teams.

The benefits of teacher-formed teams are that they:

- ensure the resources required for the team to succeed are fairly distributed across teams;
- avoid coalitions among team members who already know each other, as these voting blocs create insider/outsider divisions in a group and prevent it from ever really unifying;
- avoid a leftovers effect in which the scattered individuals "no one else wanted" fall by default into an unmotivated team of self-perceived misfits.

Further, teams must be permanent for the duration of the course. Wheelan's (2004) integrative model of group development draws on decades of research to describe a group "life-cycle" (p. 13) in which members' relationships evolve along a generally linear trajectory. Early in a group's life, a great deal of energy is consumed by the social concerns of members getting to know one another and finding their place within the group. There is a great deal of small talk, and not many resources are available for performing complex work together. After relationships and group norms have developed, more of the group's collective capacity becomes available for problem-solving tasks (for more, see Sweet & Michaelsen, 2007). Therefore, re-shuffling groups throws students back into the early getting-to-know-you stage of relationships and wastes valuable time that is better spent learning to make content-related decisions.

Finally, while many cooperative or collaborative learning strategies recommend groups of four students, in TBL we recommend larger teams of five to seven students. This does a better job of ensuring each team has the intellectual and social resources it needs to succeed in the class, even if some team members are absent on any given day.

Belonging to a permanent team can foster a critical thinking attitude and instructional engagement for at least two reasons. First, a sense of relatedness or (belongingness and connectedness) is a primary component of motivated behavior (Ryan & Deci, 2000), and this effect no doubt becomes doubly important in very large classes. Instead of being an anonymous face in a sea of strangers, students in a TBL class belong to a group that knows them and needs them and will miss them when they are absent. Second, a permanent team gives students many opportunities over time to learn about each other's strengths and weaknesses and establish increasingly effective zones of proximal development (ZPDs). As described by Vygotsky (1978) and others, the ZPD is the fertile area for new learning that lies just beyond what an individual already knows; it is bounded on the lower end by what one can learn on one's own and on the upper end by what one can learn with assistance.

A student who has just broken through a misconception into a clear understanding can still freshly recall the nature of that misconception, recognize it in his peers, and help them similarly advance their ZPD into clear understanding as well. In contrast, we as teachers can often develop blind spots in which the very depth and breadth of our content knowledge can prevent us from understanding why something is not obvious. We forget how to think like a beginner. For this reason, a student who has just learned something can sometimes be the very best teacher of it, and students who work together repeatedly over time can use their shared experience to communicate and learn together with increasing efficiency. When learning teams are strategically organized to ensure an equitable distribution of intellectual resources throughout the class, these movements happen with as much synchronicity among teams as is realistically possible, minimizing the differences between teams.

So far, we have identified clusters of learning goals and used these learning goals to organize the course into units. We then organized our students into well-balanced, permanent teams. Now we are ready to put those teams into action.

RAP at the Beginning of Each Unit

The first day of each unit is where the rubber meets the road: TBL really ignites when students come together for the RAP. The RAP does two things: First, it holds students accountable as individuals for having attempted to acquire an understanding of the assigned material, and second, it holds teams accountable for having worked together to construct a shared understanding of the material that is solid enough to start putting that material to use. Of the four practical pillars that constitute TBL, the RAP is its most obviously unique individual feature. Over the length of a course, it creates a rhythm of moments in which students' social and intellectual experiences of the classroom become interlocked and amplified.

Prior to the first day of a unit, students must have completed some preclass preparation fundamental to the unit, which can include readings, reviewing Web-based resources, and the like. The RAP consists of four sequential steps (as illustrated in

Figure 1.7), all of which typically occur during the first class session of each major unit of a course. The steps in a RAP are as follows:

1. After completing out-of-class preparations, individuals take a short multiple-choice test and turn in their answer sheets.
2. Teams then take the same test again, coming to a consensus on their team answers. Teams receive immediate feedback about their performance.
3. If teams feel they can support one of their answers that was marked as incorrect, they can then use their materials to challenge either the question or the answer by preparing a formal written appeal.
4. Based on what he or she learns from listening in on the team discussions during the team test and the preparation of the appeals, the instructor gives clarification as needed to correct any remaining student misconceptions.

If time runs out, the instructor can shift step 4 to the beginning of the next class period. In any case, he or she would give a mini lecture targeting only the topics the teams still need clarified, based on their RAP scores and the questions about the material that still remain. Figure 1.8 provides an overview of the RAP, with tips and best practices for each step.

The RAP can stimulate critical thinking and engagement beyond a normal testing situation at three separate times: during individual study, the team test, and the appeals process.

Studying the assigned prereadings in preparation for a RAP may seem like a mundane academic task, the same as preparing for a test in any course. Interestingly, however, research shows that students' expectation that they will have to justify their views likely stimulates learning in ways that preparing for a traditional individual test might not. In a meta-analysis of research on the conditions that stimulate critical thinking, Lerner and Tetlock (1999) found that expected accountability to an audience was a critical component in high-quality thinking:

> Self-critical and effortful thinking is most likely to be activated when decision makers learn prior to forming any opinions that they will be accountable to an audience (a) whose views are unknown, (b) who is interested in accuracy, (c) who is interested in processes rather than specific outcomes, (d) who is reasonably well informed, and (e) who has a legitimate reason for inquiring into the reasons behind participants' judgments. (p. 259)

FIGURE 1.7
Sequence of the RAP

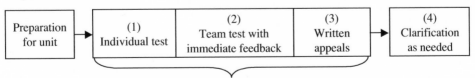

Most effective when taking place in a single class session

FIGURE 1.8
RAP: The Basics

Pre-RAP: Out-of-Class Preparation

Students must complete the required prereadings before the unit begins. This is not necessarily all the material for the entire unit but the fundamentals necessary to open the topic for discussion.

Best practice:

- Remember that students are being tested before they have been taught, so assign preparation materials they can realistically understand on their own.

- Provide a reading guide to help students focus on the most important concepts and details. Some teachers record narrated PowerPoint slide shows and make them available online to help students guide their readings.

Step 1: Individual Test

Upon arriving in class, students first take a short (5–20 questions), multiple-choice test over the readings. These individual tests are then turned in to the teacher. In a large class, use team folders to distribute and collect materials (e.g., individual answer forms).

Best practice:

- Make RAP questions basic enough for a student who has read the material to do fairly well, but with some questions challenging enough for students to need their team. Many teachers aim for average scores of 65%–80% on the individual tests and average scores of 85%–100% on the team tests.

- Some teachers allow partial credit (e.g., allowing students to answer the same question three times, with each answer worth one third of a point). If a student is confident about an answer, he or she repeats that answer three times. If not, the student splits his or her vote.

Step 2: Team Test With Immediate Feedback

Now in their teams, students take the same test again, coming to a consensus on team answers. Teams receive immediate feedback on their performance, ideally on every decision the teams make (correct or incorrect).

Best practice:

- Use IF-AT "scratch-off" answer sheets, which provide instant feedback on each team decision (available at http://epsteineducation.com).

IMMEDIATE FEEDBACK ASSESSMENT TECHNIQUE (IF AT®)

Name _____   Test # _____
Subject _____   Total _____
SCRATCH OFF COVERING TO EXPOSE ANSWER

	A	B	C	D	E	Score
1.						4
2.						2
3.						
4.						
5.						

Students scratch off an answer box, in search of a star indicating the correct answer. If a star is revealed on the first try, the team receives full credit. If not, students continue discussing and scratching until they do find the star, with their score reduced on each successive scratch.

⇩

Step 3: Open Book, Written Appeals

If a team feels it can still make an argument for its choice, now team members can open their books and notes and generate a written appeal in favor of their answer (or, if they feel the question was poorly worded, propose an alternative, with improved wording).

Best practice:

- Only teams can write appeals; individuals cannot. Furthermore, only a team that makes the effort to write an appeal will receive the points for that appeal.

- Appeals must consist of arguments and evidence. Provide a model of a successful appeal in your own syllabus, something like:

  Argument: On question 15, A and B can both be considered correct.
  Evidence: According to Johnson, p. 52, the Pilgrims did not intend to invite Squanto to Thanksgiving. However, historian Charles Sellers (quoted in Zinn, p. 74, footnote 7) asserts that Squanto said that two Plymouth townspeople had verbally asked his people to bring cranberry sauce. The evidence about whether Native Americans were welcome at the first Thanksgiving is inconclusive.

- Do *not* address appeals in class on the same day as the RAP. By the end of the RAP, students can be emotionally enmeshed with their positions, concerned with saving face, and not ready to reason beyond their own positions.

⇩

Step 4: Follow-Up, Clarifying Lecture

Scores on the team tests will tell you what students have learned themselves or taught each other versus what still needs to be clarified. (For example: "All the teams got questions 1–5 right, but 7–10 were pretty spotty.")

This synthesis is good news for TBL practitioners because for the most part it describes the conditions TBL students face as they work together on team tests. During the team test, when students must justify their views to one another and come to a consensus, they become verbally engaged in argument analysis, deductive inference, decision making, problem solving, and creative thinking—all types of thinking that are listed in Halpern's (2003, 1998) taxonomy of critical thinking skills. The immediate feedback provided on team performance enables students to quickly diagnose how well they are communicating as a team and make any necessary adjustments so they can learn together better. For example, an unprepared extrovert may once overpower a studious introvert, but if a scratch on the immediate feedback assessment technique (IF-AT) card reveals the extrovert's answer to be wrong, and a second scratch reveals the introvert's answer to be right, then everyone on the team has the evidence and motivation they need to adjust how and to whom they listen in their discussions of the following questions. In this way, team members quickly discover that failing to elicit input from every member exposes them to the significant risk of missing a question they could have answered correctly.

Finally, after team tests are completed and appeals have begun, students are motivated to take their critical thinking to the next level. Instead of arguing among themselves, they are allowed to pull out their books and notes and marshal evidence in support of an argument made directly to the instructor. Some teachers enjoy this phase the most because they have come to believe that students learn more while trying to write an appeal than they do on the entire rest of the test.

Recall Lave and Wenger's (1991) findings that opportunities for learning in apprenticeship are given structure by work practices instead of asymmetrical master-apprentice relationships. In TBL, the RAP *is* the space structured by the intellectual practices of the discipline in which learners configure their own learning relationships and take each other to the upper bounds of their ZPDs. When this has been accomplished, when the apprentices have maximized their abilities to learn on their own and teach one another, they are ready for the instructor to weigh in and move their learning collectively higher.

Application Activities in 4-S Format

With exceptions like lab sections and field trips, the college classroom setting mostly prohibits us from involving students in real, raw disciplinary practice. What we can do in the classroom is give students practice making the kinds of decisions that people in their disciplines make—to give them what John Dewey (1992) called *dramatic rehearsal* for real-world problem solving. After all, our disciplines are defined by the kinds of questions they ask and how they go about answering those questions. Application activities, therefore, are the forms of legitimate peripheral participation in our disciplines that the RAP prepares students to perform.

Effective group assignments do not require students to write a paper or make a presentation. Writing and presenting are inherently individual tasks, and charging a group with these tasks is to set yourself up for failure. On the contrary, effective group assignments simply give groups a set of data and require them to make a difficult decision, much like a courtroom jury is given a great deal of complex information and asked to render a guilty or not guilty decision.

Good application activities take the following form: Given *X*, students must decide *Y*. Of course, *X* and *Y* will vary based upon your learning objectives for the unit, but experience has taught us a few basic principles for how these activities can best be carried out. Each of these principles starts with the letter *S*, so we have come to call these the 4-S activities (Michaelsen & Sweet, 2008).

1. Significant problem: Students should work on a problem, case, or question demonstrating a concept's usefulness so they understand its impact. Instead of asking students to discuss some abstract set of conceptual distinctions, embed those distinctions in a set of concrete circumstances that would be likely to occur in your discipline. The idea here is to create a case study that grounds the experience in sets of details that would matter in your discipline.
2. Specific choice: Within the case, students should be required to use course concepts to make a decision (for example, guilty or not guilty? Should the company buy, lease, or rent? Were Carnegie and Rockefeller robber barons or captains of industry? Which essay is the best example of historicism and why?). Groups can be required to generate short, written rationales for their choice, but groups must first be required to take a position.
3. Same problem: All the students in the class should work on the same problem, case, or question so they will care about what other groups think about it and energetically engage with each other on the course content.
4. Simultaneous reporting: If possible, students should report choices at the same time so differences in group conclusions can be explored without the risk of students in later-reporting teams being tempted to simply agree with what has been said by those reporting first. It can be a powerful instructional experience when a minority of students in the room actually comes to a better answer than the rest, and when answers are reported sequentially, students in the minority can be strongly tempted to change their answers as their minority status becomes clearer.

The best application activities not only stimulate intrateam discussion, they also stimulate interteam discussion once the groups have reported their decisions. When all groups report their decisions, the teacher's job is to facilitate conversation among the groups to compare how and why they thought differently and came to different decisions. This is why simultaneous reporting is so important: When groups report simultaneously, differences between decisions are candidly revealed and can be instructionally explored.

Some teachers use cases that clearly have a right answer and grade teams accordingly, some teachers do not grade choices but instead grade rationales, and some

teachers use ungraded application assignments when they feel the discussion is valuable enough to have for its own sake. The chapters that follow contain dozens of
detailed descriptions of application activities of all shapes and kinds, many of which
have basic structures that can easily be adapted across disciplines. In fact, we feel this
abundance of specific examples is one of the primary strengths of this volume.

Application activities require students to make use of what they learned during
the RAP. When they are given significant contextualized cases and problems, they
become immersed in the content, and the experience of disciplinary apprenticeship
truly comes to life. Their learning becomes meaningful in a very specific way, as
described by Halpern (1998):

> Cognitive psychologists think of *meaning* as the way a concept is embedded in a web
> of related concepts. A concept has a rich or deep meaning when it has many connec-
> tions to other concepts. When activated, or brought to consciousness, concepts can act
> as a recall cue for the related concepts to which they are connected. One way to pro-
> mote effective organization is through the use of elaboration (and other techniques)
> that develop interconnected knowledge structures. In general, the greater the number
> of connections to information stored in memory, the greater the likelihood that it will
> be recalled.
>
> When a person elaborates a concept, he or she forms many meaningful connec-
> tions—the concept is related to other concepts. There are many techniques that can be
> used in elaboration. An especially effective technique is the use of thoughtful questions,
> which require the learners to create the necessary connections. This is also a good
> technique because recalling a fact or concept is different from learning it. The best way
> to ensure recall is to practice recall—not mindless practice, but meaningful practice
> with feedback. *The questions used to develop connected knowledge structures need to be
> drawn from real-world contexts that are frequently encountered in the workplace and in the
> exercise of citizenship* [emphasis added]. . . . Real life thinking is done in context, and a
> good learning environment provides a believable context for learning exercises. (p. 453)

As students evaluate the cases and argue the merits of one choice over another,
teachers often report that students aren't talking about history or about literature
or about anthropology. They are *talking history* and *talking literature* and *talking
anthropology*. As a teacher, it is invigorating to hear a classroom full of students
actually experimenting with the intellectual tools of one's discipline.

Student-to-Student Peer Evaluation

The fourth practical piece of TBL's frame is student-to-student peer evaluation.
Peer evaluation is perhaps the most context-sensitive aspect of TBL: Different teachers implement it differently based on the culture of their classroom, institution,
department, and discipline. There are many ways to do it right, but we make the
following general recommendations:

1. Include numbers *and* narratives. To give peer evaluation its full impact, the process should include a numerical rating and a written rationale for that rating.

Numbers give the ratings a sense of heft in the grading process, but the rationales really communicate to the student how their peers perceive them and how they can improve in their teamwork skills. In our experience the narrative prompts can be as simple as asking students for one thing about each teammate they appreciate and one thing they request.

2. Gather and distribute feedback at midterm and end of term. Feedback gathered only at the end of term can make peer evaluation feel mostly punitive. In contrast, if you gather and distribute peer evaluations partway through the semester as well, students are given the information they need and a chance to do better.

3. Think carefully about the role of anonymity. While TBL users agree that the teacher should be able to see who is saying what to whom, teachers differ on whether they feel recipients of feedback should see which of their teammates gave each specific piece of feedback. Some feel that *moderated anonymity*—in which the teacher sees everything but distributes feedback without names attributed—encourages students to be civil but honest. Others, however, feel that part of the power of peer evaluation is getting everything out in the open and that fully attributed feedback is the best way to do that.

4. Include feedback for you in the process. Regardless of whether you teach with TBL, it is always best practice to gather formative feedback about how one's course is going at midsemester so you have time to learn about problems students may be having while there is still time for you to do something about it. Including this as part of the student peer evaluation process can build a we're-all-in-this-together sense of community and equity in your classroom.

5. To maximize student acceptance of the peer evaluation process, consider including student input on what criteria peer evaluations should actually include. Some teachers let every team assemble their own criteria as a team-building exercise at the beginning of the class.

6. Consider the importance of forced differentiation in peer evaluation scores. In our experience, if you do not force students to differentiate their scores, they will be nice to the other students, and the variance in team scores will be very small. Some teachers require students to differentiate at least somewhat, either by reminding them that giving everyone the same score hurts those who contributed the most and helps those who contributed the least. Or some even require a certain point spread; for example, "You must give one teammate at least a 6, and you must give one teammate at least a 4." Think carefully about how you want the peer evaluation experience to feel for your students, in your classroom, at your school. Some teachers have found they actually had to adjust the peer evaluation practice when they moved from one school to another because the social/academic atmospheres differed greatly between the two schools.

The practical details of processing and distributing peer evaluations feedback will vary depending upon your circumstances. If you have a large class and no teaching assistant support, you might consider using some software like iPEER (see www .teambasedlearning.org). On the other hand, if you have a class of less than 100, and the peer evaluation system you design is not too complex, you can probably process and distribute the information yourself using a word processor and e-mail in a couple of hours.

Peer evaluations are a critical element of TBL for three reasons. First, they are designed to expose therefore prevent free riders who do not contribute to the team. Describing peer evaluations in this way is invaluable for getting students to buy into the idea of TBL in the first place. Most students have had the experience of being obliged to carry noncontributing group members in the past, which has soured many on the idea of collaborating in general. Describing how peer evaluations work on the first day in a TBL class can lessen student skepticism of learning teams and therefore encourage students to become engaged. Because students know peer evaluation will be part of their grade, they are more likely to interact and be on their best behavior for the course.

Second, peer evaluations fine-tune the communication relationships among teammates, thereby strengthening the community of apprentices that each team becomes. This process is apparent in examples of feedback like the following, which come from a real TBL course:

- You always read so carefully!
- Great input, keep up the good work.
- Please speak up more—you're almost always right when you do.
- You make great contributions, but please put the cell phone away!
- Please come to class more prepared.

Finally, feedback from one's own peers about how one is perceived can have a powerful effect in terms of personal development and can get students to critically reflect on their own behavior. Time and time again, we hear teachers say they could coach students until the cows come home on how to work well in teams, but when that kind of feedback actually comes from their own teammates, it really seems to sink in and have an impact. Not only does this kind of information help students do better in a given course, we also believe it can help them learn valuable collaboration skills to use in future groups for the rest of their lives.

GRADING

Having explored the cognitive apprenticeship philosophy behind TBL and the four elements that make up the instructional frame of TBL, two final but related subjects remain to be addressed: the issues of grading and getting students to buy into TBL.

A student's final grade for a TBL course must come from three sources: individual performance, team performance, and peer evaluations. How you weight each of these factors in a student's final grade is, of course, up to you. The two basic schools of thought on this matter are the straight points and the point multiplier. Each have their advantages for getting student to buy into TBL as an instructional strategy.

A straight points grading system assigns a specific number of possible points to each assignment or activity, and these points accumulate over time toward a known possible maximum (for example, 1,000 points possible in the entire course). This approach has at least three advantages. First, it is a common method of grading and makes for one less new thing to explain to students. Second, this system makes it fairly easy for students to calculate how well they are doing at any point in the term, which is an important piece of information to help learners self-regulate. Finally, in this system it is relatively simple to set up a situation whereby team performance can only help the students and not hurt them (i.e., by adding extra credit bonus points to the students' individual performance scores). Setting up the point system in this way can make students see the groups as an asset and not a threat, and encourage them to participate in the process wholeheartedly.

In a points multiplier system, all aspects of the course still have a given number of points assigned, but their influence upon the student's final grade is determined using a multiplier based on whether the points come from individual performance, team performance, or peer evaluations. The advantage of using this system is its flexibility: You let students decide at the outset how each of the three point factors should be weighted (within limits). For example, the teacher may tell the class that all three factors must be worth *at least* 10% (which would mean that the maximum for any of the three factors would be 80%), but within those limits, students can negotiate among themselves to decide what they're going to use in this course this semester. While this requires a negligible amount of class time to negotiate (via a streamlined process described in Appendix C of Michaelsen, Knight, & Fink, 2004), the sense of autonomy and real choice it gives students can generate powerful acceptance of the grading system overall.

CONCLUSION: POWERFUL THEMES IN
THE CHAPTERS THAT FOLLOW

This chapter has covered a great deal of ground in the hopes of building a solid foundation for the rest of the book. Chapter 2 and Chapter 3 strengthen this foundation by infusing detailed insights about the design of application activities and peer evaluations.

The rest of the book consists of voices of experience from TBL practitioners across curricula. As we read through these chapters and corresponded with the contributors, we saw several important themes emerge in the descriptions of how TBL is being experienced across disciplines. We feel strongly that these themes are worth identifying because they collect into the following clearly generalizable suggestions for how to set up oneself for success.

Specific learning goals developed through backward design have critical value. Many of the contributors describe the clarity, structure, and direction they felt once they had clearly identified what they wanted their students to be able to *do* upon completing an activity, unit, or course. The importance of this element of instructional design manifests itself in different ways in Chapters 5, 6, 11, 12, 13, 14, 17, and 18. This resonates with our own experience, as we often respond to the question, Is there any time when I should not use TBL? with the answer, Yes—when you don't know what you want your students to do with what they learn in your class.

One can take specific actions to make distant or esoteric course material relevant to students' own lives. In the social sciences and humanities, we must often help our students see the significance in problems and academic content that may feel quite distant or alien to them. This distance can come from many sources: The material may be in a different language from the one used in another culture, it may detail procedures of a quantitative experimental design, or it may involve cultural artifacts from a long time ago and therefore seem removed from the students' daily experience. Regardless, many of the contributors describe how they create their course around relevant themes they can continually return to, enabling students to see personal value in this horizon-expanding material. While this theme moves in and out of focus throughout the volume, it appears most prominently in Chapters 4, 7, 8, 9, 10, 11, and 14.

Help students accept TBL and take responsibility for their own learning. TBL creates a very different learning experience from what students will likely encounter at the college level. While it can provide students with a powerful, rich, and energized learning experience, it also can demand more of them than they expected. At its heart, TBL is less about what the teacher does than what the students do, and for this reason it requires students to accept a measure of responsibility for their own learning, which they may at first resist. Many contributors to the volume describe how they introduce TBL to their students in ways that reduce students' initial resistance to becoming partners in the learning process. These methods include the powerful, valuable (and marketable) social and intellectual skills that TBL cultivates; it gives them practice with TBL's procedures and even lets students participate in the grade weighting of the course. These various practices not only help students understand and perform the way the course requires of them, but they can also claim a sense of ownership in the process. Helpful details on students' taking responsibility for their learning can be found in Chapters 5, 6, 8, 10, 12, 14, 15, 16, and 17.

NOTE

1. To support each other and share resources, teachers who use TBL have developed the Team-Based Learning Collaborative (TBLC), which operates a website (www.teambasedlearn ing.org) and electronic mailing list teachers regularly use to brainstorm and help each other troubleshoot challenges as they arise in the classroom. Implementing TBL is a creative act and can feel like a lot of work, but you should never have to feel alone as you strive to create a classroom where remarkable levels of critical thinking and engagement become the norm.

REFERENCES

Abrami, P. C., Bernard, R. M., Borokhovski. E., Wadem, A., Surkes, M. A., Tamim, R., Zhang, D. 2008. Instructional interventions affecting critical thinking skills and dispositions: A stage 1 meta-analysis. *Review of Educational Research, 78*(4), 1102–1134.

Anderson, L. W., & Krathwohl, D. R. (Eds.) (2001). *A taxonomy for learning, teaching and assessing: A revision of Bloom's taxonomy of educational objectives.* New York, NY: Longman.

Barkley, E. F. (2010). *Student engagement techniques: A handbook for college faculty.* San Francisco: Jossey-Bass.

Bloom, B. S. (Ed.). (1956). *Taxonomy of educational objectives: The classification of educational goals, by a committee of college and university examiners.* New York, NY: Longmans, Green.

Collins, A., Brown, J. S., & Newman, S. E. (1989). Cognitive apprenticeship: Teaching the craft of reading, writing and mathematics. In L. B. Resnick (Ed.), *Knowing, learning and instruction: Essays in honor of Robert Glaser* (pp. 453–494). Hillsdale, NJ: Erlbaum.

Dewey, J. (1922). *Human nature and conduct: An introduction to social psychology.* New York, NY: Holt.

Glaser, E. M. (1941). *An experiment in the development of critical thinking.* New York, NY: Teachers College, Columbia University.

Halpern, D. F. (1998). Teaching critical thinking for transfer across domains: Dispositions, skills, structure training, and metacognitive monitoring. *American Psychologist, 53*(4), 449–455.

Halpern, D. F. (2003). *Thought and knowledge: An introduction to critical thinking* (4th ed.). Mahwah, NJ: Erlbaum.

Lave, J., & E. Wenger. (1991). *Situated learning: Legitimate peripheral participation (Learning in doing: Social, cognitive and computational perspectives).* Cambridge, UK: Cambridge University Press.

Lerner, J. S., & Tetlock, P. E. (1999). Accounting for the effects of accountability. *Psychological Bulletin, 125*(2), 255–275.

McTighe, J., & Wiggins, G. (2004). *Understanding professional development workbook.* Alexandria, VA: Association for Supervision and Curriculum Development.

Michaelsen, L. K., Knight, A. B., & Fink, L. D. (2004). *Team-Based Learning: A transformative use of small groups in higher education.* Sterling, VA: Stylus.

Michaelsen, L. K., & Sweet, M. (2008). Team-Based Learning: Small group learning's next big step. *New Directions for Teaching and Learning, 116.*

Nelson, J. (2005). *Cultivating judgment: A sourcebook for teaching critical thinking.* Stillwater, OK: New Forums Press.

Oakley, B., Felder, R. M., Brent, R., Elhajj, I. (2004). Turning student groups into effective teams. *Journal of Student Centered Learning, 2*(1), 9–34.

Paul, R. (1995). *Critical thinking: How to prepare students for a rapidly changing world.* Santa Rosa, CA: Foundation for Critical Thinking.

Paul, R., & Elder, L. (2008). *The miniature guide to critical thinking: Concepts and tools.* Tomales, CA: Foundation for Critical Thinking Press.

Ryan, R. M., & Deci, E. L. (2000). Intrinsic and extrinsic motivations: Classic definitions and new directions. *Contemporary Educational Psychology, 25,* 54–67.

Sweet, M., & Michaelsen, L. K. (2007). How group dynamics research can inform the theory and practice of postsecondary small group learning. *Educational Psychology Review, 19*(1), 31–47.

Tuckman, B. W. (1965). Developmental sequence in small groups. *Psychological Bulletin, 63,* 384–399.

Vygotsky, L. S. (1978). *Mind in society: The development of higher psychological processes.* Cambridge, MA: Harvard University Press.

Wheelan, S. (2004). *Group processes: A developmental perspective* (2nd ed.). Boston, MA: Allyn & Bacon.

Whitehead, A. N. (1929). *The aims of education and other essays.* New York, NY: The Free Press.

Wiggins, G., & McTighe, J. (1998). *Understanding by design* (1st ed.). Upper Saddle River, NJ: Merrill Prentice Hall.

Wiggins, G., & McTighe, J. (2005). *Understanding by design* (2nd ed.). Alexandria, VA: Association for Supervision and Curriculum Development.

CHAPTER 2

Facilitating Application Activities

Jim Sibley

Chapter 1 outlined the principles of 4-S design for application activities. While the 4-S structure is fundamental to success, it is a set of abstract principles that can often be brought into clear focus with practical advice. In this chapter, Sibley offers a broad collection of ideas on planning and facilitating 4-S activities in the classroom as well as a collection of concrete examples illustrating a range of forms that simultaneous reporting can take.

The Team-Based Learning (TBL) classroom is very different from typical classrooms. There is always more noise and when properly managed, a lot more learning. The key to turning the noise (and what otherwise might be chaos) into learning is to maintain control by designing and implementing activities that prompt team members to productively engage with the learning process and each other. Seeing teams dive into the material is probably one of the most truly joyful and initially disconcerting aspects of TBL. Swapping your role from the authoritative dispenser of knowledge to the designer of high-quality learning experiences can be a difficult transition for some.

Application activities are the keystone integration and knowledge-building events of any TBL module and must build on the foundational knowledge the students have gained during the Readiness Assurance Process (RAP; see Chapter 1 of this volume). However, unless teachers design and implement the application activities so the TBL components are clearly and explicitly integrated, students will frequently get the impression that the RAP is just about testing and not about getting them ready for the activities that follow. Probably the most reliable strategy to ensure the application activities properly integrate with the RAP and the overall course objectives is using backward design (see Chapter 1).

PLANNING AND FACILITATION

This section offers some helpful ideas about preparing for and facilitating successful application activities. The methods and processes, discussed in great detail, are only suggestions. As you become a more experienced TBL practitioner, this kind of methodical, heavily detailed planning will likely become a smaller and smaller part of your preparation. New and first-time TBL practitioners may find this structure can help them to more comfortably facilitate activities.

PREPARING BEFORE CLASS

Most of the preparation should take place before the class meets. Many TBL practitioners have found it helpful to use team folders to organize application activity materials. The folders can be preloaded with the application activities worksheets, reporting cards, and any other required materials. These team folders are critical for large classes (see Michaelsen, Fink, & Knight, 2004). However, every time you use team folders, they help you accomplish two important things: They smooth facilitation of the activity in the classroom, and having the folders prepared in advance sends the message to students that you have committed thought and effort to this activity and its preparation.

New TBL users can benefit from using the set-body-close teaching model (see Figure 2.1; W. Godolphin, personal communication, 2009) to effectively structure their TBL application activities. This teaching model divides activities into a preparatory set, an instructional main body, and a close. The set-body-close model can be successfully incorporated in everything from lectures to discussions. The instructional set is used to introduce the task and get students ready. The body is the main instructional event (application activity). The close is your opportunity to restate and reinforce what has been learned and help students organize their take-away thoughts.

The set phase of the model outlines the kinds of things you need to do to provide your students with a frame of reference that will enable them to engage with the activity in a productive manner. The elements of the set phase of the planning model are Mood, Motivation, Utility, Content, Knowledge, and Objectives and are often summarized with the mnemonic MMUCKO. The pieces of MMUCKO can be described as follows:

- Mood is established, clear, enthusiastic, supportive.
- Motivation can be a narrative or story to focus attention.
- Utility of the knowledge about to be learned is highlighted.
- Content is what will be discussed and how it will be discussed, and what activities and tasks to expect (the road ahead).
- Knowledge (prior) needs to be activated; we need to remind students what they already know and bring to the activity, including how the RAP has prepared them for these activities.
- Objectives for the activity should be clarified.

For example, following a RAP that covered basic material, an instructor in an Eastern religion course might introduce the application activity by saying something like,

Based on your RAP scores, you're all familiar with the basics of the Buddhist philosophy [knowledge]. Today we are going to examine Kamo-No Chomei's "My Life in a Ten-Foot Square Hut" (which describes a 12th-century hermit's view of catastrophic events in a much earlier period), and see [objective] if you can identify any clues [content/utility] to why the Japanese people have been so resilient in the face of the uncertainty and stress they have had to deal with in the recent earthquake and tsunami [mood/motivation].

In TBL, the body consists of the 4-S activities with the intrateam discussions, reporting, and the whole class interteam discussion. The close aspect of the model serves as a reminder of things you can do to ensure that students are told about the key ideas they should have internalized during the activity and have been exposed to because of your content expertise. The elements of the close phase of the model are to summarize, relate to the set, give a sense of achievement, and provide no new information.

FIGURE 2.1
The Set-Body-Close Lesson Planning Model

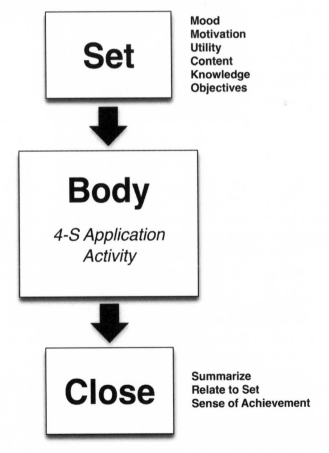

- Summarize main discussion points. If general rules emerge, the instructor should ask students for a specific application; if the discussion focused on specific cases, ask for general rules; review important strengths and weaknesses of various positions; discuss any emerging consensus or outstanding complications.
- Relate to set. Revisit motivation story and the utility of the knowledge acquired; revisit content covered and objectives.
- Achievement. Give students a sense of achievement; review everything that was learned (this can reduce student discomfort when they don't end up with a huge stack of notes).
- No new information. Resist the temptation to add new information; the final summary should clarify and expand on information already in play. Adding extra information at the last minute can reduce the overall effectiveness of the activity, and students can actually take away only the new information and not the more important large thematic elements from the activity.

FACILITATING THE ACTIVITY IN CLASS

As they think ahead to actually facilitating the activity in class, many faculty find it helpful to create a detailed discussion plan. This can help ensure that all required content is covered adequately. Although you shouldn't try to control the conversation, careful planning can help give you the mental space to facilitate the discussion in a more natural way. As we gain experience, this detailed planning becomes less and less necessary.

Introducing the 4-S Task

How you introduce a task can have an effect on the way students engage in the activity and how well they succeed with it. The application activity typically begins with the distribution of the materials and problem(s). It is important to set the students properly to task by reminding them of the applicable knowledge they bring to the problem and the length of time they will be given to discuss it in their team before reporting their decisions. You should also remind them if any worksheets or written artifacts must be completed.

Intrateam Discussion

Once properly tasked, the students are given time in their teams to discuss the questions and arrive at a team consensus on the decision. As a faculty member you should circulate around the room to actively listen to the conversations, which can accomplish two important things: You send the message that what the students are thinking and saying is important enough that the instructor will listen, and, if misconceptions or misunderstanding are preventing students from progressing, then you can intervene and provide some expert clarification at the team level or whole-class level.

Simultaneous Reporting

When the designated completion time is nearly over or when you sense the discussion in some of the teams is nearing completion, it is good to check in with the remaining teams to see how they are progressing. At that point, you need to announce that either more time (and specify how much) will be allotted for discussions or that teams should get ready to report. Asking teams to get ready to report often dramatically increases the amount of student energy in the classroom.

Once the teams are ready, it is extremely important to have them give their answers all at the same time. Although you can (and should) use a variety of methods, the important thing about simultaneous reporting is that you and the students get to see the contrasts in student thinking across the entire class all at once. These contrasts provide the richest possible starting point for a whole class discussion.

Interteam Discussion

The discussion between teams allows students to challenge each other's decisions, defend their own thinking, and thoughtfully examine other teams' decision-making process. When students are faced with contrasting opinions, their natural response is to confront, defend, and discuss these contrasts. The great thing is that, with a minimum of guidance from the instructor, the conversation focuses on why they made the decision or a judgment rather than on which is the correct answer.

When teams simultaneously report different conclusions (which is the ideal outcome), the instructor's primary function during the interteam discussions is to be sure all voices are heard and each of the possible decisions are examined. For many instructors, the hardest part of facilitating interteam discussions is learning how to get out of the way and let the students sort things out. In part, it's because, just like the students, seeing a variety of choices prompts us to think, and when we think we begin to formulate arguments about the different points of view. In addition, we feel it is our responsibility to make sure students get it right, and because of our content knowledge we usually have at least an opinion on what the right answer is.

You can do a number of things to overcome the tendency to talk too much. One way to help you limit what you say is remembering that offering your opinion too soon will often eliminate one of the students' richest learning opportunities—formulating, making, and testing decisions. In addition, figuring out ways to increase students' willingness to talk takes some of the pressure off you as the instructor. One way to increase their willingness to challenge a team's decision is to give them time to formulate their challenges. You might want to say something like, "Take three minutes and identify some questions you would like to ask one or more of the other teams." Giving them time to formulate challenges also helps in another way. Because challenging is a bit risky, students will tend to wait you out in hopes that you will do the challenging. However, if you've given them some thinking time, you can make it clear you expect them to do the challenging by saying something like, "I see you all have some questions, so who would like to go first?" Another way to increase students' willingness to challenge each other is moving around the room and away from the person who is talking, so as many students as possible are between you and the speaker. That helps in two ways: The speaker will naturally speak up so you and the rest of the class can hear what he or she is saying, and even if the speaker is directing his or her remarks to you, he or she will also be speaking to the other teams as well.

When all the teams agree on a single choice (which most often happens when the question isn't difficult enough), the instructor faces a very different problem—nothing to talk about. When that happens, one option is to take on the role of devil's advocate and ask students why they did not make other choices. Another possibility, which can even be used in a devil's advocate role, is changing the question. For example, you might ask, "Since you all agree on _____ what is the next best [or worst] choice?" or "What is the single most compelling reason (or piece of evidence) for your choice of _____ over the other choices?" or something similar. The key is remembering that the purpose of the interteam discussion is to be sure you know whether students have a sound understanding of the issues and concepts that are the key conceptual building blocks you want them to master.

Artifacts

Many instructors use some sort of team worksheets that allow teams to work through a series of problems and record their decisions and most important supporting rationales before simultaneously reporting a sequence of problems and discussing each one. Although these worksheets may or may not be officially marked, they are typically collected and reviewed by the instructor at the end of the activities and provide a valuable asset for tweaking the assignment or the process for the next class.

SIMULTANEOUS REPORTING STRATEGIES

One of the most challenging aspects of implementing TBL is figuring out how to accomplish the final S (simultaneous reporting) in the 4-S application activities. In this section, we explore the various options for simultaneous reporting. In any simultaneous reporting strategy the fundamental principle is that student teams must be able to compare their thinking and decisions to the thinking and decisions of other teams. This comparability provides the driving force behind high energy and effective interteam conversations. The more complicated the deliverable, the more difficult it is for teams to compare their thinking to that of other teams in the class, and this can result in teams being less motivated to defend their choice or challenge each other.

Voting Cards

The standard for simultaneous reporting is for each team to hold up a colored card that indicates its decision (see Figure 2.2). The visibility and comparability of this kind of reporting can be used as the starting point for a facilitated conversation where student teams defend their positions and challenge the positions of other teams. The instructor facilitates this conversation to cover all salient points and then should provide some form of summary or closure at the end of the activity to remind students of the positions, evidence, and arguments that were discussed. Reporting by holding up cards is effective even in very large classrooms ($n > 300$). In larger classes the greatest challenge is to effectively facilitate a whole class discussion that keeps all students engaged.

Some difficulty may occur in large classes when voting cards only go up for a few seconds, and the reporting conversation may take a much longer period of time. One solution to this problem is using flag holders (similar to place card holder stands used on tables at weddings) that allow teams to indicate when they have completed their worksheet and are ready to report. Voting cards can be attached to the stand so they are visible for the duration of the discussion. For example, you might want to use voting cards for simultaneous reporting in the following situation (teacher tasking student teams):

> Imagine you are an English teacher, and you are working with your students to develop their understanding of the active and passive voice. You are trying to develop their next

FIGURE 2.2
Simultaneous Reporting Cards

assignment. Which wording in the following assignments would best promote higher-level thinking and a rich reporting discussion?

1. List the mistakes writers frequently make that detract from their efforts to write in the active voice.
2. Read the following passage and identify a sentence that is a clear example of (a) active and (b) passive voice.
3. Read the following passage and identify the sentence in which the passive voice is used most appropriately.

On the count of three show a voting card indicating your team's specific choice. (Adapted from Michaelsen, Fink, & Knight, 2004).

Pushpins or Sticky Notes

When students are working with certain kinds of graphical data (maps, drawings, building plans, concept maps) you can achieve an effective simultaneous report by having student teams select a specific location that is their best answer to the question. Teams can either use pushpins or sticky notes to indicate their location choice, or each team can report a location to the instructor. The instructor then plots the coordinates to create the simultaneous report. Once each team has decided on a location and made that decision public, you can then facilitate a discussion between teams as they defend their position choice and challenge the decisions of other teams. As an example, pushpins or sticky notes can be used to answer the following questions:

You are consulting for a new business owner who wants to open a dry-cleaning store in Norman, Oklahoma. Where would you recommend locating a new dry-cleaning business (and why)?
   Use the pushpin to indicate your team's chosen location on the map.

An overweight truck has driven onto a bridge. The truck weight far exceeds the bridge's designed carrying capacity. At which specific location would the bridge structure likely fail first? Identify the specific point on the drawing, and be prepared to defend your position.
   Show a specific location with a pushpin or sticky note on the drawing.

Whiteboards

Each team can write its decision on a small whiteboard as shown in Figure 2.3. The size of the whiteboard limits the possible complexity of the report, so students can easily compare their team's decision to that of other teams. Many TBL practitioners like this kind of reporting since the choices are a bit more open ended, and alerting students to a possible subset of correct answers is reduced. A whiteboard can be used for student reporting in the following two examples:

FIGURE 2.3
Sample of Whiteboard Simultaneous Reporting

Given the following investment portfolio, investor profile, and market conditions, which stock would you sell first and when?

A patient presents at the ER with the following symptoms. What would be your first course of action? What test would you order first?

Write your decision on the whiteboard and show it to the class on the count of three.

Poster Gallery Walks

Gallery walks can be used when problems require a bit more writing. Student teams present their choice or choices (you may ask them to respond to several questions) on a flipchart or poster paper. You can prefill titles of categories on flipcharts so teams are required to structure their responses in similar ways; this aids the easy comparability of reporting decisions. This still requires teams to distill their decision to ideas that can be captured on a poster, and this public reporting helps teams take the task seriously. Typically the simultaneous reporting occurs in more than one stage. The first stage can consist of having the teams simultaneously display their posters by hanging or placing them around the room, as in a gallery. (Alternatively, the instructor can have teams hand in their posters in advance so the posters are anonymous—and the instructor can even anonymously add his or her own poster to the mix to provide an additional source of intrigue and another stimulus to promote discussion.) The next stage involves having student teams walk around and examine each other's posters, keeping in mind a particular instruction from the teacher. For example, you might ask students to identify a best idea they didn't think of or a question that would highlight the most glaring Achilles heel in the posters and use a felt-tip marker to record their choice on legal-size paper. Then the instructor would facilitate an interteam discussion of the posters and responses/questions.

Examples of gallery walk exercises can include the following:

1. Students might be asked to produce and simultaneously display a concept map illustrating concepts and relationships from the course material. Each team would then review the work of the other teams and make one or two specific choices about the others' work—for example: "Identify the most important element on another team's concept map you forgot to include on yours, and put a sticky note on it" (see Figure 2.4).

2. Students could be asked to provide organizational development plans to eliminate the kind of corruption in the New York Police Department (based on the evidence in the film *Serpico*). With this assignment, the posters would answer a series of questions that asked what was the primary cause and who would be the target of their intervention, along with a series of yes/no questions about whether specific suggestions given by *Serpico* were essential for any plan to be successful. The teams would examine each others' posters and then identify the best idea they hadn't

FIGURE 2.4
Sample of Gallery Walk Simultaneous Reporting with Stickies

thought of and the least defensible choice or the greatest conflict between the choices.

3. Students might be asked to apply a number of concepts in a production/operations course to make an integrative decision about the cost of manufacturing an origami object. In this case, teams would post their best estimate of cost per unit and several one- to two-page documents created during previous application exercises (e.g., plant layout, production stages, production time for each stage, etc.) that represent subparts of the overall cost/unit. Teams would then examine two or three other posters and identify a mistake (if they could find one) and the best idea they wished they had thought of. Next, they could have the opportunity to fix their own poster to integrate feedback from other teams. Finally, because students would have had time to process the information, the mistakes and best ideas in the other posters would come out in the debriefing discussion.

4. As a final report in an experimental design course, students learned three different data collection methods (focus groups, paper and pencil surveys, and online questionnaires) and a variety of sampling and analysis approaches. All teams could then be tasked with making a recommendation to university administrators about which action would be the most effective in reducing the degree to which students (at their university) engaged in academic misconduct. Each team would be assigned to collect data using one of the three data collection methods (meaning multiple teams use each method), analyze the data, and make posters presenting the team's recommendation and the data to support it. The posters, which might be viewed by campus administrators, would have to show the recommended action, the data collection method used, from whom the data was collected, and the procedures used to summarize or analyze the data. After viewing the posters, teams would identify the most creative (but methodologically appropriate) innovation on one of the other posters and a question that would reveal which recommendation was the most suspect because of questionable research methodology implementation.

Hot Seat Reporting

This method quickly identifies a single team to begin whole-class reporting. Putting a team in the hot seat has been used in a couple of different settings and can be done very simply by using numbered slips of paper in an envelope, a jar with numbered balls, or going high tech with an iPhone application. For example, when reporting involves a lengthier written component, such as a long worksheet, you can use either one of the low-tech method (slips of paper in an envelope or drawing numbered balls from a container; see Figure 2.5) or the high-tech version (an iPhone *Wheel of Fortune* app with wedges that can be customized by inserting team numbers or even the instructor's name) to randomly select which team will make the next report. The selected team then displays its completed worksheet with analysis using a document camera and walks its classmates through the team members' work and their thinking. After selecting more teams, there is often convergence in presented rationales and decisions, which

FIGURE 2.5
Sample of Hot Seat Reporting: Choosing a Team by Drawing Numbered Balls From a Container

gives the instructor the opportunity to facilitate a review discussion and provide effective closure to the activity.

The other application of hot seat reporting is to establish the grading key for each of the questions on an application assignment or exam. After the teams have handed in their official answers, you simply select the first team for the hot seat. Team members give their answer, and if it is unchallenged, it becomes the marking rubric for all student submissions.

Hot seat reporting is particularly useful in large classes because it is a simple way to get the discussion going. It is also very effective at keeping students engaged. In many instances, a common answer will be met with cheers from the audience, or a minority answer will prompt boos.

Scissors and Glue Sticks

This method is an excellent way to have student teams work on writing. At the class meeting, students are prompted to review each other's work using the assignment requirements and rubric and then to select passages from the different student works that best demonstrate criteria specified in the rubric. They then use the scissors and glue sticks to select, cut, paste, and assemble the best passages from various student works to generate, for them, the best compilation. This is a remarkable activity because it gets students to critically review each other's work and use a rubric to distinguish or indentify valuable parts of each document for inclusion in team submissions (Sparrow & McCabe, 2009).

For example, in a law class students may be asked to individually prepare a five-page legal brief that they bring to class, then their teams take the individually prepared documents and compile them into a final five-page team brief. The power of this activity is in the conversation as students examine each other's work and debate the strengths and weaknesses of various sections of the individual briefs for possible inclusion in the team submission.

Excel Charts

This activity is the electronic version of a pushpin in a map. Teams are asked to pick a specific location (x/y coordinate) to best answer the question prompt. The instructor then quickly enters the coordinates in Excel and displays the graphical result (see Figure 2.6). The resulting chart is the simultaneous report. The instructor then facilitates a reporting conversation based on the differences in each team's chosen location. By having the chart ready and the data entry preformatted, the entry and display of team answers can be a very efficient and quick process. Figure 2.6 is an an example of how an Excel chart can be used in team reporting.

Stacked Overheads

In this method, each team is provided with a colored marker and a printed transparency of some graphical data (demographics, maps, X-rays). Each team then answers the question by circling or delineating areas of interest on the transparency. The instructor then collects the transparencies and stacks them on an overhead projector or document camera to generate the simultaneous report. In large classes you

FIGURE 2.6
Sample of Excel Charts

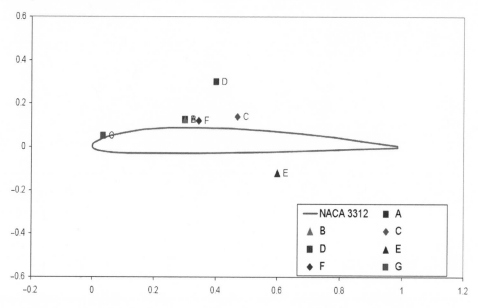

may only want to stack a subset of transparencies that capture the diversity of reporting decisions. Stacking too many transparencies can create a difficult to interpret set of data (Jones, 2009). Figure 2.7 shows two examples of how stacked overheads can be used for simultaneous reporting.

Google Docs

In very large classroom settings, Google Docs can be used to facilitate simultaneous reporting. The instructor asks that each team bring a laptop to class and then formats a table in Google Docs, typically with a team number column, a team reporting column, and a column for a short rationale or supporting evidence. The instructor then gives the password to the whole class so everyone can log on to the document and update it simultaneously. The instructor displays the resulting table on the classroom screen (see Figure 2.8 on page 48) and facilitates a discussion that examines the various positions, solutions, and evidence presented in the table (Ostafichuk, 2011).

Classroom Response System (aka Clickers)

A number of TBL practitioners are now using clickers for team reporting. When the instructor calls for the simultaneous report, each team uses a clicker to indicate its choice. There are two downsides to clicker reporting: the cost of the clickers and their anonymous nature. Since the clicker decision can't easily be attributed in real time to a particular team, the discussion can only be based on the aggregate decisions

FIGURE 2.7
Sample of Stacked Overheads

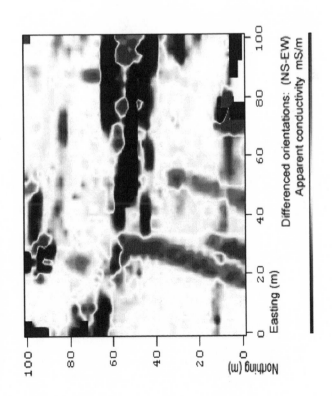

Easting (m)

Northing (m)

Differenced orientations: (NS-EW)
Apparent conductivity mS/m

Title:

Easting

Northing

FIGURE 2.8
Sample of Google Docs

223 Mechanism Design Challenge

	Team	Cost	Actuator Type	Transmission Type	Questions for this team			Cost	Team
							1st	$90.00	B2
A1	$334.33	DC Motor	Timing belt			2nd	$160.39	C3
A2	$308.19	DC Motor	Power Screw			3rd	$186.19	D1
A3	$493.00	AC Motor	Gears			4th	$217.21	C5
A4	$272.17	AC Motor	power screw					
A5	$383.25	AC Motor	Power Screw					
B1	$268.62	AC Motor	Power Screw					
B2	$90.00	DC Motor	Pulley					
B3	$290.00	DC Motor	Power Screw	Price is low - did you include motor control?				
B4	$350.45	Electric Motor	Worm Gears to Rack and Pinion	AC or DC motor?				
B5	$331.67	AC Motor	Belt&Gear					
C1	$750.00	AC Motor	Power Screw					
C2		AC motor	Power Screw					
C3	$160.39	Motor	Direct	AC or DC? Couplings used?				
C4	$293.38	AC motor	Direct	How are you reversing the AC motor?				
C5	$217.21	DC motor	Pulley system w/ manual clutch					
D1	$186.19	AC motor	Power Screw					
D2	$228.26	DC Motor	ACME Power Screw					
D3	$262.64	AC Motor	POWER SCREW					
D4	$289.43	DC Motor	Power screw					
D5	$291.52	DC Motor	Power Screw					

of the entire class. Many instructors have learned to overcome this problem by using voting cards and clickers. Using the clickers gives the instructor a permanent record of the voting, which can be used for grading purposes or to refine the activity for future classes. The voting cards ensure that each team really owns its particular decision and cannot hide behind the anonymity of the clicker results.

FINISHING UP EFFECTIVELY

The final task of effectively managing the application activities is bringing them to an effective close. The following are some of the things you will want to do:

- Remind students of the salient points or general rules that may have emerged during the class discussions.
- Identify points of view that were not considered.
- Ask if there are any questions that might still be outstanding to reinforce what has been learned and what has yet to be learned.
- Highlight, restate, and reinforce any particularly insightful observations.

One very effective strategy for bringing closure to an activity is involving the teams by saying something like, "Take two minutes and identify what you think was the most important idea that emerged from the discussion" or "What is the most important question you think still needs to be answered?" The important thing, however, is that if even a rich discussion isn't properly closed, some of its long-term value may be lost for the students.

REFERENCES

Erskine, J., Leenders, M., Mauffette-Leenders, L. (2003) *Teaching with cases*. London, Ontario, Canada: Ivey Publishing.

Jones, F. (2009). *TBL course talk* [Webinar]. Retrieved from http://vimeo.com/26639358

Michaelsen, L. K., Knight, A. B., Fink, L. D. (2004) *Team-Based Learning: A transformative use of small groups in college teaching*. Sterling, Va.: Stylus.

Ostafichuk, P. (2011, March). *Team-Based Learning in the engineering classroom: What we have learned along the way*. Presented at the 10th annual meeting of the Team-Based Learning Collaborative, Las Vegas, Nevada.

Sparrow, S., & McCabe, M. (2009, March). *Using TBL to give graduate students effective and efficient feedback on analytical writing assignments*. Paper presented at the eighth annual meeting of the Team-Based Learning Collaborative, Austin, Texas.

CHAPTER 3

Peer Feedback Processes and Individual Accountability in Team-Based Learning

Derek R. Lane

This chapter reviews the social science literature regarding the dimensions and factors influencing peer feedback and discusses the complexity of communicating peer feedback to ensure individual accountability in Team-Based Learning. It describes domain-specific skills and detailed strategies that can be used for communicating effective and constructive student-to-student peer feedback, especially when such feedback contains negative messages.

In Chapter 1, Sweet and Michaelsen describe student-to-student peer feedback as one of the four major practical elements of Team-Based Learning (TBL). They present several recommendations and describe how peer feedback can be used to stimulate critical thinking and engagement. They also say that peer feedback has the potential to reduce negative behaviors and reinforce positive behaviors. When implemented successfully, student-to-student peer feedback can certainly reduce social loafing, improve team cohesion, and reinforce preferred behaviors—or help change and improve unsatisfactory behaviors. On the other hand, when peer feedback is treated as a necessary evil (e.g., as a mechanism for justifying poor group performance, or worse, as a means for criticizing and penalizing individual peer performance at the end of an instructional sequence), it can be divisive and serve to damage the credibility and undermine the effectiveness of TBL as a viable instructional strategy.

In this chapter I embrace an inclusive view of peer feedback, consistent with the recommendations provided in Chapter 1, and extend those ideas by focusing on the dimensions and factors that influence competent student-to-student peer feedback. This chapter has three objectives. First, it establishes a context for the importance of student-to-student peer feedback—formative process feedback (provided multiple times during the course) and summative outcome feedback (provided once at the end of the course)—to achieve TBL learning objectives. Next, it describes the complexity and unique characteristics of TBL peer feedback processes and how these factors can influence individual behaviors and enhance group productivity. Finally, it identifies the skills and justifies the procedures for helping students communicate constructive peer feedback—especially when such feedback contains negative messages.

PEER FEEDBACK AS A CRITICAL COMPONENT OF TBL

The degree to which a team effectively and efficiently achieves its goals is the degree to which it is judged productive. This productivity, however, is largely dependent upon competent communication—especially in the form of student-to-student peer feedback—to provide critical information about group interactions, improve group cohesion, and ultimately to enhance group effectiveness. Peer feedback is used to accomplish the following important goals: establish individual and mutual accountability, motivate team members, create a climate of trust, manage conflict, correct inappropriate behavior of members, and develop team members' potential for future activities. Consequently, giving meaningful and constructive feedback to peers about observable behavior—and receiving and acting on that peer feedback—is a necessary component for creating an optimal TBL learning environment (Cestone, Levine, & Lane, 2008; Michaelsen, Knight, & Fink, 2004; Michaelsen & Sweet, 2008).

Successful TBL teams use peer feedback to their advantage. Individuals in productive teams use self-examination and peer assessment to voluntarily change basic operating assumptions (when necessary) and monitor their own interaction patterns and progress. Moreover, effective TBL teams are more attentive to group processes, encourage the expression of diverse points of view, and begin their discussions by attempting to analyze the problem before trying to search for viable solutions.

It is worth noting, however, that peer feedback is emotionally potent in nature. Even in successful TBL teams, students will initially resist giving honest feedback—whether the message is positive or negative—because the process of giving such feedback can be uncomfortable, and students will resent receiving any feedback that makes them feel guilty or inadequate. Students value their freedom and independence to do what they want in their own way and in their own time. A reality of TBL is that it requires students to become interdependent and function as a cohesive unit to make decisions and solve problems using course content. Therefore, student-to-student peer feedback, as a critical component of TBL, helps students understand that their actions, words, and attitudes have a profound effect—for either good or harm—on themselves, their teammates, and ultimately on team productivity.

DISTINGUISHING BETWEEN FORMATIVE PROCESS AND SUMMATIVE OUTCOME FEEDBACK

Effective peer feedback provides two types of information that are equally critical to the successful implementation of TBL. The first type of information provides student-to-student formative process feedback and serves to enhance group processes and team productivity. Essentially, student-to-student formative process feedback provides the mechanism that allows the individual team members to know whether they are on the right track and whether the team is headed in the right direction. The importance of formative process feedback can be illustrated with a simple example. If a group of people board an airplane in San Francisco and want to fly to Washington, DC, they can expect to see a mountain range within the first 15 or 20 minutes of their flight. If instead all they see is ocean, then they are obviously going in the wrong direction because there is no ocean between San Francisco and Washington. For TBL students, this is what formative process feedback in the form of peer evaluation ought to be. It should establish benchmarks for the individuals (and the team) to figure out whether their current strategies are taking them to their desired goal. When formative process feedback is less than effective, however, it can produce unintended negative consequences.

The second type of information provides student-to-teacher summative outcome feedback and serves to guard against student social loafing while reducing grade inflation. Summative outcome feedback is provided confidentially as a final assessment from individual students to the instructor and serves to describe how helpful (or not) team members have been throughout the course. Early TBL instructional materials referred to summative outcome feedback as group maintenance (Michaelsen, Cragin, & Watson, 1981) or student helping behavior because it served to inform the the teacher about the overall helpfulness of each student (www.teambasedlearning .org/resources/documents/4363-syllabus.pdf). The strengths and shortcomings of the various methods (e.g., Michaelsen's, Fink's, Koles's) and the logistics associated with administering summative outcome feedback in TBL courses have been explored in detail in several publications (e.g., Birmingham & McCord, 2004; Cestone et al., 2008; Levine, 2008; Michaelsen, Knight, & Fink, 2004). The choice of one strategy over another is largely determined by the culture and instructional environment where TBL is being implemented.

A comparison of the features of formative process and summative outcome feedback is provided in Table 3.1.

It is unfortunate that a preponderance of TBL literature tends to focus on the logistics associated with summative outcome feedback or how to assign group maintenance or helping behavior grades. The attention on summative outcome feedback is justified by the concerns of new TBL instructors about the logistics associated with TBL and grade inflation (see Cestone et al., 2008; Levine, 2008). While summative outcome feedback can guard against grade inflation, only formative process feedback can enhance group processes, foster a trusting group climate, and provide information (when it is most relevant) directly from students to their peers. Both types of feedback are useful in guarding against social loafing, but summative outcome feedback does very little to help a TBL group that may be struggling with more substantive issues (e.g., dominant team members, ineffective use of time, disorganized structure and roles, poor listening, insufficient preparation, pressure for uniformity, etc.). Therefore, students in TBL groups should be encouraged to provide formative process feedback to their teammates as a catalyst for team success.

TABLE 3.1
Comparative Features of Formative Process and Summative Outcome Feedback

Formative Process Feedback	Summative Outcome Feedback
Process feedback	Outcome feedback
Student-to-student	Student-to-teacher
Open and shared	Confidential
Enhances group processes	Guards against grade inflation
Establishes individual and mutual accountability	Reduces social loafing
Ongoing	Final
Provides information to the team about how to improve group processes and productivity	Provides details to the teacher about how to assign final helping behavior grades

When students provide formative process feedback they are giving their peers the opportunity to make adjustments and improve before the final summative outcome feedback grade is assigned. Additional pedagogical merits of effective peer assessment and evaluation in TBL teams, documented by Cestone and her colleagues (2008), include increased student confidence and control over students' learning, improvements in motivation, and enhanced knowledge acquisition (see also Dochy, Segers, & Sluijsmans, 1999). If formative process feedback is not expected or if the peer formative process feedback process is implemented as part of the TBL experience without care, the results of the peer formative process feedback process can actually be destructive. The worst-case scenario occurs when summative outcome feedback provides nothing more than an opportunity for peers to unleash the resentment they've kept bottled up throughout the course. In this case, summative outcome feedback is nothing more than retribution.

The exchange of helpful formative process feedback between students working in TBL groups is an essential communication activity that can potentially serve to increase team productivity and maintain production quality without requiring additional time from TBL instructors. Indeed, social scientists have been extremely successful in their attempts to understand the role of communication in decision-making groups (Gouran & Hirokawa, 1983) and to articulate the forces that influence group interaction (Poole, Seibold, & McPhee, 1985).

Based on interviews with over 6,000 team members and leaders, LaFasto and Larson (2001) identified eight characteristics of high-performance teams: a clear elevating goal, a results-driven structure, competent team members, unified commitment, collaborative climate, standards of excellence, external support and recognition, and principled leadership. The eight characteristics are similar to Katzenbach and Smith's (1999) six team basics that define the discipline required for team performance: small number of members, complementary skills, common purpose, common set of specific performance goals, commonly agreed-upon working approach, and mutual accountability. Peer formative process feedback supplies a results-driven structure with specific criteria that provides standards of excellence and helps to ensure mutual accountability in TBL groups. Research published by Ogilvie and Haslett (1985) and Haslett and Ogilvie (2003) describes the complexity and unique characteristics of student-to-student formative process feedback and how such feedback can be used to improve TBL group performance.

UNIQUE CHARACTERISTICS OF TBL PEER FORMATIVE PROCESS FEEDBACK STRATEGIES

Uncertainty gives feedback its value. When TBL students design and implement effective peer formative process feedback strategies for determining how well their team is functioning, the individual students are more likely to make the necessary corrections that will reduce uncertainty and ultimately enhance their overall team productivity. TBL instructors should not simply put individual students together in TBL groups and expect the students to be accountable and productive. Nor should they assume that students are prepared to provide meaningful formative process feedback to their peers. The key to individual accountability and team productivity begins with an understanding of the unique characteristics of formative process feedback in task groups.

Over three decades ago, Ilgen, Fisher, and Taylor (1979) identified four important features of feedback that are equally relevant to TBL teams in the 21st century. They suggested that individuals must perceive the feedback, accept the feedback, develop intentions to respond to the feedback, and establish specific goals for improvement. Ogilvie and Haslett (1985) conducted an experimental study that revealed three underlying dimensions of feedback in task groups that could have a remarkable impact on group effectiveness. The first dimension was related to the content of the message and included valence (whether feedback was positive or negative), clarity, accuracy, and relevance. The second underlying dimension of feedback was related to the source (self, task, peers, teachers) and whether the source was assertive, trustworthy, dynamic, relaxed, or responsive. The final dimension was related to the intended recipient of the feedback—specifically, the mind-set or frame of reference when feedback is received.

The dynamic interplay of source, message, and recipient characteristics interact to determine whether student-to-student peer feedback is communicated constructively.

COMMUNICATING CONSTRUCTIVE STUDENT-TO-STUDENT FEEDBACK

Effective student-to-student formative process feedback in TBL teams is dependent upon two related factors: individual commitment to the feedback process and the criteria used to identify the behaviors and frame the peer feedback. One of the best strategies for ensuring individual commitment to the process is to allow TBL teams to design and implement their own team peer formative process feedback strategies. After all, students will support what they help to create. The next section describes the process of establishing peer formative process feedback criteria and procedures, and details general communicative strategies for providing effective peer formative process feedback.

STUDENT-TO-STUDENT FORMATIVE PROCESS FEEDBACK PROCEDURES AND CRITERIA

Phase One: Individual Criteria Identification

The process of establishing peer formative process feedback criteria and procedures has three phases. Phase one begins with students' reflecting independently on their past group experiences. Students should be encouraged to consider positive and negative group experiences—though most will tend to recall more information about their negative experiences. Next, students should identify the four or five most important issues they feel are most responsible for contributing to the success (or failure) of their previous groups. Finally, students should generate a list of criteria they would feel comfortable using to evaluate individuals in their current TBL team. One strategy is to request that students translate their four or five most important issues into three to six specific criteria for group success. Students should record their list of preliminary criteria to be shared with their team members in phase two. Common criteria include attendance, accountability, active communication, preparation, work quality, equitable work distribution, punctuality, reliability, individual initiative, team commitment, respect, responsibility, constant communication, notification of inability to attend meetings, and leadership.

Phase Two: Generating Consensus About Team Formative Process Feedback Criteria

The second phase should ideally occur as soon as possible after the TBL teams are formed and instructed to introduce themselves, share contact information, and in some cases determine a name for their TBL team. Many TBL practitioners number their teams and refer to them using team numbers for the duration of the course, which is especially efficient in very large courses with teaching assistants (e.g., Bob is responsible for grading and meeting with teams 1–10, and Mary is responsible for teams 11–20). In contrast, I believe it is important not to underestimate the value of having the team make a decision about a team name because it is the first tangible decision teammates will make as a team. After individuals agree on a team name, they discuss their individual criteria with their teammates. Their goal is to collapse all their individual criteria into a team list of mutually agreed-upon team criteria. In my experience, students are generally surprised at how much overlap there is between their individual criteria, and they quickly generate a list of six to eight peer formative process feedback criteria that has group consensus. Again, the specific nature of the criteria is not important. What is critical, however, is for the team to agree on the most important criteria it will use to provide formative process feedback to individual teammates within their team during the course. The list generated by students typically includes generic criteria such as attendance, punctuality, attitude, respect, and preparation.

In my opinion, it is unfortunate that some instructors simply distribute specific criteria without letting teams generate their own because I feel TBL students are much more likely to be committed to, and support, criteria they create with their teammates. However, for those instructors who simply want to distribute a common set of criteria, or a form students can use to provide formative process feedback to one another, several documents could be modified to use in a TBL course.

For example, Little and Cardenas (2001) identified the following five criteria as being especially important for engineering students who are working in teams and suggested that faculty simply provide the criteria to students: quality of technical work (Is the work clear, complete, and relevant to the problem under discussion? Are equations, graphs, and notes clear and intelligible?), ability to communicate (Do students understand what is being said? Are they clearly heard? Is the team's direction clear?), ability to provide leadership (Do students initiate activities, make suggestions, or provide focus? Is the student a spark plug?), commitment to the team and the project (Does the student attend all meetings? Arrive promptly? Is the student prepared and ready to work?), and demonstrated effectiveness (Has the student done what was promised? Could the project have benefited from more, or less, of this person's contributions?).

Another useful form developed by Paul Koles at Wright State University has three clusters of criteria students can use to provide formative process feedback to their TBL teammates: cooperative learning, self-directed learning, and interpersonal skills. The form is available from the TBL Collaborative website (www.teambasedlearning .org/resources/documents/TBL,%20Peer%20Feedback%20form,%20Koles,%20RE VISED%20May%202008.doc). Koles has suggested that the form is also useful for providing summative outcome feedback at the end of the course.

Phase Three: Designing Procedures for Team Formative Process Feedback

The final step in the process requires that teams develop meaningful procedures for providing formative process feedback to all team members. Before students begin to develop a rubric for measuring each of the team criteria, I require students to read a short four-page article by Michaelsen and Schultheiss (1988) that clearly outlines seven characteristics of helpful feedback. After students have read the article, instructors provide the teams with instructions for developing specific team peer formative process feedback procedures and criteria. To facilitate the generation of a final formative process feedback system, students respond to the following:

1. Provide a statement of the team goals and objectives you intend to achieve. These goals should reflect an integration of individual team members' goals for the course.
2. Describe how you intend to collect the data the feedback will be based on. Please include a copy of a specific peer grading form that clearly indicates how data will be collected.
3. Explain details of the feedback process you intend to use.
   a. When will the feedback will given? Be specific.
   b. Who will give it? Be specific.
4. Assess the difficulties you are likely to encounter in implementing your performance feedback system.
5. How does the feedback system provide input into the helping behavior grade at the end of the class?

At this point, I make it clear to my students that I will not be reviewing the formative process feedback individuals are providing to teammates. Instead, I will simply be evaluating the extent to which the performance feedback system meets four specific criteria:

1. Are teams collecting data they will need to support the achievement of their team goals and objectives that will lead to effective learning outcomes and team productivity?
2. Will the procedures they intend to use support the achievement of their objective(s)?
3. Are the procedures they intend to use practical (i.e., can they be implemented effectively given the specific situation they will be used in)?
4. Have they accurately anticipated the problems they are likely to encounter in implementing their performance feedback system?

I feel it is critical for my students to be informed that I will only evaluate the quality of the criteria and the thoroughness of the procedures and will not be reading the content of the actual formative process feedback as it is provided from student to student during the course. Rather, the students should establish individual and mutual accountability, create a climate of trust, manage conflict, and use the formative process feedback procedures and criteria as a mechanism for improving group productivity. For this student-to-student formative process feedback to be meaningful, it must inform the final summative outcome feedback, which should account for no less than 10% of the final course grade. This is the equivalent of one full letter grade. The specific final grade is determined using a summative outcome feedback process known as *helping behavior*, explained in the next section.

SUMMATIVE OUTCOME FEEDBACK

Summative outcome feedback provides an end-of-course strategy to assess individual accountability across a semester and ensures that the students take the formative process feedback seriously. It is essential that the final summative outcome feedback score account for no less than 10% (at least one letter grade) of the final course grade. Unlike the formative process feedback, the summative outcome scores need to be confidential and shared only with the instructor. In addition, students should be required to discriminate among their teammates when giving summative outcome feedback to reduce the likelihood of grade inflation.

There are some concerns that the summative outcome feedback may have adverse effects on group cohesion. The concerns are dispelled, however, as long as the group has been diligent during their formative process feedback. The summative outcome feedback process should include parameters that allow for complete and honest disclosure.

COMMUNICATIVE STRATEGIES FOR GIVING AND RECEIVING EFFECTIVE FORMATIVE PROCESS FEEDBACK

Haslett and Ogilvie (2003) described eight specific communicative strategies for giving and receiving effective feedback that are equally applicable to TBL groups (see Table 3.2).

Three years after Ogilvie and Haslett (2003) published their original research on feedback processes in task groups, Michaelsen and Schultheiss (1988) outlined seven

TABLE 3.2
Strategies for Giving and Receiving Effective Feedback

1. Be specific and direct.
2. Support comments with evidence.
3. Separate the issue from the person.
4. Sandwich negative comments between positive comments.
5. Pose the situation as a mutual problem.
6. Soften or mitigate negative messages to avoid overload.
7. Deliver feedback close to occurrence
8. Use effective delivery that includes being assertive, dynamic, trustworthy, fair, credible, relaxed, and responsive, and must preserve the public image of recipient.

Note. From "Feedback Processes in Task Groups," by B. B. Haslett, & J. R. Ogilvie, 2003, in *Small Group Communication Theory and Practice: An Anthology* (p. 105) by R. Y. Hirokawa, R. S. Cathcart, L. A. Samovar, & L. D. Henman (Eds.), New York: Oxford University Press. Copyright 1993 by Oxford University Press. Adapted with permission.

characteristics of helpful feedback (see Table 3.3). The substantial overlap between the communication strategies described by Haslett and Ogilvie and the characteristics identified by Michaelsen and Schultheiss should not go unnoticed.

Harris (2006) published a pocket mentor guide on giving feedback that describes the basics for giving feedback from the standpoint of a supervisor or manager. The short 75-page guide explains that the purpose of feedback is to reinforce or change behavior. It then describes when and how to give feedback effectively, much of which aligns directly with the principles described in this chapter. However, for the individual receiving feedback, the guide describes six steps for receiving feedback openly that are also appropriate for students who feel defensive about receiving formative process feedback in TBL teams. The six steps (as modified for TBL students) are preparing before the feedback session begins, staying open to the feedback given by teammates, presenting a response carefully and rationally, deciding what can be learned about the feedback, working with the feedback giver(s) to develop an action plan for change, and asking the feedback giver(s) for support in following the action plan. For formative process feedback to be effective it must not be seen as a form of punishment.

Using a robust experimental design to determine the effect of combining negative and positive feedback messages, Davies and Jacobs (1985) were able to identify the most effective format for communicating constructive peer formative process feedback—especially when the feedback contained negative messages. They reported that when a negative (N) feedback message was sandwiched between two positive (P) messages (PNP), the feedback was rated as significantly more accurate, credible, and desirable, and contributed most to group cohesiveness than any of the other three format combinations (PPN, NPN, and NNP). Therefore, when it is necessary to communicate negative information, it is most effective to sandwich a negative message between two positive comments. According to the results of Davies and Jacobs's study, positive feedback containing negative messages had the greatest potential for improving performance.

TABLE 3.3
Characteristics of Helpful Feedback

1. Descriptive, not evaluative, and is owned by the sender.
2. Specific, not general.
3. Honest and sincere.
4. Expressed in terms relevant to the self-perceived needs of the receiver.
5. Timely and in context.
6. Desired by the receiver, not imposed on him or her.
7. Usable, concerned with behavior the receiver has no control over.

Note. From "Making Feedback Helpful," by L. K. Michaelsen & E. E. Schultheiss, 1988, in *The Organizational Behavior Teaching Review* (p. 112). Copyright 1988 by Sage. Reprinted with permission.

Currently, there is no general agreement in the TBL community about the role of anonymous formative process feedback. Some early adopters of TBL suggest that formative process feedback containing negative messages should be anonymous to increase honesty. Others say that anonymity makes it more likely for peer formative process feedback to destroy team cohesion. However, those in both schools of thought believe that the sender of the formative process feedback should be identified, even if only the instructor knows (in this case, the instructor knows what every student said in his or her formative process feedback to peers, even if those peers only receive anonymous collective feedback).

I began this chapter began by establishing a context for the importance of student-to-student peer feedback—formative process and summative outcome—to achieve TBL learning objectives. Next, I described the complexity and unique characteristics of TBL peer feedback processes and how those factors could influence individual behaviors and enhance group productivity. Finally, I identified the skills and justified the procedures for helping students communicate constructive peer formative process feedback—especially when such feedback contained negative messages. Instructors who are interested in adopting TBL are encouraged to make use of the strategies for facilitating respect among team members using formative process feedback procedures to improve team productivity and summative outcome feedback strategies to reduce social loafing.

Put simply, feedback—formative process feedback and summative outcome feedback—should be direct and clear, and ensure that group members are accountable to the rest of the team. The value of formative process feedback is that all the members of the team have the opportunity to discuss the feedback and make performance improvements over the course of the semester. Even if faculty insist on providing their students the evaluation criteria (see Little & Cardenas, 2001) and the procedures to use, it is vital that the sender of the formative process feedback is identified because anonymous feedback—especially anonymous negative feedback—destroys trust and group cohesion. On the other hand, when peer formative process feedback follows Michaelsen and Schultheiss's (1988) seven characteristics, TBL students are empowered to discuss their concerns, make corrections, and perform more effectively.

REFERENCES

Birmingham, C., & McCord, M. (2004). Group process research: Implications for using learning groups." In L. K. Michaelsen, A. B. Knight, & L. D. Fink (Eds.). *Team-Based Learning: A transformative use of small groups in college teaching.* Sterling, VA: Stylus.

Cestone, C. M., Levine, R. E., & Lane, D. R. (2008). Peer assessment and evaluation in - team-based learning. *New Directions for Teaching and Learning, 116,* 69–78.

Davies, D., & Jacobs, A. (1985). Sandwiching complex interpersonal feedback. *Small Group Behavior, 16*(3), 387–396.

Dochy, F., Segers, M., & Sluijsmans, D. (1999). The use of self, peer, and co-assessment in higher education: A review. *Studies in Higher Education, 24*(3), 331–350.

Gouran, D. S., & Hirokawa, R. Y. (1983). The role of communication in decision-making groups: A functional perspective. In M. S. Mander (Ed.), *Communications in transition* (pp. 168–185). New York: Praeger.

Harris, J. O. (2006). *Giving feedback: Expert solutions to everyday problems.* Boston, MA: Harvard Business School Press.

Haslett, B. B., & Ogilvie, J. R. (2003). Feedback processes in task groups. In R. Y. Hirokawa, R. S. Cathcart, L. A. Samovar, & L. D. Henman (Eds.), *Small group communication theory and practice: An anthology* (8th ed.), pp. 97–108. New York: Oxford University Press.

Ilgen, D. R., Fisher, C. D., & Taylor, S. M. (1979). Consequences of individual feedback on behavior in organizations. *Journal of Applied Psychology, 64*(4), 349–371.

Katzenbach, J. R., & Smith, D. K. (1999). *The wisdom of teams: Creating the high performance organization.* New York: HarperCollins.

LaFasto, F., & Larson, C. (2001). *When teams work best: 6,000 team members and leaders tell what it takes to succeed.* Thousand Oaks, CA: Sage.

Levine, R. E. (2008). Peer evaluation in team-based learning. In L. K. Michaelsen, D. X. Parmelee, K. K. McMahon, & R. E. Levine (Eds.), *Team-Based Learning for health professions education* (pp. 103–111). Sterling, VA: Stylus.

Little, P., & Cardenas, M. (2001). Use of "studio" methods in the introductory engineering design curriculum. *Journal of Engineering Education, 90*(3), 309–313.

Michaelsen, L. K., Cragin, J. P., & Watson, W. E. (1981). Grading and anxiety: A strategy for coping. *The Organizational Behavior Teaching Journal, 6,* 8–14.

Michaelsen, L. K., Knight, A. B., & Fink, L. D. (2004). *Team-Based Learning: A transformative use of small groups in college teaching.* Sterling, VA: Stylus.

Michaelsen, L. K., & Schultheiss, E. E. (1988). Making feedback helpful. *Organizational Behavior Teaching Review, 13*(1), 109–112.

Michaelsen, L. K., & Sweet, M. (2008). The essential elements of Team-Based Learning. *New Directions for Teaching and Learning, 116,* 7–27.

Ogilvie, J. R., & Haslett, B. (1985). Communicating peer feedback in a task group. *Human Communication Research, 12*(1), 79–98.

Poole, M. S., Seibold, D. R., & McPhee, R. D. (1985). Group decision-making as a structurational process. *Quarterly Journal of Speech, 71*(1), 74–102.

PART TWO

Voices of Experience

CHAPTER 4

Application Exercises

Challenges and Strategies in the Psychology Classroom

Karla Kubitz and Robin Lightner

This chapter serves the entire volume by describing in precise terms how the sequence of activities in Team-Based Learning scaffolds students' learning experiences from basic knowledge acquisition up through the application of sophisticated concepts to complex situations. Further, it describes how the power of Team-Based Learning can overcome common Team-Based Learning misconceptions, which are often tenacious in the face of disproval. Developing good application activities is often described as the most difficult part of teaching with Team-Based Learning, so readers from all disciplines can benefit from the wide variety of activities these authors describe, from application activities using student-generated data to videos and even posters and concept maps.

The Team-Based Learning (TBL) instructional strategy transforms teaching from a focus on telling students about the theories, concepts, and vocabulary of psychology to facilitating students' understanding and application of the course material. In addition, TBL challenges students' misconceptions and develops their critical thinking abilities. When teachers begin using TBL, most of them master the Readiness Assurance Process aspect of Team-Based Learning relatively easily. In fact, sometimes they are able to use many of their existing test items for their Readiness Assurance Test questions. However, the process of creating effective application exercises is more daunting. In this chapter, we begin by describing our rationale for adopting the TBL instructional strategy. Next, we provide tips on creating team application exercises that meet Michaelsen and Sweet's (2008) 4-S activities (i.e., the applications focus on significant problems, are the same across groups, involve specific choices, and can be reported simultaneously). We also give examples of application exercises that have worked in our psychology classrooms.

The authors thank Linda Kubitz for the extremely professional proofreading/editing.

RATIONALE FOR THE USE OF TBL IN PSYCHOLOGY CLASSROOMS

TBL Provides a Mechanism for Tackling Negative Transfer

Karla Kubitz uses TBL because the instructional strategy provides a mechanism for tackling negative transfer common in psychology classrooms. Negative transfer occurs when prior knowledge hinders the acquisition of new knowledge (Coker, 2009). Students frequently hear and use psychological vocabulary in everyday conversation, so it is already recognizable to them; this can be a problem because students come into psychology classes thinking they are already well informed about psychology. In reality, psychological terms are frequently misused in everyday conversation (e.g., "I'm going to use negative reinforcement to get that #%&! dog to stop barking."), and students often come into class with a considerable amount of misinformation (e.g., "It's best to express anger to get it out and reduce angry feelings."), which is difficult to change. As Kowalski and Taylor (2009) put it,

> Students come into our classes with a wide variety of [psychological] misconceptions. . . . [and] they also leave with their erroneous beliefs intact. . . . Although it is clear that students hold misconceptions, it is less clear how to reduce those misconceptions. Neither McKeachie (1960) nor Vaughn (1977) found evidence that the [traditional] introductory course promoted general thinking skills that allowed students to apply and generalize their learning. (p. 153)

As they suggest, traditional teaching does little to change students' psychological misconceptions. However, alternative teaching techniques have been more successful. Kowalski and Taylor (2009) examined the effects of three different instructional activities on students' psychological misconceptions, including refutations provided in lecture, refutations in readings, and refutations in lecture and readings. The greatest changes in students' misconceptions occurred when refutations were made in lecture and in readings. The instructional activities that focused on "directly refuting misconceptions . . . [were] particularly important" (p. 157), and changing misconceptions "often involved engaging students in activities or demonstrations designed to create cognitive conflict between their prior knowledge and the information to be learned" (p. 154). For example, a teacher might show a slide depicting the tongue map (to illustrate the misconception that certain areas of the tongue respond only to certain tastes) and then create cognitive conflict by explaining that "actually all areas of the tongue are sensitive to all taste qualities" (p. 155).

In the TBL psychology classroom, opportunities for creating cognitive conflict abound. Initially, misconceptions at the foundational knowledge level can be brought up and refuted by well-designed readiness assurance test questions. Subsequently, misconceptions at the application and integration knowledge levels can be directly addressed by effective team application exercises (see Fink [2003] for an explanation of his taxonomy of significant learning).

TBL Provides a Mechanism for Facilitating Positive Transfer

Robin Lightner uses the instructional strategy of TBL because it provides a mechanism for facilitating positive transfer in the psychology classroom. Positive transfer occurs when prior knowledge speeds the acquisition of new knowledge (Coker, 2009). Psychology instructors want students to build on prior psychological knowledge and apply their growing knowledge to their lives or to problems in other disciplines. With this goal in mind, psychology instructors traditionally teach key terms, definitions, and examples of psychological concepts all semester and then present challenging application problems on the final exam. Quite often teachers are surprised when students cannot make the leap between terms and definitions and the application of those concepts to the real world. Earlier in her teaching career, Lightner spent two action-packed weeks covering memory and was distressed that on the final exam her students could not follow this instruction: Write a letter to peers with study advice, based on the studies and concepts of cognitive psychology, for remembering exam material. For two weeks, the students had been engaged and entertained in the classroom, and they were familiar with psychology terms and definitions, but they couldn't apply that knowledge to a real-world situation. Instead of using the course material, many students wrote about their personal experiences with memory or gave pieces of advice they had heard all their lives, like, eat a good breakfast. Without practice, students could not transfer what they learned from in-class lectures and learning activities to the application question. Similarly, Lightner had disappointing results on a question asking students to design a teaching protocol based on the principles of operant conditioning on how to stop a dog from jumping up on visitors (less than half the students earned a B or better). Again, she mistakenly thought if the students understood the concepts, they would be able to use them when dealing with a relevant problem. Only 25% of the students used psychological terms she thought were important in their training essays.

This disappointing student performance on difficult critical thinking items is not unique. Summarizing some of the main research findings, cognitive scientists Alexander and Murphy (1999) concluded, "Transfer of schooled knowledge and procedures occurs far less often than educators and educational researchers would hope" (p. 563). To use what they have learned, students have to do more than just know the material. In *How Learning Works: 7 Research-Based Principles for Smart Teaching* (Ambrose, Bridges, DiPietro, Lovett, & Normal, 2010), the authors outline a number of potential problems for using relevant previous knowledge to solve a problem. Students need several different skills to answer application questions that require transfer of learning. First, they need to be able to access their prior knowledge, and their knowledge must be thorough enough to generate examples. Second, students need to be able to identify which knowledge applies to the problem and which doesn't. For example, when Lightner asks her students to apply the concepts of cognitive development to explain how children of different ages would play Monopoly, they need to understand that Piaget's theory is relevant, and Skinner's theory is not. In addition, the students need to know the characteristics of each of Piaget's stages well enough to be able to connect them to the game of Monopoly. Indeed, it's a lot to ask of students who are learning a new set of concepts.

A key solution to helping students develop all the skills necessary for transfer of learning is to provide structured practice and immediate feedback (Halpern & Hakel, 2003). In this way, instructors provide scaffolds or "temporary supports . . . that help students bridge the gap between their current abilities and the intended goal" (Bulu & Pederson, 2010, p. 509). A study by Bensley, Crowe, Bernhardt, Buckner, & Allman (2010) showed that practicing critical thinking skills makes a difference in student performance. The researchers compared a critical thinking–infused class to a traditionally taught research methods class. Students in the critical thinking class had to distinguish arguments from nonarguments, evaluate evidence, and analyze a literature review. Most important, students received feedback on their performance. Students with critical thinking practice outperformed students in an otherwise equivalent section of research methods on an argument analysis test. In contrast to building higher-order thinking skills throughout a course, giving tough application questions solely at the end of a course is unproductive and unfair to students. It does not provide the scaffolding (Bulu & Pederson, 2010) necessary for students to adjust their performance and improve. If the goal of the course is for students to transfer course content into their own lives, then time in class is best spent applying the material to everyday situations. The application exercises in TBL provide the structure and immediate feedback that improve students' abilities to solve real-world problems with course content.

TIPS AND EXAMPLES FOR TWO DIFFERENT KINDS OF APPLICATION EXERCISES

Multiple-Choice Question Application Exercises

Writing application exercises that meet Michaelsen and Sweet's (2008) 4-Ss (i.e., significant problem, same problem, specific choice, simultaneous reports) can be challenging—often more challenging than designing other open-ended group projects. The concepts in psychology are traditionally presented in disjointed ways, making it tough for students to understand or apply them to problems. On the other hand, forced-choice application problems that capture big themes aid in student learning but can be demanding to design. Case studies can be a problem in that instructors must be careful not to oversimplify the processes of diagnosis or behavior change.

Nonetheless, with patience and practice, the instructor redesigning a course with TBL can find some formats for writing application exercises that simplify the process. A number of existing activities can be adapted to the TBL format with relative ease. Instructors can find examples of group activities in published volumes (e.g., Dunn & Chew, 2006), publisher's supplements (e.g., Bolt, 2007), at teaching conferences (e.g., the Lilly Conferences on College and University Teaching), and in the journal *Teaching of Psychology*.

Additionally, the problem-based learning literature is filled with rich peer-reviewed problems along with descriptions of their implementation in many disciplines. The Problem-Based Learning Clearinghouse (https://primus.nss.udel.edu/Pbl/) and the *Interdisciplinary Journal of Problem-Based Learning* provide access to hundreds of problems. Generally, these are case studies or scenario-based problems students must outline, research, and answer in groups. Groups then create products such as written reports or in-class presentations. These case study problems have been routinely implemented in psychology courses (e.g., Willis, 2003). However, in their published form, most of them violate one or more of Michaelsen and Sweet's (2008) 4-S prescriptions in ways that hamper team development and limit learning. The most common and most obvious problem is that the requirement for written reports (as team products) means that students will typically adopt a divide and conquer strategy for completing the assignment. Consequently, there will be little sustained intrateam interaction on the course material. The results of this limited interaction include decreased engagement, lower team cohesion, and diminished learning. The requirement for sequential presentations (as team products) means that students will naturally tend to tune out before and after their team presentation. As a result, little interteam interaction on the course material and accompanying detrimental effects on engagement, team cohesion, and learning will occur. Additionally, with presentations much of the team discussion is centered around superficial aspects of the project, such as choosing font, colors, or clip art. Team members frequently divvy up sections and work individually on their own parts. In contrast, when the product is a specific choice, the team discussion is more focused on content. Team members have to explain, differentiate, and evaluate each option, and this conversation requires all the members to analyze all the components of the project. To convert the scenario or case to the TBL format, the final product must be changed to a specific choice rather than the open-ended presentation common in problem-based learning. So instead of being asked to present a behavioral modification treatment plan for a disruptive third-grader, students in a TBL classroom would be asked to choose the best treatment plan among four options. Thus, by changing the format of these problem-based learning assignments to require specific choices and simultaneous presentations, interaction will be increased within and between teams, and students will be more engaged, develop more cohesive teams, and learn more. Table 4.1 provides examples of multiple-choice application exercises from Lightner's classes.

As a proponent of TBL, Lightner would rather see her students discussing the pros and cons of each of several plans than talking about what font or clip art to use in their PowerPoint presentation. One of the many strengths of TBL is that the students spend more time digging into the meaning of the concepts, debating the best answer, and differentiating between the pros and cons of each multiple-choice option. A well-designed application problem requires a high level of critical thinking skills. Furthermore, the simultaneous reporting of the best treatment option creates an energized debate over the pros and cons of the various choices. Lightner has found that during the typical sequential group presentation session, nonpresenters become disinterested, particularly with less effective presenters. In TBL, students in the entire

TABLE 4.1
Multiple-Choice Question Application Exercise Examples

Problem	Worksheet Questions	Grading
Predict the correlations between the traits and behaviors.	For each correlation predicted, describe the rationale, citing studies or conceptual relevance.	Each justification is scored on a 0 (missing or insufficient), 1 (merely a definition), 2 (explanation coherent with theory) scale. The points are summed for an overall percentage grade.
Imagine Freud, Rogers, Kelley, and Skinner were playing a game of poker. Who would win?	(a) For each theorist, outline his or her strengths and weaknesses in this game, given the perspective of his or her theory. (b) At the end of the game, imagine if each theorist would lose, how would he or she explain the cause of his or her loss. (c) Who would you most like to play poker with and why? In your answer, refer to specific aspects of the theory that you find helpful or appealing.	Students are graded solely on their worksheet and not their final decision. Each question is rated on a simple 0 (missing or insufficient), 1 (merely a definition), 2 (explanation coherent with theory) scale and summed to calculate a percentage score.
What is the main problem with the experiment (video) run by the smile psychologist?	(a) Define the independent variable and dependent variable. (b) Was random assignment used, and if not, how do the researchers ensure equivalent groups? (c) Is there experimenter bias? (d) How might researchers improve external validity? (e) Define and give an example of a confound. (f) Define and give an example of a placebo.	Grading for this problem involves accuracy with each of the questions and concepts, as well as arriving at the correct conclusion. Group participation ratings are also factored into the students' points.

class have a vested interest in their group's answer, and students are interested in comparing their reasoning with that of the other groups.

Example: Personality Trait Application Exercise

For a personality class, Lightner has adapted an exercise (Dollinger, 2004) that asks students to predict the relationships between several personality traits and behaviors. Early in the course, students are surveyed anonymously on their personality traits, including extroversion, agreeableness, openness, consciousness, neuroticism, as well as optimism and locus of control. They are also given 10 behavioral statements they can agree or disagree with, for example, "I've crashed a party" or "I regularly text while driving." Later in the course, when Lightner covers trait theories, she completes the Readiness Assurance Process (see Chapter 1) and then presents a 45-minute application exercise. Students are given a matrix that lists the 10 behaviors from the survey in the first column. The personality traits are listed on the first row. The groups must predict, for each personality trait, whether the behavior will show no correlation or a positive or negative correlation. Each term, Lightner adds her new class's data to the analysis. During the group discussion, students dig into the meaning of each trait to decide if the trait is relevant to the behavior or not. They discuss the fine points about each example, such as whether optimism is going to show the same relationships as agreeableness or low neuroticism. Students use their books to review the traits and relevant theories. Frequently, they take out their laptops and look up studies about the predictive validity of the traits. If Lightner were simply lecturing about the traits (even with clever, vivid examples), she is confident that the only reason laptops would be used would be for checking Facebook.

After the group work, students report their prediction for each behavior simultaneously. If the group predicts a relationship, group members hold up one card with the name of the trait and another card to indicate the direction of the predicted correlation. Then Lightner reveals what the trait/behavior data showed. Inevitably, the results show some unexpected relationships. For example, the item, "I go out on a date almost every weekend," shows a positive relationship with trait conscientiousness. These unexpected findings allow for a discussion of third-variable confounds, probability, and sampling. The distribution of grades on this exercise is negatively skewed. Most groups perform extremely well on this activity and remember the traits and relevant research terminology on the final exam.

Example: Personality Review Application Exercise

Another application exercise in Lightner's personality class does not rely on concrete data to identify the correct answer. Instead, at the end of the group deliberations, the class votes on the most persuasive answer. This personality application activity reviews some of the major theoretical perspectives and influential leaders in the field. Students are asked the following question: Imagine Freud, Rogers, Kelley, and Skinner were playing a game of poker. Who would win? From a purely objective standpoint, a fictitious poker game among deceased theorists is not a significant problem. However, from a student standpoint (and that is what really matters), probably because it conjures up such intriguing visual imagery, it clearly meets the 4-S criterion of being a significant problem. As a result, it is highly engaging and provides many a humorous moment as students imagine such a game. Students often offer funny, creative suggestions for the dialogue for the players, so Lightner uses this activity at the end of the term to energize the class while reviewing for the final exam.

She ensures that at least one member of each group has in fact played poker and can explain the rules and strategies to teammates.

As a way of scaffolding student learning, most of Lightner's application exercises ask students to complete a worksheet that leads them through an analysis of different aspects of their theories and ideas. These types of worksheets help in application exercises because they structure discussion of the relevant pieces of the question, focusing attention on any that students might not easily recognize as applicable. Table 4.1 shows the types of questions that accompany some of the application problems as well as an approach to grading them. After a moment or two to orient themselves to a new unusual problem, students open their books to review the biographies of the theorists. Then they methodically examine poker-playing strategies as viewed through the lens of each of the theories. They talk about which aspects matter most, and after 45 minutes, simultaneously report the winner by holding up a note card with the winner's name. Though most students start and also end with Freud as the winner of the poker game, given his superior skills at making inferences from nonverbal behaviors, many switch to Skinner who might be more attentive to the consequences of the poker players' choices.

Example: Video Prompt Application Exercise

Online videos depicting content for psychology abound, and these can provide rich stimuli for application exercises. For example, in her Psychology and Law class, Karyn McKenzie (2010) shows students dramatic video clips of court cases about controversial topics. Her topics include euthanasia, faith healing, involuntary homicide, vigilantism, children as eyewitnesses, and the death penalty. Students have to differentiate black letter law and common sense justice. She structures debates on these topics, but this learning activity could easily be converted into a TBL-style application exercise by changing the student response to a multiple-choice question: Based on black letter law, the defendant in the video should (a) be found not guilty, (b) be found guilty and receive a fine, (c) be found guilty and be incarcerated for six months, or (d) be found guilty and be incarcerated for 10 years. In addition, students might use a worksheet to ensure they are considering the most important legal and psychological principles in their final decision.

Lightner uses a similar video scenario approach in an application exercise related to research methods and experimental conclusions in an introductory psychology class. In this activity, she shows students a three-minute video/infomercial about a smile psychologist who conducts a study of a brand of teeth-whitening strips. In the video, people who have used the whitening strips are interviewed and give (literally) glowing endorsements. Next, the smile psychologist introduces a study on people who have had a speed dating experience and are rated by their potential dates. Then, after whitening with the strips, participants go through the speed dating again with different partners and are rated again. This time, the ratings are higher. The same experiment is replicated in a job interview context. The smile psychologist concludes, "Whitening will get you dates and a job!"

Students then complete a short, 30-minute application exercise with the following question: What is the main problem for endorsing the whitening strips based on the preceding commercial? (a) The study has confounds, (b) the people are not a random sample, (c) the results of this sample may not apply to others, (d) people may already have white teeth, or (e) the physical attractiveness of the participants varies to begin with (see worksheet questions in Table 4.1). Students report their answers simultaneously by holding up a note card that indicates their group's choice. For this application exercise, Lightner grades the answers to the six worksheet questions as well as the final decisions of the groups. After working in groups, most students (93%) accurately conclude there are confounds, and the class frequently talks about placebo effects and whether the confidence produced is an inherent benefit of physical improvements that should be left in the experiment. In contrast, before using this video and multiple-choice questions in a TBL context, Lightner asked students to watch the video and individually answer the question in an online WebQuest. Only 15% of them were able to explain that the order in the testing of the strips created confounds. Clearly the group context and the structured worksheet allowed students to discuss the study in a way that led them to think through the various concepts and make the correct conclusion about the problem with the experiment.

In summary, video examples can provide the stimuli for a number of application exercises about psychological topics. The following is a short list of some additional examples.

- Students pick the most relevant theory of aggression that could explain events in a video of a parent who becomes violent at his son's soccer game.
- Students pick among experiments that are relevant to Bart's behavior in a *Simpsons* video (i.e., self-handicapping).
- Students watch a video of an egocentric teenager and have to use Erikson's theory to choose the best approach for his parents to help him become more empathetic.

Concept Mapping/Poster Application Exercises

Like many instructors, Kubitz's biggest stumbling block in implementing TBL was learning to create effective application exercises. Meeuwsen (2003) suggested creating poster assignments, that is, assignments that ask students to collaborate on a poster depicting their solution to a course-related problem or question (e.g., a poster that illustrates the various factors that affect information processing). Kubitz combined Meeuwsen's poster assignment with concept mapping (Novak & Gowin, 2006) and created what she calls *concept mapping application exercises*. Concept maps are "diagrams that represent ideas as node-link assemblies" (Nesbit & Adesope, 2006, p. 413). Or in simpler words, concept maps are pictures that denote ideas and the ways they can be connected. Concepts are displayed in boxes (or circles), and the concepts are connected with arrows. Linking words depict the relationship between the concepts. Sets of boxes, links, and arrowheads can be read like sentences. The appendix contains an example of the instructions for a typical concept mapping application exercise in Kubitz's class. Figure 4.1 in the appendix is an example of a team concept map.

Over the years, Kubitz has found concept maps to be especially effective as team application exercises. Concept maps meet Michaelsen and Sweet's (2008) 4-S criteria for effective TBL assignments. First, they can focus on significant problems that can include a variety of case studies, videos, or intervention design problems. Second, all teams can work on the same problem. Third, the exercises require specific choices. Students have to decide what they're going to put on the map, how they're going to draw it, and where they're going to put it. More importantly, they have to process their course material, take it out of the text, and put it into the context of the problem. As Nesbit and Adesope (2006) put it, "To construct concept maps from a text, students must more thoroughly and precisely extract the text's meaning" (p. 420). For example, students must first process the statement "self-efficacy . . . focuses on the extent to which the individual feels she will be successful in performing the desired behavior" (Lox, Martin-Ginnis, & Petruzzello, 2010, p. 50) in the text. Then students have to transfer their knowledge of self-efficacy theory to the application problem of a real or a fictitious person's sedentary lifestyle, stating, for example, "According to self-efficacy theory, having low exercise self-efficacy contributes to the non-exerciser's sedentary lifestyle." Finally, concept maps can be presented simultaneously. Team maps can be taped to a wall for display, and teams can then be asked to take a poster walk to identify the best *kudo* (correct application of course information) and the best *kvetch* (incorrect application of course information) on the maps. Alternatively, application statements drawn from team concept maps can be used to develop multiple-choice-question team application exercises. For example, teams can be challenged to select the application statement (from a list of application statements) that most deserves a kudo or a kvetch.

Research supports the efficacy of concept mapping for learning and for collaborative learning in particular. Nesbit and Adesope's (2006) meta-analysis examined the effects of concept mapping on learning. They included 55 studies and calculated 67 mean difference effect sizes. Of particular interest were the large effect sizes for concept mapping in postsecondary education ($ES = .77$) and for concept mapping in mixed groups ($ES = .95$). These data led them to conclude that

> concept maps seem to suit collaborative and cooperative learning because, like lists and outlines, they make economical use of text and can be written with letters that are large enough to be viewed by a small group. When drawn on large paper sheets or whiteboards, concept maps can often be extended with less need for reorganization and erasure than lists and outlines. Because semantic dependencies are more explicitly represented in concept maps than in text formats, they may be more amenable to concurrent editing in which different group members simultaneously modify the product. (p. 420)

Thus, concept maps likely work well in the psychology TBL classroom because they require that students think critically about psychological content, and collaboratively and concurrently create their final products.

In addition to refining her concept mapping application exercises, Kubitz has also experimented with a variety of other poster-type application exercises. Table 4.2 contains some examples of three of Michaelsen and Sweet's (2008) 4-Ss. Since all teams work on the same problem, she did not include a column for the fourth *S* (same across groups). In addition, Kubitz included a column indicating whether a product was graded, and if it was, what was graded and how it was graded. The following comments were made by students after completing one of her concept mapping/poster application exercises and highlight the effects of the exercises on course-related misconceptions.

I learned more thoroughly about negative transfer and its possible effects on your learning and performance. If you start out learning "pushcart" and then try to learn bobsledding, it could negatively affect your performance. This is because, although the two tasks are similar, they require different actions to perform them and your old learning gets in the way of the new.

I learned several things. I learned that a sauna is not a good example of the thermogenic hypothesis. I learned how to better apply many of the theories and I got to see "real life" examples of the theories. This team exercise helped to strengthen my knowledge of the course information overall.

This exercise taught me how important it is to practice in the same type of environment as you will perform. I learned this by using the information from the book and by connecting it to what was written on the team maps.

I learned a different way of looking at what a gym has to offer beyond the physical benefits, which can be obvious. I think it's important to be able to relay to potential members the important mental health benefits a gym can offer. This is not something foremost in their minds when shopping around; usually it's weight loss. When doing health screenings, a lot of people usually check off they want to relieve stress, so it's important for me to be able to communicate to them how different activities they do will help them accomplish that.

I learned that having too many attentional demands causes a decrease in performance because there is a limited attentional capacity. I learned this by reading over the various team maps, most of which used this concept effectively. I also looked in the book at the section on attentional demand to solidify my thoughts.

In summary, Kubitz has relied quite a bit on concept mapping/poster application exercises in her psychology TBL classroom. As she listens in on student conversations during these exercises, Kubitz hears students challenging one another's interpretations of the textbook and coming to new understandings of how the knowledge base might apply to the world of their future careers. In addition, students seem to appreciate the hands-on aspect of creating concept maps and posters. Thus, concept mapping/poster application exercises offer an alternative (or supplement) to the multiple-choice application exercise in the psychology TBL classroom.

CONCLUSION

Writing TBL application exercises can be a challenging aspect of implementing TBL in a psychology classroom. However, there are helpful resources. Materials from other approaches that use groups can be adapted to the TBL format, and examples of these can be found in the problem-based learning literature. Worksheets can ensure that students sufficiently consider all aspects of a specific-choice question that is used as an application exercise. Practice with well-designed TBL application exercises is the way to scaffold the important skill of transfer of learning. As the authors of a review on education concluded: "Much of the financial and human investment in education has been justified on the grounds that formal schooling helps inculcate general skills that transfer beyond the world of the academic and thus help students become more productive members of society" (Barnett & Ceci, 2002, p. 613). To meet course objectives that involve students in using and applying the material from our courses, TBL application exercises are an effective structure for guiding students through that difficult process of transfer of learning.

REFERENCES

Alexander, P. A., & Murphy, P. K. (1999). Nurturing the seeds of transfer: A domain-specific perspective. *International Journal of Educational Research, 31*(7), 561–576.

Ambrose, S. A., Bridges, M. W., DiPietro, M., Lovett, M. C., & Normal, M. K. (2010). *How learning works: 7 research-based principles for smart teaching.* San Francisco, CA: Jossey-Bass.

Barnett, S. M., & Ceci, S. (2002). When and where do we apply what we learn? A taxonomy for far transfer. *Psychological Bulletin, 128*(4), 612–637. doi: 10.1037/0033–2909 .128.4.612

Bensley, A. D., Crowe, D. S., Bernhardt, P., Buckner, C., & Allman, A. L. (2010). Teaching and assessing critical thinking skills for argument analysis in psychology. *Teaching of Psychology, 37*(1), 91–96. doi: 10.1080/00986281003626656

Bolt, M. (2007). *Instructor's resources to accompany David G. Myers Psychology, 8th edition.* New York, NY: Worth.

Bulu, S. T., & Pederson, S. (2010). Scaffolding middle school students' content knowledge and ill-structured problem solving in a problem-based hypermedia learning environment. *Educational Technology Research and Development, 58*(5), 507–529.

Coker, C. (2009). *Motor learning and control for practitioners.* Scottsdale, AZ: Holcomb Hathaway.

Dollinger, S. J. (2004). Predicting personality-behavior relations: A teaching activity. *Teaching of Psychology, 31*(1), 48–51.

Dunn, D. S., & Chew, S. L. (2006). *Best practices for teaching introduction to psychology.* Mahwah, NJ: Erlbaum.

Fink, D. (2003). *Creating significant learning experiences: An integrated approach to designing college courses.* San Francisco, CA: Jossey-Bass.

Halpern, D., & Hakel, M. D. (2003, July–August). Applying the science of learning to the university and beyond: Teaching for long-term retention and transfer. *Change, 35*(4), 37–41.

Kowalski, P., & Taylor, A. K. (2009).The effect of refuting misconceptions in the introductory psychology class. *Teaching of Psychology, 36*(3), 153–159.

Lox, C. L., Martin-Ginis, K. A., & Petruzzello, S. J. (2010). *The psychology of exercise.* Scottsdale, AZ: Holcomb Hathaway.

McKenzie, K. (2010, November). *Students as judge and jury.* Paper presented at the 30th Annual International Lilly Conference on College Teaching, Miami, OH.

Meeuwsen, H. (2003). Changing your students' learning: From apathy to engagement. *North American Society for the Psychology of Sports and Physical Activity Newsletter, 28*(3), 10–11.

Michaelsen, L. K., & Sweet, M. (2008). The essential elements of Team-Based Learning. *New Directions for Teaching & Learning* (116), 7–27.

Nesbit, J. C., & Adesope, O. O. (2006). Learning with concept and knowledge maps: A meta-analysis. *Review of Educational Research, 76*(3), 413–448.

Novak, J., & Gowin, D. B. (2006). *Learning how to learn.* London, UK: Cambridge University Press.

Willis, A. S. (2003). Problem-based learning in a general psychology course. *Journal of General Education, 51*(4), 282–292. doi: 10.1353/jge.2003.0017

APPENDIX

Concept Mapping/Poster Application Exercise Instruction Sheet

1. Read the case study about the Wimpy Weightlifter. In the case, Matt has a serious problem. That is, he is not performing optimally in his efforts to rehabilitate his shoulder injury and return to competition.

2. Using what you've learned thus far this semester, identify as many scientifically defensible causes of and solutions for Matt's suboptimal rehabilitation performance as you can.

3. Create a concept map illustrating your thoughts about Matt's problem, its causes, and potential solutions. Organize your map so that the problem (Matt's suboptimal performance) is in the middle, the causes are on the left side of the page, and the solutions (or interventions) that might help are on the right side of the page. The map in Figure 4.1 illustrates this organization. Theories and models go in the outermost boxes; solutions derived from them go in the innermost boxes.

4. Write as neatly as possible and large enough so that someone standing in front of your map looking at it on a wall will be able to read it. When you're finished, write your team name on the back of your map and essay lightly in pencil and turn your map in to me. You have the class period today to complete your work.

Note: Theories, models, and research studies may *only* be included if they have been discussed in class or included on the test blueprints. Keep in mind that words like *personality* and *motivation* aren't theories or models. Abbreviate the names of the models and theories (e.g., NAT for Need Achievement Theory), and cite studies using *APA* style (e.g., Kubitz et al., 2009).

FIGURE 4.1
Team Concept Map

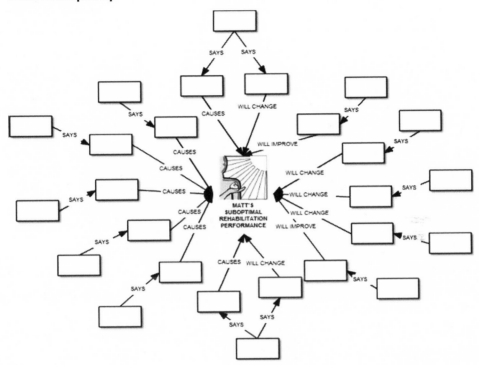

Chapter 5

Connecting Students to the Social World

Using Team-Based Learning in the Sociology Classroom

Erica Hunter and Bryan K. Robinson

In this chapter the authors candidly describe their struggles growing into a clear understanding of what they wanted their students to do after finishing certain courses. Ultimately they developed broad learning goals for use across several courses in which they want their students to use original texts to solve problems, read and use charts and data, create research proposals or conduct research, and evaluate sources and apply course content to them. Readers from any discipline can benefit greatly from the authors' comprehensiveness in describing what implementing Team-Based Learning looks like in their classrooms and what they learned from implementing certain pieces in different ways.

One of the great temptations of teaching is to talk *at* not *with* your class. After all, as instructors, we have only a finite amount of time to cover the key concepts and content our students need to learn in our courses. For many in our position, the solution to these time constraints is to simply lecture and leave or chalk and talk each class session. We spend hours of time developing lectures and assignments to help our students learn the information they expect and require from our courses. At best, this approach bores students who come prepared with the readings completed and who were looking forward to digging deeper into the material. At worst, it suggests to students that a critical reading of course materials is unnecessary because they will hear the important stuff from the reading during lecture. Given the time constraints of an academic semester, many sociology instructors may feel forced to choose between developing active learners who are engaging their sociological imaginations or taking class time to expose students to the largely unfamiliar concepts, ideas, and theories central to the discipline.

Team-Based Learning (TBL; Michaelsen, Knight, & Fink, 2004) provides instructors with a way to move beyond lecture to engage students in discussing and critically thinking about course materials while still mastering the core concepts they need to learn. The design of a TBL course moves the responsibility of learning core concepts and information—what we might normally cover in lecture—to students through assigned readings. Students are then held accountable for studying the nuts and bolts of the course on their own through assessments that enable us to know what information we need to cover further with our students. Class time is then free for students to work in teams on tasks specifically designed to foster a deeper understanding of the material, like discussions or activities. We watch our students move beyond merely memorizing course materials as they begin to use the information in ways that foster critical thinking. In our classes, students are no longer students when they start to work with course materials as sociologists would.

In this chapter we present our experiences teaching TBL sociology. As friends who co-taught our first TBL sociology course before branching into our separate careers, we hope our experiences can help not only other sociologists but also other instructors working in the humanities who are curious about TBL but are unsure where to begin. We start the chapter by discussing the challenges we found in implementing TBL in our discipline: student expectations, the culture of sociology, and how to design a course with students doing sociology. We will then share a variety of activities from our classes that successfully allow students to work with course materials on an applied level. We conclude by providing some tips for starting out with teams in your own courses, focusing on areas we initially struggled with as we converted our courses to TBL.

CHALLENGES TO IMPLEMENTING TBL IN SOCIOLOGY

The thought of redesigning your courses to use TBL may be daunting at first, but it is well worth the effort once you witness the students' level of engagement with the materials. In addition, you will find that the time put into developing TBL courses pays off in the long run with more student engagement, measurable changes in student learning, and once course plans are prepared, a reduction in the amount of time spent getting ready for each class. In this section, we discuss the challenges we found when we started using TBL and how we worked to overcome them. These challenges fell mostly in two areas: student expectations and course design.

Student Expectations and the Culture of Sociology

One of the main challenges we encountered as we developed our TBL courses is that students struggled with understanding sociology as a discipline. Prior experience in high school has exposed many students to core disciplines like history, mathematics, English, and science. Similarly, the mass media have done their share to expose students to other disciplines like criminology, psychology, and fine arts. While students taking courses in these areas often begin with a general understanding of basic concepts, such as biology being the science of life, many are unsure exactly what sociology is or what sociologists do. Although some students approach class with an open mind, attempting to visit their sociological imaginations and understand the complexities of societies across time and place, others will hold fast to the notion of sociology as common sense—there is no need to study because everything they hear, read, or otherwise could learn from the course is easily reduced to common sense and personal experience. For these students, TBL is especially fruitful because it forces them to realize that society is not always common sense, and the mental work required to truly understand the discipline is a challenge.

Student reactions to TBL tend to be twofold. Some students have an ah-ha moment when they realize that sociology is not just common sense but that societies operate in complex ways that cannot always be guessed from one's own experiences. These students tend to embrace TBL and enjoy the challenges the class presents to their current understanding of the world. On the other end of the spectrum are students who resist—sometimes greatly—the TBL framework and may even come to resent the instructor for not teaching using the chalk and talk method they are accustomed to with their other instructors. We have found, however, that these pockets of resentment tend to decrease as we work harder to make sure students understand why we use TBL and how it will benefit their experience in the course.

Perhaps one of the most useful aspects of TBL in a sociology course is the intuitive nature of using teams to teach social structures and social interaction. Although some students initially resist the new teaching paradigm, it does not take long to convince most of the merits of viewing their classmates as teammates, peer authorities, and coconspirators. Working in teams provides students with opportunities to see how their peers understand and experience the social world differently and encourages increased learning as they cooperatively navigate the course material and assignments. Many students comment in our course evaluations that they learned the most from their teammates during exercises in which teams needed to discuss material and defend a choice or propose a course of action. These discussions allowed them to see different viewpoints and understandings of course material.

Course Design: Having Students Do Sociology

A second challenge in developing TBL courses are issues of course design. While academics are accustomed to doing sociology as teachers and scholars, most of the ways sociology is taught do not require students to step into the role of a sociologist. In our experience, we found we were accustomed to teaching students about sociology instead of helping them learn to do sociology; thus our first few TBL courses were crash courses in creating a new paradigm for student instruction. For us, some courses were more difficult than others to convert to a TBL format. The easiest courses to convert were the ones in our areas of specialization and the ones that could clearly answer the question, "What do we want students to be able to do at the end of this course?" For these courses, we were able to use our experience and knowledge of teaching to design the course. However, this was not foolproof. Sometimes we struggled with what we were doing as we initially prepared a new TBL course. What could our students be doing to learn sociology? What could our students be doing for team activities?

After struggling with these problems for a while, we found it helpful to think about the outcomes we wanted to see from our students. Do we want them to be able to work with data? To provide original examples of concepts? To connect policies with theories? Once we started thinking about setting our courses up to meet specific outcomes as goals, the preparation of the course and creating activities students would be doing became easier since a context for activities was provided. Do not be afraid to create your own goals to fit the outcomes you want to see from your students. Lists such as Fink's (2003) verbs for significant learning goals are a great resource for thinking about what students might do in class. The following are some goals along with examples from our classes. Many of these work well across several areas of study in sociology.

1. Using original texts to solve problems
   a. In the course Sociology of Gender, students learned to read original theory texts (e.g. Hill Collins, 2000; Connell, 1995; Butler, 1991) and demonstrate their understanding of the text through case studies, questions, or creative activities (visual maps, interpretive drawings). For example, after reading Connell's work on masculinities, teams must discuss and select the one most important component for understanding what masculinity is in the United States today.
   b. In Nature of Crime, students are challenged to make policy decisions based on readings of original theory texts. For example, teams are asked to rank a number of crime reduction policies in a specific context in order of their faithfulness to the assumptions and conclusions of a theory piece they recently read.
2. Reading and using demographic charts and data
   a. In Sociology of Families, students learned to work with demographic trends in families to understand how families have changed over time, to predict future patterns in family life, and to develop data reading skills. For example, teams are asked to identify on a map of the United States which regions, based on course readings and experiences, they predict would have the highest and lowest marriage rates. Before the answers are revealed, teams must justify and defend their choices.
   b. In Class, Power, and Privilege, students are given statistics and charts and asked to provide liberal and conservative policy interpretations of the data. Students are then challenged to identify which policy interpretations best reflect the ideas presented in the readings. For example, after reading Reiman's (2009) *The Rich Get Richer and the Poor Get Prison*, teams are given statistics on racial differences in arrest rates and asked to consider different explanations about why minority arrests are so high. Teams are then asked to identify which interpretation of the high arrest rates fits best with Reiman's theory.

3. Creating research proposals or conducting research
   a. In Research Methods, students produce research proposals during the course that could be continued as a senior seminar project. Unit activities help students work together to apply the core concepts needed for their proposals, and team members review each other's work as new concepts are brought into their projects. For example, in the unit project that addresses research ethics, teams are asked to act as an ethics review board. They are then given several research proposals they must review to decide whether the proposal is ethically reasonable, in need of revisions, or unethical.
   b. In Introduction to Sociology, teams conduct small research projects to answer the same research question. Teams then compare their results and discuss reasons for differences in findings. For example, one project involves teams collecting data from friends about how they would describe themselves over the phone to someone they have never met. The hypothesis is that people with privileged status positions (being male and White) will be less likely to use those terms to describe themselves than individuals with less privileged statuses (being female and non-White). Teams gather their data, compile it in a chart, and summarize their findings. After teams review each team's findings, the class discusses what reasons may explain variation in findings across teams.
4. Evaluating sources and applying course content to them
   a. In Sociology of Families, students read news stories and evaluate the values presented in the story against the realities of family life in the United States. For example, students responded to a news story about a deadbeat dad who had fathered over 20 children with different women by discussing the values associated with parenting and fatherhood as well as our society's definitions of family and fatherhood.
   b. In Introduction to Sociology, students watch films and identify examples of concepts from the unit. For example, after watching an episode of the television show *The Office* ("Phyllis's Wedding"), teams had to identify the best examples of the primary and secondary groups in the show. They also were required to explain what norm the character Michael was violating that was central to the comedy of the episode.

These kinds of outcomes, alone or paired with others, can be very helpful in setting the stage for the kinds of activities you create for your students. Since each outcome can be evaluated clearly (i.e., you can see students doing the critical thinking your activity requires), it provides a strong foundation for thinking about course design. For example, when Erica set out to redesign her Sociology of Families course, an area she specializes in, she was not sure about how to make the course TBL—what would students be doing? However, once she determined she wanted students to be able to use demographic data and case studies to evaluate and solve problems, the task of putting the course together fell into place.

SOCIOLOGY IN TEAMS: EXAMPLE ACTIVITIES

Once you become familiar with the structure of well-designed TBL activities, you will find it easier to develop activities for your students that help them learn sociology by using the tools, skills, and languages of the discipline. In this section we provide several examples of activities we do in our classrooms that allow students to use course content to expand their critical thinking and creative skills. These activities are strict in following the 4-S design model outlined by Michaelsen, Knight, and Fink (2004). These activities are true cornerstones in developing TBL in courses and should be the primary focus of your classroom activities.

These activities conform to the 4-S activity model of activity design (see Chapter 1). This means the cases students investigate reflect a significant problem (real-world application vs. an abstract one) and they need to make a specific choice to defend. In addition, teams work on the same problem and simultaneously report their choice so they are involved not only in whether their choice was good but also in reflecting on the reasons behind the different choices other teams made. The strength of well-designed 4-S activities is that they allow students to try their hand at doing sociology and to reflect on how other teams approached the same problem. This combination, along with immediate feedback on their work, helps students become better thinkers.

One of our favorite activities involves giving students a case to evaluate though a sociological lens. These have included episodes of *The Simpsons* and *The Office* (both shows are great because they cover a lot of solid material), local news stories, interviews with scholars or pop culture icons, and quoted material related to the unit. Prior to giving students the materials, we provide them with a short overview of what to look for as they independently evaluate the source such as, "We have been talking about culture in this unit. As you watch this episode, I want you to keep an eye out for examples of culture. Remember that culture has material and nonmaterial components." This provides students with a reason to watch the show; they know that afterward they will be applying the concept of culture to examples they found in the show. Often we will give the students the questions they will be discussing with their team to help them prepare as they watch the show. Afterward, teams are given a set amount of time to make a specific choice, such as answering the question, "What aspect of the show do you think best illustrates the concept of culture?" before the teams reveal their choices. This provides students with practice applying knowledge about culture to the show in an environment where they can try out different answers before going public with their choice in front of the rest of the class. After teams make their choices public, the class and instructor can turn to evaluating the choices teams made, and the instructor can provide feedback on the overall strengths and weaknesses of a team's performances.

Here we provide a clear example of a 4-S activity to demonstrate how it might look in the sociology classroom. In Research Methods, students read about different sampling methods and took a readiness assessment test (RAT) on the material. In class Erica wanted to provide students with an opportunity to examine different research questions and to practice using the information they learned to decide the best sampling method for different research examples. The following is a breakdown of her activity based on the 4-S criteria.

Significant problem. She has each team determine the best method to draw a sample of participants for each of four quite different studies, which in combination represent a cross-section of the kinds of studies students are likely to pursue in doing their own work. This is a significant problem because researchers face it each time they start a study, and it is one of the key decisions Erica's students will have to work through individually in their research proposals for the course.

Same problem. All the students discuss each of the four cases in turn and pick the sampling method they think is the most appropriate for each research question. This ensures that when they report and discuss their choices, others will be interested in their answers, and they can learn from the choices other teams defend. In class, teams review the four cases one at a time and discuss their answers before moving on to the next case. This provides students with multiple chances to learn about the decision-making processes that go into selecting a sampling method. As they do more cases, students become better at narrowing and defending their choices.

Specific choice. In discussing each case, teams are required to pick the best sampling method to share with the class. Teams are given a list of sampling methods from their readings to make their selections.

Simultaneous reporting. After making their choices, Erica asks teams to hold up a colored card on cue ("Answers up in 3 . . . 2 . . . 1.") so everyone in class can see how other teams answered the question. Requiring teams to show their answers simultaneously holds them accountable for their choice. To encourage answers on cue, she requires last team up or a team that is not prepared with an answer to start the discussion. This sends the message that teams need to be ready with an answer and that teams need to have a justification for their choice—simply holding up any card is highly risky because teams will have to defend their choice publicly.

Once teams reveal their answers, Erica has teams defend their choice to the class. For example, if half the teams picked snowball sampling and the other half picked purposive sampling, she might start by saying, "It looks like teams are split down the middle on this question. Team 3, I see you picked snowball sampling. Can you explain to us why you picked that?" Additionally, she encourages teams to challenge others' answers. For example, she might say, "So you picked snowball sampling because—? Teams that picked purposive sampling, why is your choice better?" Teams that picked alternative answers then respond with their arguments to build a case why their answer is better. If needed, Erica probes and asks additional questions when justifications are weak or vague. As teams discuss each case, she provides them with feedback on their choices and arguments.

Feedback on their contributions—especially when it is from their peers—allows students to understand when their examples are good, or when they are wrong, to understand why another option is a better choice. From this example, it is easy to imagine that students will be a lot more engaged in the course than if Erica had given a lecture on which method was the best in each of the situations. The 4-S activity model is rich in providing students with methods to work with information in a way that enhances learning.

Depending on the source and the goals for the activity, we decide whether to give teams specific options to choose from or if we will require them to develop their own answer from the material. The more abstract the application, the more likely we will give teams choices so they have a general set of options to work with. For activities with clearer answers, we allow teams to develop them on their own (e.g., "Which group in the show is the best example of a primary group?").

Other examples of 4-S activities from our sociology courses include the following:

1. *Evaluate what is true or false about the source, given what students have learned in the unit.* This is a great activity for building your students' critical evaluation skills. The starting spot is exposing them to a common example such as a news story, quotation, or ideological argument, then asking a question such as, "Based on our readings, what is true about the case we are evaluating? What is false? What evidence do we have to support our answers? What is the best evidence we have to support position X? Position Y?" For example, in the Nature of Crime teams are shown political speeches and debates in which crime reduction is the central theme, and we have teams identify, based on crime statistics, which political candidate focused on the most realistic concerns.

2. *Step into the shoes of a theoretical position or author.* This allows students to think critically about sources so they can deduce the key arguments and then evaluate them against other positions presented in the course. For example, in Sociology of Families, students read a short piece that argues that the American family is in decline. They are then asked to report how a different author, who argues that American families are historically set and changing, would reply to the first author.

3. *Pro/con or support/refute lists.* Given the evidence, what can teams uncover to support or refute the position? This activity can be fun if you give students a source that is very conservative or very liberal. You will want to make the source extreme enough that students can find something to talk about that will force them to look beyond common sense understandings and dig into the readings. We also like to assign half the teams to make one side of an argument and the other half to take the opposing view. This helps prevent everyone from picking the easy list or students' feeling like they are defending their personal choices. In Sociology of Families, readings that argue for nonmonogamy or very strict definitions of what constitutes a family are different enough for most students to capture their interest. In developing lists, it is important to ask teams to identify the strongest piece of evidence from their list instead of a list of everything they can think of for a list. Their key point can then be used to frame the class discussion (e.g., teams report the best answer they have and defend it). Alternatively, after developing a list of three to five answers on the board, have teams reevaluate the question and pick the most compelling piece of evidence to defend from the list the class created.

4. *Concept maps.* These are a fun activity to do when you want students to use course materials in a creative way. We have students map out three key concepts and

then develop applications for them. For example, in Introduction to Sociology, students learn about a wild child named Genie. Students create a map that identifies three concepts that help explain what is wrong with Genie (e.g., lacks primary socialization). They then identify ways that, in an ideal world, these problems could be addressed to help her (e.g., place her in a family where she is cared for and can learn how to talk, walk, and be human).

5. *Policy think tank.* In Bryan's class, Power and Privilege, he conducts an exercise in which teams are presented with a policy problem to solve. For example, students are asked to develop new guidelines for identifying the poverty line. Students are given a brief explanation of the issue and time to propose a solution. Next, each team briefly presents its solution to the entire class. Then Bryan takes a few minutes to explain the current policy (if any) that is in use, and the floor is open for discussion about which proposed solutions are most viable and why they might work better than current policies. Finally, teams are asked to reconvene and decide which one element of the formula for the poverty line is the most important.

6. *Content analysis.* This assignment can work with any number of sources (e.g., magazines, newspapers) and is particularly suited for small enrollments because of costs of material and its open nature. Each team is provided with the same set of sources for the analysis. For example, if they are analyzing magazines, they may each get a copy of *Cosmo*, *Men's Health*, or *Ebony*. Students are then encouraged to identify examples in the magazines of a key concept from the readings (i.e., sexism, racism, classism, homophobia). Once each team has had the opportunity to identify at least three examples, teams are asked to rank their examples by strength and to write a short explanation on how they would use each one as an example of the concept. Teams then share, compare, and discuss differences in how teams approached their rankings for each concept.

With each of these activities, students must use critical thinking skills to link the information they are given to the course content. Additionally, they need to make a specific choice when answering the questions, which allows discussion and feedback. In each activity, it is very important to find a way to phrase the question so the answer will appear as a simple concrete choice that teams can defend and not a long explanation that is hard to summarize. Students can be given options to pick from, or you can ask for one best example. The key is that forcing a choice is a cornerstone of 4-S activities and allows for great team discussion since teams will have to defend their choices. Often, students may not see the sociology in such things as TV shows or a news story. This is what makes these types of activities great for developing learning skills; students gain practice in using sociology to reexamine artifacts from everyday life. After a couple of popular media exercises in class, students tell us they cannot watch television the same way anymore; they are able to see concepts from the course in a new way.

Another activity students really enjoy involves demography, a topic that used to put our students to sleep. These activities actually get the most positive mention on the course evaluations and are very easy to do. The traditional approach typically involves putting up charts and explaining them to students and maybe asking them to summarize information presented on the chart. Using TBL transforms what is usually a dry topic into a fun event by engaging teams in a 4-S activity in which teams use demographic data to make an educated guess they must defend using evidence from their course materials. We have discovered two general approaches that work really well. One is giving teams a blank chart and having them estimate the answers on a graph (e.g., draw a line that represents the divorce rate over time or fill in a pie chart with estimates of the percentage of violent vs. property crimes). With line charts, we use overhead transparencies and stack the teams' responses for a simultaneous report. After teams have time to make their estimates, it is useful to sort them into similar groups and ask one team from each group to explain the thinking behind its answer. In doing this, students' brains are activated; they cannot do the assignment well if they do not think about what they know about the topic, their experiences, and what might make the most sense given what they have learned in the unit.

The other option is to give teams a chart but to remove all labels and have each team hypothesize what the chart is showing. We find this activity drives students even more nuts than the first, and by brainstorming and thinking about the material and evidence, a high proportion of the teams end up with the right answer. For example, in Sociology of Families, students are given two different pie charts and told the data is related to the current unit on divorce. The labels on the charts read, "Several times a week," "Once a week," "1–3 times a month," and so on, up to, "Not at all." After giving teams time to label and justify the choices they made, we open the floor for discussion. Teams volunteer their answers, which are recorded on the board, along with the reasons they picked them. We usually list three or four different answers before taking a hand poll to see which teams picked what. If one answer is right, we agree and tell the other teams to go back and reevaluate the data. If none of the answers are correct, we say so and give them another hint. In doing this, it is important to confirm the great thinking teams are developing; in many ways, being right on their first try is not as important as using evidence from their studies to try to make sense of what they are seeing. You will be amazed at the sources students will pull from as they develop arguments they use to defend their understanding of the data.

USING TBL IN SOCIOLOGY COURSES:
ADVICE FOR STARTING OUT

We end this chapter by offering our advice and suggestions for implementing TBL in sociology. These suggestions come from our experiences at three different schools and are largely a result of the challenges we have had with each student body. Bryan's TBL experience has been predominately in small classes (10 to 25) at a small liberal arts college, while Erica's classroom experience has been split between large enroll-ments (80 to 120 students) at a research university and small-enrollment courses (20 to 25) at another liberal arts college. In this section, we focus on two areas. First, we offer some more tips and tricks for developing 4-S activities. Second, we focus on larger-course design and curricula concerns. These suggestions provide a good start-ing point for thinking about some issues you may uncover as you start your TBL adventure. However, even after using TBL for a few semesters, we find that each new class can provide a new surprise we had not anticipated.

Starting Out in TBL: Tips and Ideas for Instructors New to TBL Course Designs

Switching to a new teaching model can be intimidating, and we admit our first few TBL attempts were crash courses. Experience was our best teacher when we started with TBL, along with making connections with other TBL instructors who provide insight, encouragement, and creative approaches to the problems we faced. In reflecting on the best advice we can provide, it has to be, *start simple*. Keep with simpler, more proven types of activities while you get a feel for how TBL works in your course and how your students respond to it. Simple 4-S activities, such as the activity that asks students to pick the best sampling method for a research project, are an excellent way to warm up students to TBL, and as long as the 4-S criteria are met, the activities tend to be failproof. Along with the other contributors to this book, we provide a variety of ways to use the 4-S model in class. It is important to become comfortable in developing and implementing activities in class before mov-ing to activities that expand or deviate from the model.

Once students gain a feel for the rhythm of 4-S activities and being active contrib-utors in their classroom, you can look into developing larger activities that incorpo-rate the spirit of 4-S activities in innovative ways. This may be important for classes that have specific learning goals or skills students need to learn that may be better addressed with a more complex activity. For example, the research project in which students gathered, calculated, and presented their findings about how individuals describe themselves contains many more steps than a classic 4-S activity, but this project can be broken into parts and accomplished over several class periods as a series of decisions the team makes. Based on your goals and what you want your students to accomplish (we wanted our students to experience doing real sociological research), you can work to develop innovative adaptations to students' in-class activities.

The following list of tips for creating activities works well in small and large courses. We hope these tips, along with the 4-S activity framework, will provide you with ideas for developing your first activities.

1. Clear connections among course goals, concepts, and application are key. Well-designed assignments not only clearly state what the teams need to do but should

also clearly link to the readings and course objectives. If students sense the assignments are merely busy work, they will quickly lose interest in the TBL process. Similarly, if students cannot easily identify how the work relates to the readings and other course work, they may begin to take the reading less seriously. However, if the question or problem they are working with allows them to discuss and try out ideas they are working with in the course, they will have a more rewarding time engaging in the activity.

2. Keep the doing/feedback cycle in mind. Ideal activities have students doing something and receiving immediate feedback on their work. It is helpful to think about the activity and how you approach gathering team responses, group discussion, and providing final feedback. For example, teams may read a case study, make a choice, and simultaneously report their decision. This provides fuel for large-group discussion and instructor wrap-up at the end. This wrap-up is very important because it celebrates strong answers from teams and provides incentives for them to keep up the good work, highlights weaker responses and provides rationales for why it is weaker, and gives students a sense of closure to their learning. In this sense, teams see how they compare to others in their work and receive feedback that will help them learn in future sessions.

3. If possible, keep activities within one class period. This supports the immediate feedback cycle and keeps the discussion relevant to students. If scheduling or the activity require more than one class period, examine your activity to see if the break can benefit teams (e.g., "We determined the best approaches to the questions we needed to address to move forward with this activity. Between now and next class, start thinking about ideas to bring to your team for the next part of the problem."). Having activities that contain smaller steps breaks down the decision-making process and lights a fire under the team (e.g. "We only have five minutes to make a choice! Let's get to work!") and discourages engagement in other activities.

4. When asking questions students might perceive as simply opinion questions, always require evidence. Students often come to sociology thinking the correct answer is the one based on their experiences or thoughts on a topic. Since our goal is to help students become better critical thinkers in our discipline, we want them not only to see there can be different views on a topic but that some answers are more relevant or better supported than others, given a context and evidence from the discipline. These errors in judgment are simple to avoid by having teams identify the key argument for a specific viewpoint and support it with solid evidence from the course. This will force students to move beyond their gut reactions to the material to examine the potential choices in a larger context. The data collected from activities like this inevitably promote critical thinking because the class discussion consists of evaluating and making sense of teams' statements and provides students with clear feedback on how to evaluate cases from various angles. In discussing these activities, we often respond to team statements with, "Where is the proof? How do we know that is true?" to remind them that sociology is not about what they think, but they need to use evidence from their readings to support their claims.

5. Keep variety in mind. Once we find a format that works well, it is easy to fall into a pattern of doing something similar with new cases. While this works, it is likely students will become accustomed and perhaps bored with doing the same types of activities every day. This does not mean you need to reinvent the wheel for each class; instead, think about small ways to change activities.

   a. Data or cases can be presented in various ways, such as a short reading, a quote, a news story, a short video, a video clip, a picture, a graph, a comic strip, a chart, and so on.

   b. Vary the kinds of questions students are asked. For example, the first thing we ask teams to do with a case is to summarize it: What are we looking at? What are the facts? However, something as simple as summarizing can be changed to create interest. Sometimes we have students summarize in 10 words or less, develop a set of five key words, make a chart, or (Erica's favorite) write a haiku to summarize the case or problem. These activities all ask for the same final product (a good summary) but force teams to be creative in different ways. The kinds of questions we ask students to work on (e.g., ask for policy suggestions, research questions, or a comparison to another author or viewpoint) can also keep discussions interesting and different. In addition, you can explore other parts of their decision-making process by asking teams which choices they would eliminate first or asking them to explain which answer is second best and identify what led them to eliminate it from their discussion.

   c. Explore different ways for teams to report their answers. Cold call teams, ask for volunteers, use colored response cards or flags for answers, have teams write their choice on whiteboards or paper; these all facilitate simultaneous reporting while keeping things fresh.

We hope these tips have given you some more ideas for developing and building on the activities you develop for your course. While we developed some of these ideas, we do want to note that many of them were stimulated by the ideas of others. In fact, one of our favorite aspects of doing TBL is the creativity and the community of educators who share ideas on the TBL Listserv (www.teambasedlearning.org/listserv).

Preparing for and Troubleshooting Course, Design, and Curriculum Concerns

In addition to our activity design tips, we also have some thoughts on course, design, and curriculum concerns that can develop because of your particular classroom situations. Our desire is to share our thoughts here because one or both of us has struggled in these areas as we adapted our courses to TBL. The situation you have at your own institution will inform the choices you make for your courses. Here we provide some ideas on grading structure and individual versus team accountability, designing TBL courses with specific curriculum requirements, thoughts on student attendance, and insight on using TBL in exceptionally small classrooms.

Keep overall grade structure and accountability in mind. Setting up a grading scheme for your TBL course can be a challenge—we both continue to work on developing one that feels right with our goals for our students. From our experience, semesters with less individual accountability showed higher grades than semesters with more individual accountability. While it may be tempting to grade mostly group products, this can cover up individual students' low performances, especially if they are on a team that fails to assign fair peer evaluation scores. Second, it does not allow students who are going above and beyond with their learning a way to demonstrate their own work and gain credit for it on their own. As a result, be sure to balance the percentage of a student's grade that is based on team accomplishments (e.g., team RATs [tRATs], unit projects, team worksheets) and individual accomplishments (e.g., individual RATs [iRATs], individual short papers, quizzes, or exams). By ensuring that success in the course is a product of individual and team effort, students will have to work hard on their own and with their teams to earn a high grade.

To illustrate finding this balance Erica uses a TBL grading model in Sociology of Families in which students are graded both as individuals and as teams. Individual grades include five unit iRATs (lowest score is dropped), online discussions where students post relevant news stories and discuss them, and a cumulative final exam over major course themes. Team grades consist of tRATs, randomly selected team worksheets (graded satisfactory/not satisfactory), and unit projects. Students are allowed to set the weight for the RATs to determine how much of their RAT grade is based on their individual and team performance. In addition, Erica uses the peer helper score (Michaelsen, Knight, & Fink, 2004) peer evaluation method, which creates a multiplier that weights the team's grade based on each individual member's contributions, or helping behaviors. Overall, about 60% of the course grade is based on individual contributions and 40% is based on team contributions. This way, students who do not pass individually are unlikely to pass the course based on their team's effort. It helps to ensure that grades reflect the relative abilities of a student's accomplishments in the course.

However, Erica used a different grade structure for her Research Methods course, which is required for the major, and she wanted to make sure students earned grades that reflected their ability to apply research methods. Here, individual grades are composed of six iRATs (lowest score dropped), an individual research proposal paper, and individual assignments done in class (usually as a part of a TBL activity; e.g., tell the students to take five minutes to make their own choice and defend it on a sheet of paper before talking with the team). In addition, she converted the group unit projects to individual projects for this course because she wanted to evaluate individuals on their learning from the unit. The only team grade consists of those earned on six tRATs (lowest score dropped), weighted using the peer helper score. The grade distribution is 80% individual and 20% team. The day-to-day activities are done in teams, but teams are not graded for their performance on these tasks; instead, their accountability for activities comes from their individual need to learn to work with the course materials because they will need to do it by themselves when they write their research proposal. Teams function to help students learn, negotiate, and understand the material in a very low-stakes environment (e.g., team's answers are not graded based on being right or wrong).

Bryan takes a different approach with grading structure, with a heavier focus on team member evaluations of each other. In general, his class grades are evenly weighted between individual and team grades. Individual grades are calculated from five iRATs, daily attendance, and evaluations of teammates. Team grades are calculated from six tRATs, team activities, and unit projects. Team grades are also weighted by the peer helper score. The teammate evaluations are conducted at midterm and at the conclusion of the course. Students are asked to write detailed evaluations of each of their teammates' performances focusing on various team qualities such as attendance, preparedness, and contribution to teamwork. Students are then assigned two grades, one for the quality of their evaluation of their teammates and another based on their teammates' evaluation of their contribution to the team.

NEEDS FOR SPECIAL CURRICULUM GOALS

Based on specific curriculum or course goals, modifications are sometimes necessary in courses that focus on individual achievements such as writing-intensive courses, senior seminars, and honors thesis. Activities like these are poor candidates for team activities because they are too complex, and the ability for teams to divide and conquer the task creates concerns for team functioning and individual accountability. Asking teams to create team proposals would not be an effective team-based assignment. However, creating team activities that assist students in practicing the skills they need to accomplish on their own provides an excellent approach to designing these courses.

While our Research Methods classes are TBL and use many 4-S activities, we are faced with a curricular requirement that mandates that each student must individually produce a unique research proposal. To fulfill this requirement, students complete individual components of the research proposal in conjunction with the team assignments. For example, after reading about survey design, students develop several sample questions they could use as part of their research. Once teams have worked through the group exercise of identifying the best question from a list of sample questions in class, teams are then asked to evaluate their own team members' questions.

Attendance

If you are lucky and work at a school where attendance is normative, you will likely not have many issues with this creating problems for teams. However, if you are at an institution where students need some encouragement to attend, be sure to think of a way to work it into your grading system. We have found on campuses with attendance issues that some students will show up only when something is being graded, such as for a RAT or graded project. This is quite a problem since it prohibits team formation and the students' ability to gain practice using course concepts from activities during a unit. While peer evaluation can help, peer evaluations do not always penalize poor attendance, especially on teams with frequent absences or in small college settings where everyone knows everyone and teammates are likely to be friends and less critical in their evaluations.

We offer two suggestions for combating attendance issues, both of which involve adding measures of individual accountability to the grade. First, have teams track their attendance. Last semester Erica had teams take attendance at the start of class. This helped improve attendance some from the previous semester, but there were still students who frequently skipped class. Bryan has team members sign their name to every team assignment they submit. In his experience, this encouraged attendance and participation since team members feel a sense of ownership for the work when their signature is on it. When asked for ideas, students suggested to penalize students for missing too many classes (i.e., after two unexcused absences, students lose points off their grade) and allow teams to kick off members who are no-shows too often. Both ideas provide incentives to come to class and allow teams the power to remove members who are uncommunicative and who are deadweight to the team. This helps alleviate a lot of stress from teams that have a member who is causing trouble because of poor attendance.

Second, assign grades to class activities. While it might be time consuming to grade all activities, if students know, for example, one random assignment from each unit will be graded, it provides motivation to attend class and do the work to ensure they will earn credit. There are different ways you can grade these assignments, such as satisfactory/unsatisfactory, the logic behind their team's choice, or overall class performance. Alternatively, you can collect individual assignments during class to factor into students' grades. In a TBL activity, reflective writing, making individual choices before team discussions, and various assessment activities (see Angelo & Cross, 1993) can hold students accountable for attending, provide them with opportunities to reflect on materials or their learning, and provide you with information on areas students need more help understanding.

Concerns With Teaching Exceptionally Small Courses

Several challenges surface for the traditional TBL model in very small classrooms (under 15 students). For starters, small classrooms primarily are either on small campuses or in upper-level courses, both of which can result in classrooms of less than a dozen students. Additionally, this presents unique issues since many students will arrive with preconceived notions about others in the class, which may hinder the team formation process. However, these small classes can also be easier to manage since the instructor is more likely to know many of the students in advance and can better plan teams around the strengths and weaknesses of individuals in the course.

Furthermore, small classes can still benefit from TBL's structure even if you are forced to create teams with less than ideal numbers of members.

Another issue generated by small classrooms is the limited number of students available for group formation. For example, a class of 10 students would only allow for two teams of five, which limits the diversity of team answers in many assignments. A final issue arising from small classrooms is the feast or famine nature of classroom discussion. In large-enrollment classes, the odds are in your favor that at least some of the students did the readings and are looking forward to discussion, but in small-enrollment courses it is reasonable to assume there will be days when no one wants to contribute and days when everyone wants to contribute. However, our experience tells us these smaller classes are usually more engaged than the large classes because students often feel more comfortable talking in intimate numbers.

To conclude, we hope the experiences discussed in this chapter have helped you think about how to implement TBL in your courses. The most difficult part of teaching a team-based course is determining the goals and the course design that can help your students meet these goals. In the first section, we provided many suggestions for goals that can work well in a variety of sociology courses. We hope these suggestions will help you start to think about how to spark the inner sociologist in your students by creating activities that allow students to do sociology. In the next section, we provided a variety of ideas for activities that you can adapt to your unique classroom needs. We gave examples of activities we have used in small (15 to 30) and large-enrollment (100 plus) classrooms. Finally, we related a few tidbits we wish we had known when we started out with TBL in our courses. Whether you jump in feet first or start by using bits of TBL in your courses, be assured that TBL will provide your classroom with a renewed energy and allow your students to be sociologists in their everyday use of course concepts and materials.

REFERENCES

Angelo, T. A., & K. P. Cross (1993). *Classroom assessment techniques: A handbook for college teachers*. San Francisco, CA: Jossey-Bass.

Butler, J. (1991). Gender imitation and insubordination. In D. Fuss (Ed.), *Inside/Out: Lesbian Theories, Gay Theories* (pp. 13–31). New York, NY: Routledge.

Connell, R. (1995). *Masculinities*. Berkeley, CA: University of California Press.

Fink, L. D. (2003). *Creating significant learning experiences: An integrated approach to designing college courses*. San Francisco, CA: Jossey-Bass.

Hill Collins, P. (2000). *Black feminist thought*. New York, NY: Routledge.

Michaelsen, L. K., Knight, A. B., & Fink, L. D. (2004). *Team-Based Learning: A transformative use of small groups in college teaching*. Sterling, VA: Stylus.

Reiman, J., & P. Leighton. (2009). *The rich get richer and the poor get prison: Ideology, class, and criminal justice*. Upper Saddle River, NJ: Prentice Hall.

CHAPTER 6

Team-Based Learning in Economics
A Pareto Improvement

Molly Espey

Molly Espey provides a clear depiction of how dabbling with only pieces of Team-Based Learning or adjusting the system away from what is recommended actually created a worse classroom experience for her. In contrast, she then describes how her implementation of Team-Based Learning matured in ways that were localized but still in keeping with best practice. She offers excellent examples of how she uses Team-Based Learning to cultivate students' quantitative reasoning and critical thinking skills. The result? "It was not until I recently looked back at assignments and tests from the time before I started using TBL that I realized how much depth I have added to my course."

When I first learned about Team-Based Learning (TBL), I was not seeking a new way of teaching, I was not dissatisfied with my classroom experiences, nor was I particularly frustrated with the students. Sure, I might have desired more engagement from the students, or more intrinsic interest; I was teaching economics primarily to nonmajors after all. Decent attendance with open eyes in the room was an accomplishment. Really, I was pretty pleased with how things had been going and how I had adjusted to a new university with a different student and academic culture. But I continued to attend teaching workshops, always excited to find new techniques to incorporate into my classes. Attending an all-day workshop on TBL was the beginning of the most significant change to my teaching in my career.

MY TBL ODYSSEY

I began the transition in my teaching to TBL by implementing most of the big pieces right away and was quite pleased with the results—but over time I adapted it in ways that actually made things worse, teaching me important lessons about the value of all the pieces of the system. In the fall of 2002, I was scheduled to teach a new course on the economics of the interface between agriculture and the environment. I had already planned this as a case-based course, so in a sense the structure lent itself well to adaption as a TBL course: I had the end in mind; that is, I had used backward design (see Chapter 1) so I knew what I wanted the students to be able to do by the end of each unit. I selected five cases, and I knew what concepts the students needed to understand before they could successfully analyze those cases. Course enrollment included agricultural economics majors, community and economic development majors, and environment and natural resource economics majors, which allowed me to capitalize on this diversity in the formation of teams. I implemented individual and team readiness assurance tests (iRATs, tRATs) at the beginning of each major unit and peer evaluation at the end of the semester, and the students engaged in application activities and discussion encompassing the course material and case studies in their teams fairly regularly in the classroom.

Overall, the students gave a very positive evaluation of the course. However, even though I had attempted a full-fledged TBL implementation, I now realize there were a few weaknesses in what I did that were based on either my previous experiences with group work or my limited understanding of the nuances of TBL. While I deliberately created diverse teams based on academic majors and kept the same teams throughout the semester, each team only had four members. Based on my pre-TBL experience with group work, five to seven students in a group just seemed too big because I hadn't yet experienced the impact of using the Readiness Assurance Process (RAP; see Chapter 1) with immediate feedback assessment technique (IF-AT) answer sheets. I feared groups of that size would make it harder for quiet students to give their input and that it would also provide a greater opportunity for free riding. In this particular course, four students per group worked reasonably well because most of the students were seniors, and they were taking the class because they wanted to be in it; hence attendance was near 100%. Thus it was another semester before I realized the value of having groups of five to seven rather than just four.

While I used beginning-of-unit iRATs and tRATs with conceptual-level questions, I did not provide a reading guide. I did not allow students to split points on answers for partial credit on their iRATs, and I did not use the IF-AT forms for the tRATs. As a result, scores averaged only 61% on iRATs and 77% on tRATs. I had actually forgotten about the IF-AT forms and the idea of allowing partial credit on multiple-choice questions by giving students four points to distribute among the four or five possible multiple-choice answers. So instead of attributing the low scores to the lack of guidance, the lack of partial credit on individual tests, or the lack of instant feedback and second-chance opportunities on the tRATs, I decided the idea of beginning-of-unit tests was just crazy. How can students succeed on tests over material that has not been covered in class?

The following semester, I took a stab at TBL again, really just using a different mixture of elements of TBL, this time in an intermediate-level natural resource economics course, one I had taught successfully for years using interactive lecturing and evaluating students on homework, tests, and a term paper. With a mix of majors and class levels (sophomores to seniors), I was able to make diverse, permanent teams, but given my previous experience with a highly motivated, advanced group of students, I kept the team size at four students. Also based on my previous experience, I decided to dispense with the beginning of unit iRATs and tRATs, essentially omitting a critical aspect of TBL, the RAP. I also continued to primarily lecture, with a few graded team activities interspersed throughout the semester, including short end-of-unit quizzes individually and in teams. Finally, in contrast to what TBL recommends, each team conducted a market analysis of a different local natural resource business and made a presentation of its findings.

What regression! I quickly discovered that the RAP is the critical first step for creating individual accountability to oneself and to one's team, for establishing the content foundation to ensure the class is ready for application activities, and for weaving together the learning interdependencies that enhance the teams' ability to tackle more complex problems. I also learned that groups do not become teams with only sporadic interaction and that the RATs are just the starting point. If teams don't have to work together until an end-of-unit activity or quiz, they will still be in the early stages of team development when faced with important graded assignments. TBL is not TBL unless there is daily interaction among students in their teams and some degree of interaction among teams. As a result, I now use daily ungraded activities to teach the basic application of concepts and build team cohesiveness, allowing for a stress-free environment in which teams can learn how to work together, building up their ability to handle more complex, integrative applications.

In addition, while not all of my group projects were disasters, and many were a (mostly) positive learning activity for my students, my experience set the stage for realizing the wisdom of having the teams do their work in the classroom and the value of using 4-S team assignments (see Chapter 1). Because my teams' deliverable was a presentation (not a specific choice), many of them divided their work into parts, and I ran into a number of challenges in trying to grade their work fairly. In many cases, it appeared that students learned little, if any, beyond their part of the whole, and I found it impossible to discern who on a team had done what and what individuals had or had not learned. Further, while the presentations were not poorly done, allowing students to pick their own topics reduced learning and created additional problems in grading the group work. From a learning standpoint, I was hoping students would learn from challenging each other. Unfortunately, the fact that the groups chose their own problem meant they had neither the knowledge nor the motivation to challenge each other's conclusions. From a grading standpoint, I had each of the groups expound on a common set of themes (e.g. market demand, production methods, costs of production, and the size of the industry, etc.) so that I would have a basis for across-group comparisons. Unfortunately, that strategy turned out to be a problem rather than a benefit. Because of the commonality in the structure, students appeared to learn more about presenting in spite of the fact they gained very little understanding of the content of the presentations. As a result, it was clear that groups scheduled for the second or third day revised their presentations based on the earlier groups' presentations, and I was left with the challenge of figuring out how to incorporate that reality in assigning grades for the group projects.

At that point I was in somewhat of a quandary. I still liked the idea of TBL, but I knew something wasn't quite right about how I was doing it. Further, I did not have a colleague at my institution to consult with about TBL, and I had not read Michaelsen, Knight, and Fink's (2004) book. Fortunately, I had made arrangements to attend a TBL workshop at my professional association's annual meeting that summer. So I ended the spring semester looking forward to the workshop, vowing to make improvements and try TBL again the following spring while I coasted through the fall teaching my introductory-level microeconomics course in much the same way I had done in previous years. The thought of using TBL in my introductory-level course never crossed my mind, not until I sat through the workshop for the second time.

During the workshop I realized how I could use TBL in my introductory-level class and how I could improve my implementation of it in upper-division courses. On the plane ride home from the meetings, I read the TBL book (Michaelsen, Knight, & Fink, 2004) and began planning an overhaul of my introductory-level course that was to start in two weeks. I increased the team size to six and reinstituted the RAP with beginning-of-unit RATs, allowing for partial credit on iRATs and tRATs with the use of the IF-AT forms. Teams engaged with the material every class period. I incorporated public reporting of choices on application activities, and that in turn generated ample opportunity for cross-team discussion and further engagement with the material. The following semester I incorporated an additional aspect that took team cooperation to another level: having teams evaluate each other on several team assignments.

CHALLENGES AND APPREHENSIONS

My greatest concerns about using TBL dealt with covering content, basic-level applications, and quantitative analysis. At the intermediate level, there are fewer new concepts, and it is easier to think about significant assignments or activities that could engage a group of students that would not simply be completed by the brightest student in the group. At the introductory level, however, students must obtain the basic knowledge and skills to be able to eventually tackle these larger problems—making it quite tempting to lecture at the introductory level. But, as I explain in more detail shortly, I discovered I could cover the content I normally delivered in lectures by using questions and activities for teams, allowing the students to discover cause and effect, compare outcomes, and make inferences for themselves. Even many quantitative problems were relatively easy to convert to team-based choices by giving common miscalculations or wrong approaches as alternative answers for in-class multiple-choice team activities.

I was also concerned about the amount of information the students would be responsible for reading for each unit. Once I broke it down, however, and really thought about the key concepts they needed to know to be prepared to apply the material, it did not seem so unmanageable. For a while, I allowed the students to bring in one page of handwritten notes to use on the RAT, but I soon realized they spent more time trying to get every detail in the text down on that one page than they did focusing on understanding the key concepts. RATs are not the place for nitpicky questions or complex detail, so I stopped allowing cheat sheets. But the real breakthrough came when I started providing a reading guide listing key topics; the students did not do any better on the RATs, but they were less intimidated and felt more prepared. They also engaged more with each other rather than consulting their cheat sheets during the tRATs.

CORE COMPONENTS

I have used TBL in five different courses ranging in enrollment size from six to 110. Two of these I teach every year, Introductory Microeconomic Theory and Intermediate Natural Resource Economics. Since converting to TBL in 2003, I have taught the introductory-level course nine times in classes ranging in size from about 20 to 110 students, but most often in the 45 to 55 range. I have taught the intermediate-level course using TBL eight times, in classes ranging in size from about 25 to 35 students. In both courses the material is divided into five units, with a RAT at the beginning of each. Basic applications are introduced using multiple-choice questions on the board in class, with team activities building in complexity throughout each unit. Integrative applications are introduced about midsemester to tie together material from earlier units with the later units. The biggest difference between these two classes in how I use TBL is the amount of time spent on basic versus more complex applications, with more time spent on the basics in the introductory-level course. Using TBL entails thinking differently about what it means to teach. Rather than imparting knowledge, the TBL instructor guides the learning process, enabling students to learn through trial and error, discussion, or experience, by establishing an environment of discovery for the students.

From the first RAP to the final exam, grades provide some incentive for students to learn. But to really learn, students must *do*, and a successful TBL class will get students involved in the learning process on a daily basis. Instead of telling students what's what in economics and showing them how to solve this or that type of problem, I strongly recommend designing assignments that get the students teaching each other and working together to solve a problem. Always keep the end in mind. Ask yourself, "What is it that I really want the students to be able to do at the end of the unit or the course? What skills do the students need and what concepts do they need to make use of those skills?" The RAP is the first step in their acquisition of the knowledge of the basic concepts, and each activity after the RAP should further their understanding of those concepts or require them to apply their new knowledge to answer a question or solve a problem that is relevant to the goal. I don't keep any of this a secret from my students either. I tell them the RAP allows us to spend more time in the classroom working on more interesting applications and building their understanding of economic principles and their skill in applying those principles to a variety of interesting natural resource and environmental issues. Although some of the activities take more time than simply covering the same material in lecture, overall

I am able to cover at least as much if not more content than I did pre-TBL, and I am able to go into more depth with greater integration across concepts than before. As a result, students are learning more. Comparing exams and grades from my pre-TBL classes, early stages of TBL, and now after nine years of using TBL, I confirmed what I suspected: Exams are more challenging, requiring more precision, integration, and demonstration of understanding through detailed explanations, and grades are higher.

TBL APPLICATIONS IN INTRODUCTORY MICROECONOMICS

So what does an Introductory Microeconomic Theory TBL class look like? In terms of course structure and content, it looks nearly identical to a lecture-based course. Unit 1 primarily covers supply and demand but also includes introductory concepts such as opportunity cost and beginning models such as production possibilities curves. Unit 2 goes into more depth on consumer demand theory, including consumer surplus and demand elasticities, while Unit 3 covers production theory and production costs. Unit 4 includes perfect competition and monopoly, while Unit 5 covers some basics of resource and environmental economics, as my course is specifically designed for natural science majors. Alternatively, I have taught the course with the final unit covering imperfect competition.

After the RAT, there is still a great deal of basic material to cover, and this is where using TBL requires thinking differently about teaching. Instead of defining opportunity cost and giving some examples, or even asking the students what the opportunity cost of action X is, I write a multiple-choice question on the board such as the following:

The opportunity cost of coming to class today is:

1. the value of what you learn in class
2. the money you waste if you skip class
3. less time to spend sleeping in
4. less time to study for another class
5. there is no opportunity cost of coming to class

Each team has a set of colored, numbered cards, and after a short time for team discussion I tell them to hold up their choice. Sometimes such questions will have only one correct answer, while other times, such as in this example, there is more than one possible correct answer, requiring teams to not just identify the answer that fits the definition but to learn through discussion that opportunity cost can be relative. I try to include common misconceptions or miscalculations as wrong answers. For example, for some reason, many students confuse opportunity cost with benefit (answer 1), or invert the example (answer 2). Many of these will get cleared up in team discussions, but it is also not uncommon for a team to select an incorrect answer. This allows for class discussion to focus on the thought process that led to the incorrect answer and what process would lead to the correct answer, thus getting the students to think about their thought process and not just what the right answer is. This also helps to quickly demonstrate to the students that class time is for learning, that they can learn from their peers, and that wrong answers are not always bad when you can learn from them. Daily interaction within teams engaging in ungraded problem solving also helps to build team cohesiveness without any pressure.

Multiple-choice problems like this can also be used to teach graphical interpretation or even how to draw graphs. For example, I might draw the production possibilities curve shown in Figure 6.1 on the board, then ask the students, "What is the opportunity cost of moving from A to B?" Options might include 200 board feet of timber per month (the benefit instead of the cost), 400 board feet of timber, 600 wilderness visitor days per month, and 300 wilderness visitor days per month. I can also make them think more deeply about the shape of the curve by asking why the curve has a negative slope or why it is bowed out, still giving multiple choices that include the correct answers (because of limited resources and specialized resources) as well as incorrect answers that bring in other relevant concepts such as efficiency or growth. And while one should not lean too heavily on having teams make lists, I am not averse to some basic brainstorming, such as thinking about things that would make a currently unattainable level of production possible. This can be used to precede an activity requiring a specific choice, for example, by having students decide what they think would be the most likely cause of growth in an economy's ability to produce more of a particular good without sacrifice of other goods or services.

FIGURE 6.1
Production Possibilities Frontier

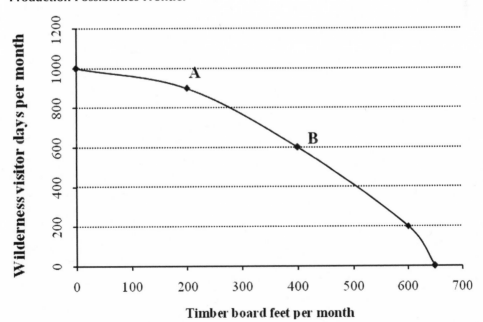

Once they have completed the RAP, I know that students have read the book and taken a test on basic concepts, so I do not need to spend class time redefining terms. However, because there may be a week between the first RAP and when I begin with supply and demand, I want to ensure that the students remember the basic concepts, but I can still address these topics without simply repeating what they've read. For example, I might draw four graphs on the board and ask which best illustrates an increase in demand; one graph might show a decrease in demand, one an increase, one a change in supply, and one with two demand curves intersecting showing that quantity demanded is greater over some range of prices but lower over another range of prices. In the process of debriefing team answers, I can review that demand curves slope down and supply curves slope up and why an increase in demand is shown as a rightward shift of the curve. In addressing price controls, I ask where an effective price ceiling should be set relative to market equilibrium and what impact it has on the market, requiring a choice from among such options as "above, cause a surplus"; "above, cause a shortage"; "above, no impact"; "below, cause a surplus"; and "below, cause a shortage." To make this choice, students must recall what a price ceiling is, when it will have an impact on the current market equilibrium, and what sort of impact it will have. As the students solidify their understanding of the basic concepts and applications, we can move on to tackle somewhat more detailed applications.

While Introductory Microeconomic Theory is necessarily content heavy, the ultimate goal of learning economics is to understand everyday economic problems and to be able to evaluate alternative economic policy proposals. Thus many of the activities in my introductory class involve interpretation of current events. Some of these might be simple, for example, asking teams to determine the impact of an economic recovery on the price of gasoline and explaining why the price would change. Some might be more complex, for example, determining why cotton prices would rise in spite of increased planting or why there might be a surplus of wind energy capacity. Teams compare relative elasticity, not just for price elasticity but also income elasticity and cross-price elasticity, choosing which of two goods (or pair of goods in the case of cross-price elasticity) would be the most elastic and why. This sort of example can also be used to demonstrate the relationship between elasticity and revenue with a link to public policy, for example, by having teams discuss the impact of a given percentage tax on two goods of differing elasticity, say, cigarettes and yachts. A key in TBL is to shift from simply discussing such an example in class to presenting a situation (e.g., "Suppose a new a 10% tax is imposed on these two goods. For which would tax revenues increase the most?") and letting teams figure it out.

I have found that students often have more trouble grasping supply-side concepts like inputs and costs than they do with demand-side concepts. Therefore, rather than speaking in the abstract about inputs and costs of production, I find a business the students have some experience with or can at least visualize. For instance, the majority of my students are interested in outdoor recreation, so I have had them consider such businesses as kayak rental, guided fishing, and summer camp operations. Early in the semester, teams consider the variety of resources needed to operate such a business. As they report the results of their brainstorming, I list their ideas on the board in three columns that they soon come to recognize as human, capital, and natural resources. This lesson returns to them when I cover production theory, as they again must consider inputs required to operate a different business, distinguishing between fixed and variable inputs. Similarly, more grounded knowledge of costs generated by a deliberate business analysis enhances their understanding of the short-run decision to shut down versus operating at a loss.

At times, I require students to prepare for a team activity in advance. For example, toward the end of our unit on supply and demand, I give the students a copy of four current news articles and tell them to read each article with a view toward understanding what is going on in terms of supply and demand. The next class period, each team must choose the article its members think is the best example of rising prices resulting from an increase in demand. I try to include more than one article discussing increasing demand but perhaps one that anticipates rising prices, one that includes a change in supply as well, and one article that discusses a price rise resulting from decreasing supply. Teams must justify their choice, including why they did not choose the other articles. I have a similar assignment addressing the impacts in competitive markets of changes in demand or input costs, and for this activity I require teams to choose the article that best reflects long-run impacts. To make these choices, teams must understand the basic economic change occurring, then differentiate between short-run and long-run changes and choose from among several articles presenting long-run changes (for example, closure of a factory because of low demand).

At the end of the 2010 fall semester, I asked the students in my introductory-level course what types of team activities they thought were most helpful to their learning. Sixty percent of the students mentioned the multiple-choice application questions on the board as being most helpful while 40% said it was the RATs (many students included more than one activity). When asked about specific activities or applications they found particularly interesting, the majority of the students mentioned some activity that involved a current event. More than anything, I use these multiple-choice questions to build and solidify the foundational disciplinary content, so the students' perception that these were most helpful in learning is indicative of the significance of basic concepts and applications at the introductory level. The more complex applications build upon this foundation, so establishing the foundation is vital at this level.

APPLICATIONS IN INTERMEDIATE NATURAL RESOURCE ECONOMICS

In my intermediate-level course with fewer new concepts to introduce, I am able to spend more time on more detailed applications. I still use multiple-choice questions fairly extensively to build the foundation of new vocabulary and new tools such as discounting. The true heart of the course, though, is in understanding those situations when markets fail to achieve efficient outcomes, why that is, and what might be done about it. This material entails discussion of property rights, valuation, externalities, open access resources, public goods, Coasian bargaining, and analysis of policy alternatives. Instead of walking through these concepts, defining each, graphing it, showing the deadweight loss, then giving some specific examples, I may start with an example and have the students identify the most likely source of the inefficiency and even brainstorm a policy to address the problem. Many of these activities lend themselves well to the gallery walk in which students post their answers on poster paper around the room and evaluate the choices of other teams. Once the foundation of economic thinking is firmly established, the possibilities for interesting and thought-provoking applications are endless.

Early in this course, it is important for students to be able to distinguish among types of goods and the characteristics that contribute to efficiently operating markets. On poster paper, teams make a grid as shown in Table 6.1, with one appropriate natural resource example for each block. Students complete the grid with the appropriate placement of each of four types of goods.

These grids are then posted on the wall around the room, and each team evaluates the others, placing a sticky note on the weakest example of each type of good with a brief explanation of why the example is weak (or even inappropriate). Students learn to recognize the characteristics of each type of good (private, public, club, and open access) and evaluate degrees of excludability and rivalry in consumption in choosing the weakest examples.

To take this a step further, I present more difficult to evaluate examples such as America's food waste problem ("A Hill of Beans," 2009) or the High Line, a New York City park built on a section of a former elevated freight railroad line. In case of the food waste problem, teams must decide whether the problem described in the brief article is a good example of an externality. When discussing the High Line Park, teams decided whether it is a good example of a public good. To make their decisions regarding food waste, students must recognize whether costs are internalized and which costs are relevant to consider. In the case of the park, they must debate whether rivalry in use is significant and discuss the ease or difficulty of excluding people depending on how the park can be accessed. Both discussions reinforce students' understanding of the characteristics of each type of good but with more complexity or subtlety, and both can also lead to a discussion of policy options to address each situation.

An example like the park can also be revisited if valuation is a component of the course, with teams challenged to choose and argue for one method for valuing the

TABLE 6.1
Team Activity: Private, Public, Club, or Open Access?

	Rival in consumption	Nonrival in consumption
Excludable		
Nonexcludable		

park among three: the travel cost method, hedonic valuation, and contingent valuation. All three methods can stimulate rich discussions about the values captured by each, data necessary to make a choice among them, how time or budget constraints might influence the choice, and how the value of each can be expressed to the general public or to policymakers in the city. Similarly, revisiting certain examples of externalities segues nicely into valuable analysis of Coasian bargaining. I require students to choose from among three very different examples of externalities to select which would be most conducive to a Coasian solution. Examples I have used include boaters harming Florida manatee, grizzly bears preying on cattle, and pollution in the Hudson River. In choosing which would be most conducive to a Coasian solution, teams must consider transaction costs and what affects those costs, what property rights are relevant, and how parties could negotiate a solution. In the end, students have acquired a clear understanding of what is relevant to private solutions to externality issues; when solutions might be found in spite of high transaction costs; and why private negotiations might fail to produce a Pareto improvement, a situation in which at least one person is made better off and no one is made worse off.

As the semester advances, and students have more disciplinary tools in their intellectual tool kit, I use applications to integrate several concepts into a decision-making framework. For example, the citizens of South Carolina debate burying the power lines that are above ground after each major ice storm—population growth keeps the debate in front of them as new lines are built. A specific location can be chosen for teams to analyze and decide whether new power lines should be put in above or below ground. Short- and long-run considerations, fixed versus variable costs, and discounting all emerge as issues and inform discussion about the decision. The issue can be made more complex by having teams determine which would be the more socially efficient option, as they would then also need to take into account such things as disruption of habitat and diminished value of views. A multitude of public decisions can be used in a similar fashion, pulling together private and external cost and benefit considerations, discounting, and valuation.

I have found that asking students to play the role of a nongovernmental organization decision maker can help engage them with the material, particularly in courses with many nonmajors who eventually end up in positions with conservation organizations. For example, I may present teams with an option on a piece of land, and they need to decide whether to spend the resources to acquire it and state the most compelling reason why they made the decision they made. Alternatively, I may give them an organizational goal such as sustainability and have teams determine the single best policy to support that goal in a specific location. Conservation organizations such as the National Wildlife Federation and the Rainforest Foundation provide a wealth of real choices that have been made; teams can be presented with background information, and the actual choice made by the organization can be revealed after the team activity. In these sorts of activities, I have found it works very well to have teams evaluate the decisions and rationales of other teams, choosing the most compelling policy or argument presented other than their own. Students really seem to enjoy evaluating others and getting evaluated by others, especially when their poster is selected as the best by the others.

GOING DEEPER

My implementation of TBL is an ongoing experimental odyssey, but it has gradually enabled me to cover more content more deeply. Designing effective team assignments takes thought and creativity, and not every assignment works out as planned. Some fail because of unclear directions, some take much more time than anticipated, and others simply don't stimulate the students as I thought they would or don't generate the learning I had hoped for. Each semester I use TBL, I include more team activities, keeping effective activities and dispensing with less effective ones, and adding new activities to reach and challenge the students. When I discover a truly effective team activity, it frees up class time because I no longer need to go through several examples and require similar homework; a truly effective application activity gets the point across the first time and more often than not can also cover more than one key point. Significant assignments will be remembered by students, so I often find myself referring to them later in the class to connect new material with the old, allowing reinforcement of the old material while also providing a solid anchor for the new.

It was not until I recently looked back at assignments and tests from the time before I started using TBL that I realized just how much depth I have added to my course. My students don't just memorize an elasticity formula and crunch through numerical problems. They can do that, but they are also expected to understand and be able to explain why the demand for one good would be more or less elastic than that of another good, and what the implications of a change in supply would be on consumer expenditures. We have come to be able to examine the connection between supply elasticity and price paths over time, linking elasticity with expansion and contraction of industries, allowing students to predict or explain price changes over time in dynamic industries. I also have students make more linkages across topics to reinforce material from earlier units, such as examining how price controls affect consumer and producer surplus and profits.

In the past, concepts such as increasing or constant cost industries and the shutdown point seem to be things students memorized, spitting a definition back out on a test or locating a point on a graph. In contrast, having worked through a team activity identifying an industry as one of increasing or constant cost, most students now seem to have a firmer understanding of these concepts and are able to explain why an industry would be one or the other and what it means for prices over time if the industry is growing or contracting. Similarly, once the students have analyzed a business operation, differentiated between variable and fixed costs, and identified the most significant fixed cost constraining production, the shutdown point means more than just minimum average variable cost.

In my intermediate-level course, I have also begun to integrate more basics, keeping students responsible for recalling the relevance of elasticity and differences between short-run and long-run changes, for example. Instead of discussing deadweight loss only in terms of a reduction in net benefits, we also break it down into change in consumer and producer surplus and analyze how elasticity relates to the relative size of changes in surplus or loss. Over time, I have gradually covered the analysis of natural resource use in more and more depth, particularly in terms of quantitative analysis, in part to better prepare a minority of the students for a subsequent required course. But by linking the mathematics to a relevant application and pushing the quantitative analysis earlier in the semester, I have been able to reiterate the lesson in subsequent applications, reinforcing the learning and bringing along more students who are generally math averse. As part of this, instead of having students work through several different discounting problems, they must make a choice based on data that will require them to discount but also determine which information is relevant in the decision and what the resulting numbers mean.

This level of understanding was not an expectation of mine for my pre-TBL classes. The top students may have been able to answer test questions, but only the very top students would have really grasped the relevance. Now I expect this level of understanding and ability to connect from *all* of my students, and the majority of students are up to the challenge. My tests are more difficult now in both classes, yet average test scores are significantly higher, by as much as half a grade (five percentage points).

FLESHING OUT THE FRAMEWORK

Chapter 1 presents the framework of TBL as strategically formed, permanent teams; readiness assurance at the beginning of each unit; 4-S applications; and peer evaluation. These are necessary components for the successful use of TBL, but these are not to be simply layered onto a traditional lecture-based course. TBL means teams are the basis of the learning process and as such must interact with each other, engaging with the material every class period, not just as a supplemental exercise but as an integral part of the process. Individuals must be held accountable to themselves and to their team, through iRATs, homework, tests, papers, or whatever sort of assignments are relevant to your particular course. They are accountable to their teams daily via tRATs and activities. Teams must be held accountable to themselves and to the rest of the class. Not every activity needs to be graded by any means, but there must be more to the team grade than just the RATs. Public reporting by teams of their choices and team-to-team evaluation increase team accountability to the class as a whole. RATs should cover basic concepts, ensuring preparation for applications. Allowing students to "split their vote" on the iRAT (as described in Chapter 1) is akin to using the IF-AT forms for tRATs and makes students think more carefully about what they do or don't know about each question. Effective team assignments require teamwork and choices and create significant learning of application and analysis, not just abstract conceptualization. These are qualities that flesh out the TBL frame, moving the experience from one of using teams in the classroom to teams being the basis of learning daily.

One last note about whether TBL might be right for you. TBL requires the teacher to relinquish some control in the classroom. You must be flexible to address whatever students might come up with, perspectives and ideas that may be very different from what you expected. You must be willing to let a good discussion continue longer than you thought it might and adapt when activities don't go as well as planned. You must be prepared to guide students in their own discovery rather than hold their hand and drag them along behind you all the way. But in my experience, it is more than worth it. TBL leads to greater student participation and increased ownership of learning by students on an individual level, as teams, and even as a whole class.

REFERENCES

A hill of beans: America's food waste problem. (2009, November 26). *The Economist.* Retrieved from http://www.economist.com/node/14960159

Michaelsen, L. K., Knight, A. B., & Fink, L. D. (2004). *Team-Based Learning: A transformative use of small groups in college teaching.* Westport, CT: Greenwood.

CHAPTER 7

Team-Based Learning in Social Sciences Research Methods Classes

Sarah J. Mahler

Mahler vividly describes her efforts in implementing Team-Based Learning in a research methods course in which students are expected to produce complex final products. Readers from many disciplines will appreciate how she tackles head-on the challenge of making seemingly esoteric academic skills directly relevant to students' own lives. Further, she details clearly how she mixes individual work and 4-S application activities to help prepare students for the subsequent course and move them through the stages of a term-long project, ensuring that students complete those stages with rich and accurate understandings.

Those of you choosing to read this chapter probably know what I am going to start with: Students *dread* taking research methods (RM). In my department (global and sociocultural studies) this course causes the most anxiety, with the possible exception of the course that follows it—the senior capstone seminar in which students must apply their skills acquired in the methods course by designing and carrying out their own research project. Obviously, their success in capstone depends upon their success in methods. What is less obvious but no less true is that our majors are assessed in capstone; consequently, their success is also a direct measure of our curricular success.[1] In sum, a lot is riding on the RM course. Similarly and not surprisingly, not so long ago when students were performing below expectations on their capstones, my department's undergraduate curriculum committee was tasked with seeking a remedy. We decided to work to improve their performance in capstone by strengthening their experience in RM. We came up with three strategies: coordinating the faculty who teach the course to increase harmonization of expectations, tying the course tightly to the capstone curriculum, and in some but not all cases turning to Team-Based Learning (TBL). I led the latter implementation because I had another reason to implement TBL in my courses.

I have several reasons for adopting TBL. My first reason was necessity. I had to adopt TBL for a new undergraduate requirement in global learning (GL) being implemented at my university. During training for this new requirement, Larry

Michaelsen conducted a two-day workshop with us to introduce TBL, and we were asked to use TBL in these courses. I immediately saw its usefulness but also recognized that I would have to retool my teaching approach into strategies to encourage student learning. Fortunately, I did not have to teach the large 120-student GL course for another year, so I decided to try out TBL in undergraduate RM, a new course for me, though I had taught similar material for graduate students.

A second reason for adopting TBL has been increasing course size caps—the outcome of budget cuts and rising enrollments. We were pressed to raise caps above 50 even for critical courses in our major. How could we ensure student learning and training with such high numbers, especially in labor-intensive courses like RM? Employing TBL in at least social science RM appealed to me as a way to stem this rising tide of mediocrity. Additionally, TBL seemed to me like it could actually be fun. Less lecturing, more learning, more interaction, and fun. Worth a try.

The third and, arguably, most practical reason for adopting TBL for the RM course was that I had to teach this course at the undergraduate level for the first time, which was a prime opportunity to design and implement it as a TBL course from the start. Another colleague who also had to teach it for the first time that semester and who had also been exposed to TBL during the GL training, Hugh Gladwin, agreed to try it with me. He and I would have to figure out how to teach the course to undergraduates—students who were majors, but unlike our graduate students probably were not going to pursue social science careers. As I started to plan the course, this fact presented me with a set of important questions to think about and that worked well with the planning processes involved in TBL. For example, I had to ask, What are my goals for this course? How do they differ from my goals in teaching this course to graduate students? What skill set should I emphasize so that students graduate with marketable skills? Additionally, as students take RM immediately before and as a requirement for entry into our senior capstone seminar, I had to ask, What do students need to learn from this course to make them more successful in the capstone in which they are expected to do their own mini research projects?

Fortunately, my summer planning for the GL course introduced me not only to TBL but also to the use of backward design (Wiggins & McTighe, 1998) in course planning. Backward design is the opposite of what faculty typically do when planning courses (in my experience anyway). Most of the time when planning a new course, faculty proceed from the introduction and move forward chronologically. We design a course from day one onward to the last day. In backward design, you figure out what you want your students to have learned, to be able to do, at the end of the course and then design the course from that point backward to meet those learning goals. What did I want students to have learned at the end? That took some work to figure out. When I teach the graduate version I emphasize the importance of four skills: research design, creating or finding valid research instruments, being able to collect valid data, and performing appropriate data analysis. All four are difficult and labor intensive, so to somewhat lighten the load, I would offer my students the option of working with one or two partners, that is, in groups. Then I had to transform this group-oriented course into an appropriate-level course for undergraduates.

I did not want to eliminate their learning any of the four skills, so the course would be intense. Would they work hard? Yes, I reasoned, if they can see the direct relationship between the course's skills and their lives. That would be my sales pitch. "You're learning this not to torture you," I repeat during the semester, "but to equip you with valuable skills that few other students graduate with and that will open more job doors to you." At the end of the semester I tell them, "Look at what you can now do. Your résumé will now stand out." Getting to that glorious point, however, takes effort.

When implementing social science methods with TBL, I reached out to the Team-Based Learning Collective Listserv and received no responses from faculty already teaching this course with undergraduates. While disappointed, the reality that I was a pioneer in adapting RM for TBL obligated me even more to think about my main goals and objectives, talk with colleagues about them, and plan the course using backward design. As I did these things, I realized I could not possibly cover all the material included in RM textbooks and contemplated what content I could skip and how much time each skill would require. I thought about what I knew were methods most frequently used in the world outside academia, including what professional data crunchers use, and I decided I would expose students directly to only two widely used data collection methods—surveys and interviews. I decided these would yield the most critical skills and involve students in learning about numerical (quantitative) and text (qualitative) data. With these skills they could also conduct focus groups and content analysis with a bit more training or learning on their own. The result was a course in which half the semester covered research design issues (such as stating and refining research problems, conceptualization, different types of data and measurement, validity, reliability, human subjects protection, sampling, etc.), and the second half involved data collection, analysis, and report preparation.

CHALLENGES I FACED (AND OVERCAME) IN DESIGNING AND IMPLEMENTING THE COURSE IN TBL FORMAT

Teaching RM is demanding for students and instructors, in no small part because students do assignments every week that force them to apply the content knowledge they are acquiring. To learn RM is to do RM, but I know many courses only teach how to do methods while fewer expect students to actually do research. I insist on the latter and also insist that students not only collect data but that they learn to analyze data they collect. This is all hugely time consuming and demanding. To prepare students for this I write them an e-mail prior to the beginning of the semester, explaining what they are about to go into and also stating that if they put in the effort they will be rewarded with marketable skills. I also open class the first day stressing these points, and I keep referring to them during the entire semester:

You are learning how to design a survey online. Not everyone knows this. It is an item for your résumé. You will be among the very few people in the whole country who know how to analyze qualitative data. This will make you far more marketable to employers than someone who only knows how to do some quantitative analysis.

I pepper my course with these types of counsel during the whole semester to keep students motivated. Over the years many of my students have been hired to do research after taking this course or have told me years later that they have used these skills more than any others they gained in college even if not directly linked to research (critical thinking skills).

In short, I try to sell not the course itself but the course as a means to acquiring marketable skills. This strategy works better than just acknowledging that taking RM is a necessary evil in the major. Still, the fact remains and probably always will that students do not relish taking RM. Dealing with student motivation toward the course is just one of many challenges an instructor faces even without trying to implement it as a TBL course. TBL presents special additional challenges and opportunities I explore now.

Apportionment of in-class time. I have colleagues who use most of the available class time in their methods courses for lecture. When not listening, students work individually on tasks in computer labs. While I was planning for this RM course in TBL, my colleague, who coplanned with me, and I were reluctant to do away with lecture but needed to set aside time for the Readiness Assurance Process (RAP; see Chapter 1) and for in-class team-based activities. When to lecture? When not to lecture? We decided on a Web-based approach to content delivery that would free up more class time for examples and explanations by the instructor, the Readiness Assurance Tests (RATs—see Chapter 1), and in-class team-based activities. For example, although we did not have time to do voice-over PowerPoints, we did write online lectures (OLL) that explained the class content in great detail and gave many examples; we also frequently posted videos online that covered lecture topics. These were housed in the course website and were organized pedagogically alongside the required readings to introduce the material and aid student comprehension. That is, as illustrated in Figure 7.1, the material appears in the module beginning with the foundational readings, then the OLL(s), followed by additional readings in their order of difficulty and any other items for students to cover. Thus, each week of the course had its own learning module in the learning management system, a self-contained area where all the week's requirements and assignments were housed in the recommended order to promote students' readiness for that week. To guarantee that students used these resources, we wrote RATs that covered each item we required students to know in the module.

RATs took up approximately one third of each week's class time, leaving two thirds to be divided between lecture/clarification and in-class team-based activities. Our experience, however, is that the team-based application activities rarely if ever conformed to our time expectations (they required more time than we budgeted largely because they required a lot of knowledge and critical thinking), leaving little time for lecture. We compensated with highly developed OLLs.

FIGURE 7.1
A Typical Week's Module in the Learning Management System

Table of Contents for Week 4 Research Design II: Types of Data and Data Collection, Refining Research Problems, Conceptualization

1. Research Design II: Types of Data and Data Collection, Refining Research Problems, Conceptualization
2. Required Readings for this week
    2.1 Text: Chapter 4 on Conceptualization and Chapter 11 on Applied Research
3. Online Lectures for this week
    3.1 OLL: Linking Theory and Methods
    3.2 OLL Research Design II Types of Data and Research
        3.2.1 Research Purposes Typology
        3.2.2 Major Qualitative Research Contributions Maxwell 1998
    3.3 OLL Refining the Research Problem and Conceptualization
        3.3.1 Conceptualization Example
4   Additional Recommended Readings: On Applied Research
    4.1 NAPA Patton 2005
    4.2 NAPA Crain and Tashima 2005
    4.3 NAPA Butler et al. 2005
    4.4 Overview of Program Evaluation PPT

RATs. As no one on the TBL Listserv responded to my inquiry about the use of TBL to teach RM, my colleague and I had to develop our own RATs. In my experience, writing good RAT questions is a major challenge, particularly since I do not see the TBL Collaborative offering guidelines for RATs, just examples. Over several semesters I have realized that guidelines are really important since RAT questions are unlike typical multiple-choice questions. A whole chapter of a TBL book should be written on writing good RAT questions across different disciplines; I offer just a couple of suggestions here. First, in the question itself I direct students to select the best or worst choice of answers, or the one that most exemplifies the concept I want them to have learned. This way they have to decide among competing possible choices, not a single correct answer. (I deliberately capitalize these superlatives in the questions for emphasis.) Second, provide in the question the issue, topic, principle you are asking them to know (e.g., random vs. nonrandom sampling or designing an interview instrument), and use the response categories to test their understanding of that concept. This reinforces their learning of that concept in the course of doing the RAP. Third, I highly recommend you work collaboratively with another faculty member when implementing TBL so you can take turns drafting the RATs; my colleague and I also had two teaching assistants (TAs), and we all took turns drafting questions then edited them collaboratively. Once the RAT is fielded, you should examine the questions that students had most difficulty with—perhaps even challenged—and consider revising them for clarity.

Providing time in the term for doing research and analyzing data, not just learning about them. In many undergraduate courses, students learn about doing research; I have always required that they also do actual research. The reason behind this is that most people learn by working on actual tasks in the vicinity of someone more skilled than they are. This is learning in the *zone of proximal development,* a concept developed by psychologist Lev Vygotsky (1978) to describe how young children learn. To learn RM, then, students should do RM. The critical difference with TBL is that it offers a consistent semester-long zone of proximal development—the team. As one or several students learn the material, they are in the best position to help other teammates learn it, too, since not only is the content fresh in the learners' minds, but the way they learned it is also fresh. Students who have just figured out the material are the best ones to help others. One way I facilitated peer-to-peer teaching and learning in the course was to ensure that the existing skills students brought to the course were equitably distributed among the teams. To explain this I now cover team formation since it directly relates to ensuring peer-to-peer teaching in RM courses.

Given that most students enrolling in RM courses are not in their first year of college and often are juniors or seniors, they tend to bring useful skills into the course. Some have taken an RM course in another discipline (e.g., psychology) but have switched their major so they need to take the sociology or anthropology version of the course. Others have learned software packages that are different from those we use in the course, particularly Excel or another type of spreadsheet. I show students how to use software to graph their data, a technique that helps them see patterns. This way they do simple univariate and bivariate quantitative data analysis of the survey data and translate the analysis into visual formats such as graphs and tables. Excel can also be used to do qualitative data analysis by making rows or columns into codes and locating the text data into the cells by respondent and code. Thus, on team formation day, I ask students who have had RM previously to line up first, followed by those with spreadsheet experience, and then any other software or skills I want to distribute among the teams. I also have students take a short online personality test called True Colors (www.truecolorstest.com) in which students discover their dominant personality—their "true color." In team formation, I distribute these personality types by having students group themselves by their true color in the line before we count off to create teams. On team formation day I also have team members introduce themselves, but I also require that they write a short online introduction that is posted on the course management system (in Moodle this is easy to do as a glossary). This way students can get to know their teammates a bit easier outside class. Finally, I provide them with name tags and also give them a team contract and team responsibility assignment papers to work on. The contract is a set of principles for how to work in teams (check the TBL Collaborative website at www.teambased learning.org for examples), which the students must agree to abide by (and they affirm this by signing it); I also give them space to include their own principles unique to the team. The responsibility sheet is where students sign up to be team leader; individual RAT (iRAT), team RAT (tRAT), and voting card coordinators; correspondence manager; attendance taker; and so on. Each team member has a responsibility to the team and to me. These team documents are housed in the team's document folder, a plastic folder that includes files for iRATs, tRATs, voting cards, attendance sheet, in-class projects, and one file for assignments to be handed in. Teams arrive in class and pick up their folder, returning it at the end of class.

I now return to pedagogical strategies I use to get many students into the zone of proximal learning, with or without TBL. An additional strategy I have always used when teaching RM, regardless of level, is to have all students in the class undertake the same research project and have them periodically and formally show their work to all students in the class. If I'm using a learning management system, I ask the team(s) up for peer review to submit their work a day or two before it's due and ask other students to review it individually via a bulletin board function in the management system. This asynchronous strategy does not preclude additional constructive criticism in class; it helps me assess, however, how well students understand the course content as it is applied in assignments, saving scarce classroom time while building critical thinking skills. These analytical tools are sharpened by doing constructive critical peer review as well, such as through exposure to multiple ways of solving problems. If all students work on the same project but approach it in different ways, students learn more by seeing what others do—what they do better and what they do worse—than if they only experience their own solution to the assignments.

So far you may like what I do, but there is definitely a TBL angle to my pedagogical strategy:

- My course is very content heavy at the beginning in order for it to involve hands-on data collection, analysis, and report writing at the end. I easily break it up into 5–7 content units as recommended by Michaelsen in his workshop and in the TBL text (Michaelsen, Knight, & Fink, 2004). However, because the coverage would all occur in the first seven weeks, I was concerned I would face the problems Michaelsen et al. warn would arise from giving too many RATs. In the end, I stayed very close to one week per content unit, even though that meant close to one RAT per week. This schedule resulted in time at the end of the semester for teams to apply their learning to a real research project. During the last weeks they had no RATs, diffusing student grumblings about having so many RATs during the first weeks of the semester.
- I encountered special challenges with team projects because the nature of RM involves steps, not all of which I was able to formulate into true 4-S in-class team exercises, as described in Chapter 1.
- Finally, as this RM course is the precursor to the senior capstone seminar, faculty in my department wanted it to prepare students *solidly* for their upcoming individual research projects that result in papers and formal oral presentations; I faced a dilemma. From what I had learned about TBL, I couldn't figure out a way to prepare students for their capstone research projects without undermining team solidarity by requiring reports and team presentations—both of which are explicitly warned against in the TBL literature (e.g., Michaelsen et al., 2004). In an attempt to minimize these problems, I decided to use Web-based project management platforms such as Google Docs and wikis that enable asynchronous

team collaboration, but I still wondered if I could implement TBL faithfully while fulfilling my course and major-specific obligations.

What I am trying to communicate so far is that I did not experience discipline-specific challenges to or problems with implementing TBL (with one possible exception that I discuss in a moment). I wasn't teaching from a singular disciplinary perspective anyway. But I did, however, encounter challenges harmonizing the different expectations from my course structurally with conventional or orthodox TBL pedagogy. While a typical TBL unit opens with a RAP and closes with some type of synthesizing exercise like a unit test or assignment, I faced having to get students to read and apply a great deal of new content each week in the first half of the course so they would get the nuts and bolts of doing research. I could think of no other way to obligate students to do the reading (which I knew they would not do unless I tested them on it) than by beginning each class for the first six weeks or so with RATs. However, I did maintain the foundational framework of TBL by having students use the material they were learning in any given week by applying it to some type of exercise between the week they learned the material and the following week. Thus, consistent with TBL practice they would immediately apply new content. Unlike TBL, however, some applications involve individual assignments, others are done in pairs, and less frequently they are team assignments done primarily in class. In the individual and pair assignments (such as problem-statement refinement, conceptualization and operationalization tasks, sampling strategies, literature reviews, etc.), I expect students to show at least a basic individual mastery of the course content. During these weeks I also lecture more than I do later on.

My class meets once a week or in some cases twice a week. Therefore, the typical class schedule, as illustrated in Figure 7.2, at least for the first third of the course, is the RAT followed by a bit of clarification of any issues arising in the RAT. After that I might lecture for a while until we reach the midpoint of the class and give students a 15-minute break. Just before the break I typically give out a team-based assignment relating to the material they are learning; as team members return to the classroom, they use the time to begin that assignment. Sometimes the assignment is designed to be finished in class and other times it continues asynchronously outside class facilitated by a Web-based collaboration tool such as a wiki. On the course website I provide examples from past semesters, so students get an idea of what is expected of them.

When the research design phase of the course ends, for two weeks we cover data collection methods—surveys and semistructured interviews. These two weeks follow a rhythm similar to that of the research design phase, RATs and in-class team assignments. Teams help design research instruments for the surveys and interviews. However, I, the instructor, provide the final instruments and go over them with students prior to commencing data collection. Having them try to design their own valid instruments is the most intellectually demanding assignment of the semester, but the critical thinking they learn here lasts a lifetime. (More students come to me years later talking about how they analyze questions posed to them on surveys more than

FIGURE 7.2
Typical Class Schedule for Each Stage of the Semester

Stages I and II—Research Design, Data Collection

This is the typical use of class time during the first 7–8 weeks of class:

1. iRAT followed by tRAT followed by clarifications (45 minutes)
2. Short lecture to emphasize content (15–30 minutes). These lectures were typically short because students already had exposure to the content in the online lectures, which are written lectures they read prior to class and cover in detail the class content.
3. Assignment of in-class team-based assignment related to module topic(s)
4. Short break
5. Teams work on in-class assignments
6. Teams report on their assignments using the voting cards; most of these are graded

Stage III—Data Analysis

This is the typical use of class time during the last 5–6 weeks of class:

1. Lecture demo on how to download and analyze data in Excel (quantitative and sometimes qualitative) and MaxQDA (qualitative)
2. Students practice skills in class individually
3. Team meeting time to collectively decide on data analysis approaches to survey and interview data
4. Teams analyze data from surveys and then interview individually and collaboratively with the objective of testing team-developed hypotheses (quantitative) and research questions (qualitative); instructor and assistants, if any, circulate among students and assist with data analysis

---

on any other topic.) For surveys, we use online data collection software such as SurveyMonkey or, my favorite, Qualtrics. Students are responsible for two interviews and two to four survey completions. They recruit appropriate research subjects, typically among students at the university. When these instrument design and data collection weeks are over and we shift to data analysis, use of class time also shifts. For this last part of the semester, we move from an Internet-ready classroom to a computer lab environment in which students learn how to download and analyze their data. There are no more RATs; instead, class flows from instructor demonstrations of data analysis using software (e.g., online survey software such as Qualtrics; Excel, or another type of spreadsheet software for the quantitative analysis; and later, qualitative data analysis [QDA] using spreadsheets or a special software for QDA, such as my favorite MaxQDA) into students practicing data analysis on computers in class. Teams sit together so those members who understand the software or assignment help the others (zone of proximal development or peer-based learning), and the instructor and TA (if there is one) circulate from student to student and team to team. In these classes the instructor's emphasis is on keeping students collectively on task while ensuring that each student learns the skill set. It is not an easy balance to keep, but the computer lab environment creates a new zone of proximal development, and students find analyzing the data they have collected to be exciting albeit challenging.

We spend about 4–5 weeks on data analysis, which is directly oriented toward teams' final projects. These projects work in the following way. Consistent with TBL practice, the entire class is involved in the same research project, but in terms of data analysis and reports, I allow teams to specialize in a subset of the research. For example, if the class research project is studying why students major in a particular discipline, teams specialize in analyzing certain factors (variables/concepts) we have collected data on and that relate to the question. Here is a specific example: The research problem the class is studying is the same, namely, What should the university do to improve undergraduate education? Each team, however, focuses on one of the factors the whole class brainstormed as needing improvement—advising, food, school spirit, physical condition of buildings, instruction, class size, and so on. All students collect data on all these factors via interviews and surveys. However, each team analyzes the data for only one factor (i.e., advising or class size). I do this because the analysis is more manageable than with all teams analyzing all data, yet gives them all the same skill set, and it is more realistic for how they will handle major projects in jobs in the future, for example, at companies where teams focus on one or more aspects of a larger project. The result is that the teams' final projects differ a bit, yet the overall class project remains common. Thus, they stay engaged with the whole project and are excited to see other teams' findings when they are presented at the end of the semester. I recommend the following: Make the research projects feasible for students by having them relate to campus life so that finding research participants is quite easy, and assign the class research project yourself instead of having them invent one. That way they tend not to personalize it so much, resulting in more attention to learning the course content than fretting over a project chosen by the students.

Balancing team assignments with individual assignments/assessments. Over the time I have been teaching with TBL, I have noticed that as much as the tRAT scores tend to be of higher quality than the iRATs, the same can be true of teams' assignment performance over individuals' assignment performance. That is, weaker students (not necessarily slackers, but including slackers) benefit from being in teams by participating in zones of proximal development; they can also benefit in terms of grades if most assessments are team-based assessments. During my first semester teaching RM with TBL, I did not anticipate this phenomenon and ended up with grades skewed too high because I did not have enough individual assessments. I figured I could measure students individually via the iRATs and peer evaluations. However, I was concerned that all students acquire key skills because they would have to use them in the capstone. Therefore, in later semesters I added individual assignments (sometimes permitting two students to collaborate but not a whole team) such as a literature review, a sampling assignment, and a take-home midterm in which students had to do the research design for their own anticipated capstone project. This produced the desired effect—greater individual effort and accountability. The midterm also served as a type of end-of-unit exam on research design. I allowed each team to select one member to describe in writing the research design from the class's project as his or her midterm; this yielded a draft of the research design teams would have to produce for the final reports, and in so doing cut down on the stress on teams producing those final reports later on. Similarly, the take-home literature review individual assignment became the foundation for the team's literature review section of its final report. To make this assignment more efficient for students—and to emphasize their ability to synthesize information over their ability to find appropriate resources—I created a short bibliography of important sources for the students to consult and housed these resources in the course website so students had easy access to them. All students had the same resources (though they were encouraged to find additional ones), which facilitated evaluating their ability to synthesize the information instead of trying to establish whether they had appropriately interpreted the materials they had found (and that I might not be familiar with). In short, I followed the TBL pedagogical strategy of learning through doing even when employing a variety of individual as well as team assignments. This also helped correct for weaker students' benefiting disproportionately from team-based assignments, given that a common project grade was assigned to all team members. And that, in turn, helped foment team esprit de corps.

Creating in-class 4-S team assignments and cross-class critical thinking team assignments. I have already indicated that I faced time constraints across the term overall and within each class period. The reasons have also been covered to a great degree: the large amount of content that had to be learned to prepare students for individual capstone research projects the following semester, the time-consuming nature of the RATs, and leaving sufficient time for in-class team assignments. What I have not discussed is examples of these 4-S assignments. To be sure, and I want to stress this, I am still not an expert in the 4-S application exercises and would identify this as my weakest area of TBL expertise for the RM course. I found it easy to invent good 4-S application exercises for my GL class, but the content in RM is more complex and that resulted in greater difficulty breaking down complex learning items like conceptualization and operationalization into 4-S exercises, but this can be done. The following are some examples I used during the first two phases of the class; I have incorporated them into a typical class schedule for a three-hour once-per-week class format to help readers plan for their own courses. Examples of in-class assignments that meet the 4-S model include

- *Refining problem statements.* Students start off the semester with a problem statement for the common project the whole course will research. This statement contains concepts and terms that need to be clarified and conceptualized. The statement must be refined. I started out by assigning each team to identify concepts and ambiguities and to go through the process of conceptualization leading to a more succinct problem statement. This took too long and also did not follow the 4-S model. I then moved to a 4-S-style assignment in which teams were given refined problem statements and had to choose the best of these and justify their choice. This can be done in a class application time slot.

- *Sampling.* In this 4-S exercise, I provide the students with three to five sampling scenarios, and they must decide which one is best and why, given our research project.

- *Stat spotting.* One of the texts I assign is *Stat Spotting* by Joel Best (2008). This book teaches students how to identify questionable uses of information in everyday life, especially quantitative information. To practice these skills I usually have students do stat spotting outside class; that is, they find examples of poor or misleading statics and explain why they violate the principles in Best's (2009) book. I have also brought in a stat spot and have student teams identify the violations in class. We use the voting cards and go through the principles; teams vote on whether they have found a particular violation and are prepared to substantiate their vote.

The following are examples of cross-class team assignments:

- *Drafting research instruments.* One of the most successful and difficult assignments I give student teams is to develop survey questions and interview protocols that will collect good data given our research project. Designing instruments is one of the most demanding critical thinking assignments in the course, yet I have found it is the lesson that sticks longest with students. When they must come up with good ways to elicit data, they become very good at seeing the flaws in others' instruments. However, this assignment is too complex to be accomplished in one class and could occupy several classes. I do not have that luxury. So I have adapted it for Web-based collaboration tools in which team members contribute to the instrument outside class, and their instrument is peer reviewed in the following class so that all teams are exposed to various solutions to the same problem. I started out having students collaborate in Web-based pages such as Google Docs and then turned to wikis—either inside or outside the learning management system—because wikis, unlike Google Docs, have history tabs that enable instructors to view and assess the input of each individual student into the process of developing and editing their team's instruments. Some course management systems have wikis built in, but many Websites offer free wikis, and I typically use those (being careful, however, to require students to log in with their real names and to permit me to log in to them as an administrator so I can delete them after the course is done—else future students can copy past students' work).

- *Quantitative and qualitative data analysis.* For quantitative data analysis, teams begin by brainstorming hypotheses involving one demographic variable and one research-related variable. For instance, drawing on the overall research problem and team specializations mentioned previously, they might hypothesize that freshmen and sophomores will be less happy with the advising they receive than upperclassmen for X and Y reasons. They must provide a logical rationale for each hypothesis. Once they develop three hypotheses, they have to analyze the data from the survey to test each. I do not require statistical significance testing, though they are exposed to it, but I do have them provide graphs and tables of the different variables they use, and then have them do bivariate comparisons. They support or refute their hypotheses based on what they see in these graphs. Do they see differences between the lower- and upperclassmen respondents? Does this match their hypothesis? Why or why not? Teams write up these analyses and conclusions and report them along with the tables and graphs in the quantitative data analysis section their team's final report. Thus, each team's data analysis report relates to the class's overall research problem (how to improve the university) yet specializes in the team's factor (e.g., advising). For qualitative analysis, I have all students go through their data and code it only for the factor or factors they are specializing in. Once they do that (each student or pair of students does the coding on transcripts of interviews the students have done and have been stripped of any identifying information so they are confidential), they go back through the coded data and look for themes or patterns that they turn into subcodes. The team develops the coding scheme, and students help each other apply it systematically to their qualitative data. This is done with the QDA software or on a spreadsheet. I then teach them some simple techniques for representing their findings visually and using good quotes toward the development of their final report's qualitative analysis section. Teams have two to three weeks of in-class time to produce each of these data analysis sections. They write these in the wiki (so each team member asynchronously can contribute and I can access them online), and I give them feedback in the wiki itself on how to improve their texts for the final report. Teams then have the final weeks of the term to edit their reports as well as edit the literature review and research design drafts team members did earlier in the semester. This is all done via wikis, making it very easy for me to evaluate the quantity and quality of individual members' inputs as well as the team's overall report.

- *Final research reports: Written and oral.* This RM course walks students through the entire process they will follow for their capstone including the written report and in-class team oral presentation of their team's specific research findings. This aspect of the course contrasts with typical 4-S in-class TBL applications. It requires a lot of team coordination to divide up and reassemble the pieces. As a result, students end up dividing up the work, which not surprisingly often opens up fracture lines between the teams' highly grade-conscious or alpha members and their more relaxed members. Yet I require the reports because I believe that working on and preparing reports is a real-world experience. So how do I mitigate team stress? First, I provide teams weeks of class time to work on their data analysis and coordination of written reports. Second, my TA and I circulate among teams constantly during class time to monitor their progress. Third, we provide in-class assistance and a lot of feedback on drafts of reports, and fourth, teams use wikis to put their work in writing. As Web-based collaborative tools in which every student's contribution is recorded under the history tab, wikis permit me to continually see individual and collaborative work and to evaluate individual students as well as overall team performance objectively.

- *Final team presentations.* The final team presentations present another challenge to the 4-S assignment model—particularly having teams work on the same problem and report simultaneously. Although each team focuses its data analysis on only one of the different factors or areas of the research, having the team reports address the same overall research problem creates enough of a commonality that the majority of the teams are genuinely interested in each other's reports. Unfortunately, although the oral reports can't be given simultaneously, having all the teams present sequentially on the final day of class seems to have worked reasonably well. However, I am also considering experimenting with an alternative reporting method such as the gallery walk in which team reports would be transformed from PowerPoint into posters to see if I can stimulate a higher level of interteam discussion focusing on how their research-design decisions may have affected their findings. I am also considering wiki reports and having teams visit them simultaneously via the Web on the final day. Each option has its advantages and disadvantages. I like the oral presentations as this skill is very important in the workplace, but so is learning collaborative research and communication formats such as wikis. In short, I aim to balance the requirements for effective TBL against course-specific needs and objectives. This is a work in progress. Ideas are welcome and much appreciated.

PEER EVALUATIONS ARE ALSO A CHALLENGE

The fourth essential element of TBL is peer evaluations. The rationale behind peer evaluations is that students will be more cooperative with others than they might be otherwise if they know their peers will evaluate them and that these evaluations are graded. I have found this to be the trickiest part of TBL largely because team esprit de corps becomes so strong. Even in teams where some students obviously do more than others, students still dislike evaluating each other, and regardless of what point-based peer evaluation system I have tried, they find a way to comply with the requirement while avoiding real differential peer evaluation. Solution? I do not have a solution but I do have recommendations.

First, I include on my syllabus a TBL caveat stating that any team issues have to be worked on within teams (peer accountability) before being brought to the TA and then, as last resort, to me. Second, I have implemented team contracts that everyone signs after reviewing the principles and adding in any particular team's additions. These contracts communicate how important team dynamics are and how I expect students to handle them. Third, students fill out a midsemester anonymous evaluation (I do mine online) where students rate their feelings toward their teams, the instructor, and the course itself. I use some in-class time after this evaluation data is analyzed to discuss it with students and to emphasize that they should bring forth team problems, if any, at that point. A check-in at this point is critical because the second half of the course relies heavily on team esprit de corps, so team problems, if any, should be aired and solved now.

End-of-term peer evaluations, however, are still difficult, though with team projects developed using wikis, students easily can see who is contributing more than others. My fourth solution to peer evaluation is based on realizing that the purpose of peer evaluation goes above and beyond providing a grade. Requiring peer evaluations is about holding each other accountable and providing constructive feedback. To that end, I give students an end-of-term peer evaluation assignment in which each team member writes a kind of annual performance review summary of his or her teammates' performance, positive (one paragraph) and negative (one paragraph), followed by a standard grade assessment. I read and evaluate these with 75% of each student's peer evaluation score reflecting the quality of their performance reviews of the *other* team members and only 25% reflecting the average of the grades given a team member by his or her teammates. Each student receives all his or her teammates' feedback stripped of any personal identifiers. The result? Most students still provide an overly rosy assessment of their teammates' performance qualitatively and quantitatively, but now they are held accountable for avoiding truly meaningful feedback to their peers. And there is an unintended benefit for me as well; the compiled feedback is extremely helpful for me when, inevitably, I am asked to write letters of recommendation for these students later. I can truly speak about their teamwork experience in addition to their grades. The time I dedicate to compiling the evaluations saves me time later on, and I feel much more satisfied with peer evaluation.

RECOMMENDATIONS TO THOSE STARTING OUT WITH TBL AND RESEARCH METHODS

I have several recommendations for anyone starting out with TBL regardless of the course. I recommend finding a mentor (the best but not only place is the TBL Listserv), someone who can help you understand the difference between planning for teaching students and enabling student learning. You need someone who can help you figure out the logic of RAT questions. I became much better at these when I started embedding the principle I wanted students to know inside the question itself and asked students to choose which response was best or worst at illustrating the principle. Similarly, figuring out good 4-S application exercises is an art best learned from someone who is already an artist. I would also recommend practicing each of the different TBL elements (RATs, 4-S activities, etc.) with students before beginning to assess them. Larry Michaelsen taught me how to practice the RAT with students by creating a RAT on the syllabus. This serves two important functions the first day of class—it gets students reading the syllabus and it introduces them to RATs. Do it! You will not regret the syllabus RAT. Also, practice 4-S exercises with voting cards before you assess teams on them. I also highly recommend launching TBL with a smaller upper-division course with four to five teams of five to seven students. This way you can know each team and get a better feel for TBL before trying it out on larger classes.

In terms of recommendations more specific to using TBL for RM, I stress that you cannot cover everything typically covered in an RM textbook, nor is it wise to try especially when implementing TBL. Have a conversation with yourself about the content you feel is most important to cover and the skills you want all students to be able to perform upon leaving the class. What skills will enhance their learning overall (critical thinking) and which ones will improve their labor market prospects? What skills do they need for the next phase(s) of their curriculum? Focus on those and let students know why you chose to cover/emphasize what you chose. Be up front with them that this is a demanding course, which is one reason it is great to have a team; they can ask for help from teammates in addition to asking you. Finally, I cannot stress enough the value added to my students' learning experience of including peer review. That is, students view how their peers handled the same assignment and learn to provide constructive feedback to each other. As Halpern (1998) argues, seeing is believing. Students have a very difficult time evaluating their own work unless it is juxtaposed with the work of others. In courses such as RM where there often is no one way to do something, let alone no right way, exposure to different ways, each of which has merits and demerits, is among the most important tools in any person's toolkit.

NOTE

1. At the time of writing this chapter, these statements were true. However, now and owing to budget cuts and staffing shortages, we no longer require a senior capstone seminar. We still require students to take research methods.

REFERENCES

Best, J. (2008). *Stat spotting: A field guide to identifying dubious data.* Berkeley: University of California Press.

Halpern, D. F. (1998). Teaching critical thinking for transfer across domains: Dispositions, skills, structure training, and metacognitive monitoring. *American Psychologist 53*(4), 449–455.

Michaelsen, L., Knight, A. B., & Fink, L. D. (Eds.). (2004). *Team-Based Learning: A transformative use of small groups in college teaching.* Sterling, VA: Stylus.

Vygotsky, L. S. (1978). *Mind in society: The development of higher mental processes.* Cambridge, MA: Harvard University Press.

Wiggins, G., & McTighe, J. (1998). *Understanding by design.* Alexandria, VA: Association for Supervision and Curriculum Development.

CHAPTER 8

Team-Based Learning for Critical Reading and Thinking in Literature and Great Books Courses

Bill Roberson and Christine Reimers

In this chapter, Roberson and Reimers break new ground in their description of how they have implemented Team-Based Learning in a required general education literature course. Specifically, they address how they overcame their own resistance to using the multiple-choice format in teaching literature by developing high-quality questions and using them with intention. Further, they describe how in-class, team-writing micropaper activities enable teams to generate small pieces of writing that no single student could produce on his or her own.

We came to Team-Based Learning (TBL) by way of a quest to deepen students' engagement with difficult often obscure texts whose immediate relevance to students' lives is not clear, a problem that is compounded by older writing styles. For our students, reading Hobbes, J. S. Mill, or Rousseau is much like reading in a foreign language, even when the original is in English. Reading effectively in these circumstances requires high levels of motivation, and since the Great Books (History of Ideas) course was a stand-alone general education requirement for all students, motivation was not intrinsically high. We were struggling with this challenge just at the moment when we first became exposed to the arguments and techniques of TBL. We were a bit daunted at first but were so dissatisfied by traditional approaches that over five years we persisted in complete makeovers of our literature courses, transforming them into fully developed examples of the method. This chapter describes the latest and culminating efforts but should be understood as a synthesis of various iterations over a period of time.

Overall, we have found that the structure and process of TBL are highly compatible with the goals of most literature courses: analytical reading, critical reflection, and analytical-argumentative writing. However, for many teachers and students of literature there is a strong cultural resistance to several dimensions of TBL, the two most pronounced being the notion that authentic assessment can never take the form of a selection-style (multiple-choice) test, and individual students should never be held fully accountable for team-generated products. Adapting TBL required us to rethink the assumptions behind both of these forces of resistance and design courses where the gains in learning through teams were equally expressed in the gains in learning of individuals.

We made peace with multiple choice when we realized we were not using it for summative assessment but rather were exploiting the decision-making format to induce our students to think more analytically. Having to choose among three competing explanations or interpretations of something—knowing that your choice will face scrutiny in conversation with well-informed peers who also had to make the same choice—is much more dynamic than simply being asked to offer your own explanation. The former forces students into authentic conversations about what something might mean; the latter opens the possibility for lazy, vague language that obfuscates whether a student has fully engaged with the reading.

We overcame our concerns for the second form of cultural resistance (fairness of holding individuals accountable for their team's work) by realizing that the team assignments in no way interfered with individual accountability. We discovered that the quality of student writing—our primary means of assessing individual performance—significantly improved as a result of the TBL experience. Students simply became more analytical and articulate as a result of engaging and challenging each other in class throughout the semester. This showed up regularly in their individual performance.

DESCRIPTION OF THE COURSE

Before coming to the University at Albany, State University of New York, we taught at the University of Texas at El Paso (UT-El Paso). Humanities 3303 at UT-El Paso is the third component of a three-course humanities requirement for nearly all undergraduates that covers the history of thought from classical times to the 20th century. This third course covers the late 17th century through the 20th century. Philosophers covered in the course include such thinkers as Montaigne, Galileo, Newton, William Wallace, Bossuet, Hobbes, Locke, Rousseau, Madison, Adam Smith, Marx, Carnegie, Huxley, and J. S. Mill. Artists include, among others, David, Delacroix, and the Impressionists. Literature can include, among others, Voltaire, Shelley, Chekhov, Sartre, Camus, Kafka, Woolf, and Chopin. A requirement of this course is that students read whole texts or substantive excerpts to investigate the concepts, theories, arguments, and assumptions upon which modern Western (i.e., European) ideas about society are constructed. Students are supposed to study the writings of past thinkers and artists, and track how those ideas resurface in contemporary politics, economics, science, art, and literature.

To raise expectations in the course (and thereby improve motivation), we took the given learning objectives that focused on cultural literacy and supplemented them to make them more active, more student-driven, and more specifically related to student collaboration. Key learning goals for the course included the expectations that students would work to

- master and reflect seriously on the historical ideas that have shaped their own beliefs, attitudes, and values;
- think independently and systematically to be able to support with confidence a valid point of view using solid evidence and reasoning;
- develop cultural literacy, particularly with regard to those thinkers most influential in shaping our culture, society, and values;
- become critical readers who can take an unfamiliar text of almost any type, read it closely, and pull from it the key ideas, arguments, and assumptions;
- become less self-conscious and fearful about what they don't know, so they can learn more quickly;
- learn to teach themselves, so they'll be able to teach others; and
- collaborate productively with their peers by fostering contributions from others and capitalizing on those contributions in team productions.

To ensure that students were aware of these expectations, and to communicate to them that we were serious in our approach, the first Readiness Assurance Test (RAT) we conducted was a review of the syllabus.

CREATING COHERENCE IN A SURVEY COURSE

Survey courses like this are extremely difficult to teach for obvious reasons, the most important one being the limited time to deepen understanding of philosophical ideas when looking at 350 years of thought. A critical challenge of these surveys is, therefore, developing thematic coherence. Unless care is taken in choosing texts that can be compared in meaningful ways, the analytical process (which is founded in comparison and contrast) is stymied. To deal with a course that covers such a large territory, and to make intelligent, coherent choices of texts, we developed the idea of imposing a focusing, organizing theme to see and compare meaningfully the various works we read.

The theme we chose was Power and Responsibility, which involved answering the following questions posed to all our authors and artists:

- What is the relationship between power and responsibility?
- Where does power come from?
- How does a person acquire responsibility and what is it?
- What happens when individuals get together in society; who has power and responsibility then?
- Are justice and responsibility different for individuals than for societies?
- What is a personal identity? Can it be real?
- What is an individual? (Why does it matter?)
- What is a community? (Why does it matter?)
- Why is society the way it is, and how might it be different?

Our intention in choosing this particular theme was to connect the instructional method and the student experience in class to the themes that would emerge from the readings. In this way students would be working in ways that directly underscored the relevancy of the texts.

READING ASSIGNMENTS IN A TBL LITERATURE CLASS

Adapting TBL to a literature class presents a specific challenge in figuring out how to pace the reading assignments. In traditional TBL, the readings are front loaded for each unit and immediately assessed, so that students have key information at their disposal as they proceed to work on applications and projects. Teachers of literature require an alteration/adaptation of this practice while maintaining the original goal of getting students to take responsibility for their preparation. In literature courses it does students very little good to study a large body of reading (e.g., more than one novel, play, or extended essay) for subsequent work that will be done over several class meetings. The reason for this is that one major purpose of reading literature is to experience and respond to what the author does rather than read simply for direct understanding of and familiarization with content. Reading for the experience means that the assessment of readings (RATs) will be more focused, more specific, and will apply not only to accurate retention of concepts but also to the reader's preliminary independent analysis of the text. For this reason reading assignments—when the goal for students is to develop analytical reading skills—have to be shorter and more frequent.

At first we tried to address this challenge by maintaining the reading and Readiness Assurance Process as described by Michaelsen (Michaelsen, Knight, & Fink, 2004) for all reading assignments. As one might imagine, in our first attempt this led to a profusion of RATs. After four or five RATs within the first few weeks of the course, students became demoralized by the excessive assessment. In addition, this accelerated assessment plan also took up a large amount of class time, so much so that the application tasks in class had to be limited to stay on schedule.

Our struggle led to the strategy of no longer trying to include every reading in a RAT. Instead, we began to conceive of RATS as being for only the hardest, densest, or longest readings, or for clusters of shorter but related readings. Additional readings would be assigned from day to day between RATs and assessed in smaller ways, such as by individual minute papers, or microquizzes. This decision forced us to more clearly delineate thematic units of the course so the reading clusters would make sense in light of course progression.

By the end of the revision process, a semester of reading in the course included five or six large readings (whole books) or reading clusters (several essays or stories followed by RATs).

WRITING RATS ON LITERATURE

The first time we tried to adapt multiple-choice and true/false formats to literature, we were quite surprised by how well it worked and how engaging it was for the students. Questions that we believed to be simple recall and verification of reading turned out to provoke discussion. Especially in reading literature, simple recall is never as simple as it looks, as it often is a function of relations among comprehension, perspective, analysis, and interpretation. The select-response format of multiple-choice and true/false questions itself, because it forces a clear decision, can be the trigger to start a lively discussion about what a text really says.

Practically speaking, we invented questions that fell into three categories:

1. Low: basic reading comprehension (Which character did what? What did so-and-so say? What is the best definition of classicism?)
2. Medium: analytical-interpretive (What did so and so mean by X?)
3. High: Inference and analysis (extrapolation to or from something not seen before; How does this new text reflect or conflict with the thoughts of the author(s) in our most recent unit?)

We used the higher-order questions to make the transition to larger discussions. These were naturally subject to appeals, so we had to be ready to award points for multiple answers if students made an effective argument. We allowed appeals freely on those questions. We also added the technique of sometimes finishing a RAT with an open-ended analysis-judgment question the group had to answer in a short paragraph. This allowed for more complex questioning but was more focused and disciplined than what one might expect, as the RAT forced the teams to come to reasoned conclusions within a short period of time while still encouraging the team's knowledge and effort to take precedence over a single individual's contributions. In this section we present examples of some basic formats for literature questions.

Comprehension and Recall

- Which of the following (A B C D E = descriptive statements) is true/not true of the narrative/poem/essay, etc.?
- Which character utters this statement: ". . ."? (A B C D E = characters)
- Which character does the following? (A B C D E = actions)
- What are the consequences of character X's action (A B C D E = consequences; this could also be an analytic question depending on the distracters)

Example

Anny's relationship to time can best be described as
  (a) passively accepting the passage of time
  (b) fighting to keep it in the present as perfect moments
  (c) indifference to the whole topic of time
  (d) actively looking and working toward the future

Analytical-Interpretive

- Which of the following statements best summarizes the author's purpose for writing this essay? (A B C D E = various global statements)
- Which of the following characteristics is common to all? (characters, authors, narrative voices)
- Which of the following is the most accurate characterization of this novel?
- The best description of the author's narrative strategy in this novel would be which of the following?

Example

Rousseau would agree with
(a) Carnegie, that some people should have more wealth than others for the good of society
(b) Huxley, that we should share our property with others
(c) Locke, that the goal of joining society is to safeguard property
(d) Hobbes that outside society, stealing another's property is not unjust
(e) two of the above

Inference and Analysis

- Which of the following is the author's/artist's/character's reason for saying/doing X?
- This statement (invented by the professor) is consistent with the perspective of which character in the story (or in the case of comparing multiple works, which author)?
- The following passage represents whose point of view? (A B C D E = various characters or the narrator)
- Which of the following sequence of events represents the true chronological sequence of events (when the narrative is told out of chronological order; A B C D E = different sequence possibilities)
- Which of the following statements is consistent/not consistent with the writer's (or narrator's or character's) argument/perspective/worldview?
- Which of the following events is the pivotal turning point of the narrative?
- Which of the following ideas/themes is suggested by the recurrence of X motif/image?
- Which of the following images are associated with X theme?
- Why is character X continually associated with image Y? (A B C D E = possible explanations of Y's symbolic relationship with X)

Examples

Montaigne would admire the way the American court system works because it
(a) allows the public to save on costly trials by allowing settlements of cases and plea bargains

(b) gives every citizen a good opportunity to fight for his or her rights in court

(c) allows people to admit they were wrong and to make up for it by paying a settlement to the injured party

(d) none of the above

(e) two of the above

This painting (which students haven't seen before), *The Intervention of the Sabine Women* by David, shows clearly his concern about

(a) rational, emotional balance and calm in the wake of revolutionary disorder

(b) the value of revolution to overthrow tyrannical governments

(c) the role of women in a warlike society

(d) two of the above

(e) none of the above

IN-CLASS APPLICATIONS

In class, once students completed the RAT, we structured team tasks to deepen understanding through comparisons and contrasts among different thinkers' perspectives. In some cases the format of the questions for these discussions closely resembled the multiple-choice format of questions for a RAT to give students extra practice comparing texts for their essential ideas and working in teams to make decisions and find evidence. We also found true/false questions to work well in this context. We would display the question in PowerPoint and ask teams to make a determination, then discuss and find evidence (with page numbers and quotes) for their answers. All teams showed their answer on a colored card at a given point, and then we facilitated a class discussion/debate about how teams came up with different answers to the question, and each team provided what evidence it could muster for its point of view.

In other cases teams did not vote but had a specific time period to find the evidence for the answer they had decided was the best one. Then each team was responsible for reporting its answer and participated in the discussion about why it was the best answer. For example, we would ask, "What would Madison think about the fact that in the aftermath of the attacks of September 11th, 2001, the U.S. attorney general has been allowed to change how laws are applied in order to arrest, charge, and imprison people suspected of being terrorists?" or "What would Locke and Marx say about the system of health care or Social Security?"

Yet another format for team tasks was an in-class exploration of new texts by authors we had not read or current events that had not been represented in the reading assignments.

Examples

In Clarence Page's op-ed piece "The Problem With Trashing Liberty", where does the responsibility for a civil and safe society lie? Which of these three philosophers (X , Y, and Z) does Clarence Page most agree with on these fronts?

You have now studied the ideas of Bossuet, Hobbes, Locke, Madison, and Rousseau in regard to what the nature of man is and how government/society should therefore be organized. You know what they think about what benefits a society brings its citizens, how the society should be organized in order to guarantee those benefits, and what responsibilities the government and the individual citizen have to one another.

Your task today: Analyze the Declaration of Independence.

The question you are answering: How would the five philosophers we have read respond to the Declaration of Independence? What parts of the document are consistent with their thinking? What parts of the document would they disagree with? Why?

As a second-phase discussion, and to encourage broader integration and synthesis of the course material, we developed a tag team version of the traditional fishbowl debating method. These rather raucous capstone events followed two or three days of teams' processing multiple thinkers in a unit of the course. Each team sent a representative to the center of the room to sit at a debate table, while all other students sat in a ring surrounding it. A debatable question (focusing on the key divisions expressed by the thinkers) was projected on a screen with PowerPoint, and students at the debate table were asked to take positions and defend them, similar to what happens at a political roundtable. Students at the table and in the outer circle could tag one another to request a substitution, either to relieve a student who had run out of arguments or to admit a student who was eager to bring a new argument to the discussion.

TEAM EXAMS AND INDIVIDUAL EXAMS

We debated over several semesters the best way to validate team effort in the larger assessments and at the same time hold individual students fully accountable for their work. This resulted in a process that replicated the individual-then-team format of RATs but at a higher level. We therefore instituted team exams or team exam components of a larger exam that included individual components.

Individual Exam Components and/or Essays

To prepare for the individual applications, we first conducted team application tasks in class in which teams read a text we had never discussed in class and applied the content to a current event so they could practice dealing with new texts they had not seen before. These were not written assignments but drivers of in-class discussions along the lines of the various team discussion formats mentioned previously. We found that individual exams were more engaging for students when the essay questions followed a team task. We scheduled a team application in class to elicit from all the teams a focused analysis of ideas from the readings. Then we assigned (either for the following class or as a take-home assignment) an application essay in which individual students were asked to respond to a new scenario or text related to the same set of ideas. A variation included requiring students to read contemporary opinion columns in newspapers, examine their basic assumptions and the philosophical background of the opinions about where power and responsibility lie, and write an essay to justify how the authors we studied in the course might respond to those assumptions.

Team Exam Components

In team exams (administered as short time-limited team writing assignments during the class period) students were asked to compare the ideas of the authors and artists we covered and to apply them to contemporary issues. An example of one such assignment was to create a time warp in which five of our thinkers suddenly appeared in our time, in our town. They have now lived here for two years, have read newspapers regularly to try to understand this strange new society they were now stuck in, and regularly meet at a local watering hole. We chose a current events issue discussed in the media that week, provided a short newspaper article that captured the issue, and asked the students to create a conversation about that issue among our five philosophers. What would the philosophers think of the dialogue happening right now in our country on this issue? Where would they come down on the issue? Why?

This is one example of a complex writing assignment that was truly beneficial by being carried out as a team. No one student—even among the best ones—had sufficient mastery of all five philosophers to develop this conversation. Through this exercise, which forced students to insert pieces into a whole to make a single coherence, individuals were able to represent in the discussion those thinkers whose ideas they had best mastered. As not all students achieved equal mastery of all the thinkers, the construction of the conversation allowed each student to contribute an idea that he or she completely understood and that seemed relevant to the assignment.

Team Writing Assignments

The TBL literature on assignment design warns against long writing assignments or presentations, as students will inevitably resort to a divide-and-conquer strategy, thus undermining the dynamic of focused team decision making at the heart of the method. Respecting this principle, we experimented with various alternatives to getting students to produce something complex and of substance in a time-restricted but open-ended format. This resulted in the creation of micropapers, which are focused writing assignments in which teams write down a decision and then add their argument, with evidence, for making that decision. This process took place in class and under time constraints.

While the micropaper approach solved the problem of dividing and conquering, it remained a challenge to find enough time in the semester to schedule regular team papers, given all the other assignments and in-class exercises we administered. As a result, students had insufficient practice writing as a team to produce very polished results. While the team process of debating and writing a short text was very instructive for teammates, the short time frame was insufficient for the final written product to reflect the sophistication of the thinking that went into their prewriting in the form of internal team debates. We have been fascinated by how little of a team's rich, intense discussion is expressed in that same team's written statement about that same discussion. We have not yet found a way to improve team papers, although we believe they are valuable.

CHALLENGES REMAINING

Plagiarism

With the use of TBL, instances of plagiarism have actually decreased in our classes. However, one of us did have one case of plagiarism on a take-home exam in which students were assigned to write an essay comparing a new text with readings we had done in class. In this case, the student took the risk of plagiarizing from the Web because she was under pressure from other classes and was worried about not being able to graduate in time. TBL has definitely raised our standards for the performance of students, and we believe that such raised expectations for intellectual engagement and application of new ideas may heighten the pressure on some students and helped push this student toward a decision to take the easier way out. We have a clause in the syllabus about plagiarism, and we assign a graded activity early in the semester on how to cite and attribute others' ideas properly, so students cannot say they do not know about plagiarism or how to avoid it. We are not sure what else could be done to avoid this problem because we do not want to lower our expectations of students to pre-TBL levels.

Magic Teams and Normal Teams

We have been frustrated about the difference among team performances. Some of the teams are what we call Magic Teams: Students fully engage, all team members participate, and the teams raise the intellectual level of discussions and the grades of individuals. Other teams are what we call Normal Teams: TBL works well, but students still do not completely challenge one another to reach as high as we think they could. We rarely have failed teams at all, for which we are thankful, but we wish we could turn all Normal Teams into Magic Teams. At this point, we do not have strategies to do so, partly because we cannot identify the actual difference between these two types of teams. One of us took the time to interview students from both types of teams at the end of the semester, asking them questions about their experience in the teams and why they think the teams performed as they did. But the result of these interviews was inconclusive—the students themselves did not understand what produced particular success in their teams, and usually told us, "We just clicked" or "We became friends." We are unwilling to accept that some teams are just lucky to have better leaders—we will continue to inquire into the difference between Magic Teams and Normal Teams, and eventually implement strategies to help the Normals become more Magic.

FINAL RESULTS AND ANALYSIS

It took several iterations over several semesters, but we were very pleased with the quality of interaction in our classes once we adopted TBL as the main way the course was organized. When we speak of quality of interactions we do not only mean the level of civility of the participants, although that was a significant factor in our satisfaction. The civility in the course was driven by a team contract: At the beginning of the course, each team collaboratively chose a team name it would be known by throughout the semester and then drew up its own constitution that governed how team members were to behave during the course. Each team signed its own contract, and we made copies for each person and then also stapled a copy to the team folder so that each team could see its constitution on a daily basis.

However, quality of interactions also means that we saw students engaging—enthusiastically and with energetic use of evidence—in class discussions about very difficult philosophical, political, and literary texts. During in-class discussions, the team competition to get the best answer during the voting process drove the students back to their texts, and we heard impassioned arguments about what they thought the key ideas of an author were. Students routinely marked up their texts and were able to quote evidence and cite page numbers to support their points of view. This level of engagement with texts as difficult as those from Montaigne, Rousseau, Sartre, Dostoevsky, or Woolf was something we had never seen before. We believe it was because the teams were working as real teams (as opposed to groups of students completing assignments) and competing with other teams on questions that mattered to them that led to a higher level of engagement. The team competition gave students a cover to debate ideas: They did not have to stand out as individuals who were debating their own ideas but could work collectively to defend the best ideas they had developed within their teams.

From our perspective, the initial groups we set up seemed to become strongly collaborative because of their identification with their teams and through the pressure for individual and team accountability fostered by the structure of in-class applications, RATs, team writing assignments, and individual and team exam components. We were pleased to see that even in situations where the teams had problems, the structure of the course supported greater student independence and responsibility.

In one case, one of the teams was slightly too large (because of a snafu with registration and a desire to get teams set up early in the first week of the semester). In addition, this team had one problem-causing team member who was struggling with issues that had nothing to do with the course but affected her interactions with her teammates and her contributions to class discussion. In the 11th week of the course, the members of this team approached us, without the team member who was causing problems. The students described the challenges they had had with this team member and expressed their worry that her awkward in-class contributions would be understood by us as the team's contributions. We assured them that we understood their challenges and we could see that sometimes this student reported things the team had not discussed. We asked them whether they had taken this up with her directly. They said that they had indeed had discussions with her, but the behavior had not changed. We then asked them what they thought we should do about it. Taken aback, they suddenly realized that if we were to do or say anything to the student in question it would be evident they had gone behind her back to talk with the instructor. This was clearly inconsistent with their team constitution. They asked us not to do anything at all and left, relieved that we understood their problem. We never again heard about that team's problems, and the team as a whole did quite well in the class by the end of the semester, although the student in question did not perform quite as well as her teammates.

In another case, the grading scheme we had imposed became a source of concern among the students, specifically the percentages we had assigned to individual and team performances. At about midsemester, one of the students who contributed actively to all discussions came to our office to ask us to change the grading system in the class. We were quite surprised by this, having thought through the percentages carefully and having ensured in advance that our grading scheme was equitable. The student insisted that given all the time students worked as teams in class, the percentage of the grade for the teams should be greater, at the expense of individual grades. Again, we were quite surprised because this was one of our strongest students, and we would have expected him to be happy that his individual work counted. But the student came prepared; he made the argument that we spent significantly more time in teams than as individuals doing the work of the class. Then he showed us, based on his own team's performance, how the team was performing at a higher level than the individuals that made it up. Then he described the change he wanted us to make. As we looked at his proposal, we realized that we agreed with him. In fact, were we to make this change, it wouldn't change our grading scheme to such a degree that we thought the grades would be skewed, but indeed each individual's grade would rise by a small percentage. Next we discussed the problem of the syllabus as a contract. We pointed out that all the students in the class saw the grading scheme as the one they and we were bound to, and we couldn't just change it because one student wanted it changed. We came to an agreement—if he could convince every single other student in the class that this was a good idea, then we would change the grading scheme. We agreed to give him 15 minutes at the beginning of the next class to make his arguments and put it to a vote. The next day this student gave an impassioned argument, calculating the difference out on the board for all teams to see. All the students voted in favor of the proposal, and we changed the grading scheme. We were entirely delighted. In this course about power and responsibility, the students had taken responsibility, argued with power by taking on the professor and the grading scheme, and had done so in a completely rational and civil way based on the evidence they had.

On the whole, students' grades improved because we were grading on the quality of evidence being offered for any particular idea. The team exercises helped the students gain practice at finding and offering evidence in support of an argument, and the safety the teams offered individual students allowed them to reach higher and make riskier contributions than we had ever seen in class before.

REFERENCE

Michaelsen, L. K., Knight, A. B., & Fink, L. D. (2004). *Team-Based Learning: A transformative use of small groups in college teaching.*Sterling, VA: Stylus.

CHAPTER 9

Team-Based Learning in the First-Year English Classroom

Roxanne Harde with Sandy Bugeja

In this chapter, Harde describes how she has implemented Team-Based Learning principles into a writing-intensive English literature course. Her smaller class size enables her to creatively adapt Readiness Assurance Process procedures and enmesh student writing and feedback on that writing throughout the course, tightly coupling her approach to Halpern's (1998) critical thinking framework. In addition to quantitative data from her class and a colleague's class, this chapter contains more student voices than the others, documenting many of the specific ways students find positive meaning in the experience of Team-Based Learning.

In the fall of 2008, I had an encounter with a colleague that juxtaposed dramatically different teaching experiences. Having used Team-Based Learning (TBL) with great success in a senior English course, Feminist Theory and Women's Writing, the previous winter, I was in the midst of piloting TBL in two sections of our freshman survey course, English Literature From the Romantic Period to the Present (English 103). I had hoped that converting the course to TBL would increase student preparation and participation, enhance students' knowledge of the material, and sharpen their critical thinking and communication skills. I could not have been more pleased with the results. I had just led both sections through our initial class on *Jane Eyre*, a novel that first-year students generally find challenging. My students had all read the entire novel to prepare for the Readiness Assurance Test (RAT), and the team and class discussions were simply stellar. As I headed to my office in the state of joy that seems to come only from a great teaching experience, I ran into Sandy Bugeja, who was teaching with me in the English program at Augustana, a small liberal arts faculty of the University of Alberta.[1] Sandy had also just led freshman classes in work on *Jane Eyre*, or tried to, and she was disappointed and annoyed that her students had not read the novel. In short, our experiences with the same text in the same course, and with classes drawn from a fairly homogeneous student body, were polar opposites. I credited TBL with my success and encouraged Sandy to adopt it in the following term, which she did with the same positive outcomes. I continue to use TBL in first-year and senior English courses with consistently good results. In what follows, I discuss my learning objectives for English 103. I also explore how I meet these goals by adapting a pedagogy commonly used in professional schools and the sciences to my first-year English course. I then detail the methods I use and the resulting outcomes. Along the way, I include some reflections on Sandy's experiences with TBL.

KNOWING WHAT THE ANSWERS MEAN: LEARNING OBJECTIVES

As Donald Bligh (2000) and Stephen Brookfield (1999) noted, there is ample empirical evidence that students learn more effectively from participating in discussions (or almost any form of active learning) than they do from lectures. I understood the social nature of learning, that it happens in context, requires time and repetition, works better when students are active, and that motivation is a component. Even as a graduate teaching fellow and a postdoctoral adjunct lecturer, I knew from experience that lectures did not teach my students what I wanted them to know, so I had always incorporated a variety of active learning strategies. Still, I was casting about for a teaching strategy that would meet my course objectives, as stated in my syllabus:

> English 103 has three objectives. The first is to familiarize students with literary study of the Romantic, Victorian and contemporary periods. To that end we will chronologically read influential texts by leading and lesser-known authors from these three periods. The second objective is to help students develop their reading skills. As readers, we need to be aware of a text's potential meanings and to learn how to discriminate among them, and to that end we will cover some of the ways in which authors and texts generate meaning. For example, we will take into account literary strategies and conventions, and various theoretical approaches; students will develop a set of critical tools for further study and for everyday life. "Critical tools" refers partly to a vocabulary for discussing and understanding literary forms and genres, and partly to the skills of theorizing and contextualizing the text at hand. Most importantly, these tools provide the methods by which literary texts and other texts—including the "texts" of daily life like information and entertainment media, politics, religion, or friendship—can be interpreted. The third objective is to help students develop effective communication skills through the use of Team-Based Learning. In terms of oral communication, discussions will be key to the learning process. You must, therefore, come to class prepared to talk and write about what you have read and to ask questions. To develop written communication, students will work on their writing in frequent "grammar moments" and a number of writing exercises and assignments.

In short, I want all my students to gain familiarity with the literature and its cultural milieu, to become acute critical thinkers, and to develop superior communication skills. I do not want them, as Diane Halpern (1998) cautions in her work on critical thinking, to be "in danger of having all of the answers but still not knowing what the answers mean" (p. 450), and their comments in Figure 9.1 demonstrate that they do learn what the answers mean in their teams. I first used TBL in my third

FIGURE 9.1
Student Comments on Critical Thinking

I did not see how poetry would help me with a business major. What difference does it make if I can understand what someone wrote two hundred years ago? Well, my attitude has changed. Now I believe that if I can break down and understand what a poem is saying, then I will have a skill I can use in everyday life.

The writers of the literature we studied did not sit idle with their thoughts nor am I called to sit idly. There are new truths being shared, subtly and explicitly in works today and in works from the past. I can choose to be challenged by these works, or I can leave them. I will take the challenge. . . . Writing is still writing even if it is I behind the pen. I am just starting to understand that I have a voice as well. I am allowed to make choices and have opinions, and I am allowed to share them.

I feel I have developed as a critical thinker because of my RATs, and have steadily made progress throughout the semester. The RATs forced me to analyze every aspect of the literature assigned and develop my thoughts in order to be prepared for the evaluation. The team RATs only added to my development in that they forced me to listen to my teammates' ideas.

With these new skills from English 103, I will be able to understand the world in an entirely new way.

While I may prefer memorizing terms over writing essays, I recognize that I cannot completely omit English and the arts from my life. I need and want to continue to think critically about the world around me.

The RATs did stress me out, but as the semester progressed, I was able to thoroughly figure out how to study properly for them. I personally think that the groups were invaluable to my learning process; I improved my critical thinking skills with the assistance of my team members.

I have learned how to be a better critical thinker because of this class. My term paper establishes arguments and defends them.

---

year of full-time teaching when I piloted a senior feminist literary theory course in the winter term of 2008. TBL strategies ensured that students did not just learn the theory; they learned to use the theory. They performed the action that is necessary for critical thinking as TBL motivated them to actually do things connected to their learning and to think about what they are doing. Learning outcomes were so impressive that I adapted my courses for the next term—two sections of the first-year survey and a senior course on ecofeminist theory and women's environmental literature—to TBL, and I applied for ethics approval to study the outcomes.[2]

NOT QUITE THE WHOLE ENCHILADA: ADAPTING TBL

Adapting TBL for a humanities classroom was something of a negotiation. Fink (2004) emphasized the ability of this pedagogy to transform learning because it turns small groups of students into effective learning teams, it changes the technique of group work into a profoundly effective teaching strategy, and it enhances the quality of student learning. Michaelsen (Michaelsen, Knight, & Fink, 2004) noted that using all the components of TBL works better than using only some, but he also pointed out that while disciplines in the humanities may be more difficult to adapt to TBL, "the answer to whether or not Team-Based Learning is appropriate for the subject matter is an unequivocal 'yes,' and the key . . . is having a clear picture of what you want students to do with the material" (p. 211).

From my experience in the senior course, I was certain that TBL could help my students achieve the desired learning objectives, but for the practice to work in a literature classroom, I was reluctant to adopt the whole enchilada that Michaelsen (2009) recommends. In particular, I was not comfortable with using multiple-choice questions on the RATs because I think they lead students by feeding them too much information, which in turn tends to focus their attention on the more superficial details of a literary text and narrows their line of inquiry. I therefore based my RATs on the short essay and grammar-fix questions students had always found provocative in my traditional lecture-style courses. As a result, I chose to forgo using the immediate feedback assessment technique (IF-AT) answer sheets and settled for in-the-same-class as opposed to the choice-by-choice instantaneous feedback on the RATs.

PURPOSEFUL, REASONED, AND GOAL-DIRECTED: METHODS

I developed a series of 15 RATs for the course; I include two examples in Figure 9.2. Each RAT has five questions, four based on the readings for that day, and the fifth is a grammar exercise requiring students to identify and correct the errors in a sentence. (The grammar sentences provide a running narrative about my dogs, something my students seem to enjoy.) Daily readings are drawn from *The Norton Anthology of English Literature* and are grouped thematically to some extent. Themes are not necessary, or even usual for a freshmen survey, but because I want my students to become adept critical thinkers, I find it useful for them to think about something, most often literary considerations of social justice. As Halpern (1998) noted, "[t]he goal of instruction designed to help students become better thinkers is transferability to real-world, out-of-the-classroom situations" (p. 451). Therefore, I choose mostly texts in which the authors, from whichever period, are writing as critical thinkers, such as Percy Bysshe Shelley's criticism of the monarchy in "England in 1819," Elizabeth Barrett Browning's discussion of child labor in "The Cry of the Children," or William Butler Yeats's view of the Easter Rising in "Easter 1916." Following Michaelsen's suggestion that every reading be important, I cut my old syllabus by a third. Everything my students read is crucial to their understanding of each period's literature and culture. Thus, for most classes they read either two or three short poems or a short story or essay. I prompt them frequently to budget their time when one of the three major texts is an upcoming required reading. Students know in

FIGURE 9.2
Examples of RATs

English 103—RAT #1   Name:

1. What kind of poems are William Blake's chimney sweeper poems?
2. Choose one of them, explain what the poem is about, and then explain why the form matters.
3. What is the most important image in each poem, and how does it matter to Blake's message?
4. In "London," Blake uses several running metaphors or tropes. Discuss one of them and its effectiveness in making meaning.
5. Identify the problem with the following sentence and fix it in two different ways: Browning, my chocolate lab, has degenerative arthritis, Franklin, my golden retriever puppy, is in perfect health.

English 103—RAT #8   Name:

1. Discuss the form of *Jane Eyre*. How do Brontë's various strategies of narrative form and speaker make meaning?
2. Does this novel attempt to answer the Woman Question? How so or how not?
3. Does class matter in this novel? How so or how not?

advance the readings and grammatical problem they will be tested on. They are also given relevant key terms, such as *metaphor* or *narrative*.

Classes with RATs begin with students' taking up to 20 minutes to answer the questions on their own; then they hand in their tests and move into their teams to answer the same questions. Teams discuss and come to a consensus on their answers, written down by the team recorder for that day. We then reconvene as a class and discuss each team's answers. This is the point at which I revise TBL practice. Instead of teams' receiving decision-by-decision feedback (by using the IF-AT answer cards), I provide the feedback by leading the class in a discussion of the answers. I ask each team in turn to answer one of the questions first and then encourage the other teams to offer their answers or to build upon what has been said already. As we go through team responses, I offer mini lectures that provide missing information, clarify and expand on the topics under discussion, and challenge students to work on richer and more detailed interpretations of the texts. I also take questions. During the whole-class discussion, I invite teams to change the teams' student recorders and ink colors and to continue to make notes on the team RAT, and I copy those larger RATs for each team member, which are graded and returned with the graded individual RATs the next class. By the end of a 75-minute class, students have gone over the questions three times and generally come away with a sense of ownership of the material, which is demonstrated by their almost uniform ability to discuss on the final exam months later the details of texts they read in September.

Classes that do not begin with RATs include a variety of learning strategies; I intersperse mini lectures with team or class discussions of one of the longer works—novels such as Charlotte Brontë's *Jane Eyre* or Harper Lee's *To Kill a Mockingbird* or a play, such as Brian Friel's *Translations*—in which students must examine the text with some depth and detail. These discussions enhance students' ability to think and communicate, and often help them focus their ideas for the term paper they will have to write on one of the major texts. My courses are all necessarily writing-intensive courses, so the classes that do not include RATs often include writing activities that require peer review and teamwork. Term papers go through a series of drafts that are read and evaluated for grades by team members. I provide a rubric for grading and comments (see Figure 9.3), and students appreciate the chance to read and be read by their teammates before handing in their major assignment. Peer response to writing works well as a component of TBL, but writing also goes hand in hand with critical thinking as it makes students active agents in their own learning process. Halpern's (1998) description of critical thinking as "purposeful, reasoned, and goal-directed . . . the kind of thinking involved in solving problems, formulating inferences, calculating likelihoods, and making decisions" (pp. 450–451) works just as well to define the processes and outcomes of essay writing. Working on term papers requires students to engage in the effortful thinking that Halpern sees as the heart of the critical thinker, and it builds many of the skills she lists as necessary: reasoning, argument analysis, hypothesis testing, likelihood and uncertainty, and decision making and problem solving. Further, I insist my students' term papers be thesis driven. They must argue about something they take from the texts, which requires that they work to become able critical thinkers. The work students do on

FIGURE 9.3
English 103: Term Paper Peer Review Form

Title of Paper: _____

Author of Paper: _____

Peer Reviewer: _____

Draft #: _____   Grade: _____ /2.5

Comment on

1. Content: argument, insights, thinking, depth

2. Detail: supporting and relevant evidence, handling of sources, use of quotations

3. Organization: focus, guiding the reader, paragraphing, structure in relation to content

4. Language: syntax, wording, voice, diction, concision

5. Correctness: spelling, grammar, punctuation, usage, proofreading

the RATs complements the thesis-driven essay by obligating them to work at revising, building on, and developing their original answers. The RAT process is similar to the one used in developing an effective thesis.

Three classes are devoted to *inksheds*, an exercise in freewriting in which I guide students through a series of writing prompts.[3] *Freewriting* is a prewriting technique in which a person writes continuously for a set period of time without regard to spelling or grammar. Betsy Sargent and Cornelia Paraskevas (2005) describe ink-shedding as a social, rather than private, freewriting exercise that uses writing "as a tool for thinking, exploring, learning, and understanding" (p. 4). I inkshed along with the students, and we have the freedom to choose a primary text as the subject of our writing and a number of thematic topics to help focus the writing. The first inkshed is about team building and is carried out early in the course; the second and third inksheds are meant to help students dig into their term papers. Cheryl Glotfelty (2008) recommends including freewriting assignments early, noting that "writing creatively draws students out of their shells and into the course. . . . By sharing these pieces in class, mutual interest in one another develops that creates a climate of respect and boldness when we discuss the later literary works and issues they raise" (p. 351). Students write for about 50 minutes, and then in teams, they respond on the inkshed report sheets that I provide (see Figure 9.4). Students read some of their work out loud, and we include time for written peer response. I emphasize observational feedback (students summarize what was read, orally and in writing), and they are asked to note on the inkshed report the points that surprised or puzzled them, among other things. As the teams work through their inksheds, I circulate and sit in on as many of their discussions as possible. This is a low-stakes writing assignment, with no grades attached, and my students have universally enjoyed these sessions and

FIGURE 9.4
English 103—Inkshed Report

Name: _____   Team Name: _____

Most eloquent or humorous sentence(s); copy them here and name the author(s):

Most surprising sentence(s), ideas or connections I had not thought of; copy them here and name the author(s):

Weirdest or most puzzling ideas; copy them here and name the author(s):

A question that should be addressed for class discussion; name the author(s) if it/they came from an inkshed:

Sentences or passages that confused me; copy them here and name the author(s):

Summary, comments, or reflections (inkshed on your team's inksheds; continue on the back):

learned from them. They create the rich climate of respect and boldness that Glot-felty describes, and they build teams that are comfortable, confident, and happily collaborative. Students comment that they enjoy the inkshedding as a process that is creative and productive; one noted that "it was fun to just write and get down my thoughts with low stakes," and another pointed out that "inkshedding for Jane Eyre gave me more ways to get ideas and concepts together in a more manageable, orga-nized manner for the term paper."

MY TEAMMATES RELIED ON ME: ACCOUNTABILITY

Even though no grades are involved, the inksheds are another way students become accountable to their teams. Michaelsen (2004) stressed accountability as cru-cial in TBL; of his four key components—significant problem, same problem, spe-cific choice, simultaneous report—the final two are invested in accountability. Accountability makes TBL effective: Members of a group are accountable to the professor; members of a team are accountable to each other. With inksheds students are asked to take risks and to hold each other accountable in group discussions on what can be a highly personal piece of writing. Accountability is more obviously invested in graded peer evaluations, like the peer review of the term paper drafts. In my TBL courses, 30% of the final grade comes from TBL work: RATs (15%), peer review (5%), and participation (10%). I provide a team participation guide (see Figure 9.5) that team members use to assign each other participation grades at the end of the term.

FIGURE 9.5
English 103—Team Participation Grade

We agreed as a group that team members would assign 10% of the final grade by assessing their teammates' attendance and participation. This is a closed marking system; no one will know how you grade your teammates. I will take an average of the grades assigned by members. Write the names of your teammates below and give them each a mark out of 10.

Signature: _____

What grade do you think you deserve?

Because it works to "assess interpersonal skills, foster insight, and promote professional behavior," Levine (2008, p. 110) contended that peer assessment is an essential tool for reinforcing individual accountability in TBL: "Students *need* peer review to feel comfortable that their teammates are contributing their fair share of the group work" (p. 110). Student comments in Figure 9.6 demonstrate their appreciation for peer review. To ensure accountability, peer review and grading has to reflect the work of team members and make a significant impact on the course grade; my course involves peer review in every aspect of teamwork and in individual writing assignments. Students are accountable, but more importantly they are engaged with a learning experience they consistently describe as transformative.

A BETTER CHANCE TO SUCCEED: OUTCOMES AND ANALYSIS

TBL outcomes can be qualified and quantified, and both sets of results are important. I begin with comments from the students themselves, with the ways they express their reactions to and evaluations of English 103 as taught with TBL. While I have included student comments on accountability and writing assignments, the following comments qualify my students' reactions to TBL. Comments gathered from their course evaluations and term portfolios are universally positive and quite specific about what they find most valuable.

Comments were taken from year-end student course evaluations. When asked what they enjoyed about the course, students said the following, and I include comments from Sandy's students in Figure 9.7:

• "The team-based work, and all the feedback that was given throughout the term"

FIGURE 9.6
Student Comments on Accountability

Team-Based Learning makes you accountable to your teammates. I found knowing my teammates relied on me to be prepared for class, I made it a high priority to try to have an understanding of the readings that were going to be taken up in class. Team-Based Learning is something that I enjoyed doing; it was a great way to meet new people, and better my writing process.

When I failed to read the proper text, I felt bad for my team. Sometimes I just couldn't read it and I hated those classes because I really dragged down my team.

As you begin to read my RATs, it will become apparent that as the semester gets further along, my involvement in the group increases as well. At the beginning, I would do well on my individual RAT, but my ideas were usually left off the team RAT. As I got more comfortable in interpreting [the literature], I became more vocal in my group.

FIGURE 9.7
Comments From Sandy Bugeja's Students

In general, my group was surprisingly hard working. Nearly every class, everyone had completed the readings, and came prepared with their own interpretations as well as with questions they would pose towards other members of the group. Instead of passively allowing one person to control the group discussion, various members of our group would offer suggestions that others would support or debate. Often times, we would get carried away interpreting a question only to hear Sandy inform us that we have a minimal amount of time to finish. . . . yikes!

I felt a lot more comfortable speaking in the small group and it became a bit easier to talk in the large class discussions.

- "The very good class discussions are the best part about this course. I had a fantastic term with my teammates who were almost always prepared and willing to share their opinions."
- "The Team-Based Learning was not only a very useful learning experience, but it was enjoyable as well."
- "We are involved in the discussions. [Professor Harde] doesn't just tell us what everything means but also listens to what we think it means."
- "The lack of a lecture"
- "The RATs really encourage you to find your rhythm of working at home."
- "Working with people in class and not just sitting there"
- "TBL was a great experience, taught me a lot about how useful study groups can be."
- "I found [TBL] to be very productive and efficient. It allowed those who don't do well speaking in front of large groups to give their input. I found that in my group, all of us noticed different aspects of the [literature] and during out group RATs, we were allowed to work together and teach each other. On the negative side, those who didn't do the work the night before can depend on the group to provide them with marks, and abuse the system. But in the long run, those who do this will not receive a high mark on their participation evaluations by their teammates. Overall, I am a huge fan of working in teams because it allows a social aspect in class that satisfied the social craving of some students and the intellectual craving of others."

When students were then asked what the professor could do to help them make progress, they responded with the following:

- "Continue with the group work."
- "Provide more questions that require us to fix punctuation problems."
- "Nothing more could be done; the rest falls to my own initiative."

Another way I had students qualify their experience in the course was through portfolio cover letters. The portfolios themselves encourage students to think reflectively and critically about their work in the course. Due the last day of classes, the portfolios must include students' individual RATs, inksheds and inkshed reports, both short essays, the peer-evaluated drafts of the term paper and the grading rubrics, the final term paper, and the cover letter. I ask that their letter be one to two pages and that it reflect on the work that has gone into the portfolio, and that they discuss their experiences with TBL and with a writing-intensive course. The following are excerpts from the portfolio cover letters:

- "Team-Based Learning has also been an interesting, and unexpected, part of English 103. When I first began the course, I was skeptical, because I don't usually like group work with people I do not know. However, I have grown to appreciate my group and I love that it connected me to new people. We are not really close, but they are people that I appreciate because we have different perspectives. The group taught me more than I would have learned on my own."

- "What really helped my transition [from high school to university] become smoother was Team-Based Learning. My peers helped me through the texts and gave me a better chance to succeed. A few weeks in, I found myself giving my thoughts on the answers to RATs. It felt good when we got a good mark on our team RATs because we all gave our input into them. I learned to listen too. If I did not understand what a team member was saying, they had no trouble explaining their answer to me. I think that this was a very good way to learn, especially in a first-year course."

- "I never thought I would say this but the RATs are good. The mark was the reason I read most of the poems; if we were not marked I would not have read much at all."

- "This is the only class I can say that I have looked forward to attending this semester, and I think that is based largely on my eagerness to exchange ideas with my peers."

- "Everyone in the team took something from someone else. After hearing the different points of view and interpretations, I started to interpret differently. I do not think that this particular trait could have been gained from a lecture. I think that practicing what we are supposed to be doing worked much better than listening to a lecture. Quantitative analysis confirms the effectiveness of TBL in every respect."

Figure 9.8 shows a comparison of students' final grades in my four TBL sections with the previous eight sections of English 103 in which I did not use TBL. Student numbers are on the left, grades are indicated by colored bars, and sections are ranged along the bottom divided by year. There are two fairly radical changes in final grades because of TBL. First, in the four sections taught using TBL, only one has any failures at all, and then only two, for an average of .5% per year. This result compares

FIGURE 9.8
Final Grades

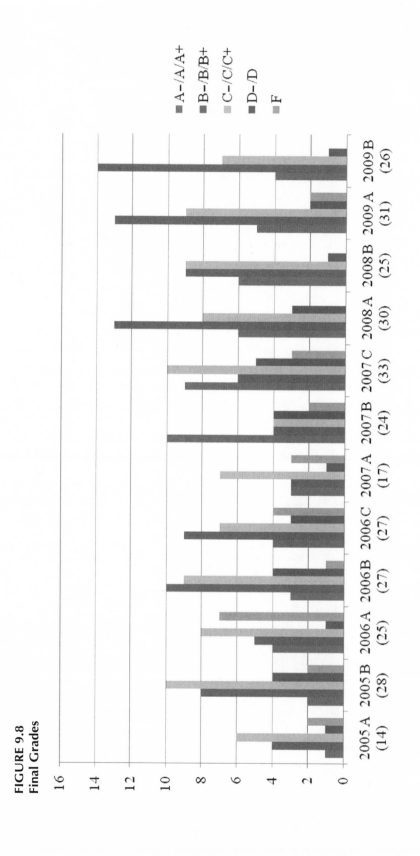

favorably to the previous eight sections, which range from a low of 1 to a high of 7, for an average of 3. In short, fewer students fail a freshman survey in English when TBL is used. Second, the increase in the number of students earning a grade in the B range is astonishing. There are marginal increases in students' earning a grade in the ranges of A and C, with and without TBL (5.25/4.25% and 8.25/7.625%), and a slight decrease in the students earning a grade in the D range (1.75/2.875%). However, the number of students earning a B minus, B, or B plus almost doubled (12.25/6.375%). In short, students used the team setting to scaffold themselves into a richer learning experience and knowledge base.

Figure 9.9 displays student responses to an end-of-term evaluation. The questionnaire was administered by support staff and held until final marks were released to students. Students understood that their responses could in no way affect their grades, and they were encouraged to be candid in their comments when responding

FIGURE 9.9
Term Evaluation/Questionnaire

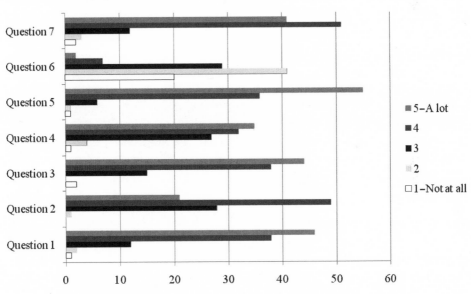

	Not at all				A lot
1. I enjoy working with my team	1	2	3	4	5
2. I have worked hard to prepare before classes	1	2	3	4	5
3. Preparing for the RATs helps me understand the material	1	2	3	4	5
4. I learn more with team-based work than I would with a lecture	1	2	3	4	5
5. Redoing the RATs with my team helps me understand more	1	2	3	4	5
6. I would prefer a typical lecture format	1	2	3	4	5
7. My team works more effectively as the term goes on	1	2	3	4	5

to the evaluation. The table groups responses from the four sections of English 103 that were taught using TBL. Responses to questions 1, 2, 3, 4, 5, and 7 ranged from neutral to "a lot," while responses to question 6 earned numbers on the negative to neutral end. In this end-of-term survey, even first-year students have enough experience with both TBL courses and those with a traditional lecture format to demonstrate a clear preference for one over the other.

Attendance in my classes tends to be high. I take attendance at the beginning of every class, and I make it clear that I expect my students to be in their seats. However, as Figure 9.10 demonstrates, attendance in my TBL sections is extremely high and consistent. Moreover, the sections marked 2008 A and 2009 A took place in the first time slot of the day, 8:00 a.m. to 9:15 a.m., which makes this rate of attendance even more remarkable. With the exception of one section, only one student in each missed more than six classes. The one section with more than one student with habitual absences is also the TBL section with the only failures, and, not coincidentally, the students who missed class were the students who failed. The highest numbers were for students who missed one to three classes or none at all, and in the two classes taught in the afternoon, the number of students with perfect attendance was the greatest.

Overall, TBL is a continuing and profound success in my teaching, and Sandy found it equally successful, as shown by her comments in Figure 9.11. I finish my first-year courses with students who have good working knowledge of the material, who are adept critical thinkers, and who are confident lifelong learners. Moreover, TBL taught me a number of things I needed to learn, such as the patience to withdraw and simply manage the discussion, to put my students' ideas well ahead of mine, to demonstrate openness to their contributions and enthusiasm about what

FIGURE 9.10
Attendance

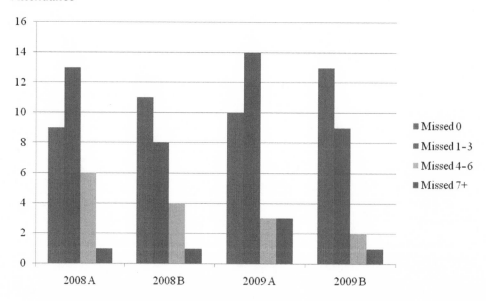

FIGURE 9.11
Sandy's Observations

- I noticed that students were better equipped to discuss literary works in conjunction with previous texts studied in the course.
- Attendance throughout the term was exceptionally high—it was typical to have at least 90% of students in each class.
- I noticed a dramatic improvement in the quality of class discussion.
- I had no issues in terms of class management—I felt that the students used their group time well and were consistently on track and focused.
- I held several out-of-class readings and the attendance for these was remarkable—almost 50% of the two 104 classes attended the readings. I've done the extra reading sessions of *Paradise Lost* each year that I taught the poem in a first-year course, but attendance was usually limited to the "usual suspects"—the very diligent students. I believe that the Team-Based Learning improved the classroom dynamic and encouraged greater participation.
- I had several students this term who had taken classes with me in a previous term; these students commented on how the Team-Based Learning improved the class experience for them: "The RATs made this term much better than last term." "The RATs added to the quality of the class and my learning."
- I've used the Team-Based Learning in 3 classes, although the amount of marking was increased and I needed to devote extra time to preparation, if I were to use Team-Based Learning in future classes, the prep work would be reduced. Team-Based Learning is a bit of a trade-off: your marking time is increased, but actual lecturing time decreases.

they have to say, to slow down the pace, and to allow silence or a lot of noise. My students become well-connected and well-prepared citizens of this campus, and I look forward to seeing them in my senior courses.

NOTES

1. Bugeja has since left Augustana to pursue a career in communications. She is a fine teacher, colleague, and friend, and she is missed by her students and the faculty. Sandy was kind enough to share her TBL experiences with me and contribute to this chapter, and I am in her debt. I am also indebted to Paula Marentette for introducing me to TBL and mentoring me in my trial run, to Larry Michaelsen for his work in pioneering this pedagogy, and to Larry and Michael Sweet for their work on this volume.

2. Student comments and all reported results are used with permission and approval from the University of Alberta Research Ethics Board.

3. For the definitive text on inksheds and other writing exercises, see Sargent and Paraskevas (2005).

REFERENCES

Bligh, D. (2000). *What's the use of lectures?* San Francisco, CA: Jossey-Bass.
Brookfield, S. D. (1999). *Discussion as a way of teaching: Tools and techniques for democratic classrooms.* San Francisco, CA: Jossey-Bass.

Fink, L. D. (2004). Beyond small groups. In L. K. Michaelsen, A. B. Knight, & L. D. Fink (Eds.), *Team-Based Learning: A transformative use of small groups in college teaching.* Sterling, VA: Stylus.

Glotfelty, C. (2008). Finding home in Nevada? Teaching the literature of place, on location. In L. Christensen, M. C. Long, & F. Waage (Eds.), *Teaching North American environmental literature* (pp. 345–353). New York, NY: Modern Language Association.

Halpern, D. F. (1998). Teaching critical thinking for transfer across domains: Dispositions, skills, structure training, and metacognitive monitoring. *American Psychologist, 53*(4), 449–455.

Levine, R. E. (2008). Peer evaluation in Team-Based Learning. In Michaelsen, L. K., Parmelee, D. X., McMahon, K. K., & Levine, R. E. (Eds.), *Team-Based Learning for health professions education: A guide to using small groups for improving learning* (pp. 103–117). Sterling, VA: Stylus.

Michaelsen, L. K., (2004). Frequently asked questions about Team-Based Learning. In L. K. Michaelsen, A. B. Knight, & L. D. Fink (Eds.), *Team-Based Learning: A transformative use of small groups in college teaching.* Sterling, VA: Stylus.

Michaelsen, L. K. (2009, March). *Plenary: A conversation with Larry Michaelsen.* Presented at the Team-Based Learning Conference, University of Texas, Austin.

Michaelsen, L. K., Knight, A. B, & Fink, L. D. (2004). *Team-Based Learning: A transformative use of small groups in college teaching.* Sterling, VA: Stylus.

Sargent, M. E., & Paraskevas, C. C. (2005). *Conversations about writing: Eavesdropping, inkshedding, and joining in.* Toronto, Ontario, Canada: Thomson Nelson.

CHAPTER 10

American History Learned, Argued, and Agreed Upon

Team-Based Learning in a Large Lecture Class

Penne Restad

In this chapter, Restad describes her process of overhauling a large survey course using backward design so students can learn to think like historians. But how does one get a lecture hall full of students to do history, and what does that look like? "Three features emerged as key to the structure of the redesigned course: testing at the beginning of a unit to ensure everyone's familiarity with the basic historical narrative when we began to work with it in class; considering history as an ongoing, contested, and revisable narrative; and using the power of team collaboration to investigate interpretations, explore primary sources, and practice a series of critical thinking moves associated with thinking critically in the mode of historian."

Villainy, glory, struggle, triumph, and defeat just begin to describe what we search for among the mountains of names, dates, and places that structure our study of the past. We also want history to teach us citizenship, morality, patriotism, and who we are. Ken Burns's documentaries, Tom Hanks's war heroics, Oliver Stone's fantasy history movies, the *History* and *Discovery* television channels, even conversations at a family reunion in their various ways fulfill some of these demands (Edgerton, 2001; Jefferson, 2009; Ravitch & Finn, 1987; Rosenzweig, 2000; Sturken, 1997). Yet despite our exposure to American history in school, at home, and in the media, it has been proved repeatedly that no one apparently remembers much of any of the history he or she was taught in middle or high school (Wineburg, 2004). Part of the problem may be that against the color of popular renderings, the names, dates, and places of formal history instruction don't have a chance. It also may be that the real

This chapter reports on an ongoing project, Large History Survey: Redesign, funded by a University of Texas System initiative, Transforming Undergraduate Education. I want to thank especially Michael Sweet and Doris Adams, University of Texas Center for Teaching and Learning, who have been, and continue to be, most generous with their time, support, and sound advice as the redesign develops.

benefit of confronting history in school—learning to think like a historian—is rarely emphasized.

The college-level American history survey course may be the last chance to get it right, to go beyond memorizing vivid particulars and bold dramas to present history as a negotiable narrative that can be evaluated and given the deeper meaning professional historians seek. The challenge is to bring home the importance of history to classes made up of every sort of major and student, many enrolled under duress from their advisers, who represent wide disparities of preparation and motivation. Traditionally, this has meant giving a polished set of lectures. There are good reasons for this. A good lecture delivers impressive quantities of information efficiently. Even less-than-inspired lecturing can provide good enough coverage as student and teacher settle into traditional roles in which one speaks and the other listens.

While this works for some, we have no way to calculate the experience of significant numbers of students who feel lost and too intimidated to seek help, often stop attending lectures, and do not fill out evaluations. Even more discouraging, neither learner nor teacher can be assured that the payoff will be any greater once the lecture has been revised, PowerPoint vivified, anecdote enhanced, and user-friendlied. Excellent and highly motivated teachers and potentially engaged and successful students now encounter each other in a learning structure forged during an era when teaching methods, goals, and student expectations and needs were significantly different. The impact of widely available information and communication technologies has remade the entirety of our environment, including the one in which we teach and learn. According to Tapscott (2009), students now

> expect a two-way conversation. What's more, growing up digital has encouraged this generation to be active and demanding enquirers. Rather than waiting for a trusted professor to tell them what's going on, they find out everything on their own from Google to Wikipedia.

Tapscott (2009) perhaps overstates the case. The existence of a good search engine and an encyclopedic website does not offer a compelling enough case to abandon a good set of lectures that make sense of past and present. Nonetheless, the democratization of educational goals and student constituencies has moved higher education, especially at large and accessible state universities, from a process of Darwinian winnowing to one of responsibly seeking successful learning environments for all students. The lecture, a leading feature of what Tapscott has called the "industrial model of student mass production," has not become obsolete, but neither does it replicate or encourage contemporary discourse—scholarly or popular—as it once did.

Most professors are acutely aware of this. They also know that students, at least in a survey of American history, have access to plenty of information. The pressing need is to help students develop strategies to make sense of a rich abundance of often contradictory or superfluous facts or narratives revealed in historical sources and an array of media, and to make reasoned judgments concerning their meaning and reliability. In short, students' need to learn to think for themselves has grown exponentially. And as a consequence, the teacher's knowledge and skill in validating or interrogating speculations, refining understandings, and guiding the active learning process in real time become even more important to the learning experience.

DEVELOPING A NEW MODEL FOR THE LARGE SURVEY COURSE

Most of us have long understood, at least intuitively, that traditional approaches to teaching a history survey tend to miss the critical element that makes history a discipline, not a memory project: the process of evaluating the significance of the events and ideas of the past. In seminars, when 15 students discuss a book they've read, they bring to the table 15 different interpretations. The intrinsically collaborative process centers learning within the circle of participants. When gaps in understanding reveal themselves, as they inevitably do when working in such close range, a short, on-point minilecture exploits the teachable moment. By the end of a class, the 15 have actively negotiated a much richer body of knowledge and insight than a single, albeit more informed and polished, lecture might have imparted. Over a term, individuals build a more complex working vocabulary and conceptual grasp of the topic, grow more confident in their ability to participate ably in an intellectual discussion, and write and reason more cogently. The question that nagged me was simply this: How could the multiple benefits of a seminar setting be transferred to students in a large lecture class who usually had no intention of taking more than the minimum of required, most basic history courses?

Although encouraging class discussion figured high on a list of qualities I wanted to import into the survey, there were other characteristics typical of a big class that begged for remedy. Many are situational: Students enter with a wide variation of preparation in writing a good argument and interest in history. For some, it is their first semester in college; many more are seniors, ready to graduate with degrees in engineering or natural science or business. The A tends to go to the more experienced older students or the new ones who graduated from good high schools. Another problem is that students often regard lectures as a substitute for reading, or at least they wait until just before an exam to open their books, which brings up another issue: those textbooks with their double columns, important points in bold ink, beautiful color pictures, excerpts from original sources, time lines, and helpful questions to ponder already installed. A text is a wonderfully designed, closed system. And it tends to remain closed. Attrition adds to the mix. Even when attendance is taken, the audience in large lectures tends to dwindle over the course of a term. All in all, it was time to rethink every aspect of the survey. Or, as one of my colleagues phrased it, to "blow up the course." A generous grant from the University of Texas System gave me that opportunity.

My goal was to present history as a particular way of thinking in an atmosphere of open questioning, discussion, debate, and negotiation about the past, and Michaelsen and Sweet (2008) suggested a viable framework for doing so. Students working collaboratively and with clear guidance from the professor could themselves explore and explain the important why as well as the what happened. The collaborative and analytical dimensions of this revised American history survey would, I believed, create an environment in which students actively and even enthusiastically learn that history is more than an arbitrary set of facts or an overly simplified narrative.

Three features emerged as key to the structure of the redesigned course: testing at the beginning of a unit to ensure everyone's familiarity with the basic historical narrative when we began to work with it in class; considering history as an ongoing, contested, and revisable narrative; and using the power of team collaboration to investigate interpretations, explore primary sources, and practice a series of moves associated with thinking critically in the mode of historian.

The plan I set out looks like this: Working in permanently assigned teams, students solve carefully designed problems that require them to assess sources, weigh evidence, and draw conclusions from two texts and numerous primary sources. One text takes a nationalist, what some might call a triumphalist, viewpoint; the second provides a challenging, populist perspective. Newspaper and magazine articles, government reports, statistics, essays, manifestos, films, and television ads serve as some of the sources for primary documents.

The class meets twice weekly in 75-minute sessions. The course is divided into five units, each of which is divided into five parts. Each unit begins with a readiness assurance quiz, followed by a general lecture on major themes and tensions of the time period. The remaining three days of the unit address three separate questions and sets of documents, designated as Projects 1, 2, and 3, related to the lecture and general reading assignment. This sequence (Figure 10.1) gives a predictable order and rhythm to the course, making it relatively easy for students to know where to be and what to do for any given class.

TEXTS AND UNCOVERAGE

As I worked to transfer the action of learning to the students, to enable them to engage with the material of history more independently and at a more complex level, I quite unexpectedly found myself reexamining some of my own ingrained habits of teaching. Deciding which if any text to use set up the first test. I don't know anyone who claims to cover everything, but a hefty book feeds an illusion that at the least

FIGURE 10.1
Sequence of an Instructional Unit

One Unit	Readiness assurance quizzes individual/ team	Lecture	Team Project 1	Team Project 2	Team Project 3

the student has been provided access to everything. On the other hand, students tend to fixate on the sheer amount of information presented in a history course. Give the typical student a section to read on the New Deal, and the student's first question is, "How do we know what's important?" By "important," he or she means "What do we have to memorize?"

History classes from kindergarten through 12th grade often emphasize building historical knowledge through memory. This approach has its advantages, especially as one begins to learn history. However, a microfocus on facts effectively obscures the big picture. In the past decade or so, a number of professional historians and master teachers have taken a hard look at this big picture problem, challenging the notion that history, at its base, is an exercise in managing and memorizing material.

"Many of the assumptions historians make about learning have been shown by cognitive scientists to be quite wrong," Lendol Calder (2006, p. 1361) wrote. He asserted that educators, especially historians, subscribe to "what Sam Wineburg calls the 'attic theory' of cognition" (p. 1361). That is to say, they believe that collecting information equals learning. New understandings of how we learn argue otherwise. Learning takes place when a person develops a method for sorting information, a way to make sense of names, dates, and places.

Such an approach argues for teaching students how to think historically, to assimilate what has been described as history's signature. Lee Schulman (2005) said, "Signature pedagogies are the forms of instruction that leap to mind when we first think about the preparation of members of particular professions" (p. 52). They are "important precisely because they are pervasive. They implicitly define what counts as knowledge in a field and how things become known. They define how knowledge is analyzed, criticized, accepted, or discarded" (p. 54). Calder (2006) explained: "A signature pedagogy, then, is what beginning students in the professions have but history beginners typically do not: ways of being taught that require them to do, think, and value what practitioners in the field are doing, thinking, and valuing" (p. 1361). Students need to read history, not a manual, to learn to evaluate and appreciate a diversity of interpretation.

American history surveys cover, at least in Texas, what is required to graduate from high school. Ostensibly, if a student already knows the basics of that history, it seems wasteful not to take the opportunity to enhance his or her knowledge. And if a student can't remember history after two years, it seems pointless to teach the same thing in essentially the same way and expect a different outcome. This observation had prompted me earlier to experiment with supplementing an excellent if conventional textbook with Howard Zinn's (2003) *The People's History of the United States*, a book that usually carries with it the adjective *leftist*. Students were delighted to discover the other side of the story. Their comparison of the two books generated truly lively and informed discussions. Calder (2006) pushed the idea of contrasting historical narratives further. Along with Zinn's book, he assigned Paul Johnson's (1999) *The History of the American People*, whose conservative institutional and national history counterbalanced Zinn's interest in the people. The point was not to cover everything, but to let students participate in a process of uncovering history (Calder; Hall & Scott, 2007; Hynd, 1999; Wiggins & McTighe, 2005).

Assigning Johnson (1999) and Zinn (2003) has its points. Foremost, it deprives students of a single, definitive authority. Putting two plausible interpretations of the same history before them destabilizes their reliance on the reinforcing authority that text and teacher traditionally supply. Reading Zinn next to Johnson, students find themselves sandwiched, sometimes uncomfortably, between two estimable historians with sometimes wildly divergent takes on the past. Second, the contrast lays open for comparison important qualities about the actual way in which historians think, write, and argue. Uncoverage opens a view onto the historian's signature. Third, these trade paperbacks are much less expensive than a textbook.

Choosing texts was only one step in reenvisioning the survey course. Team-Based Learning (TBL) suggested important structural changes. The idea of giving students a test on reading assignments before we began a unit seemed useful. Their early preparation creates a knowledge context for all subsequent lecture, discussion, and readings. It also puts the student in a place where he or she would have to bite into the reading, something each is capable of doing but often is able to delay or avoid in a big lecture class. Facing a history text on one's own, though, can be daunting. Reading two textbooks doubles the problem of answering the well-worn questions, "Do I have to know everything?" and "What do I have to know?" So I created a guide to aid them. The first part offers four to six Big Questions to ponder for each unit. One, for example, states: "Zinn characterizes capitalists (and their business dealings) in the late 19th century as 'robber barons,' but Johnson asks, 'Was it robbing?'" The reader needs to decide and explain. The second part, Just the Facts, lists about 20 specific terms, people, or events students must become familiar with.

SOME REVISIONS

I found that students are not used to reading history for interpretation first and fact second. The reverse feels more comfortable. Moreover, quizzing them on what they've read on their own before a lecture or discussion heightens anxiety about learning all the information offered by Zinn (2003) and Johnson (1999). In the second iteration of the course, I added a third text, a short *Outline of U.S. History* (available from www.america.gov/publications/books/history-outline.html), supplemented with short selections from Zinn and Johnson, as the basis of the opening readiness assurance quiz. The outline is succinct and dry but reasonably reviews the major narratives high school history covers. I also edited the reading required in Zinn and Johnson, focusing more closely on their contrasting views of a particular era or event. Additionally, I used several of the guide questions as the basis for team applications exercises.

GENTLY WEANING STUDENTS FROM
THE EXPECTATION OF LECTURES

Malcolm Gladwell (2007) contends that we have only a few seconds to make the critical first impression (p. 50). I try to stack the deck. Two or three weeks before the semester begins, I send a friendly short e-mail to the class and attach copies of the syllabus and "Course Sequence and Rules," which explains in detail how the course works. I don't expect that either document will be closely read at the time, but I intend to begin to set students' expectations for the class. I send a second message just before the term begins, again using phrases such as "collaborative format," "register your i>clicker," "course website," and "primary sources." No one likes to be blindsided, especially on the first day of class when everything else is so intense.

The first day of class offers another, more direct chance to revise students' ideas about what a history class should be like. I take the precious Gladwellian (2007) few seconds to initiate a conversation with them about history, asking, "Well, tell me, why are you in this class?" I have come to rely on students to respond eagerly and bluntly (but always politely): "Because the state legislature requires us to take six hours of Texas or U.S. history." From there, they fill in their side of the dialogue. This exercise in class conversation yields two main points. First, memorizing facts about dead people and events long past has little appeal. And second, an agreement with a mangled but essentially correct version of Santayana's warning that "those who cannot remember the past are condemned to repeat it" (www.gutenberg.org/files/15000/15000-h/vol1.html), which at least one student inevitably invokes. Throughout this seemingly casual discussion, they agree with but are surprised by my suggestion that they already know some history. Meanwhile, I try to rephrase comments using, and introducing, what Thomas Andrews and Flannery Burke (2007) have designated the five C's of historical thinking: contingency, causality, change over time, context, and complexity. (We return to these throughout the term, using them to help bind our historical understanding.) In the next step, students discover that each of them has, at least to some degree, a basic if implicit philosophy of history already in place, one that they have been bringing forward throughout the meeting. Some are progressives. Some see history as endless repetition. Most put forward more complicated interpretations. As for me, I'm pleased to see that the class has moved easily from relating the details of history to arranging them in an interpretative framework, albeit a very loose one.

Whereas the first day is devoted to American history, the second covers the nuts and bolts. It begins with an ungraded quiz on the syllabus and course sequence, then students take the same quiz in teams. For this quiz only, I form ad hoc teams of five or six. Each team's members introduce themselves to their teammates and discuss a silly topic, say, comparing the worst restaurant meals they've ever eaten. A little more comfortable with each other, they tackle the quiz together. This is an opportunity for the class to try out aspects of the course that are most likely quite unfamiliar to them. They learn more about the syllabus, experience that being certain doesn't necessarily mean being right, and perhaps argue successfully that theirs is a better answer than the official one. Most likely, they will also discover their team score is better than that of any individual. It is all fairly chaotic, but the real first day goes much more smoothly because of the rehearsal.

TEAMS

One of the most difficult aspects of the TBL design for students to accept is taking a readiness assurance quiz at the beginning of each unit before the material is discussed in class. Earning grades for work done as a team poses another. Students often hold an unexamined belief that when working alone they are masters of their own success. Yet the business world, in fact most all of adult life, puts high value on an ability to work in teams and great store in the quality of work a good team produces. Most if not all the class will experience this as they move out into the wider world. Nurses, doctors, families, engineers, real estate brokers, teachers, venture capitalists, volunteers—name a calling or community and you will find that most successful individuals meet new challenges and find more success by drawing on the success of a team working on the same problem. The TV show *House* demonstrates the point. Dr. House is the smartest (and nastiest) of the team, but the members sharpen his brilliance, and he hones theirs. In the end, the patient lives (or usually does) because of the team's collective intensity and diverse inquiry.

Pedagogically, the team idea is sound. Students trust each other more than they trust professors (which might be wrongheaded, but it's true). Like most people, they look to their peers for information before, or more frequently instead of, seeking an authoritative answer. Working together, a team can tackle the harder problems of thinking about history and achieve a much higher level of comprehension than most individual students. Their arguments, revisions, and reformulations of ideas at each point add to their own mastery of history—skills that will be very helpful at exam time at the very least, and most likely far beyond then. I admit, though, to being somewhat perplexed about the best way to explain the advantages of collaborative work to a class. To spend too much time on the topic sends a message that this is risky business and the instructor is overselling the approach. To gloss over it devalues its importance as a learning strategy. The main point to convey is that students should expect to work in permanently set teams. As a team, they are dependent on one another. As individuals, they cannot succeed unless the group succeeds.

No matter how one pitches the idea of teams, expect that more than a few students will express some resistance to the idea. Some might be even vocal. One senior, even after two e-mails and two days of class in which I'd explicitly said that everyone would be working in teams, protested in front of his new team members: "I don't like this one little bit." (He later became a staunch advocate of the practice.) Of course, everyone has experienced being dragged down by the group slacker, who must exist as a stereotype. But there's usually another problem person, the one who tells everyone what to do, or worse, hijacks the whole project out of fear of not getting a perfect A. Now is the time to exercise some finesse and firmness. Make it clear you are committed to this team strategy and that you'll continue to make every effort to ensure each student's individual as well as team success. But if anyone feels at this point that he or she cannot give the team and course a fair try, that person should find another, more suitable class.

Once the roster has a stable list of names, just before the third class, I organize everyone into the teams that remain the same throughout the term. A team of five to seven seems optimal. The number is sufficient to protect a team's effectiveness if there are absences but small enough to ensure accountability among teammates. There is a great deal of literature on how to form teams (Davis, 1993). Some use questionnaires, standardized or self-crafted, to sort students, but the main idea is that the more diverse a team, the better its chances of success. In any case, experts advise against letting students choose their own teams. They will clump together for social reasons or, worse, individuals will be rejected, excluded, or ignored.

This is how I approach forming the teams: Accepting the wisdom that diversity makes the best team, I make a cursory inventory of a classes' majors and levels. Typically the survey is among the last courses majors in other fields take; with graduation looming, they sign up. In last spring's class, for example, 46% were seniors (in the fall, only a third). I can always count history majors on one hand. To the degree possible, I want to ensure that a team's members are strangers to each other and hope they will find each other a puzzle at first but come to some appreciation that other minds work in other ways and have something to offer. I have drawn additional conclusions, which may or may not be fair. It seems that engineering and natural sciences majors tend to make up the older half of the class. Female or liberal arts majors dispense with the history requirement earlier. Given a fairly limited amount of personal information officially available, I try to construct teams that are as similar as possible in their imbalances: seniors countered by freshmen, liberal arts pitted against engineering (and other major incongruities), male versus female.

The rest of the task is mechanical but goes fairly quickly. Set out an index card for each team. Print out a numbered roster. Begin by distributing the biggest category of majors among the teams. Last term it was male seniors in natural science, then senior females (science also), ensuring that each team has roughly the same number of older students. My experience is the older ones tend to mentor younger students. One freshman told me the senior on his team had showed him how to read more effectively. A 30-year-old, at first impatient with callow youth, recanted a few weeks later after she began actually listening to them. Assign first-year students and undeclared majors next. Once you've gone through the entire roster, correct the most obvious misplacements. This system doesn't guarantee perfect teams (nor do any of the other methods I've found), but it's easy to do and, importantly, easy to explain to the class. They will want to know what your system is.

Some teams will be stronger than others, some more cooperative. Sometimes personalities clash. My impulse is to rush in and fix it, but that's wrongheaded. The short answer to the problem is that the members need to work out a solution. Reassigning individuals simply doesn't work. Certainly other teams don't want to take in new members who may be the cause of the difficulties. Also, it sets a precedent in the class that you might not want to maintain. Here's what you might try with a troublesome team: Ask, "If you were working for a company, what would you do in this situation?" (Complaining to the boss is not the best answer.) Or try sitting in on a meeting to help the team focus on the work before them. Peer evaluations (described in Chapters 1 and 3) allow a team to air its grievances anonymously and can be especially helpful if a person recognizes his or her own culpability in a team's imperfect dynamic. In any case, avoid breaking the group up, even if the teammates request it (see Figure 10.2 for tips on succeeding as teams). Also, I am finding some success in daily rotating the responsibility for being the team scribe, or reporter, and encouraging students to assume different conversational roles such as skeptic, harmonizer, and sheepdog. This seems to keep teams from settling into comfortable routines that freeze roles and power positions in which the same person always does the writing or another always reports conclusions to the class at large.

HOW IT ALL GOES TOGETHER

Day 1: Readiness Assurance Quizzes

On the first day of each unit, students demonstrate individual mastery of their reading by taking a 20- to 25-question multiple-choice readiness assurance quiz based on the reading assigned in the study guide. When writing quiz questions, try to include those that require the flat-out right answers as well as ones that require reasoning; for example, "X was more important than Y and Z in enabling Q." The

FIGURE 10.2
How to Succeed as a Team

Success in the professional world is influenced by three things: your own effort, the effort of the people you depend upon, and the way you work together. The same is true in this class. After our observations of the behaviors of high- and low-performing teams in other courses, we offer these suggestions:

1) Sit close, in a circle.
This enables easy communication and eye contact, which is very important to team performance.

2) Come prepared.
Read and write as assigned. Bring your books and readings to class, complete with your underlining, marginalia, and other notes.

3) Prepare to share three things with your teammates:
        what answer you chose as an individual
        why you chose that answer
        how confident you are about it

4) Deliberate as long as time permits. Unless a team is full of all-stars, we have found that teams that deliberate longer (especially at the beginning of the term) do better in team activities.

5) Keep an open mind and a willing attitude.
You are responsible for the success of the entire team.

---

collection of verbs associated with Bloom's taxonomy (descibed in Chapter 1) has proved invaluable in creating quizzes that work across various cognitive levels. Web versions of Bloom's taxonomy and its associated verbs, in graphic and text formats, are easy to find (see, for example, www.odu.edu/educ/roverbau/Bloom/blooms_taxon omy.htm). Students record their answers using i>clickers, a small wireless device that allows short questions to be answered and scored immediately, and the grades are recorded on a spreadsheet. I don't return graded copies; I'd like to discourage students from thinking that memorizing old quizzes is of special value. And because quizzes and exams tend to circulate, I want to avoid writing a completely new set of questions each term.

Only rarely does a student score 100% on the individual quiz, so I curve grades. For me at least, this creates the unexpected result of making students produce better work. It removes what some perceive as a near-impossible standard and installs a competitiveness buoyed by possibility. In past classes, the average rose for each of the five quizzes, except for one term. But I think the fact that nearly half of the class was graduating seniors and it was spring had something to do with that.

Immediately following the individual quiz, students collaborate on the same quiz in their assigned teams during the second part of the class. To avoid at least some confusion, I tape large sheets of paper with team numbers on them to chair backs spaced evenly throughout the room the first time. Printed copies of the team roster and a document camera also help, and I also post the information on the course website.

The team quiz is not simply a chance to compare answers. It involves talking about history, where sentences are parsed, facts recited, interpretations aired, and consensus achieved. The first time I watched negotiations over potential right answers, I was taken aback. Nearly 80 students (14 teams) argued with each other about what they'd read. One team, for example, carried on a lively discussion about the development and impact of refrigerated rail cars. In another, I overheard a heated conversation about the definition of socialism. It is a noisy process.

Once a team agrees on an answer, it is recorded on an immediate feedback assessment technique (IF-AT) card (see www.epsteineducation.com for more information on IF-ATs), which works like a lottery scratch-off ticket; scraping the correct answer reveals a star. Students like this. It builds anticipation, has a small payoff, and allows second chances. In practice, it often plays out like this: Six people hunch over the answer card. One person, pinching the edge of a quarter, poised to scrape the silvery paint away from a square, nervously scans faces to get the go-ahead. "Do we all agree B is the answer?" "B?" "Yes?" "Okay." If there's a star, you might hear a great sigh or, sometimes, a collective shout. If a star doesn't show up, talk resumes, and a new square is tried. The IF-ATs allow a team to make second, third, and even fourth attempts, effectively returning students to a discussion in which they try to figure out what went wrong. Perhaps they bowed to the will of an overconfident student. Maybe the team second-guessed itself. It could be team members misunderstood the question, or a poorly worded phrase confused them. Each additional try costs the team points, so it's important to get the answer right with a minimum number of tries. Yet what matters most is that throughout the minidramas, six people continue to explain history to and learn from each other.

Appeals for a better grade. The appeals process adds another dimension to the team quiz. If a team thinks the official answer is wrong or misleading, it can protest in writing. Appeals are not simply a chance to dig the question for more points. They are an opportunity for teams to make scholarly arguments for their collective position; all arguments must be supported by evidence from the text or lecture notes (see Figure 10.3 for an example of an appeal). If an appeal protests an allegedly ambiguously phrased question, the team must suggest better wording. The decision to grant or refuse an appeal will be made later by the instructor, and the team is informed at the following meeting. (I've learned never to make a ruling on the spot. Too much emotion is invested in the outcome, sometimes mine as well as a team's.) The decision is final.

At the end of class, each person who took the test writes his or her name on the back of the team's answer sheet and staples any appeal, the scratch-off, and all the individual quizzes together to be filed in their folder.

Bonus points. The best team quiz scores earn bonus points for members. Two points are added to each individual quiz scores on the highest-scoring team. So a score of 13 on the individual quiz is raised to 15 if the team outscores the others. Individuals on the second-place teams each receive 1 additional point. If teams tie, they get equal points added to personal grades, which are the ones that count for their course grade.

Day 2: Lecture

The second day is devoted to a lecture that introduces major themes and draws together critical points. I e-mail a PowerPoint outline of the presentation to the class the day before, which some students say helps them take better notes. Preparing these lectures has pushed me to synthesize and bring to the forefront historical threads, such as the increasing presence of a middle class, the changing role of the government, and growing expectations concerning personal rights, which are certainly discussed in any reputable text but tend to hide in small paragraphs. Having read about

FIGURE 10.3
Example of a Successful Appeal

Argument: Question 15: We feel that A, rather than B, should be the correct answer.

Evidence: According to Johnson, p. 52, the Pilgrims did not intend to invite Squanto to Thanksgiving. However, historian Charles Sellers (quoted in Zinn, p. 74, footnote 7) asserts that Squanto said that two Plimouth townspeople had verbally asked his people to bring cranberry sauce. This would lead us to conclude that, at best, the evidence about whether Native Americans were formally invited to the First Thanksgiving is inconclusive.

the time period on their own, taken an individual readiness assurance quiz, and discussed some of the material while completing the team readiness assurance quiz on Day 1, students have at least some familiarity with the information, and therefore are more open to seeing the interplay of larger forces that give shape to historical periods and are more ready to ask questions.

i>clicker warm-up. I begin each of the lecture days, as well as the three teamwork days that follow, with two or three i>clicker questions that link ideas from course readings or documents to a bigger picture. Sometimes I allow students to discuss the answer with those around them first. Sometimes they answer individually and again after discussion. Because the i>clicker software graphs and displays votes, students can readily gauge their knowledge against that of the class. And I can too. This exercise prompts student questions, reinforces knowledge, and can reveal important gaps in understanding, all of which can be addressed right then. I don't score the answers, but a secondary benefit of the i>clicker's record of responses allows me to check attendance if I choose to.

Days 3, 4, and 5: Teamwork

During the final three days of a unit, students work in teams to solve problems based on a set of primary documents or passages from Zinn (2003) and Johnson (1999). The work begins at the class website where teams find a general question, a selection of documents that I have edited to a reasonable length (usually no more than four or five pages), and notes about how to distribute the work among team members. In one exercise, for example, they find a prompt: "This project examines a small sampling of evidence concerning the McCarthy era. You will be asked to evaluate the following documents in terms of this proposition: The hysteria and restriction of civil liberties during the early 1950s were justified." Everyone is instructed to read selected passages from Zinn and Johnson and watch two short videos. The remaining documents are assigned to individuals who will annotate their copies and summarize orally what they found when the team meets. Each document has a letter next to it, so it is easy to assign, for instance, "team members 1 and 3 to read document A."

As of yet, I have not found an entirely satisfactory way to ensure that everyone completes work ahead of time. Peer evaluations and direct observation provide some form of checking. The example of others' conscientious work and a desire to be well thought of motivates many but not enough or always. I am currently working out a system for students to keep an ongoing electronic journal of their work, one that I can read on a random basis. However, one aim in redesigning the course was to lessen the amount of paperwork and grading detail, and to shift responsibility for learning more squarely onto the student. Clearly, work completion is an area that needs to be carefully balanced between student autonomy and instructor responsibility to the class as a whole.

Before the class starts on a teamwork day, I post a short list of what I intend students to be able to do. In pedagogic terms, it is a list of objectives. I've been calling it The Point (see the example in Figure 10.4), and admittedly it is a bald attempt to underline for the students that there is indeed a point or purpose to their work. I have found that writing The Point has been especially helpful to me in clarifying my own reasons for an assignment and in assessing how it fits into the overall scheme of building critical thinking skills. Lately, I've been writing The Point in two tiers. The first is more general, intended to remind students of the types of historical thinking that will be emphasized on that day. The second tier speaks to the topic at hand.

Class starts with a few i>clicker questions, a quick introduction to the day's work, and each person reporting to his or her team. Teams then begin work on an application exercise, a set of questions that lead a team to synthesize individual work, evaluate it in some way, and arrive at a conclusion. Teams might be required to agree or disagree with a proposition set before them, take a multiple-choice quiz, or rank their conclusions according to some criteria.

At the beginning of the course, I concentrate on the importance of using evidence to support an interpretation, a basic move that will come into play throughout the remaining units. As the term progresses, the tasks become more complicated. For the first exercise, though, students are assigned relevant passages from Zinn (2003) and Johnson (1999). As a team, they must select and quote passages (with page numbers) about Carnegie, Morgan, and others, and sort them into positive and negative columns. At the bottom of the page, they are directed to review the evidence they have amassed and using only that evidence, choose a simple one-or-the-other answer to the question: "Were the late 19th-century industrialists captains of industry or robber barons?" They must explain their reasoning in 25 words or less. As the teams work (loudly) I roam, as does my teaching assistant, ready to prod discussion, answer

FIGURE 10.4
The Point

Use primary documents to identify the variety of motives and solutions existing within a given movement. (causation)

Evaluate documents in light of potentially conflicting historical interpretations (complexity)

Draw conclusions based on primary documents about
a. what Progressives saw as "progress"
b. what Progressives saw as "problems"

Synthesize conclusions in order to articulate these Progressives' goals and concerns in the form of a written manifesto.

Given three valid historical interpretations of the Progressive Movement, discern which best describes the Progressives revealed in the manifesto your team wrote.

---

questions, and provide minilectures to the class at large when we spot teachable moments. For example, because several teams asked for a definition of *Victorian values*, a term Johnson uses in reference to some of the late 19th-century moguls, I gave an impromptu five-minute explanation (along with a truly amateur illustration of Victorian dress) to the class at large. These have now been dubbed *flash lectures*.

We reconvene as a class in the last 15 minutes to discuss the application exercise. This is a time to pull the disparate voices and activities together. Sometimes I begin by polling teams for their yes/no answers. But there are numerous paths. You can talk about why a simple yes or no answer is difficult to declare, or how Zinn (2003) and Johnson (1999) use evidence and how it accumulates into an interpretation. A small debate can be orchestrated. "Which teams concluded that Harding was a better president than Wilson? Why?" or "Team 7 ranked the causes of McCarthyism as A, B, C. Team 9, which ranked them B, D, A, will explain why it rejected the A, B, C answer." Then, "Team 7 will respond." These peer critiques foster competition between groups and a motivation for cooperation within groups. They also demonstrate the variety and test the validity of interpretations possible from a single body of evidence. At the conclusion, it's easy to suggest that the teams have just worked out an argument based on evidence, just as Zinn and Johnson did, and just as they will do independently on exams.

There is a lot of room for inventiveness in creating application exercises, but some points bear consideration. Decide what goal or outcome you intend the class to achieve. The levels (and verbs) of Bloom's taxonomy (as described in Chapter 1), the five Cs of historical thinking (Andrews & Burke, 2007), and Calder's moves (Calder, 2006) are currently my working set of references. Figure out what steps you take instinctively to think like a historian, then transfer those steps to the team applications. (This is curiously challenging.) Keep in mind that students work slowly. Teams are good at keeping track of specific facts but need time to work out how to select, synthesize, and evaluate them. You are asking them to do something new; the exercises will probably have to be shorter than you had thought. Also, students are remarkably agile at splitting work into parts to be worked on individually. This effectively negates the value of collaboration. Keep them working with each other by creating a situation in which they have to share information. If everyone brings part of a puzzle to the table, they have to pool their knowledge to reveal the big picture.

Argument templates: Application exercises. The idea for argument templates originated when I experienced a cold moment of fear envisioning what would happen when I told a big class to discuss the documents they'd just read and to keep at it for 20 or even 10 minutes. Issuing an instruction to examine or analyze didn't help. How does one actually perform these tasks? Of course, we do it all the time, but we've had lots of practice. Students are understandably perplexed about how they should proceed. Consider a conversation I've had with nonhistory majors, mystified that history is a discipline and more than just names and dates. A chemist or an engineer, they argue, can prove an idea. (My solemn answer is that, whereas mathematicians solve for multiple variables, we solve for multiple variables to the fifth power.) These and similar experiences led me to try to break the historian's action of analyzing into component parts. Each day's team application exercise is a tabloid-size set of prompts that guide a team as it pulls apart, reorganizes, builds, compares, evaluates, contextualizes, ranks, or in some way thinks systematically and critically about historical information (see the appendix for an example of an application exercise).

Scoring teamwork. Teamwork counts 15% to 20% of the course grade in my class, but I offer this only as information, not advice. Students bristle at the idea of being saddled with someone else's grade—apparently even when the team consistently performs better than the individual. Organizing the application exercises to require a bottom line or a final answer means you can quickly scan the work to assess its quality. So far I've been impressed by the work, enough that I have announced that the standard grade is an A or B. The catch is that students have to participate in their team's work. If they are absent, they get an F for the day. (Remember a side benefit of the warm-up questions? i>clickers generate a record of student attendance.) One or two absences over the course of a term won't significantly harm a grade average, but if a person is not there to help the team, he or she can't share the rewards in either points or experience. In any case, the rule is that all team members get the same grade, and no missed teamwork can be made up.

PEER EVALUATIONS

Approval motivates us all. In a class setting, peer approval is more important than a teacher's. Peer evaluations make good use of this possibly curious observation. They let team members hear what others expect of them and how they are perceived. They give students the opportunity to tell slackers on the team to get into the game, smart but shy people to speak up, bossy people to retreat, and the most helpful to carry on. Feedback helps them answer, "What can we do to make our team work better?"

I hold two peer evaluations during the term. The first one, completed at the end of Unit 1, gives teams an early chance to make the adjustments that can ensure a smoother working relationship for the remainder of the semester. It also sets an expectation squarely before the group. In the later stages of the term, when everyone feels the pressures of impending finals and is wearied by school in general, the second evaluation helps refocus teams. The evaluation form I use (courtesy of Michael Sweet; see Figure 10.5) has several features that help students get over their wariness about judging one another. Each person has a total of 25 points to distribute to his or her teammates, which provides a framework to evaluate relative contributions. Second, by asking for a compliment and a request, the form emphasizes the need for help and courtesy. It works. Students make remarkably positive comments; I have yet to read a rude one. However, they are direct in a way that leaves little room for interpretation. For example: (I appreciate) "You have really good ideas" and (I request) "Please stop checking your text messages all the time."

The question is how to use the information. I make each individual's comments available to him or her as soon as possible. I also establish a generous curve and count the evaluations as 5% of the course grade. If a person receives 24 or 25 points, I

FIGURE 10.5
Partial Peer Feedback Report

Team Reflection and Feedback

To help your team become more effective, give your teammates some *anonymous* feedback.

Consider such things as:

Preparation: were they prepared when they came to class?
Contribution: did they contribute to the team discussion and work?
Gatekeeping: did they help *others* contribute?
Flexibility: did they listen when disagreements occurred?

You have 25 points to distribute among your teammates. These are anonymous, so be honest. :-)

	Points
1. Team Member Name: [add a box for each name] *Things I appreciate about this team member:* *Things I would like to request of this team member:*	

TOTAL (must = 25): _____

assume he or she met a standard that indicates the team is in balance, and I assign an A for that evaluation. Another way might be to use the scores for bonus points. In any case, this peek into team dynamics yields, at the very least, insights for the teacher, student, and team alike.

ESSAY EXAMINATIONS

Our department places high value on the ability to write a history essay. I agree, and so I have kept this perhaps quite conventional element in the redesigned course. In the survey, I give two midterms and a final that emphasize the knowledge and use the skills that have been practiced in class. Throughout the application exercises I point out the ways that students are performing in their teams as well as the sorts of analysis, use of evidence, and awareness of argument strategies that they will be using in their history exams. The first midterm counts a mere 10%. If a student doesn't do well, she or he has plenty of opportunity to correct whatever went wrong—reading habits, time organization, lack of good evidence, poor writing skills. The second and third exams each raise the stakes. By the close of the term, some students will be better at thinking critically about history, organizing their thoughts, and writing them down, but each will have grown more confident, skilled, and accustomed to thinking about history critically and less passive in his or her acceptance of people, print, and media that assert an unexamined viewpoint.

CONCLUSION

Before the culture wars got well under way, Frances FitzGerald (1979) wrote:

What sticks to the memory from those [1950s history] textbooks is not any particular series of facts but an atmosphere, an impression, a tone. And this impression may be all the more influential because one cannot remember the facts and arguments that created it. (p. 47)

But times change. Neither textbooks nor teachers can lay claim to the sort of power they once held or tried to hold. Perhaps, though, the atmosphere remains the salient feature of a history class. If so, it would seem all the more important to foster an environment that encourages students to master for themselves the process of evaluating the facts and arguments. In their participation, they will find they will not only remember names, dates, and places but also will be able to understand how these facts and arguments relate to their own lives and futures.

NOTE

1. A description of i>clickers can be found www.iclicker.com. A number of similar devices are available, but at present this is the most reliable system. Because the devices don't allow a person to answer questions out of sequence, I distribute hard copies of the quiz.

REFERENCES

Andrews, T., & Burke, F. (2007). What does it mean to think historically? *AHA Perspectives*, *45*(1). Retrieved from http://www.historians.org/perspectives/issues/2007/0701/0701tea2.cfm

Calder, L. (2006). Uncoverage: Toward a signature pedagogy for the history survey. *Journal of American History*, *92*(4), 1358–1370. doi: 10.2307/4485896

Davis, B. G. (1993). *Tools for teaching*. San Francisco: Jossey-Bass.

Edgerton, G. R. (2001). Television as historian. In G. R. Edgerton & P. C. Rollins (Eds.), *Television histories: Shaping collective memory in the media age* (pp. 19–36). Lexington: University of Kentucky Press.

FitzGerald, F. (1979, February 26). Rewriting American history: Part I. *New Yorker*, 41–77.

Gladwell, M. (2007). *Blink*. Boston, MA: Back Bay Books.

Hall, T. D., & Scott, R. (2007). Closing the gap between professors and teachers: "Uncoverage" as a model of professional development for history teachers. *History Teacher*, *40*(2), 257–263.

Hynd, C. R. (1999). Teaching students to think critically using multiple texts in history. *Journal of Adolescent & Adult Literacy*, *42*(6), 428–436.

Jefferson, R. F. (2009). Whose war is it anyway? Ken Burns' *The War* and American popular memory. *Oral History Review, 36*(1), 71–81.

Johnson, P. (1993). *History of the American people.* New York, NY: HarperCollins.

Michaelson, L. K., & Sweet, M. (2008). The essential elements of team-based learning. *New Directions in Teaching and Learning, 116,* 7–27. doi: 10.1002/tl.330

Ravitch, D., & Finn,, C. A., Jr. (1987). *What do our 17-year-olds know: A report on the first national assessment of history and literature.* New York, NY: Harper & Row.

Rosenzweig, R. (2000). How Americans use and think about the past. In P. N. Sterns, P. Seixas, & S. Wineburg (Eds.), *Knowing, teaching, and learning history: National and international perspectives* (pp. 262–83). New York: New York University Press.

Schulman, L. S. (2005). Signature pedagogies in the professions. *Daedalus, 134*(3), 52–59. doi:10.1162/0011526054622015

Schweikart, L., & and Allen, M. (2007). *A patriot's history of the United States: From Columbus's great discovery to the war on terror.* New York, NY: Sentinel Trade, Penguin Group.

Sturken, M. (1997). Re-enactment, fantasy, and the paranoia of history: Oliver Stone's docudramas. *History and Theory, 36*(4) 64–79.

Tapscott, D. (2010, December 30). The impending demise of the university [Web log post]. Retrieved from http://www.edge.org/3rd_culture/tapscott09/tapscott09_index.html

Wiggins, G., & McTighe, J. (2005). *Understanding by design* (2nd ed.). Upper Saddle River, NJ: Prentice Hall.

Wineburg, S. (2004). Crazy for history. *Journal of American History, 90*(4), 1401–1414. doi: 10.2307/3660360

Zinn, H. (2003). *A people's history of the United States.* New York, NY: HarperCollins.

APPENDIX

Example of an Application Exercise

The McCarthy era: What were the fears? How real were the fears?

I. What fears do each of the following primary source documents call into play? Be as precise as possible in describing each of the fears. Indicate whether the fear expressed implicitly (I) or explicitly (E) (see Figure 10.6).

II. The best evidence. Rank the "sources" 1 (strongest)–6 (weakest) in response to each of these statements (see Figure 10.7):

1. The most balanced and reputable information about the early Cold War period.
2. The most useful for understanding the era.

FIGURE 10.6

SOURCE	Specific fears	I/E
A. "Duck and cover"		
B. Communism		
C. "Hiss and Chambers"		
D. "Is this tomorrow"		
E. "Communists should not teach in American colleges"		
F. "Iron Curtain look"		

FIGURE 10.7

Source	1. Most balanced . . .	2. Most useful . . .
A		
B		
C		
D		
E		
F		

III. Historicism versus presentism

Referring to the previous documents, the readings in Zinn and Johnson, and your knowledge of Cold War events, agree or disagree with the following statement. Write a short (no more that 25 words) justification for your answer that reflects the team's best "history essay" style.

"The hysteria and restriction of civil liberties during the Cold War were justified."

HISTORICISM

Agree/disagree

PRESENTISM

Agree/disagree

CHAPTER 11

Discerning the Elements of Culture

A Team-Based Learning Approach to Asian Religions and Cultures

Joël Dubois

In this chapter, Dubois writes with deep introspection about how he has learned to help students develop a working relationship to course material that is at the outset dense and alien to them. Readers from any discipline can benefit from considering his metaphor of learning as the exploration of a new landscape and some clear navigational aids we as teachers can provide to support students in finding their way. Further, the specific examples he provides of application activities in his field can serve as exemplars for adaptation in many fields, as can the deep thought he has put into the alignment of his readiness assurance tests and application activities, and where he is planning to take them next.

I have long been drawn to pedagogies that engage students in actively analyzing sources rather than simply repeating scholarly assessments of what those sources mean. In graduate school, I was most impressed with the case-based discussion teaching method pioneered by Roland Christensen (Barnes, Christensen, & Hansen, 1994; Christensen & Hansen, 1987) at Harvard Business School. However, this method proved difficult to implement effectively with classes of 25–50 undergraduates encountering premodern Asia for the first time, and whose ability to decipher sources documenting ancient and foreign cultures were at best highly variable. The richly textured, case-based discussions I had savored as a graduate student occurred only rarely and serendipitously in such classrooms—until I began using Team-Based Learning (TBL). TBL can provide the "structured work practices" (Lave & Wenger, 1991, p. 15) needed for students to explore difficult sources independently, yielding rich discussions that bring individual insights to light for the benefit of the entire class.

It took considerable patience and discernment, however, to adapt existing applications of TBL from science- and practice-oriented disciplines to my classroom. At the time I began with TBL nearly seven years ago, many were successfully applying TBL in business, clinical practice, and engineering, as documented in Michaelsen (2008) and Michaelsen, Knight, and Fink (2004), but these disciplines focus on widely appreciated practical and technological problems solved by directly analyzing broadly observable natural and social processes. In contrast, humanities and many social science disciplines focus on the less widely valued analysis of sources viewed as artifacts revealing the dynamics of human culture; a few faculty in these disciplines were just starting to experiment with TBL. I could see the distinctive critical thinking skills promoted in humanities and social sciences (as per Donald, 2002) require designing distinctive assessments and application activities, but there were no clear models for doing so.

Not surprisingly given this context, my first semester of applying TBL to my "Arts and Ideas of Asia" course included a student mutiny over poorly constructed readiness assurance tests (RATs) and many ineffectual team activities. Yet considering what they endured, students showed remarkable goodwill overall. I decided the method deserved another try and kept going. Like many faculty adopting TBL who lack an on-site mentor familiar with the method, I availed myself instead of sympathetic on-campus mentors, peers doing problem-based learning with groups, the TBL Listserve, and long-distance mentoring with TBL experts, slowly but steadily refining my approach.

In the past few years I have gained considerable confidence as I see the four practical pieces of TBL bringing about with increasing efficiency the dynamic and insightful student discussions I had always wanted to see. Though I cannot claim expert status, in what follows I report on a work in progress, noting important mistakes to spotlight my rationale for approaching the four framing pieces of TBL (see Chapter 1) the way I do now. Since readiness assurance and application activities have required the most significant deliberation and modifications, I begin with these, concluding with more minimal adjustments and contributions to team formation and peer evaluation. Some of the insights I describe in this chapter are very recent, some adaptations I am still vetting, and some issues I am still unsure how to resolve. Yet my hope is that by drawing on the principles and examples included in this chapter, interested teachers will more efficiently[1] learn to guide students in analyzing sources that reveal the evolution of culture.

READINESS ASSURANCE: ORIENTATION TO PRIMARY SOURCES FOR THE STUDY OF CULTURE

In applying TBL, I have taken as the foundation of student learning the analysis of primary sources, defined as artifacts, writings, and visual media created by people in the cultures we are studying. I tell students on the first day that familiarity with such sources is the prerequisite for the application activities that are the heart of the course. I compare such sources to materials or data used in science labs, without handling which students cannot effectively learn course concepts. As pointed out in Chapter 1 of this volume, we cannot typically take students out to excavate ruins or interview members of a culture, but available primary sources provide a glimpse of worlds outside the classroom and an opportunity for dramatic rehearsal of real-world problem-solving. As suggested by Bain (2004, p. 50), highly effective college teachers build their courses around questions that students are likely to care about. Formulating relevant questions is also the first of Paul and Elder's list of critical thinking skills (see Chapter 1). In my courses, I tell students the central question is, "What makes a culture, and what forces change it?"—which anyone who wants to change the world or improve his or her community must ponder. Primary sources created by people in cultures far and near are the essential evidence for investigating that question.

This centrality of primary sources makes the meticulous reading and viewing of available sources the single most essential task for structuring and refining a course to frame "legitimate peripheral participation" by cognitive student-apprentices most effectively (Lave & Wenger, 1991; see Chapter 1). I have made it a priority to dedicate the necessary time to reviewing and selecting such sources, assigning 12–18 of them averaging 5–20 pages each for a 15-week course, to be read alongside a brief (60- to 70-page) general survey of the topic.[2] When I feel responsible for exposing students to a broader range of sources, I require reading and analysis of one additional source from a list provided for each unit and give extra credit for making use of such sources on individual assignments.

THEORETICAL CHALLENGES AND A USEFUL ANALOGY

Clarifying this focus on primary sources has helped me discern the two most significant challenges involved in applying TBL to analyze sources as cultural artifacts. First, most students in general education courses like mine find primary sources dealing with foreign cultures and distant periods highly disorienting. Even apart from difficulties with pronunciation of foreign words, such sources assume familiarity with radically different cultural practices and social structures. A subtler and more serious challenge, however, is the notion that the Readiness Assurance Process (RAP; see Chapter 1) is an opportunity to familiarize students with discrete introductory concepts, clearly distinguishable from the application of such concepts to specific examples. When preparing students to analyze sources as artifacts of culture, I have come to see that there are in fact (A) just a few broad concepts applicable to all the sources assigned for a given course that students can easily understand without repeated review in each RAP, and (B) a plethora of specific details related to individual sources that no beginning cognitive apprentice could hope to understand in its entirety the first time around. Michaelsen (2004, p. 218) does present very helpful suggestions for dealing with difficult readings prior to RATs. But these appear designed for disciplines that feature application of discrete introductory concepts, which can reasonably be learned in the time available between the end of one unit and the RAT at the start of the next.

Aware of (B) the complexity of sources which are difficult for beginners to understand how to read on their own, I have from the start been unwilling to ask students to prepare for RATs without in-class guidance from me; instead I have settled on scheduling in-class reading orientations for students. I began with one class period and have in recent years stretched this to two class periods.[3] To clarify for myself and students the relationship between the two types of preparatory knowledge (A) and (B), I have come to rely on the analogy of mapping a territory for the purposes of navigation and study. To study a region, one must first (A) know why one would want to study it, what one hopes to achieve by doing so, and some general terms useful for describing any region, such as *landscape*, *topography*, and *elevation*. Beyond this, however, one must then (B) familiarize oneself with the distinctive landscape and topography of each region studied, which often escape any neat categorization, to know what features are where and how to get around from one place to another. All of this must take place before one is ready to (C) analyze those features, the forces that produced them, and the relationships between them.

In initial reading orientations of the course, I explain to students that they must create maps of the primary sources. Through readings and discussion during the introductory unit of the course, (A) I introduce them to the idea that all the sources we examine provide clues about the interrelationship of three essential elements of human culture: reflection about things one can't immediately see, habitual practices that provide a way for people to reflect about such things, and communities that preserve and pass on such practices. I ask them to revisit one or more of these elements in every team application activity. In the period leading up to each RAT, I then ask them (B) to focus primarily on figuring out how to get around in the sources assigned for a given unit, that is, how to locate all the important features and the details of each, which often seem quite disorienting. The study guides I provide (more on these later) are in essence instructions for such map making, which means a general outline of the major regions in each text and key features in each region I expect them to look for and locate. Although visually inclined students may sketch diagrams and flow charts that map each source's landscape and topography, I point out that for many students mapping simply means highlighting and annotating the course reader; yet I want them to understand such activities as a kind of map making. I also note, however, that the orientation provided by my study guides, assessed via RATs, is just the foundation for (C) the deeper analysis undertaken in the team application activities. At that stage their notations and sketches will help them discern the elements of culture that shaped the creation of each source.

DESIGNING RATs

The theoretical framework just described did not pop into my head while planning my first TBL course; rather it evolved over several years of only partially successful attempts to prepare students adequately for team application activities. I describe this messy evolution next to highlight key features of the reading orientations and RATs I now use.

My initial attempts did assume a clear-cut distinction between discrete introductory concepts and application to examples. I asked students to read a broad overview to locate 10–14 terms naming the historical periods during which primary sources were written and the key cultural or religious ideas characteristic of those periods, most of which were not explicitly referenced in the sources themselves; based on these terms I composed the initial 5–7 questions for the 10-question RAT. I based the other 3–5 questions on unidentified primary source passages that I posted on my course website and asked them to locate beforehand, from which I selected two. These questions asked not only about titles, authors, places, and dates of sources of the passages but also about people referred to in the passages and what occurred before or after them.

Over time, however, I observed several problems with this RAT format. First, overview readings containing terms and concepts typically provided much more details than students needed to know, often oversimplifying the more messy reality reflected in the primary sources themselves. This made the supposed introduction to basic ideas anything but introductory or basic and gave students even less time to sort through equally, if not more, complex primary sources. Such overview term/ concept questions also did little to prepare students for reading primary sources. Students often failed to locate and answer the RAT questions about the primary source passages, and it was clear during team activities that many were still unfamiliar with those sources.

A year ago I began to transform the RATs to focus more directly on primary sources. Instead of assigning terms and concepts addressed mainly in overview readings, I now draw terms only from primary sources and the translator/editor introductions that precede them. I also increased the number of terms to several dozen, highlighting these as important landmarks embedded in the landscapes of the assigned sources, rather than as broad concepts to be thoroughly grasped before applying them (for example, see Figure 11.1).

Where an important term is used without being adequately clarified in the assigned primary sources, I did add briefer secondary readings for clarification, often online encyclopedia summaries. The 5–7 RAT questions addressing these terms thus now overlap significantly with the questions about unidentified passages, to which students are now better prepared to respond.[4]

READING ORIENTATIONS AND STUDY GUIDES

While refining RATs, I experimented with a variety of approaches to pre-RAT reading orientations. The main hurdle in this exploration has been that, regardless of the label, students tend to expect I will tell them what they need to know for the test. This problem was aggravated in earlier years when I wrote study guides that focused largely on defining terms only distantly related to the primary sources. In an

FIGURE 11.1
Comparison of Old and New Approaches to Writing RAT Questions

OLD WAY: asking about a broad concept described by a secondary overview

1–5. According to Thanissaro, the Buddha's approach to the issue of karma was unique in that he:
 (a) looked at skillful mental action in and of itself as a means to release.
 (b) assumed that all action was a form of violence.
 (c) stressed that correctly performed ritual action led to happiness after death.
 (d) insisted that human action is totally subject to fate.
 (e) concluded that good and evil were illusory social conventions.

NEW WAY: assessing awareness of key terms in the context of a source:

1–5. According to legends and sutras assigned for this unit, during the night of Shakyamuni Buddha's unbinding he:
 (a) saw with a divine eye all beings passing away and being reborn according to their karma.
 (b) became painfully aware of how much his father, wife and other family missed him.
 (c) fell asleep under the Bodhi Tree and dreamt of beautiful women tempting him.
 (d) observed for the first time the inevitability of ageing, illness, and death for all beings.
 (e) articulated the eight steps of the noble path that he taught as part of his dharma.

effort to avoid a lecture posture, I would alternate between reviewing key definitions from handouts or PowerPoint slides, reading important passages out loud, asking teams to locate terms in the readings, and showing short video clips related to the subject under consideration. Yet however engaged students were during team activities, they remained largely passive during such orientations and in midsemester and end-of-course feedback, many asked for more standard lectures that presented the information in a linear way. I thus concluded that such an approach was inherently counterproductive.

Nevertheless, remaining convinced that some type of in-class reading orientation was necessary, if only to give students a bit more time with difficult readings, I consulted colleagues and observed their ways of engaging students in examining assigned readings. I wanted something more in harmony with the mapping analogy presented earlier: given a list of important landmarks, mapping apprentices must locate each and determine which are most important rather than having their guide walk them along every route and tell them what to map. The most attractive option initially seemed to be assigning participation credit to students who brought in notes about key details addressed in the reading. During reading orientation sessions I projected sets of terms on the screen, addressing one primary source at a time, and asking students to call out a page number for any term they were able to locate, along with a brief description of whatever they had discerned. In return I offered extra credit points for any contribution, however minimal. I could feel immediately that this approach was shifting responsibility onto students in a productive way. Short videos and reading key passages out loud continued to help break up the intensity of such sessions.

Yet by midterm, getting even prepared students to volunteer information felt like pulling teeth. Thus I also experimented with allowing students to look for terms independently for most of the class period, offering extra credit for written notes rather than oral participation. At the end of such sessions I allowed 15–20 minutes for questions and answers, with mixed results. During the first day of each unit's reading orientation, many teams were focused and asked clear questions, but on the second day most of this energy dissipated.

As a result of this experiment with locating terms as a whole class and in teams, I hit upon the idea of injecting the specific choice focus of formal team activities into the reading orientation process. This signals from the start that I am guiding students in locating for themselves features of the textual landscape rather than just telling them what is on the test. I home in on one or two sections of a single primary source and ask teams to consider which of these terms (or pair, or set of terms) is most important (sometimes adding an additional qualifier, such as "for understanding the practice that inspired this source"), and why? Polling the results of such informal team investigations helps prepared students assimilate details and themes but also models for less-confident or unprepared students a way to draw on the study guide on their initial run through each source.

I now perceive that formatting and presentation of study guides are key to getting students to understand the task before them. I begin each study guide with a list of three content objectives for each unit (see the example in Figure 11.2) to orient students to the big picture of ideas, themes, cultural regions, or historical periods to be investigated via the primary sources; this substitutes for the inefficient overview reading I used to make them do.

I also make it a point to omit all definitions of terms from these study guides, to divide each primary source into 3–4 sections with a brief phrase describing each, to list relevant terms separately for each section (as shown in Figure 11.3), and to include a separate list of terms treated in translator/editor's introductions to those sources.

Finally, I provide the 4–5 unidentified passages from primary sources that students must locate and study ahead of time.

Early in the course, after the content objectives and prior to the list of terms in the study guide itself, I introduce the mapping analogy described earlier. Most students are at first baffled by the analogy between the source and the territory to be mapped. I therefore first compare the initial study of a given primary source to putting together a puzzle, which they find appealing.[5] But I then caution that this idea masks the fact they likely will find many missing pieces and may on the first go-round feel their source puzzle is disturbingly incomplete. I explain the advantages of

FIGURE 11.2
Sample Unit Learning Objectives

CONTENT OBJECTIVES FOR UNIT 1a: ANCIENT INDIA

By the end of this unit you should be able to describe, for an interested peer unfamiliar with these topics:

1. the influence of Vedic culture in 2nd & 1st millennia BCE north India, glimpsed through hymns composed for its fire-offering rituals.

2. the ideology of the mid-3rd century BCE emperor Ashoka Maurya as reflected in his widely dissemintated stone-carved edicts.

3. expansion and spread of the Hindu *Mahabharata* epic in the centuries following Ashoka's reign, illustrated in its most famous episode.

[+ see *practice* reinforcing (and/or undermining) *community*]

FIGURE 11.3
Sample Primary Source Reading and Vocabulary Guide

(a) Ashoka asks the Sangha for help (pp. 188–89)
   • Asoka
   • bhikkhus
   • Sangha

(b) enter Upagupta (pp. 190, 194–95)
      [+ details of monk's ordination (pp. 190–93)]
   • [Phra] Upagutta (= Upagupta)
   • naga
   • upasampada

(c) Upagupta gets ready (pp. 196–200)
   • almsfood
   • Asoka

(d) the showdown and Ashoka's offering (pp. 200–1)
      [+ details of the river festival (pp. 202–204)]
   • Mara
   • yakkha
   • binding

---

the map analogy because effective maps need not be complete at the outset and may be adjusted as one goes along. The mapping comparison also suggests that their notes will help them glimpse a world that would otherwise be inaccessible.

RAP LOGISTICS

Prior to the first several RATs, unfamiliarity with the language and genres of primary sources stresses many students. To lessen this, I have over time made all RATs open note and open book and counted RAT scores as only a small percentage of their grades. While open-book tests are generally not recommended because they decrease preparation, I found that allowing notes and books seemed to motivate many students to more thoroughly annotate their reading materials. Prior to this I experimented with closed-note, closed-book tests, as well as various combinations of allowing books and notes, and found that essential details needed to respond to RAT questions simply did not stand out for most students.[6] Regarding grade percentages, I now set the total for individual performance on RATs at 5% to 7% of the total grade, with team performance totaling 35% to 40%, and the remainder of the grade derived from peer evaluation, individual assignments, and tests.[7] I point out to students this means they could skip all the RATs and still get an A in the course. I then also point out that I have never known any student who did so and ask them why that might be. They quickly realize that the study assessed in the RATs is foundational for the rest of the course. These disclosures do not eliminate all student stress but do allow students permission to do their best without feeling they must perfect a map of each source prior to the RATs.[8]

I have also over time adjusted my expectations of what is possible immediately after a RAT. The form I provide to focus student appeals specifies the need for evidence from the reading and alternative wording for questions deemed too difficult or unfair. But I also provide instructions on the back of the same form inviting students to submit an alternative RAT question dealing with some assigned term not fully treated, providing an outlet for students still daunted by the primary sources yet wanting to show and get credit for whatever reading they have done.

Last, but perhaps most important, I find that the final 15–20 minutes of a RAP session are best used to highlight the connections between the RAT and upcoming application activities. Attempting to remediate lingering student misunderstandings and confusions revealed by the RAT is about as productive as it would be to critique the sketches of a group of travel-weary mapping apprentices just in from their latest tour of a region. I find it more helpful to review a RAT by assigning a short, informal (mini) 4-S team activity (see Chapter 1) that asks students to make a specific choice about some significant problem related to the test, which can then quickly be simultaneously reported and discussed. For example, which of several test questions dealing with a particular source is most helpful for addressing the focus of the upcoming application activity? Or, more broadly, which of the historical periods, concepts, or cultural practices encountered through the sources is most significant in relation to the focus of the unit in question, or the evolution of the single tradition that is the focus of some courses? Such discussions remind students that each RAT prepares the way for imagining more fully the culture that created the sources.

APPLICATION ACTIVITIES: REVEALING CULTURE AND DISCERNING ITS EVOLUTION

Based on my experience using TBL over six years in nearly a dozen courses, I strongly recommend that anyone designing application activities to analyze sources as evidence of culture take seriously the need for repeated and explicit spotlighting of broad concepts used to analyze elements of culture, taking this as the central focus of the course for which such activities are designed. I have long pointed out to students the importance of the elements of culture (see p. 182), but I only recently realized these are the primary concepts of every TBL course I teach. With each team activity and each course unit, I now loop back to consider which of these elements is most influential and how they influence one another. With such spotlighting, students now consistently perceive that the repeated analysis of primary sources adds up to heightened discernment of all that culture involves and what drives its evolution—a theme that had previously been dimly discernible only to the perceptive few. In describing application activities here, I emphasize the way that repeated and explicit spotlighting of such concepts, as well as the analytical skills used to discern them, guides the structuring of all my courses.

Additional Preparation for Application Activities

The RAP ensures that students are largely ready for team activities, but I have found a few additional prompts are needed to make sure students are fully prepared. During the class prior to each application activity—following the team RAT at the start of the unit and then at the beginning of each subsequent class—I post a two-sentence statement specifying the focus of the upcoming activity. Several years ago, based on one student's suggestion, I also began requiring each team member to bring a page of notes to each activity with the focus statement written at the top, three examples from different parts of the reading, and page numbers specified for each example (I now provide an optional worksheet for students). Students must bring notes to receive full credit for the team's score on a given assignment; otherwise they receive half credit, though I allow them to miss one day of notes without penalty.

Such notes accomplish two things that were not happening on their own before I began assigning them. First of all, they explicitly move students from summary/description to deeper analysis of the same sources. Prior to requiring notes, students tended to focus on description/summary in team assignments rather than on selecting and justifying their choice of the most relevant details. Second, notes provide an additional measure of accountability; students who barely looked at a given source for the RAT can partly catch up to the rest of the group. This was especially important before I modified RATs to focus more on primary sources, but even now I find it essential to provide reinforcement for going beyond knowledge of terms and passages to real analysis. As a bonus, checking notes during application activities provides an excuse to listen to and interact with team members as I move around the room, marking missed notes and absences in team folders. Other teachers working with similar activities will no doubt discover further refinements to the process. As described in Chapter 1 such a backward design is a valuable part of applying TBL to new courses.

Formats for Application Activities

The format I use for application activities is best discerned by viewing the sample included in Figure 11.4. To clarify the logic of the way these assignments are structured, here I describe the evolution of this structure. To encourage student focus I provide highly condensed instructions on the worksheets, so wording is important. In designing each activity, I observe the same and significant problem principle by relating each analysis to the central question: Which elements of culture are most influential in its evolution? I spotlight the relationship of each activity to this question by explicitly naming the elements—practice, reflection, and social context—and what in the primary source under consideration provides evidence for one or more of these.

As with refining RATs and study guides, it has taken me years to figure out how to apply the specific choice principle effectively. Looking for something concrete for students to choose, I began the experiment by asking them to select the passage from an assigned source that would best illustrate the significance of an element of culture, or the way that two or more elements influence one another. For example, to use a widely known example, what passage in the *Bhagavad Gita* best illustrates reflection about the nature of Krishna's divinity, and why is that passage the best example? Because I did not want students to perceive application activities as meaningless cookie-cutter exercises, I varied the assignments quite a bit, and because I wanted students to be exposed to as many primary sources as possible, I often asked them to analyze several during one activity. Sometimes I asked students to select one best passage from each of three sections of the same source, and then asked them what all three had in common. Sometimes I asked them to identify the best contrast or best parallel between one passage from each of two different sources to illustrate the way those sources viewed some practice, concept, or social role very differently. I often asked for a reference to yet another source in the justification of the choice. And often I asked teams to sketch a poster, using symbols, drawings, and words arranged spatially on the page to illustrate practices, concepts, or social roles in the best possible way.[9]

All these variations produced team and whole-class discussions that were far more interesting than any I had previously elicited, so I continued experimenting. Yet all along, the parts of the assignments seemed slightly misaligned; while they generated many interesting responses, too many students were too often stressed and confused. Feedback forms and evaluations also showed that students remained unclear about the details and significance of key ideas, practices, and social realities addressed in the activities.

Several years into TBL, I chanced upon submissions to the TBL Listserve regarding TBL in the humanities. One of these by Jim Sibley (personal communication, March 8, 2011) suggested that application activity questions for humanities disciplines could ask students to determine the most powerful example of a concept, such as the most powerful example of a Jungian archetype in a Shakespeare play. Sibley's suggestion made me realize that asking students to choose the best is too vague, and that asking for passages was letting them off the hook too easily. All they had to do was quote something and then come up with some reason why it addressed the activity prompt. So I also began asking for the most powerful, and later also the most dramatic, examples. Students picked out the most powerful scene (e.g., illustrating the relationship between kings and ascetics in medieval India), moment in a ritual (e.g., showing the way that symbolic actions and words support reflection about the unseen forces affected by the ritual), or sequence of steps in an argument (e.g., showing the importance of a certain practice for a given community). I also typically required students to note briefly the details that followed and preceded such examples in the source, as otherwise students often homed in on an unnecessarily narrow set of details.[10] With these refinements in place, teams immediately became more focused on, first selecting a relevant set of details from the primary sources, and then, justifying that those details offer the most powerful or dramatic example of the element(s) of culture in question

Observing such increased focus clarified for me that these two interdependent skills deserved more consistent spotlighting throughout the course. I thus reworked assignments that asked for contrasting examples or several related best examples so that each activity required just one choice of a most powerful or dramatic example. For the justification, I rewrote prompts to insist that each example explicitly reference a contrasting less powerful or dramatic example from a different part of the source; I also emphasized the need for an explicit reference to the element(s) of culture being analyzed, which students often forgot. If I felt strongly that students needed to consider two primary sources in the same activity, I asked them to choose one example from one or another source rather than requiring a contrast or parallel, discovering that I could highlight contrasts and parallels myself during simultaneous reporting. I still varied the activities by alternating between verbal description and posters of the most powerful or dramatic scene, ritual, or idea. But I made sure that all assignments required the same kind of justification because I noticed that the complex nature of the analysis I was guiding them to do called for such repetitive practice. With this change I soon observed students' stress decreasing once they knew exactly what to expect from the format.

The most recent breakthrough in my ongoing TBL experiment came less than a year ago when I learned of Penne Restad's work (see Chapter 10). At the time teams were on the whole approaching application activities with focus, animated discussions, insightful choices, and skillful justifications. But I was hearing dedicated students who valued the activities express persistent disorientation with having to delve into foreign source material day after day. Then I examined one of Restad's activities for history courses, which guided students in identifying McCarthy-era fears called into play by various documents; she asks students to consider the fears that each source addresses, listing these explicitly, and then rank how useful each source is for understanding the fears of the Cold War era. This model mirrors Paul and Elder's sequence of thinking skills as described in Chapter 1 (p. 8): Precisely formulating an application question leads to showing students where to gather relevant information and how to use the abstract ideas to interpret that information, and the ranking process leads to drawing well-reasoned conclusions. Studying this example made me realize what was missing from my team activity worksheets that made them more disorienting than necessary: a clear list of all the options to choose from. Seeing Restad's format, I also realized what I could gain by providing such a list: requiring students to evaluate each option carefully before making a choice rather than just choosing the first thing that seemed to work.

Students immediately expressed relief when I applied these principles to team activities in my courses. Several who were present in class when I first used such activities were concurrently enrolled in another of my courses and asked if I could apply the same format there. Although the work was still intensive, I perceived and heard from many students that they now had clearer guidance on what to do at each step. The main challenge has been to get students to articulate explicitly in part one of the worksheet the way(s) each section of the source(s) in question illustrates some point about the elements of culture. Their tendency at first was to fill each space with minuscule descriptions of every possibly relevant detail without much analysis. I now limit analysis of each reading section listed in part one to 30–50 words and require students to incorporate one or more of the terms in boldface in the initial prompt to their statements (for example, see Figure 11.4).

This formatting of application activity worksheets, which will undoubtedly continue to evolve, still allows for variations. For activities that focused on a single source, I divide that source into four to five sections. When I feel students can handle two clearly related sources, I identify three sections in each source and ask that they address two in each for a total of four. And I now list all such divisions for students as part of their study guide. I continue to ask for a poster sketch for the analysis part of some activities, though ranking sections of the reading or of distinct sources must still be explained in writing. I also plan to experiment with moving from explicitly listing and ranking of options in the first half of the term to the more open-ended format I was previously using to assess the extent to which students transfer the listing and ranking process to new contexts—the third aspect of critical thinking identified by Halpern (see Chapter 1, p. 8–9).

SIMULTANEOUS REPORTING AND FOLLOW-UP DISCUSSIONS

Having explicitly spotlighted the elements of culture in application activity worksheets, I can easily spotlight which lessons were learned about the culture's evolution when I call teams together for simultaneous reporting. I do everything I can to get

FIGURE 11.4
Sample Analysis Worksheet

"History of Buddhism"

Team Assignment #4a

1. Analysis: The *Lokapaññati* records the practice of experienced monks telling stories to novice monks and laypeople in medieval Burma, which Strong's analysis suggests also refers to and elucidates monks' and layperson's rituals. Specify below ways(s) that these **social and ritual context** influences the storytellers' **reflection** on Upagupta's clever use of supernatural powers.

IMPORTANT: consider some person, event, dialogue and/or setting from **each part of the story (a)–(d) and incorporate some detail about rituals mentioned in EITHER (a) OR (d)**

(a)　Ashoka asks the Sangha for help (pp. 188–90) [20–40 words]
　　　[+ details of monk's ordination (pp. 190–93)]
(b)　summoning Upagupta (pp. 194–95) [20–40 words]
(c)　Upagupta gets ready (pp. 196–200) [20–40 words]
(d)　the showdown & Ashoka's offering (pp. 200–1, 207–8) [20–40 words]
　　　[+ details of the river festival (pp. 202–204)]

2. Ranking: using ROMAN NUMERALS next to each of the above (a)–(d), rank them as **(I) most dramatic–(IV) least dramatic** examples of **social and ritual contexts** influencing the storytellers' **reflection** about Upagupta's powers; then explain your choices (use back as needed).

* "Choice I is the most powerful example of social and geographical context influencing the storytellers' reflection on Upagupta's powers because, **in comparison to choice II** . . ."
* "Choices III and IV are the least powerful examples of this because . . ."

3. For Informal Discussion: What do the scenes from this source suggest about the relationship among ascetics, settled monks, and laypeople? To what extent does this source seem to you historically useful for studying Southeast Asian Buddhist history, and in what ways?

---

team activities under way within the first 10–15 minutes of class so that teams can finish working and post results within 50–55 minutes to allow 20–25 minutes for discussion.[11] The format I use for simultaneous reporting has changed little since I began. I determined from the start that the most effective way to report is to list the sections of the source(s) being considered horizontally like a time line, identifying key details in each section and citing page numbers. A representative from each team then draws an arrow from the part of the source where he or she located the most powerful or dramatic passage, scene, and so forth, either above or below the time line of the source, and then writes 5–10 words describing the selection and leaves the team's name in parentheses.[12] Now that I list and require ranking of options, reporting is even easier via a chart with columns for each section of the reading—sometimes just two columns when related sources are being compared—where each team representative puts his or her team name in one column. Including ranking on the activity worksheet has the added benefit of allowing reporting of the least powerful or dramatic choices; to show this I divide the chart into two rows, labeled "first" and "last" choices, and then have representatives place their team name once in each row to show these choices (as illustrated in Figure 11.5).[13]

Based on the recommendation of a colleague who observed one of my classes, I have started getting my student assistants to take pictures of these charts, which I will be posting online to document the cumulative work of the class for students and outside observers.[14]

Despite the general effectiveness of these simultaneous reporting formats, my use of these reports now contrasts starkly with what I initially did. My first impulse following team activities in early years was to guide student discussion the way I was trained in graduate school. I asked each student who offered to describe his or her team's choice to elaborate by pointing to page numbers and details from the source. When a given team was silent, I prodded its members to speak up. When someone hit on what I felt was an important point, I would often read related passages I wanted to make sure everyone noticed. But despite the high energy evident among students working in teams, that energy quickly dissipated once such questioning began.

At the time I made the transition to a more consistent focus on extracting details from the text and justifying their selection in contrast to at least one less-powerful example, I realized why the approach just described failed to capitalize on the hard

FIGURE 11.5
Sample Simultaneous Report of Rank Choices

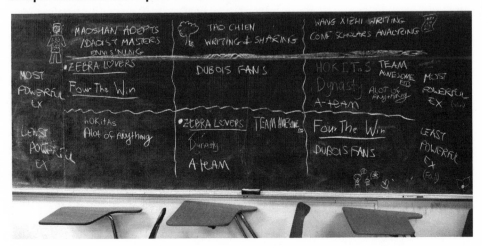

work students had just done in their teams. The team-by-team interrogation I had been doing is just the thing that simultaneous reporting is designed to avoid. Just as students are not up for hearing a lecture about details of complex primary sources after each RAT, they also need a break from the meticulous analysis of textual details during application activities.

What students are ready for is a broader consideration of what the class has achieved as a whole. So I started closing my book at this point, not asking for page number references, focusing instead on patterns revealed by variation in student responses. I began to focus attention on how interesting it was, for example, that some teams felt the role of the priest was most important in the source under consideration, whereas others chose the laypeople served by him. Increasingly I reminded myself to bring the discussion back repeatedly to the issue of justification: Why is this or that scene, ritual moment, or sequence of points the most powerful illustration of this or that element of culture at work? Now that I chart the distribution of the most and least powerful/dramatic examples, I sometimes start by noting cases in which all or nearly all teams picked one example as their last choice. Why did everyone agree that example was least powerful? When students initially mention key details from the relevant section of the source, I repeat the most important; but if students begin to offer extended summaries or explanations of the source, unless they mentioned some detail that all seem to have missed, I gently ask, "But why is that the more powerful choice?" Having heard one side's justification, rather than asking for more details from the source, I have learned to turn immediately to those who chose a different option and ask, "What is it about this other choice that makes it more powerful?" I have begun to ask, "Having heard the other side's rationale, would you change your mind? Why? or (as more usually happened) Why not?" Though thoughtful answers often took some time to emerge when I began to lead discussion in this way, student engagement noticeably increased. And in the midst of such discussions, I could spotlight when outlying teams had picked up something important or interject my own observations about important details no one had noticed.[15]

From guiding such discussions I observed the kind of preparation that made them dramatically more effective. From the start I had noticed that the more time I gave to reviewing primary sources just before an application activity, the more focused I would be in the ensuing discussion. But now I discerned clearly the importance of preparing by doing the required analysis: explicitly identifying the most powerful/ dramatic examples in the source and the advantages of each. After all the work I do selecting sources, creating study guides, and composing activity worksheets, this step has not usually taken much further reflection, especially now that I explicitly list the three to six sections students are to consider in their analysis of the assigned sources. But it is the crucial ingredient, like the salt or sugar in a recipe, which when forgotten spoils the entire dish. When I understand clearly the advantages of the choices teams are making, I can easily underscore the strengths of each choice as the discussion proceeds, including the advantages of examples that few and sometimes none of the teams have noticed. For example, everyone feels that fantastic legends describing deities coming down to help the Buddha escape his father's palace provide a dramatic example of reflection about his supernatural power, but few notice that in more realistic, autobiographical accounts, the Buddha mentions a brief visionary experience of divine beings advising against his decision to stop eating all together. When I have such contrasts firmly in mind, there is always a moment in the discussion to bring them up at a point when students are able to see its importance.

Last but not least, I now remind myself that the final minutes of every discussion should loop back to the elements of culture. Most importantly, I can highlight the ways that close analysis of culture helps open the mind and heart to the sincerity and insights of those who throughout history have worked for a greater good. In these moments the true strength of TBL shines through. With students still alert, minds filled with their own experiences of the primary sources, I can confidently deliver points that in an extended period of lecture might otherwise be lost to all but the most attentive.

Since humanities scholars typically showcase their insights via some form of individual written analysis, I have felt it important to require individual students to produce such analyses as part of my courses. But I have made sure that such individual projects build directly on skills explicitly modeled in application activities. Students in my Asian culture survey class, for example, must individually select a practice identified in assigned sources and then select the terms and passages that most powerfully illustrate the reflection that practice inspires and the social context in which it thrives. Students studying Hindu or Buddhist traditions must first visit a worship site and then identify three similar practices found in assigned readings, ranking them to point out the most striking resemblance. Just as team member interactions during RATs and application activities intrinsically motivate students to work at analyzing difficult sources when they see that others care about and are interested in them, so, too, have I found it motivating to share the best products of individual assignments with the course community in some meaningful way, as pointed out by Bain (2004, pp. 31–42, 60–67). Students in my Asian culture class read preliminary drafts of each others' analyses of a practice, and the best products of their efforts are featured in displays of student work that represent the department to the campus community. In other courses, I select the best student reports on Hindu or Buddhist worship sites and make these required reading for the final team activity, which uses this data to assesses the extent to which surviving traditions preserve essential elements of their historical roots.

STRATEGIC TEAM FORMATION AND PEER EVALUATION: CREATING A COMMUNITY OF CULTURAL INVESTIGATORS

At the start of every semester, I acknowledge that students are probably not expecting to build team skills in a humanities or religious studies class, and that I don't feel teaching such skills is a primary responsibility of our department. But I emphasize that including teamwork in my courses is the most effective way I've found to motivate and guide engaged learning. In the same vein, my adaptation of the standard

TBL team formation and peer evaluation processes has been much more minimal, and in fact in the second of these two areas I am somewhat deficient. I nevertheless mention my experience of these here since they are key parts of TBL.

The categories of experience I use to form teams begin with identifying students in majors that emphasize analysis of sources as artifacts of culture—generally majors in my department, but also those from art, music, philosophy, history, English, music, theater/dance, sociology, and anthropology. I also consider two other kinds of experience, direct familiarity with other cultures and student workload, and include additional categories that reflect these. Because awareness of stark differences between even closely related cultures is a significant asset, I ask students to identify themselves if they are directly familiar with practices, social networks, and ideas of another culture, gained either from living abroad or from growing up in or living in close relationship with European, Asian, Native American, and African subcultures embedded in American society. Workload is equally important because students with packed schedules are much less likely to complete all reading assignments. Therefore I ask students to multiply the number of course units they are taking by 3 and then add the number of hours per week they work; a number over 65 (equivalent to a 15-unit load plus 20 hours of work per week) puts them in the overstretched category. I distribute students who are overstretched, from preferred concentrations, and familiar with other cultures evenly between teams. I have mostly used Michaelsen's (2004, p. 217) line-up method to form teams, though I use surveys form teams outside of class for large sections (over 70–80 students).[16]

I have found peer evaluation essential for motivating teams, collecting data for a trial score at midterm and a final score at the end. I use Michaelsen's (2004, pp. 229–231) approach, which forces differentiation between team members and constrains the points allowed by setting a maximum total. I pitch the 70–80 peer evaluation points, which amount to 7% to 8% of the total grade, as 5 extra points for each team assignment all collected together, except that peer evaluations can increase or decrease this amount for each person. But I do allow students to score all team members the same if they provide a separate two- to three-sentence description that separately describes each team member's contribution. I have also found that I need to eliminate students from team evaluations if they have missed more than half of team assignments. Such students by default get a very low rating from others, which then unfairly inflates the scores of the students doing the rating.

I have so far, however, been stymied by lack of an adequate system of automation. Because of the numbers of students I teach, without such automation it has been practical only to report student scores without comments. There is to my knowledge no easily accessible survey software that imposes a constraint on total number of points. Although iPEER (described in Chapter 1) sounds great, it requires the support of professional information technology staff to run, which my institution has so far been unwilling to commit to. Now that other TBL elements of my courses are working efficiently, I have been experimenting with the WebCT/Blackboard system, which includes the possibility of rating a team's contribution in anonymous discussion posts by others in the team, though this doesn't allow constrained scoring, and using the assessment format to ask each student to rate team members, thus allowing for more streamlined compilation of data, especially the written comments, though this requires more work than discussion posts.

CONCLUSION

My experiences over seven years have convinced me that TBL is a uniquely potent tool for structuring cognitive apprenticeship in courses that focus primarily on sources analyzed as artifacts of culture. I hope my descriptions of the way I adapted the four practical pieces of TBL will make it easier for teachers in similar disciplines to apply this tool. If the details sound overwhelming, I ask readers to keep in mind that the work involved is also deeply fulfilling. I have found that drawing students into close examination of the kinds of fascinating sources that initially drew all of us to our disciplines repeatedly yields fresh insights, reducing the disillusionment induced by mindless grading tasks, and inspiring my own research in unexpected ways.

From what I have seen, TBL's potential to help students perceive the forces driving the evolution of human culture has barely been tapped. In addition to the wide variety of humanities and social science courses that could be effectively taught using this format, I plan to explore two new foci in the future: information literacy and field research. On the one hand, TBL application activities could be a powerful tool to guide students in discerning what makes a source authoritative in a given field, beginning with comparison of selected samples, then sending students out to collect their own sources and applying the same criteria to them, and finally requiring students to rank collected sources based on the potential to answer a particular analytical question. On the other hand, I hope to explore bringing students as a group to museum sites and local worship places to gather data, asking them to analyze and rank segments of an art exhibit or the steps in a ceremony to discover which are most relevant to understanding one or another element of culture. I hope this chapter will inspire others to follow these leads and to think of other ones.

NOTES

1. To offset the added workload of intensive grading and logistics that TBL courses involving analysis of difficult sources necessarily require, I strongly recommend enlisting the help of a student assistant (two for larger courses).

2. The only printed source I have found to be sufficiently concise is Armstrong's *Short History of Myth* for my World Mythology course. For other thematic courses I have gathered short pages and longer articles from the online version of *Encyclopedia Britannica* (www .britannica.com), which my university subscribes to; for courses dealing with Buddhist and Hindu religious traditions I have written my own overviews.

3. Most of my courses consist of four units of three weeks each that include two orientation days, one day of RAP, and three application activities. My broader Asian cultures survey course requires six units of two weeks each, with only one application activity in each.

4. I have also considered a middle-ground approach to having RATs focus entirely on primary sources: assigning only translator/editor introductions and summaries of primary sources rather than the sources themselves, thus testing on a more limited range of readings—which might eliminate the need for the in-class reading orientations described in the next section—and then requiring students to go back and read the entirety of the relevant source(s) just prior to each application activity. However, several teaching assistants have steered me away from assigning less reading initially, pointing out that this will make it even harder for dedicated students to get others to prepare by doing the full extent of the reading.

5. To draw them in with humor I often display a copy of *Find Waldo Now*, which includes numerous scenes from past historical periods. I point out that locating the terms and unidentified passages is much like trying to find Waldo: Along the way, one notices many other interesting things in the picture, and the terms listed in the course study guides provide additional guidance about what to notice.

6. As I continue to refine study guides to focus more precisely on such details, I may well experiment with allowing students to take the test with only the notes they have added to their study guides. Nevertheless, the analogy of mapping disorientingly unfamiliar territory suggests that in many cases it may not be reasonable for novices to remember every detail of the landscape.

7. Partly because of the need to introduce the essential elements of culture in the introductory unit of the course, and partly because of my own desire for a point system that makes computation easy, I have set grade points for students rather than allowing them to do it themselves; but I have based the relative weighting of RATs and team activities on Michaelsen's (2004, p. 245) report of a roughly 1:2 or 1:3 weighting of individual performance to team performance when students set their own grade weights.

8. Though I defer here to the wide acceptance of the acronym RAT, because of the complexity of the study process described previously and in line with student input received during the past several years, I have now switched to calling them team readiness assessments. I have made this change to highlight more emphatically that the tests assess team members' readiness to apply a few broad, central concepts to the highly complex foreign source materials described in in this chapter; this is in contrast to the idea of free-standing assessments that require each student to construct a complete map of disorientingly unfamiliar territory prior to each test. I found that *assurance* is the last thing that good students feel after taking this test; rather, the numerous errors, misperception, and disorientation experienced as they struggle to map these sources bears fruit only gradually when they take the test as a team and then go back to review the primary sources in preparation for application activities. It is this *process* that *assures readiness*; hence I do emphasize the acronym RAP.

9. To mitigate the understandable student exhaustion when I still offered only one day of reading orientation and four days of team assignments one after the other in each unit, I also alternated informal lecture/discussion days with days during which I attempted two separate application activities on each of the alternate days, postponing discussion for the following class. In light of the importance of follow-up discussion, I would now strongly recommend against such a sequence.

10. I am also now incorporating Penne Restad's use of the phrase "best evidence from the reading" in assignments that she has shared with me (personal communications, 2010 and 2011), which focuses attention on the way sources provide evidence for some interpretation of history or culture (see the following paragraph regarding her overall influence in my use of activities).

11. I teach all my courses in 75-minute class periods twice a week. I have had great difficulty with once-a-week (150 minutes) sessions and have not tried shorter ones because RAP and application activities could not be carried out effectively in 50 minutes.

12. This also works for getting students to put posters on the board, though in this case I draw the source time line at the top of the board. This did not work well when students had selected the best contrast between two examples—another good reason for getting rid of that format.

13. When students contrast two related sources by sketching posters, I have also on some occasions had teams put up basic versions of their sketches of the most powerful/dramatic of the two sources, placing them on opposite sides of the board.

14. Though colleagues in my department have been highly supportive of my efforts, in my experience TBL courses receive comparably lower scores, no doubt in part because of the added demand on students but also because traditional evaluation questions like "Does the instructor clearly communicate class material?" favor the delivery of information in a lecture format. My hope is that visual documentation of the products of TBL, including videotaping of team deliberations and whole-class discussions, may help clarify for outside evaluators the dynamic learning opportunities that occur in our classrooms. This is especially important to document since the value of choices made will be less apparent to outsiders than comparable problems addressed in practical disciplines, for example, best business practice or the most effective design solution or treatment.

15. On some occasions, whether because of insufficiently precise wording on my part or simple student exhaustion, students were slower to participate. Yet even then I could always move the discussion forward by asking, "Why should we care about these sources? Why have I asked you to analyze them? What do they show us about this culture's evolution?" I would sometimes joke that I know making such choices isn't as fulfilling as the game of *Jeopardy!*, where there are clear right and wrong answers. Yet as with any kind of debate, being forced to make such choices is part of learning to represent sources, which in turn makes us go back to look at them more closely.

16. I ask students to create name signs and turn them in after each class for the first few weeks until I learn names; it is easy for them to write details that will help me sort them into teams on the back of these signs.

REFERENCES

Armstrong, K. (2005). *A short history of myth*. New York, NY: Canongate.

Bain, K. (2004). *What the best college teachers do*. Cambridge, MA: Harvard University Press.

Barnes, L. B., Christensen, C. R., & Hansen, A. J. (1994). *Teaching and the case method: Text, cases, and readings* (3rd ed.). Boston, MA: Harvard Business School Press.

Christensen, C. R., & Hansen, A. J. (1987). *Teaching and the case method: Text, cases, and readings* (Rev. ed.). Boston, MA: Harvard Business School.

Donald, J. G. (2002). *Learning to think: Disciplinary perspectives*. San Francisco, CA: Jossey-Bass.

Handord, M. (2002). *Find Waldo now*. Cambridge, MA: Candlewick Press.

Lave, J., & Wenger, E. (1991). *Situated learning: Legitimate peripheral participation*. Cambridge, UK: Cambridge University Press.

Michaelsen, L. K. (2008). Team-based learning for health professions education: A guide to using small groups for improving learning. Sterling, VA: Stylus.

Michaelsen, L. K., Knight, A. B., & Fink, L. D. (2004). *Team-based learning: A transformative use of small groups.* Sterling, VA: Stylus.

Paul, R., & Elder, L. (2006). *Critical thinking : Tools for taking charge of your learning and your life* (2nd ed.). Upper Saddle River, NJ: Pearson/Prentice Hall.

CHAPTER 12

Applying Team-Based Learning With Mexican American Students in the Social Science Classroom

Kristin L. Croyle and Edna Alfaro

One reason Team-Based Learning is so powerful is because it taps social relationships to fuel academic effort. However, no social relationships exist in a vacuum, so students' cultural backgrounds inevitably influence in-class teamwork. In this chapter, Croyle and Alfaro describe some of the preferences and needs Mexican American students bring to the classroom and offer specific suggestions on how to communicate well with this population. Further, they describe specific application activities they have found to be successful in their classrooms.

I (Croyle) began teaching at the University of Texas-Pan American (UTPA), a Hispanic-serving institution in south Texas, in 2002. This was my first faculty position, but I had excellent teacher mentoring, formal graduate work in teaching, and independent teaching experience from a strong graduate program in the Northwest. I was ready to go and excited to get back in the classroom. Because of my strong teacher training, I did not experience any dramatic shock when entering the classroom again. Instead, I experienced a quiet, growing dissatisfaction. My students just did not seem to be developing the skills I thought were important and I thought I was teaching them, particularly critical thinking and analysis skills. This chapter is a description of how I am addressing this problem by developing a Team-Based Learning (TBL) approach in class and adapting that approach to UTPA's predominantly Mexican American student population.

Edna Alfaro has graciously contributed her expertise in Latino educational issues to this chapter. The experiences with TBL described here are my own. General issues in the education of Latino students are discussed by both of us. I begin by describing the setting where I work, including suggestions based on research literature for working with Mexican American students, and my path to using TBL. I then give specific examples of TBL activities I use in the classroom.

MY TBL CONTEXT

UTPA

UTPA is located in Edinburg, Texas, 14 miles north of the U.S.–Mexico border. It was formed in 1927 as Edinburg College and joined the University of Texas system in 1989 to become one of nine universities in the system. Current enrollment is about 18,800 students. It is the 10th largest university in the state and is highly rated in university rating systems that take into account the "bang for your buck," including indicators of student learning, student accumulated debt, and student satisfaction. For example, in 2009 *Forbes* magazine ranked UTPA 32nd in the country and 3rd in Texas in a top 100 list in "America's Best Public Colleges" (2009). UTPA enrollment reflects the region and is 89% Hispanic, with the third highest Hispanic enrollment in the United States among institutions of higher learning. UTPA was an open admissions university until 2005, when minimum admission standards were introduced and have been gradually raised each year. Our students range widely in academic preparedness.

The Rio Grande Valley, where UTPA is located, is often rated as one of the poorest regions in the United States. Recent census data indicate that Hidalgo County, where UTPA is based, has a median household income of $30,076 (in contrast, the median U.S. household income is $51,425; U.S. Census Bureau, 2009). Additionally, the county has low educational attainment levels, with only 60% of residents ages 25 and above holding a high school diploma or higher and 15% holding a bachelor's degree or higher. In this context, UTPA serves a critical mission of serving Hispanic students and improving the standard of living and economic outlook of the region. UTPA faculty are often devoted to their role in higher education and in the community. We believe we are doing important work in our teaching and our research.

Teaching University-Level Mexican American Students

Since the vast majority of students I work with are Mexican American, it is important to understand the cultural values of these students and how they affect the college classroom before discussing how TBL can be adapted to Mexican American students. While the Latino community is made up of various subgroups that differ based on nationality, socioeconomic status, generational status, and immigration history (Umaña-Taylor & Fine, 2001), the university's location in deep south Texas means the student body is primarily composed of Hispanic individuals of Mexican origin. Although we would prefer to cite research and make observations specific to Mexican American students, the data that is currently available does not always differentiate between Latino subgroups. Instead our observations include a combination of information regarding Mexican American students specifically and Latino students in general. We have chosen not to include coverage of second language issues here, particularly since most of the students we work with are fluent in English, though a large proportion are also fluent in Spanish.

The ethnic homogeneity of the Rio Grande Valley helps foster cultural values, one of which we believe influences our students' classroom behaviors: *respeto*, which can be defined as deference to authority figures in general and more specifically to educators (Gaitan, 2004; Tyler et al., 2008). Consistent with this notion, we have noticed that our students demonstrate a great deal of respect for their professors in and outside class and are uncomfortable calling professors by their first names, even when specifically asked to do so. A potential negative consequence of respeto is that students are hesitant to ask questions during class and contact professors for help outside class. Students may perceive asking questions to be a disrespectful action (Smith, Stern, & Shatrova, 2008). They are also unlikely to complain about assignments or classroom situations they perceive as unfair. This can be mistaken by professors as a lack of appropriate assertiveness.

Although respeto is generally directed toward authority figures, it has a reciprocal quality as well. Treating students with respect may be more highly valued by Latino students than Anglo students. An attitude of disrespect by professors toward their students may negatively affect Latino students' course work and attitude. Similarly, communicating a devaluing of aspects important to Latino students, such as commitment to their family members or a professor's personal opinion of the student, may damage the relationship between the professor and student. When I (Croyle) first moved to south Texas, I was perplexed by students telling me things that could have a negative impact on a successful academic career, and that family relationships weighed more heavily than academic success. For example, students would tell me things like, "I can't make it to class because I have to take my cousin to the doctor" or "I can't leave the area to attend a good graduate program because I am supporting my family" or "I can't leave the area to attend a good graduate program because my parents won't let me" (in the case of a bright single female student; her parents would have let her move if she was married). I am fortunate that my students treated my confusion as ignorance rather than as a personal insult or as disrespectful of their values, which could have had a negative impact on my relationship with them. Similarly, on more than one occasion, students I accused of academic dishonesty placed a high priority on my personal opinion of them as honest/good people, almost separating my accusations into two components: their dishonest action and my opinion of them. Pursuing action with respect to the academic dishonesty was tolerated as long as I clearly communicated to them that my personal opinion of them as worthwhile people was not affected (which is not difficult for me because it is consistent with my worldview that all people have worth, even if they plagiarize).

Latinos are also often characterized as having a strong relational orientation that emphasizes social relationships inside and outside the family (Cooper, 1999; Shweder, Goodnow, Hatano, LeVine, Markus, & Miller, 1998). This emphasis on interdependence and group harmony has the potential to influence students' willingness to engage in conflict and controversy in the classroom (more on that later), as well as their preferences for how groups are formed inside the classroom. Specifically, Brown (2008) noted differences in Latino and Anglo students' preferences, such that Anglo students were more likely to report they preferred to select their own group members. Conversely, Latino college students were more likely to prefer being assigned to groups "so no one is left out" (p. 109). Brown suggests this difference may be a direct reflection of Latino students' value of group harmony in that group harmony is maintained by ensuring that no one feels left out.

This emphasis on group harmony may also influence students' in-class participation. For example, White students were more likely than Latinos to report they would respond immediately in class if they knew the answer to a question the professor asked (Brown, 2008). Latinos, on the other hand, were more likely to report they would wait for other students who normally participate to respond, even if the Latino student knew the answer to the question. Further, Latinos were more likely to believe that in the majority of instances students "who participate in class are showing off" (p. 110) when compared to their White counterparts. Thus, not only does participation vary by ethnic group, students' perceptions of participation vary by ethnic group.

The orientation toward strong social relationships also has an implication for the relationship between student and professor, and the institution more broadly. Personal and professional relationships in Mexican American communities are often characterized by a more personal connection than is the case in Anglo communities (Alegría & Woo, 2009). Although this has some disadvantages (political favoritism, nepotism), it results in close-knit communities and a strong social network. An academic environment that expects Latino students to connect more strongly with the material in class than with their peers and professor, and to navigate a faceless bureaucracy outside class rather than interact more personally with university staff may conflict with what has been an adaptive relationship style for Latino students. It prevents them from exercising their strengths, may communicate to the students that the institution and their professors are uncaring, and potentially reduce academic success and retention of these students. A more personal interactional style from the professor in the classroom may encourage Latino students to become engaged with the material and participate in class. For example, Brown (2008) reported that Latino students were more likely to indicate they would participate in class if they felt they knew more about what their professors were like outside the classroom.

Gender and cultural socialization may work together in women of Mexican origin in increasing the emphasis on social relationships in Latina students. Specifically, girls of Mexican origin are more likely than boys to spend time at home with their families (Updegraff, McHale, Whiteman, Thayer, & Crouter, 2006), which may provide more opportunities for parents to transmit their traditional values to girls (Buriel, Perez, De Ment, Chavez, & Moran, 1998). It is possible that one of the traditional gender socialization messages Latino parents transmit to their daughters is the belief that girls should demonstrate good behaviors (Feliciano & Rumbaut, 2005), which with regard to interpersonal/group dynamics may translate to girls' focusing more on fostering relationships and less on competition within the group or on individual academic achievement.

These observations lead to several concrete suggestions for college professors working with Latino students.

Foster interdependent classroom environments. Latino students tend to prefer classroom environments that promote group solidarity as opposed to individual achievement (Brown, 2008). Consequently they may take to TBL easily, as long as it is structured to encourage the success of the team and the class as a whole, rather than emphasizing pitting one team against another.

Be open to sharing information about yourself. Latino students prefer relationships that have a personal aspect. Sharing information about ourselves as professors (of course, in an appropriate fashion) may encourage Latino students to participate more in class (Brown, 2008). This helps Latino students feel more connected with the course experience and encourages them to see us more as individuals and less as unapproachable authority figures.

Consistently communicate respect to students. Latino students may be more sensitive to subtle communications of disrespect than Anglo students. Consistently try to manifest respect for students, as well as their worldviews and personal values. Recognize that their family relationships may be particularly strong and important to them, and show your respect for those relationships as well. If those relationships conflict with academic priorities, help the students resolve those conflicts without appearing judgmental or discounting.

Accept students' respect for you. In my experience social science professors often strive to create at least something of an egalitarian relationship with their students. It is not uncommon for social scientists to want to be called by their first name or to encourage their students to call them at home or on their personal cell phones if they have questions. If some of your Latino students cannot do this because they perceive it as disrespectful, even if they cannot verbalize the reason for their discomfort, accept their respectful treatment without misunderstanding it as being cooler or more standoffish than your other students.

Tests and Measurements in Psychology Courses

I teach in the Department of Psychology and Anthropology, which has about 800 undergraduate psychology students and 60 graduate students (emphasis is predominantly clinical). My specialty area is clinical psychology. I typically teach applied clinical courses at the graduate level and a required undergraduate course, Tests and Measurements in Psychology. The discussion in this chapter focuses on the undergraduate course because it has been my greatest teaching challenge; it is also the course in which using TBL has been the most helpful. Psychology students generally begin Tests and Measurements with the attitude that it is a painful course to be endured. It certainly has a boring title. They expect it to be dull, with little relevance to their future careers. Given that most psychology students use their undergraduate degrees as general liberal arts degrees and do not pursue a graduate degree, they are correct to some extent. Knowing details about the construction, administration, and interpretation of the Wechsler Adult Intelligence Scale, for example, is not useful to them since use of that knowledge is restricted to practitioners with graduate degrees.

My students come to the course expecting to never need to use a psychological test or measure and therefore to never use the course content. The intrinsic interest most psychology students have in their major courses is not something I can use to capture their attention in this course.

MY PATH TO TBL

When I was first asked to teach Tests and Measurements, I was somewhat at a loss. It was a course with primarily clinical content, so the experimental psychologist who had been teaching it was eager to pass it along to a clinical colleague. However, my undergraduate and graduate institutions did not include that course and I didn't understand its role in our undergraduate curriculum. The content I found most valuable in the course I had learned as a graduate student, and it was, ethically, graduate-level material because of its emphasis on practical clinical assessment skills. What in the world was I going to teach undergraduate students that they would find useful?

I started, as I believe is not uncommon, with the textbook survey approach, which was tried and true and followed in the footsteps of my esteemed colleague who had previously taught the course. I am a skilled lecturer, able to inject enthusiasm into even the most boring topics, and the course was moderately successful. I received no student complaints and I covered a great deal of material. I included ambitious homework assignments to ensure that students would have experience applying the ideas I was teaching (which I now believe most students did not really understand or retain). Given that I was new and didn't know what I was truly teaching these students, my homework assignments were all adapted from an excellent instructor's manual (Nicolai, 2005). The advantages of this approach were that the course covered a lot of material; was appropriately rigorous and familiar to students, resulting in high teaching evaluations; appeared rigorous to colleagues; and was easy to teach. Once those lectures were prepared, I was set forever. But I was unhappy. I didn't believe students were learning things that would be useful to them, and if I didn't think so, I couldn't see how they would think so. Further, most students seemed inattentive on a regular basis, though I was successful at engaging a brave minority of students every day.

Luckily for my students, UTPA offered extensive training sessions in cooperative learning strategies (Johnson, Johnson, & Smith, 2006), which I had the good fortune to attend. Here I learned the formal skills I needed to incorporate productive small-group work in class on a regular basis and to ensure that all students were participating in class every day. No loafing allowed. I completely redesigned my lectures to incorporate cooperative learning frequently. This was a major improvement. The advantages of this approach were that the course still covered a lot of material (actually the same amount as the all-lecture-all-the-time version), was still appropriately rigorous with enough lecture time for the class to feel familiar and with enough cooperative learning for it to feel exciting and supportive, still appeared rigorous to colleagues because the course covered the same content as the all-lecture version, and was even easier to teach. Once the cooperative learning activities were added, course preparation was a breeze. Plus, students then injected so much enthusiasm and energy into class that I came out of class energized rather than tired out. But once the shiny newness of cooperative learning wore off, I realized I had only gone halfway. I now was using techniques that improved student engagement, but I still did not know whether I was teaching my students useful material or whether my learning objectives were appropriate. Adding cooperative learning was like building a beautiful house on a rotten foundation.

Then TBL arrived to save the day. I read an article about TBL (Michaelsen & Sweet, 2008), purchased a book on it (Michaelsen, Knight, & Fink, 2004), and was sold. I revised my course immediately from the ground up. What I found most exciting about TBL is that it provided a framework for me to clearly identify the course objectives I had been lacking—what I wanted my students to do, not what I wanted to cover. It also showed me how I could continue to use cooperative team-based techniques to achieve those objectives. TBL helped me crystallize my growing awareness that learning objectives, focused on critical thinking skills important to the discipline (Halpern, 1998), are the top priority for any course. These objectives take precedence over the style of course delivery, particular assignments, or the particular content covered. I began to recognize that I wanted my undergraduate students to begin to think like psychologists, including using the scientific analysis it required, even if they didn't end up being psychologists. Those critical thinking skills are useful on a day-to-day basis regardless of career path. In this way the course content became the avenue I was using to teach critical thinking skills rather than being primary in importance.

To illustrate this change in my approach to the course, I provide examples of learning objectives from each of my three course iterations in Figure 12.1. These are, admittedly, reconstructions because I didn't have formal learning objectives for the first two approaches. What is immediately obvious is that in the TBL approach I actually know what I am trying to teach to my students and why. The driving force has become the thinking skill, not the content.

Admittedly, with TBL I am not as able to cover as much material as I did with previous approaches because I now focus much more intensely on practicing important thinking skills. But covering a wide range of material seems to have little value to my students because once the material is *covered*, it is likely never to be *uncovered* again without the application practice. I also find that my students are more hesitant to accept TBL than the previous two approaches, probably because it is more unfamiliar. However, presenting it with confidence while appearing highly organized and in control helps to overcome their skepticism. Finally, I have also found that my teaching evaluations are now slightly lower than they were with previous approaches, though they are still very strong. I believe this is because my students no longer see the hard work I put into teaching them. Instead of my working hard in class and students passively receiving, I now require them to work hard in class with my work on course design taking place primarily outside class.

FIGURE 12.1
Learning Objectives

Approach 1: Lecture

Example learning objective—Students will be able to list and describe the ways to evaluate reliability and validity of a test.

Translation—I will cover this in lecture. Students will listen and take notes. They will then write those notes on homework and tests.

Approach 2: Lecture plus cooperative learning techniques

Example learning objective—Students will be able to list and describe the ways to evaluate reliability and validity of a test.

Translation—I will cover this in lecture supplemented by cooperative learning techniques that will engage all students. Students will listen, take notes, and be more engaged and more aware of whether they understood the material because they will need to explain or work with it in some way in class. They will then write those notes on homework and tests.

Approach 3: Team-based learning

Example learning objective—Students will be able to evaluate the reliability and validity data on a given test and critique test results based on the test's reliability and validity. Students will further understand that all information about the world comes from data sources. All data sources should be evaluated for reliability and validity.

Translation—Following exposure to reliability and validity information via out-of-class reading, students will have multiple, increasingly difficult practice opportunities for evaluating reliability and validity of data sources, supported by the instructor and by their teammates. Applicability to real-world decision making will be practiced and emphasized.

CHALLENGES IN IMPLEMENTING TBL:
AKA THE RACE TO THE MIDDLE

In the process of implementing TBL, I had difficulty with challenges I thought were related primarily to characteristics of the course content and difficulties generating controversy and encouraging achievement.

First, I initially found it difficult to create strong application activities. In fact, this remains my greatest challenge, probably because I see it as the most important part of the course. With my initial learning goals for the students related to covering material and having them recall it, application activities were difficult to initially generate. Additionally, I was stuck in a mind-set that the application of assessment course material was really limited to master's-level students because psychological assessment as a skill is practiced only by master's- or doctoral-level practitioners.

When TBL helped me to reexamine my goals for my students, I was able to identify what I wanted them to be able to do as a function of having taken my course, focusing on using scientific thinking (as illustrated by assessment topics) when approaching information about the world. With that new mind-set it became easier to adapt application activities from previous homework assignments and an excellent instructor's manual, and generate new activities.

Second, I had difficulty implementing activities that required competition and controversy. My impression is that TBL is most easily implemented in contexts in which interteam competition can be encouraged. Interteam competition stimulates higher achievement within teams, and by giving team members a common enemy, it encourages team cohesion. Team competition can be fostered by using application activities that inherently contain controversial material or by explicitly encouraging team competition through instructor intervention (guiding teams toward differences that must be resolved through whole-class discussion or awarding points or some other incentive to a top team on an activity). A highly competitive university context also encourages team competition. My teams did not compete; they were content to agree to disagree. My students were fine if another team had a different understanding of an application activity than they did, even if the implication was that one of them was wrong. Even within teams, there was very little jockeying to be on top. Rather than racing to the top within and across teams, students seemed to be racing to the middle. The unfortunate result of this was that it pulled team achievement down overall as stronger members tried to accommodate weaker members rather than trying to pull them up. Also, I am naturally conflict averse, so generating conflict or controversy across teams was difficult for me to initiate, and particularly, to sustain.

What was responsible for this race to the middle? Initially I thought this may be a common experience among TBL instructors, even though it was not mentioned in the otherwise very thorough TBL book (Michaelsen, Knight, & Fink, 2004). However, it became clear to me when attending the annual TBL conference in 2009 that this was not the case. Most instructors I spoke with had highly competitive teams of students who were frequently trying to display their mastery of the material as well as trying to pull up their teammates so their overall team performance would be higher. My experience appeared to be somewhat unique. I now attribute my students' behavior to three potential driving factors: a relatively noncompetitive educational environment, Latino cultural values, and gender socialization (the majority of psychology majors at UTPA, and across the country, are women).

First, undergraduate psychology is not typically a highly competitive major. The majority of psychology students view their degree as a terminal degree and plan to use it as a general liberal arts degree. Only a small proportion will eventually attend graduate school. With this orientation, top grades are not critically important, which contrasts with other disciplines in which TBL is frequently applied. For example, many of the instructors I interacted with at the TBL conference were teaching in medical schools where students highly value their own intellectual strengths and where superiority over peers may have concrete payoffs. Additionally, UTPA, as a public university with a strong mission to educate the populace, does not have high admission standards and thus admits a large number of students whose primary goal is to graduate, not get straight As. Their self-concepts may not be as closely tied to strong academic achievement as you may find, for example, in a private liberal arts college with high admission standards.

Second, Latino cultural values, which emphasize group harmony and strong social relationships, may discourage individual achievement within teams and competition between teams. Within teams, group harmony norms may encourage some adaptive group behaviors, such as patiently explaining important concepts and treating team members respectfully. However a norm that highly values group harmony may reduce team members' willingness to disagree with each other and point out errors in reasoning. Across teams, strong social relationship values may make students unwilling to disagree with other teams. If students are very inexperienced with intellectual debate and conflict, it may also be upsetting to them to be in an environment of conflict. They may have difficulty separating the relationship conflict from the intellectual controversy.

Third, gender socialization of female students may be important in social science classrooms. In my latest semester of teaching this course, 61 of the 75 students were women. It has been frequently documented that women students are socialized to not appear too smart to maintain an attractive female gender role, with this first appearing most clearly in the middle school years (see Helgeson, 2009). Additionally, female students may be more oriented than male students toward maintaining strong relationships with and protecting the feelings of their team members (Whiffen & Demidenko, 2006).

Of course, lack of competition within and across groups has its positives. My students typically develop into cooperative teams very quickly. Though they do not have much interteam competition to encourage them to bond quickly, they tend to work well with each other without requiring much instructor intervention nor a great deal of formalized team reflection to assist with group formation. Additionally, facilitating my students' work in teams helps them feel more comfortable in the classroom because the teamwork plays to their relational strengths.

My first response to the lack of competition in the classroom was to struggle against it by trying to create controversy and conflict. When that was spectacularly unsuccessful, I restructured my application activities to not require interteam competition for a successful outcome. I also removed most rewards for team competition (such as giving the best team extra points on an activity) since it went against the grain of my students' preferences. This has resulted in a pleasant and supportive "we're-all-in-it-together" atmosphere; however, it means I also have to work against a pull toward mediocrity within teams. One way I do that is by using immediate feedback assessment technique (IF-AT) forms for the team readiness assurance tests (tRATs). This gives teams immediate feedback about which teammates are most prepared or knowledgeable without requiring team members to more forcibly assert their own knowledge over their peers. I also frequently circulate among the teams when they are working on application activities. When student questions arise, I often assign the question to another team member whom I believe has a good understanding of the material. By assigning a student to respond, I am giving the student explicit instructions to excel and bring his or her teammates along. This combats the tendency of stronger students' allowing the team to function with an adequate, but not excellent, understanding of the material. I also require some kind of artifact from each team after each application activity, such as written notes on the team discussion, so that students feel their teamwork is under evaluation.

MY TBL IMPLEMENTATION: THREE EXAMPLE APPLICATION ACTIVITIES

This section contains three examples of application activities I use, including one from the beginning, middle, and end of the course. I believe all three activities incorporate the TBL 4-Ss (see Chapter 1), which help to guarantee a successful experience: a significant problem, the same problem for all students to work on, a specific choice as a team outcome, and simultaneous team reporting of that choice to the class. I use all these activities in the full TBL context, including heterogeneous team formation, the Readiness Assurance Process, and peer evaluations. I am convinced the activities would not be as successful without those components.

Application Activity: Who Is the Better Teacher?

This is the first application activity I use in the course and is very enthusiastically received by students. At this point, students have already engaged in a grade-weight-setting activity (as described in Michaelsen et al., 2004, pp. 242–248) and so have had an opportunity to begin to bond with teammates. They have also read a statistics review from their text and taken an individual readiness assurance test (iRAT) and a tRAT on the material. The activity is designed to give students a review of basic statistics content (a prerequisite to the course), engage them in team-based problem solving in a way that is relatively familiar, and give them an introduction to the use of data in decision making. It takes about two hours of class time, including class discussion.

The activity is a case of two first-grade teachers. They have each given a spelling test to their classes, and the number of words spelled correctly for each student is given (10 students per class). Teams are asked to graph the test results, compute basic descriptive statistics (mean, median, mode, standard deviation, percentile of a given score), and use the graph and statistics to answer two questions: Which teacher should be nominated for a teaching award? Which teacher should be given the option to teach an after-school remedial spelling class for extra pay? The two distributions of test scores have identical means, but one is a highly skewed distribution so that a few students are excelling and several are failing, while the second is a relatively symmetrical distribution so almost all students are passing but none are excelling.

When all teams have answered both questions they simultaneously report their decisions on the two questions, and we then discuss the issue as a class.

This activity is highly successful because it allows the students to use their existing knowledge, which they are comfortable with, paired with statistics practice, which they are very uncomfortable with. Students are remarkably sophisticated in their thinking about what constitutes a successful teacher. They have already thought through issues such as whether a teacher who encourages excellence is more skilled than a teacher who develops competence in all his or her students. They are also already aware of the ambiguities in that question and deeply understand that, although there are clearly great and terrible teachers, the issue of teaching excellence is more nuanced and controversial in most cases. Using this case for students' first introduction to the use of statistics in decision making helps them see the role good data can have, while recognizing their limitations as well.

Application Activity: Communicating Psychological Test Results

This application activity is used midway through the course. At this point in the semester, we have been working on intelligence test design. I include this content because intelligence tests represent important breakthroughs in psychological test construction, and because intelligence testing is so present in the culture it is important for psychology students to have a strong understanding of what an intelligence test can and cannot tell us. Students have read text material on intelligence testing, been individually (iRAT) and team (tRAT) tested on the material, and we have done one or two previous application activities and mini lectures. The activity requires about 40 minutes of class time, including class discussion.

In this activity, students select the best statements to include in a psychological report. They are given the profile of intelligence test scores of a 10-year-old child and are asked to select one sentence each among three groups of four statements the evaluating psychologist should include in the testing report. I provide the statements to the teams as handouts for their discussion. I also post the 12 statements on the classroom walls, and the teams indicate their choices with sticky notes that have their team numbers written on them. They post their choices simultaneously after all teams have reached a decision. An example of one of the groups of statements is shown in Figure 12.2.

This activity is successful with students and well received. I believe they take to it with enthusiasm because it has a professional feel and seems significant to them because it is clearly tied to the work of a clinical psychologist. But it is important to me because it ties data-based interpretation to the real world. It requires a solid understanding of the basics of intelligence test design (as well as basic statistics), so it allows me to check on their knowledge by listening in to their discussions. It also requires students to make the leap from psychological test results to real-world recommendations, which introduces issues of certainty/uncertainty in applying data to real-world decision making. In whole-class discussions, other points of interest to

FIGURE 12.2
Application Activity: Communicating Psychological Test Results

---

Choose the best statement to include in the
report recommendations regarding Dominic's weaknesses:

1. Dominic's difficulty with processing speed indicates that his teachers should give him extended time on tests and assignments. However, given extended time, he should score near the top of his class on most assignments.

2. Dominic is capable of learning all class materials but may have difficulty expressing his knowledge on tests and activities that emphasize quick initial mastery or completion.

3. Dominic's teachers should be aware of his poor processing speed ability in order to accommodate his difficulties.

4. Dominic performed well on all areas of the intelligence test. No areas of performance were significantly below average. No special accommodations are necessary for Dominic to be successful in class.

---

students are often raised. For example, statement number 4 in Figure 12.2 is the seemingly nicest and would be the easiest thing to say to Dominic's parents. Unfortunately, it is also incorrect. This allows us to discuss the importance of accurate data to society and to us individually, even if the data are unpleasant or bad news in some way.

Application Activity: Test-Bias Debate

This is one of the last application activities I use in this class. It requires about 90 minutes of class time, including class discussion. In this section, we discuss bias in psychological testing, which I believe is the most complex topic of the course because it requires a very firm understanding of test reliability and validity (which I have been emphasizing throughout the course), and it requires students to overcome the idea that if person X (or group X) scores lower on a test than person Y (or group Y), then the test must be biased against that person (or group). More fundamentally, it requires students to examine their beliefs that all humans are created equal and what the implication of this idea is in reference to individual differences, such as intelligence, in which all people are not equal in ability.

Prior to this application activity, students have read textbook content on test bias and been tested on it individually (iRAT) and as a team (tRAT). They have also completed a homework assignment on a specific test-bias case that requires review of evidence related to the case. For the in-class activity, I give them the case that was reviewed as part of the homework assignment as a court case to argue in which a minority child has been potentially inappropriately tracked into special education based on psychological test results. In the case, the parents of the child are suing the school district. Two team members argue for the parents, two argue for the school district, and the remaining one or two team members are judges. I assign the roles so that the most talkative and strongest contributing team members are the judges, requiring the more retiring team members to strongly contribute to the activity. (However, I do it in a fashion that appears random, by counting off team members.) I provide a structure for the debate, including the amount of time allocated to each side. At the end of the debate, the judges make a decision and communicate their decision and the rationale to their teammates. After all judges have made their decisions, teams simultaneously report whether they voted pro or con, and we follow up with a whole-class discussion on the most important issues raised in the debates. Case instructions, tasks, and the structure of the debate are shown in Figure 12.3.

I display case instructions, tasks, and the structure of the debate as slides in class to keep the teams on track. Although the structure of the debate appears somewhat complicated, I have no difficulty getting teams to adhere to it relatively closely. I emphasize that each side gets two turns and the judge talks last.

This activity is well received by the students, again I believe because it feels authentic and professional. It also assists students with humanizing the test-bias issue by applying it to a single case in which they have an advocacy role. Although the activity appears to focus on conflict and controversy, which is not particularly successful with my students, they take to it very easily. I believe their assigned advocacy roles give them permission to engage in the conflict so they are more easily able to tolerate the controversy than they would be if the activity were more loosely structured. Also with this activity occurring at the end of the semester, teams are comfortable with working together and may thus be more tolerant of conflict.

FINAL COMMENTS

TBL has helped me to entirely reconceptualize my role as a college professor. It provides a tried-and-true framework to easily adapt teaching critical thinking skills in psychology courses. Although my students are generally initially skeptical because it is unfamiliar, they are willing to try it out and participate enthusiastically in each activity. It is particularly satisfying to me that I regularly have students return after a semester or two, telling me that they had no idea how much they learned in the class until they moved on to more applied settings, such as internships, which are relevant to their future careers.

Using TBL at UTPA has been a fulfilling experience. I find that I am most successful when working with Mexican American students when I foster an interdependent classroom atmosphere, share information about myself with the students, treat the students with respect, and accept their respect for me gracefully. My ability to effectively use TBL also improved when I reduced the emphasis on competition in the classroom. Mexican American college students easily adapt to the TBL classroom and

FIGURE 12.3
Application Activity: Test-Bias Debate

Case Instructions

Terrence L. is a 12-year-old African American boy who lives in a poor section of Detroit. Early in his elementary school years, Terrence was not performing well in school. He was referred for psychological testing and was administered several tests including the WISC-IV. Based on the results of the testing, he was diagnosed as mildly mentally retarded and placed in special education classes.

Terrence's parents are now suing the school district, claiming that the WISC-IV is biased against African American children so that his diagnosis was inaccurate. They further claim that if an African American school psychologist had administered the test to Terrence, he would have performed better on the test and not been diagnosed as mentally retarded. The school psychologist who worked with Terrence was White.

The school district has responded that the WISC-IV is the best available tool to assess intelligence in children, that the evaluation included several components (interview, other testing, etc.) and not just the WISC-IV, and that the race of the examiner does not have a significant effect on test scores.

Team Member Tasks

1's (Pro). Advocate for Terrence's parents' position that the WISC-IV is biased and should not be used for diagnosing mental retardation in African American children.

2's (Con). Advocate for the school district's position that the WISC-IV is not biased and is the best available tool for assessing intelligence.

3's (Judge). Weigh the strength of each set of arguments made in the debate and decide which set is stronger. Provide feedback to both sides regarding your decision and the basis for it.

Structure of the Debate

5 minutes preparation time
2 minute presentation of the arguments supporting Terrence's parents (Pro)
1 minute preparation time for Con
2 minute presentation of the arguments supporting the school district (Con)
1 minute preparation time for Pro
1 minute rebuttal from Pro
1 minute rebuttal time from Con
1 minute preparation time for Judge
2 minutes for the Judge to provide feedback to the two sides regarding the decision and the basis for it

may be more comfortable and feel more supported with a team-based approach than with an approach that more strongly emphasizes individual performance.

REFERENCES

Alegría, M., & Woo, M. (2009). Conceptual issues in Latino mental health. In F. A. Villar-ruel, G. Carlo, J. M. Grau, M. Azmitia, N. J. Cabrera, & T. J. Chahin (Eds.), *Handbook of U.S. Latino psychology: Developmental and community-based perspectives* (pp. 15–30). Thousand Oaks, CA: Sage.

America's best public colleges. (2009, August 5). *Forbes.* Retrieved from http://www.forbes .com/2009/08/06/best-public-colleges-opinions-colleges-09-top.html

Brown, A. V. (2008). Effectively educating Latino/a students: A comparative study of partici-pation patterns of Hispanic American and Anglo-American university students. *Journal of Hispanic Higher Education, 7*(2), 97–118.

Buriel, R., Perez, W., De Ment, T. L., Chavez, D. V., & Moran, V. R. (1998). The relation-ship of language brokering to academic performance, biculturalism, and self-efficacy among Latino adolescents. *Hispanic Journal of Behavioral Sciences, 20*(3), 283–297.

Cooper, C. R. (1999). Multiple selves, multiple worlds: Cultural perspectives on individuality and connectedness in adolescent development. In A. S. Masten (Series Ed.), *The Minnesota Symposia on Child Psychology: Vol. 29. Cultural processes in child development* (pp. 25–57). NJ: Erlbaum.

Feliciano, C., & Rumbaut, R. G. (2005). Gendered paths: Educational and occupational expectations and outcomes among adult children of immigrants. *Ethnic and Racial Studies, 28*(6), 1087–1118.

Gaitan, D. G. (2004). *Involving Latino families in schools: Raising student achievement through home-school partnerships.* Thousand Oaks, CA: Corwin Press.

Halpern, D. F. (1998). Teaching critical thinking for transfer across domains: Dispositions, skills, structure training, and metacognitive monitoring. *American Psychologist, 53*(4), 449–455.

Helgeson, V. S. (2009). *Psychology of gender* (3rd ed.). Uppper Saddle River, NJ: Pearson.

Johnson, D. W., Johnson, R. T., & Smith, K. A. (2006). *Active learning: Cooperation in the college classroom* (3rd ed.). Edina, MN: Interaction Book Company.

Michaelsen, L. K., Knight, A. B., & Fink, L. D. (2004). *Team-Based Learning: A transforma-tive use of small groups in college teaching.* Sterling, VA: Stylus.

Michaelsen, L. K., & Sweet, M. (2008). Team-Based Learning. *Higher Education Advocate, 25*(6), 5–8.

Nicolai, K. (2005). *Instructor's manual for Kaplan and Saccuzzo's Psychological Testing: Princi-ples, applications, and issues* (6th ed.). Belmont CA: Thomson Wadsworth.

Shweder, R. A., Goodnow, J., Hatano, G., LeVine, R. A., Markus, H., & Miller, P. (1998). The cultural psychology of development: One mind, many mentalities. In W. Damon (Series Ed.) & R. Lerner (Vol. Ed.), *Handbook of Child Psychology: Vol. 1. Theoretical models of human development* (pp. 865–937). New York: Wiley.

Smith, J., Stern, K., & Shatrova, Z. (2008). Factors inhibiting Hispanic parents' school involvement. *Rural Educator, 29*(2), 8–13.

Tyler, K. M., Uqdah, A. L., Dillihunt, M. L., Beatty-Hazelbaker, R., Conner, T., Gadson, N., . . . Stevens, R. (2008). Cultural discontinuity: Toward a quantitative investigation of a major hypothesis in education. *Educational Researcher, 37*(5), 280–297.

Umaña-Taylor, A. J., & Fine, M. A. (2001). Methodological implications of grouping Latino adolescents into one collective ethnic group. *Hispanic Journal of Behavioral Sciences, 23*(4), 347–362.

U.S. Census Bureau. (2009). *Hidalgo County, Texas. Selected social characteristics in the United States: 2005–2009.* Retrieved from http://factfinder.census.gov/servlet/ADPTable?_bm =y&-geo_id=05000US48215&-qr_name=ACS_2009_5YR_G00_DP5YR2&-ds_name =ACS_2009_5YR_G00_&-_lang=en&-redoLog=false&-_sse=on

Updegraff, K. A., McHale, S. M., Whiteman, S. D., Thayer, S. M., & Crouter, A. C. (2006). The nature and correlates of Mexican-American adolescents' time with parents and peers. *Child Development, 77*(6), 1470–1486.

Whiffen, V. E., & Demidenko, N. (2006). Mood disturbances across the life span. In J. Worell & C. D. Goodheart (Eds.), *Handbook of girls' and women's psychological health: Gender and well-being across the life span* (pp. 51–60). New York, NY: Oxford University Press.

Chapter 13

Using Team-Based Learning to Meet the American Psychological Association Recommendations for Undergraduate Psychology Education

Herb Coleman

Our professional organizations are where we as members of our disciplines meet to participate in and continually redefine our fields. This chapter is therefore especially valuable for how it models important linkages between Team-Based Learning and the instructional principles identified as best practice by the academic/social heart of Coleman's field. At a more practical level, Coleman describes how Team-Based Learning can flow in a community college classroom, with helpful depictions of specific application activities.

Like other contributors to this book, my journey to Team-Based Learning (TBL) began years before I discovered it. By the time I encountered TBL, my own process of experimentation as a teacher had led me to a collection of practices that did not take a far leap for me to adopt TBL. My experience had prepared me to recognize in TBL the mechanisms for engagement I had been moving toward on my own.

In this chapter, I first describe the evolution of my teaching practice into full-blown TBL, culminating in a brief description of how I currently organize each unit in my courses. I then explore how I see TBL aligning in my classroom with recommendations for undergraduate psychology education as specified by the American Psychological Association (APA, 2011) and Diane Halpern's (1998) principles of critical thinking. I conclude the chapter by describing some of the specific application activities I use to teach Introduction to Psychology.

MY GROWTH INTO TBL

When I prepared to teach my first psychology class over 20 years ago, all my mentor told me was, "Teach something from every chapter." This meant I could emphasize or de-emphasize any aspect of the 22 chapters I wanted, but it also meant I had to cover a great deal of material without much depth. This was my first frustration as a teacher. We cover so many fascinating topics that some necessarily get short shrift. I sensed this superficial coverage also frustrated my students, a suspicion that was later borne out by students in my course evaluations—they also wanted to spend more time on some topics and less on others. Worse still, I made the typical first-year mistake of treating my freshmen like upper-division or grad students. By this I mean that my exams consisted exclusively of essay questions, and my students had to review research articles and write a term paper. Surprisingly, most of my students were successful, and I had a fairly normal grade distribution. It was only when my students petitioned to have my course counted as writing intensive did I realize I needed to make a change.

To reduce the amount of writing in my class, I introduced a modified multiple-choice exam format. I had avoided multiple-choice testing from the outset because as a student I had always disliked the fact that multiple-choice exams did not allow me to explain why I chose a particular answer or argue why two or more answers could be correct. As a compromise, I gave a traditional multiple-choice exam, but I also picked several items (usually five) that required students to explain in writing the rationales for their answers. They also had the option of explaining their answer to any item they felt was ambiguous or had more than one possible correct answer. This type of testing enabled me to evaluate students' understanding of at least some of the material much like the essays did but took less time to administer and grade, and students no longer felt the course was writing intensive.

Shortly thereafter, a colleague introduced me to the concept of collaborative testing, in which students paired up, discussed their answers, and together turned in a single Scantron answer sheet. When I introduced team testing, I had students test individually for the first two exams to establish an individual baseline. Then for the third and fourth exam they could choose to pair team testing with a partner or continue to test individually—though I still required students to explain some of their answers individually in writing, whether they chose to test together or not. Because of my point structure in the class, not every student needed to take the final exam at the end of the term, but those who did could choose to take the test as one large team consisting of all those wishing to team test or they can choose to take the test individually. To my surprise, while students testing in pairs did not seem to help students much beyond their individual abilities, the scores on the final from those who took the test in larger teams were consistently high. This would be my mode of assessment for 10 years.

The educational literature at the time argued that group projects could help provide relevant experience and more authentic learning, so I also had my students do a group project that involved presenting both sides of the issue in a roundtable-style discussion. Students received 25% of their grade on the student panel from their fellow group members, another 25% from the class, and I gave them their final 50% of their grade. In all three cases a rubric was developed that rated each student from one to five on five different aspects of their presentation. While this project sometimes produced lively class discussions, it suffered many of the usual problems with poorly designed group assignments.

In 2004, I introduced a student response system (clickers) in my classroom. With these systems every student gets a response pad, while a receiver attached to the professor's computer collects the responses. I had always wanted something like this to help with polling student responses to sensitive topics in my human sexuality classes. Along with polling students' opinion, I used the system to conduct knowledge checks on lecture material and multimedia presentations in class. I would lecture for 10–15 minutes, then ask a few questions over what I had just covered. If fewer than 20% of the class missed an item, we would continue. However if more than 20% missed an item, then I would remediate right then before going on. I would do the same with video and audio presentations. This immediate assessment of student learning helped me focus on the areas students needed the most help on and not dwell on the concepts they clearly understood.

The particular system I was using also allowed for formal individual assessment. Students were given a copy of the test and their assigned clicker. Then they would complete the test at their own pace by clicking in their answers instead of using a Scantron form. Their answers were captured immediately, and their scores were immediately available, though I still had them use the blue book to explain their answers in writing. I also still allowed testing in pairs on the third and fourth exams. Likewise, for the final, they would use a single clicker for the larger group team testing and write their explanations in their individual blue books.

Now I was fairly satisfied with my instruction and my assessment of student knowledge of the material. By having to explain some concepts, letting them share their understanding with classmates, and incorporating immediate knowledge checks, I felt they were going to a sufficient depth in the material while covering a great deal of it. The immediate feedback provided by the clickers helped us spend more time on the things not entirely understood and less time on the more easily understood concepts.

So on my own, I had begun assembling some of the basic components of TBL: My students were working in groups, testing in teams and getting immediate feedback, presenting their learning publicly, choosing a side on a complex issue, and being held accountable to group members and peers.

In 2007, I encountered TBL and was enamored by what I heard because it encompassed many of the processes that had produced some of the outcomes I wanted but took them further. For example, I already used permanent teams, but I had been letting students pick their own teams instead of strategically organizing the teams myself. Furthermore, my teams had not all been working on the same problems; they had each been discussing a different issue, but I saw the value of all of them discussing every issue, and I made that change. Similarly, I left paired testing behind and made every collaborative test a team test, adding more students into the mix and thus bringing in more points of view. The clicker system I was using not only allowed individual testing but also immediate feedback. Finally, I liked very much how

Michaelsen, Knight, and Fink's (2004) 4-S application activities of significant problem, same problem, specific choice, and simultaneous reporting enabled us to address
a number of concepts and put students much deeper into the material by forcing
them to use course concepts to take a position that was based on carefully considering
the data from the text or research articles to back up their choices.

THE RHYTHM OF A TYPICAL UNIT IN MY COURSES NOW

I teach classes of 25–35 students, so I usually have five or six teams of five or six
students each, and each of my five units follows the rhythm recommended for TBL:
guided out-of-class preparation, readiness assurance with feedback, and team decision
topics (application activities).

Guided out-of-class preparation. I organize my units around application activities,
which I call *team decision topics*. To prepare for these activities, students are assigned
chapter readings and given a journal assignment to reflect on issues related to the
topic. They are also given a list of vocabulary terms related to the topic that they
must learn.

Readiness assurance. On readiness assurance day, students arrive at class and first
take the individual Readiness Assurance Test (iRAT) by entering their answers with
their clickers. Then they take the same test in their teams using a designated team
clicker. The software allows me (but not the students) to see immediately how many
items they got correct and which items they got incorrect. Along with using the
clickers, each team marks its team answers on one team test form. When the team is
finished, a team member brings the test form up to me to get feedback on how the
team has done. I quickly go through the test and circle the number of each item they
got wrong and draw a line through the incorrect answer. They then return to their
teams to discuss the items they missed and try answering them again for half credit.
When they finish, they again bring me their team test form and instead of circling
the incorrect items as I did last time, I now place an X next to them and draw a line
through their latest incorrect answer. They then get one more chance to correct any
missed items for one fourth of the original points. By the third try, most teams have
all the answers correct. If they failed to identify the correct answer, I circle the correct
answer and give the team representatives a quick explanation of why the answer is
correct. They then take the test back to their team for review. Either through their
combined work or my correction they now have all the correct answers. Also, at this
time, if a team feels that the answer identified as correct disagreed with the information from the readings or if the test item was ambiguous, it could appeal by identifying the inconsistency or rewriting the item to remove the ambiguity.

Even though this procedure doesn't provide the decision-by-decision feedback
the immediate feedback assessment technique (IF-AT) answer sheets provide, I've
continued to use it for two reasons. One is that it works well enough that I haven't
felt the need to invest in the IF-ATs. The other is that it is free or at least uses

technology that I already have. Students still go through the process of discussing the items and explaining why one answer is a better choice than another.

Once the team RAT (tRAT) is done, teams can appeal any item they feel was ambiguous or that disagrees with the readings, and I let them turn in their appeals at the next class meeting. Before the end of readiness assurance class, I introduce students to the topic of the upcoming application exercise (the team decision topic) and give them the opportunity to begin discussing and researching. The next class meeting begins with a review of the items from the individual assessment that 40% or more of the class missed. Students are also made aware of where the concepts are located in the textbook. Team appeals are also reviewed during this time. Then students are asked to get into their groups to work on the team decision.

Team decision topics (application activities). As teams discuss the topics of their team decisions, I circulate and listen in, making suggestions that will either get more of the team involved in the discussion or challenging the assumptions behind a position or statement. I usually leave them with the admonishment, "As long as you can find data or facts to back you up, . . ." After 30 to 45 minutes I ask each team to make its decision and send a representative to the front of the room to serve as a panel member representing his or her team. I used to call the panel discussion phase of class the fishbowl, but the students have playfully renamed it the Supreme Council. Members of the Supreme Council write their team's decision on the board, and I ask each of them to provide one fact supporting his or her position (that hasn't already been stated). Then I question them about their responses, why they disagreed with teams that answered differently, and so on. This goes on for 35–40 minutes, depending on whether council members need to caucus with their team (which I allow for two minutes) and potentially change their answer. After I've exhausted my questions, or the Supreme Council has come to a consensus, I open up questioning to the rest of the class for another 5 or 10 minutes.

When discussion ends, we thank the council members, and teams turn in a brief report stating their final position and providing the following forms of evidence:

- three citations from the readings,
- one psychological theory or phenomenon,
- one culturally related example, and
- one personal example or case study of behaviors or events that support their position. (The personal example does not have to come from a team member. It can come from a subject in a study or an example mentioned in the text, for example, Lil' Albert, Phineas Gage, amnesia patient HM, or other classic example from the psychology literature.)

In addition to the team decision report, each student turns in a unit review form that indicates what facts he or she contributed to the discussions, how the team came to a decision, and what the team and individuals can do to improve.

At the end of a unit, students also turn in peer evaluations that rate their team members on preparedness, contributions, and cooperation. They are not allowed to give everyone the same rating, but they are allowed to give one member up to three bonus points for extraordinary contributions or leadership.

TBL, CRITICAL THINKING, AND "PRINCIPLES FOR QUALITY UNDERGRADUATE EDUCATION IN PSYCHOLOGY"

After several semesters of using TBL, and based on my positive experience with it, I wasn't surprised to see the high degree of fit between recommended TBL practice and the 2011 revision of the APA's "Principles for Quality Undergraduate Education in Psychology" (see www.apa.org/education/undergrad/principles.aspx). The five principles each address a different population with several associated recommendations. The first two principles deal most directly with the aspects of education that are influenced by TBL: students and faculty. Therefore, this section explores the recommendations associated with each of these principles, and how TBL aligns with those recommendations.

> Principle 1: Students are responsible for monitoring and enhancing their own learning.
> Principle 2: Faculty strive to become scientist-educators who are knowledgeable about and use the principles of the science of learning.

Principle 1 about the students' relationship to their own learning, or as Halpern (1998) described it, acquiring a critical thinking disposition, and when properly implemented, TBL clearly addresses the overall principle, and the first three, and to some extent, the fourth bullet points shown in Figure 13.1. The Readiness Assurance Process (RAP; see Chapter 1) is specifically designed to accomplish the two things needed for students to accept responsibility for their own learning: opportunities

FIGURE 13.1
Principle 1

Students are responsible for monitoring and enhancing their own learning.

Recommendations:
- Students should know how to learn.
- Students assume increasing responsibility for their own learning.
- Students take advantage of the rich diversity that exists in educational institutions and learn from individuals who are different from them.
- Students are responsible for seeking advice for academic tasks, such as selecting courses in the approved sequence that satisfy the institution's requirements for the major and general education. They are also responsible for seeking advice about planning for a career that is both realistic and tailored to their individual talents, aspirations, and situations.
- Students strive to become psychologically literate citizens.

From *Principles for Quality in Undergraduate Education*, No authorship indicated. American Psychologist, Aug 29, 2011, No Pagination Specified. doi: 10.1037/a0025181 (and incentives) to learn on their own and the feedback they need to track their progress. Students learn very quickly that they cannot just take another team member's word that a particular answer is correct on the test. In no time at all, they learn to ask, "Why do you think that?" "What is your confirming evidence?" or "Where was that in the text?" Since they receive timely feedback on their team answers, it doesn't take very long for students to be willing to challenge each other's opinions. In addition, students who typically hold back soon realize that not speaking up hurts their team score (and their grade). This interaction leads students to at some point exhibit all the five behaviors associated with Halpern's (1998) description of a critical thinking attitude:

- willingness to engage in and persist at a complex task,
- habitual use of plans and the suppression of impulsive activity,
- flexibility or open-mindedness,
- willingness to abandon nonproductive strategies in an attempt to self-correct, and
- an awareness of the social realities that need to be overcome (such as the need to seek consensus or compromise) so that thoughts can become actions. (Halpern, 1998, p. 452)

In addition to encouraging students to acquire a critical thinking attitude, TBL also operationalizes each of the recommendations associated with Principle 1. Students help each other learn how to learn as a natural consequence of the discussions that occur during readiness assurance and application activities. When students share and challenge their understanding of course material, they often describe how they mastered the material they are arguing about. Given the fact the preparation for the RATs takes place before any lectures, there is no question that TBL motivates students to accept an active role in their own learning.

Finally, because I do my best to ensure students will have a semester-long interaction with other students who have a different background, every discussion has the potential for enabling students to discover the value of a diversity of input. In any given course, the diversity of input in part results from the team formation process. I typically have between five and seven people who are over 30, between five and seven who are currently raising children, between five and seven people who grew up in a home where a language other than English was spoken, and so on. Operationally, I ensure that each of the teams is diverse in culture and life experience by forming my teams using the standing line process described in Michaelsen et al. (2008, pp. 32–34).

However, diversity does not just lie in backgrounds or life circumstance; exposure to a diversity of ideas is also important. During the first phase of the Supreme Council panel discussion, students are initially exposed to a diversity of opinions and ways of addressing the application exercise topic. Furthermore, after the Supreme Council has reached a consensus or sufficiently explored the topic, I open up the discussion to the rest of the class. This goes on for another 10–15 minutes. Through the classwide discussion, students are further exposed to a variety of opinions and interpretations of the data; I am pleased to report that in my end-of-course surveys, the thing students say they like most about TBL is learning from other students.

One of the natural consequences of the team development process is that over time team members develop friendships with each other and as a result end up supporting one another in many ways. They often chat about matters not related to their class, for example, before class begins, that often deal with larger educational issues. I frequently hear students discussing how they are doing in school in general, including talking about courses they have already taken or ones they are thinking about taking as well as registration and deadlines. Students frequently advise or remind each other of program requirements and the need for academic advising. So although not directly part of TBL, the fourth recommendation under the first APA principle is addressed partly by the camaraderie that builds within a team over the course of the academic term.

Principle 2 is about the need for faculty to support student learning by being familiar with and applying the principles of the science of learning. In fact, faculty who use TBL are following educational best practice and as a result end up using approaches that are consistent with each of the bullet points that are part of Principle 2 (see Figure 13.2).

For example, using backward design (see Chapter 1) as the starting point for crafting TBL modules virtually ensures that teaching is always focused on "the critical thinking skills and abilities [teachers] wish to promote in their classes" (see Figure 13.2, fifth bullet point). Likewise setting the class tone and addressing problems fairly and transparently as they arise, for example, in how they respond to appeals on tRATs, professors model ethical behavior and establish an ethical tone in class (first bullet point). The RAP and the 4-S team applications promote active engagement and expose students to different interpretations of the material (second bullet point). I emphasize science over opinion and data over conclusions by having students use a variety of sources when they are researching their application exercises to back up their choices with scientific data from the text, peer-reviewed journals, or viable (and vetted) web resources (third bullet point).

Many of the key features of TBL focus on using "iterative inquiry into the success of their instruction in generating appropriate learning and use that evidence to refine instructional practices" (see Figure 13.2, fourth bullet point). For example, students' responses on the iRAT provide a guide for the lectures I present. Items and concepts that 40% or more of the class miss are the ones I review in class, so in this way I am using what I have learned about the success of students' instruction so far to shape the follow-up experiences I provide students to fill in the gaps.

In addition, TBL promotes the cultivation of students' critical thinking skills (fifth bullet point in Figure 13.2)—among which Halpern (1998) lists verbal reasoning, argument analysis, hypothesis testing, considering likelihood and uncertainty, decision making, and problem solving (p, 452). The combination of the RAP and 4-S application activities clearly involve most if not all the kinds of thinking on Halpern's list as a matter of course. Because the scores count, team members are motivated to

FIGURE 13.2
Principle 2

Faculty strive to become scientist–educators who are knowledgeable about and use the principles of the science of learning.

- Faculty provide instruction in the ethical standards that undergird our discipline and model this behavior across professional settings.
- Faculty understand and apply a variety of learning principles and modes of learning such as spaced practice, generation of responses, active engagement by students, group exercises, and explaining as a way of understanding, among others.
- Faculty make the same commitment to using the science of learning in their teaching as we require of scientist-practitioners who use the scientific findings of psychological research in their practice with clients and in other aspects of their professional lives.
- Faculty engage in continuous, iterative inquiry into the success of their instruction in promoting appropriate learning and use that evidence to refine instructional practices in ways to enhance the success of future students.
- Faculty foster critical thinking by identifying the critical thinking skills and abilities they wish to promote in their classes and in the psychology major as a whole. Faculty periodically review these skills and abilities throughout the term and through all years of undergraduate education.
- Faculty ensure that students develop basic skills in communication, numeracy, working cooperatively with others, and in acknowledging and respecting diverse perspectives.
- Faculty ensure that diversity issues are carefully considered and infused throughout the curriculum.
- Faculty become proficient in their use of commonly used technologies as a means to promote learning and encourage their students to develop these proficiencies as well.

From *Principles for Quality in Undergraduate Education.* No authorship indicated. American Psychologist, Aug 29, 2011, No Pagination Specified. doi: 10.1037/a0025181

challenge each other's views during the tRAT. In addition, using 4-S application activities (significant problem, same problem, specific choice, and simultaneous report) creates a situation in which teams are motivated and prepared to challenge each other if they fail to employ critical thinking. As a result, they learn from creating challenges and responding to challenges from other teams.

With respect to the final three bullet points in Figure 13.2 , students must practice communication skills and working with others during every phase of TBL, and many of my application exercises require interpretation and explanation of numerical data (sixth bullet point). Since TBL uses permanent and purposefully formed teams, students have the opportunity to work with and benefit from diversity built into their teams. Finally, I use a variety of technologies in ways that are consistent with recommended TBL practice. These include the use of the learning management system, the clicker system, requiring students to use outside resources to support their decisions, and allowing teams to go to the library or the computer lab during class to further their research.

As we've just seen, the practice of employing TBL demonstrates sound pedagogical practice by enhancing critical thinking skills. In addition, the activities engaged in through the implementation of TBL also support the recommendations of APA principles for quality. The activities of standard TBL practice provide the experiences students need for them to take responsibility for their education, as well as the opportunity for professors to demonstrate scientific principles applied to education. This provides two more reasons to recommend TBL as an education strategy, particularly for students enrolled in psychology courses.

SOME APPLICATION EXERCISES FOR INTRODUCTION TO PSYCHOLOGY

Probably the most difficult part of adopting TBL can be developing application exercises that meet the 4-S criteria as laid out by Michaelsen, Parmelee, McMahon, and Levine (2008). In this section, I list examples of what I use in my Introduction to Psychology course and in my Human Growth and Development course. The application exercises require students to apply the concepts covered in the chapters used in the RAP. The best question to ask when designing 4-S activities is, "What do I want my students to be able to do with this material?" Fortunately, I had previously used controversial or challenging issues for my student panels, so I was clear on what I wanted student to be able to do (apply the knowledge they've gained to real-world issues) and modified them to fit the 4-S model.

My courses are divided into five units. Each unit covers three to four chapters from the text. As mentioned earlier, the application exercise draws upon the concepts found in these chapters. For example, my first unit covers the introductory chapter on the history and science of psychology. In addition, I include the chapters on personality and learning behavior because they go deeper into the perspectives. The first unit outlines seven psychology perspectives, and I wanted students to be able to articulate the similarities and differences among them. With this outcome in mind, I created an application exercise that requires teams to decide which of the seven psychology perspectives is most scientific and which best represents human behavior and mental processes. I allow them to pick the same perspective or choose two different ones. To complete this assignment, they must first become familiar with the seven perspectives. They must also decide what it means to be scientific and develop a clear picture of what is meant by human behavior and mental processes and find data to support their position. I provide thought-probing questions to get them started, such as:

• What do we mean when we say a perspective is scientific?
• What makes one perspective more or less scientific than another?

- What do we include in human behavior and mental processes?
- How can you tell if one perspective addresses this better than another?
- If psychology could have only one perspective, which one would you pick and why?

Quite often the greatest amount of time is spent in teams' arguing over their choice. Once the choice is made, they conduct the research. After they compile their research, they are ready for the Supreme Council activity. The remaining topics for the application exercises in the intro course are the following:

- Is alcoholism a result of bad genes or bad behavior?
- Do we recommend that intersexed babies (born with ambiguous genitalia) be surgically altered shortly after birth?
- Should eyewitness accounts be accepted as the sole evidence in serious crimes?
- Should we continue to have the not guilty by reason of insanity defense in courts of law?

Each of these questions is based on the concepts found in the chapters and in the RAP to ensure that students are ready for the applications. So for the second exercise they will have studied genetics, heredity, biology, altered states of consciousness, narcotics, and alcohol. For the third exercise they have studied prenatal development, human development, sexual orientation, and gender. The fourth exercise requires them to have studied not only memory, but intelligence and creativity, as well as social psychology including conformity, prejudice, love, and attribution theory. The last exercise uses abnormal behavior, therapy, health, and stress as a background.

APPLICATION EXERCISES FOR HUMAN GROWTH AND DEVELOPMENT

Most of the students in Human Growth and Development, or the lifespan course, are allied health or nursing majors. So to make their application exercises more relevant (thus, significant), I couch them in terms of establishing hospital policy. For many units, I have students make their policy recommendations based on the factors presented in a specific scenario. Typically, I play the role of a hospital administrator seeking advice from the Supreme Council to make a recommendation to the hospital board. As with the intro course, the exercises are based on the concepts studied for the RAP. The application exercises for the growth and development course are as follows:

Unit 1: Prenatal and early childhood development. When, if ever, should health care workers recommend genetic counseling? What is the goal of genetic counseling? What happens if a couple shows a high probability of having a child with serious problems? What happens if the pregnancy shows serious complications? How far should health care workers' recommendations go?

Unit 2: Childhood development. What should health care providers' response be to the issue of spanking? When is it appropriate (if ever)? When is it to be discouraged (if not always)? How should undesired behavior in children be treated? What happens when those measures fail?

Scenario: Last week a 12-year-old who had broken her arm in a soccer game was brought into the emergency room by her father. Because they had come directly from the game, her 5-year-old brother was also with them. Because of the wait, the 5-year-old became restless. He began running around the emergency room and even climbed on the snack machine. Despite warnings from his father, his behavior did not cease until the father swatted him on the bottom two times with an open hand applying moderate force. One of our clerks witnessed this and called protective services.

Unit 3: Adolescent development. What should health care workers recommend as the age of consent for sexual activity? (You must pick an age.) Take into account biological, psychological, cognitive, and cultural issues to make your recommendation to the state board. Also consider age differential. For example, if you say 15 is the age of consent, does that mean a 15-year-old with anyone 15 and older or a 15-year-old only with anyone between 15 and 18? Finally, just as we have conditions for teens to drive, feel free to add conditions to your decision.

Unit 4: Adult development. How should health care procedures accommodate non-monogamous relationships? Please resist the temptation of choosing foreclosure and simply say they shouldn't (if you do, you still need to back up your position with six pieces of supporting data). Consider issues of visitation and information sharing as well as decision making.

Scenario: Imagine a situation in which a man and a woman are brought into a medical facility as victims in a car wreck. The man is severely injured and floating in and out of consciousness; the woman is injured but lucid. From their conversation you gather they are in a relationship (he calls for her and refers to her as "Honey," which is not her name. She calls him "Sweetie" and "Darling" and is obviously very concerned about his injuries). You further note that he is wearing a wedding band on the third finger of his left hand. She is not wearing a ring at all.

She provides you with all his information, including a list of his allergies and the name of his hometown doctor, verified by information in his wallet and a phone call to the doctor. Because she's not allowed to use her cell phone, she asks if you can please contact his wife, who lives in another town. When you ask what her relationship to him is, she answers that she is his "secondary" and that they are a poly family just before she passes out. It's determined that she has internal bleeding and will need an operation.

The staff member at the front desk has contacted his wife and she's on the way but it'll take about an hour for her to get there. After she's told about her husband's condition, she asks about Sherry, the other woman. What should health care workers do as far as information sharing goes? Do you consider this a family? Whom do you consider as being related to whom? What about decision making? Visitation? Spending the night?

Unit 5: Late adult development/death and dying. This is the one all medical professionals must sometimes face. At what point do we cease efforts to prolong life and allow a patient to die? Even more, is it ever appropriate for a medical professional to actually provide care that deliberately hastens death? Dr. Kevorkian became (in)famous because he wanted to put this issue that had long been under the table out front. For decades (centuries?) doctors have been providing their terminal patients with drugs or treatments with the intention of ending pain and suffering and their patient's life. Should we continue to operate in the shadows like this, or should we bring it to the light of day and establish formal policies?

The students in Human Growth and Development go through the same processes described previously. Their discussions are often more involved because they have a vested interest in this career and many have strong personal convictions. However, since we are actually talking about hospital policy and not just students' own personal position, it is fascinating to watch them build a deep understanding of the content while they struggle with resolving their cognitive dissonance as they work to make a team decision.

In both courses the application exercises challenge students at the analysis, synthesis, and evaluation level of Bloom's taxonomy (1956) of cognitive learning. Instead of merely reading the material and completing test and homework assignments, students must take their learning further by having to explain what they've learned to their teammates. In addition, the application exercises force them to analyze their own and their classmates' learning, synthesize the results into a single presentation, and evaluate it along with the other team's responses to determine which one has merit or which one is the best answer. This deep exploration is experienced at least in part by every student, and every student is asked to respond to the challenge at hand. Through the application exercises, I feel I can honestly say that all students who have been in class have not just attended but actively participated in their own educational process and assisted in the educational processes of their fellow students.

REFERENCES

American Psychological Association. (2011). *Principles for quality undergraduate education in psychology*. No authorship indicated. American Psychologist, Aug 29, 2011, No Pagination Specified. doi: 10.1037/a0025181

Bloom, B. S. (Ed.). (1956). *Taxonomy of educational objectives: Handbook I: The cognitive domain.* New York, NY: David McKay.

Halpern, D. (1998) Teaching critical thinking for transfer across domains. *American Psychologist, 23*(4), 449–455

Halpern, D. (2011). *National conference on undergraduate education in psychology: A blueprint for the future of our discipline.* Retrieved from http://www.apa.org/education/undergrad/blueprint.aspx

Michaelsen, L., Knight, A., & Fink, L. (2004). *Team-Based Learning: A transformative use of small groups in college teaching.* Sterling, VA: Stylus.

Michaelsen, L. K., Parmelee, D. X., McMahon, K. K., & Levine, R. E. (Eds.). (2008). *Team-Based Learning for health professions education: A guide to using small groups for improving learning.* Sterling, VA: Stylus.

CHAPTER 14

Using Teams in an Interdisciplinary Technology and Society Course

Team-Based Learning in Interdisciplinary Courses

Sunay Palsole

Palsole provides an inspiring description of how he integrated Team-Based Learning into a course designed to help students make important connections from material from many disciplines with problems faced by society and in their own everyday lives. His use of backward design to map his specific assignments to his larger goals for the class is an excellent model for teachers in any field. Like many teachers, his transition to Team-Based Learning was not perfect the first time, but he describes specific steps he took to improve upon his first attempt and has data to show how well they helped. A stunning result of Palsole's instructional design is how it supported the social evolution of a very large and diverse student population into clusters of close friends.

Instructors of interdisciplinary courses are often faced with significant challenges. In addition to the common challenge of making sure students are prepared for class, they must also encourage and enable students to see connections between disciplines, help students learn to think within broader frameworks, and make students comfortable grappling with issues that may not have exact answers. In an attempt to meet these challenges, my colleagues and I at the University of Texas at El Paso (UTEP) tried different techniques to modify an interdisciplinary course taught to all students at UTEP. Over time, we gradually wound up adopting Team-Based Learning (TBL), which helped transform our course and meet its special interdisciplinary challenges.

This chapter describes the background of our course, problems we dealt with during its evolution and solutions we developed, and the results we finally achieved. Finally, the chapter concludes with a getting started guide for faculty who wish to adopt TBL as a strategy in their own interdisciplinary courses.

THE COURSE

Interdisciplinary Technology and Society (or University 2350) is part of the core curriculum requirement at UTEP. The class is described in the university catalog as follows:

University 2350–Interdisciplinary Technology and Society is a 3-hour credit course created to help you critically examine the effects of technology on societies. In this course, you will be introduced to methods for assessing technology, and you will examine the many social, cultural, and environmental consequences of technology. In small groups you will problem-solve, research, analyze, discuss, and arrive at possible solutions for a broad range of topics and problems related to technology and society.

Because this class is required of all UTEP students, several sections must be offered with enrollments ranging from 50 to 300 sophomores, juniors, and seniors from all colleges in the university on any given roster. This highly heterogeneous mix of students creates the challenge of meeting all students where they are in their academic progression and training, and encouraging them to think critically about technology.

MY FIRST ATTEMPT

This first time I taught University 2350, I had 120 students with little teaching assistant (TA) support. From the outset we took pains to make the value of the course clear to the students, pointing to the course catalog and emphasizing on the syllabus that they would acquire knowledge about a variety of technology tools and learn to engage in higher-order thinking about technology. Though the course was designed to be useful to them, students objected to taking yet another required course, and they typically arrived in class viewing it as another obstacle on their path to graduation. In fact, the course had achieved the unsavory distinction of being the most hated course on campus. Student motivational problems aside, I also faced challenges typical to many large classes: student anonymity, difficulty in tracking student progress, lack of in-class student engagement, and a meager range of assessment options. This course faced an uphill battle from day one.

Realizing the course needed a shot in the arm, I took sage advice from various authors, such as Biggs (1999), McKeachie (1999), and Angelo and Cross (1993), and adopted a few techniques to broadly engage the students. These techniques included opening the class with quick summaries and a think-pair-share exercise; lecturing for 20 minutes at the most, followed by a quick student poll (either show of hands or holding up colored papers); two-minute papers; muddiest-point exercises; and so on. A few classes also took pop quizzes delivered in the style of the game *Jeopardy!* with prizes awarded to winning teams. The most popular exercise was a between-classes scavenger hunt. I would display a hints page at the end of a class session to encourage students to do some research and the readings in preparation for the next class, which would begin with a small problem based on those readings; the first three people to turn in the correct answer were awarded extra points. While this energized the dynamic of the class to some extent, there were still issues with class assessment because of the large—and growing—number of students in the class each semester.

With such large enrollments and the need to make the classes feel smaller, I created permanent collaborative groups to participate in group work during class time and online. In the first session after formation of teams, each team was required to read a short one-page document on team behavior that included important advice for working well on diverse teams. I encouraged students to keep the document at hand and bring it to each class so they could use it as a reference if frustration levels got too high. Following Slavin's (1989) research, I incorporated individual and group accountability into my assignments, and this change made a marked difference in the experience of the class. Instead of being alone in gutting out the course, students would sit in their groups and interact with one another as members of a team.

THE NEED FOR EVOLUTION

At this point, I had used a collection of active learning techniques and group work to address some of the large-class problems like student anonymity, but I still faced the problem of engaging students in critical interdisciplinary thought and philosophical frameworks for examining the use and effect of technology. Students weren't checking out and waiting for class to be over, but they also weren't really sinking their teeth into the course content in an energetic way. I wanted to increase the positive pressure on the groups so they could mature into high-performing teams and generate focused excitement to keep the class fresh.

At a conference in 2003, I was introduced to TBL as a comprehensive instructional strategy—beyond a collection of active learning techniques—designed to transform good enough groups into high-performing teams. TBL called for diverse team members (the more diverse the better), provided a process for ensuring that all teams and team members were prepared, incorporated methods to ensure individual and team accountability, and provided a framework to engage students in significant learning tasks (Michaelsen, Knight, & Fink, 2004).

INTERDISCIPLINARY CHALLENGES
AND THE REDESIGN PROCESS

From the outset, one of the challenges I encountered while considering TBL was the discipline-specific nature of most TBL literature. Very practical and detailed materials about implementing TBL are available in subject areas ranging from management to languages to science, technology, engineering, and math, but not much has been published on implementing TBL in interdisciplinary courses and the wide-ranging nature of their content. For example, one portion of the class examines the frameworks of technology adoption within the context of determinism, social constructivism, and technological momentum. Given the philosophical breadth of even this one piece of the course, I was unsure whether I could generate multiple-choice questions that had correct answers but were also interesting enough to stimulate useful discussions about the answer choices.

Similarly, the course already employed strategies for interdisciplinary implementation as identified by Haynes (1998) and Jacobs (1989), who advised designing a series of smaller assignments to help students learn and practice skills in one or more subject areas and then build up to a larger, summative, integrative assignment in which students combine what they have learned in an interdisciplinary way. Therefore, a second challenge was to envision a final, integrative assignment that would build upon the overhauled TBL versions of these smaller assignments. It seemed to me the course would need to fit together like a jigsaw puzzle to ensure that each smaller assignment was helping the students and teams discover tools that would help them develop, represent, and tackle the final assignment. Nonetheless, the experiences described by others using TBL made the effort of reshaping the class seem like a worthwhile experiment.

Rather than lose myself immediately in the endless details of trying to meld the interdisciplinary scaffolding framework I already used into the activity sequence of TBL, I took a few steps back and relied on the basic tools of Wiggins and McTighe's (2001) method of backward design. Backward design is a sound and powerful method of course design.

Following the backward design process, I outlined the main goals of the course and wrote down key assignments that matched to, aligned, and measured the key goals and objectives of the course. This ensured that every assignment I had in the course addressed one or more of the course goals and objectives, with the ultimate goal being that the final assignment would map most if not all the goals and objectives of the course. Table 14.1 shows part of the resulting assignment and goals map. Once this was done it became relatively easy to sequence the topics with learning activities so the students could practice and build the skills needed.

THE RESULTING CLASS EXPERIENCE

At the beginning of the semester, we formed teams and distributed the usual how-to-work-in-teams handout, but following this we asked teams to each create their own team contract that had to address the following issues:

- rules for team member behavior
- handling of due dates and work time lines
- work distribution and accountability
- individual team member strengths

We provided teams with template contracts they could customize to their own needs, with a draft due by the end of the first class. The final version of the contract was due two weeks later.

Like many TBL instructors, I feel strongly that students need a low-stakes practice round executing the stages of the Readiness Assurance Process (RAP), which includes the individual and team Readiness Assurance Tests (iRATs and tRATs; see Chapter

TABLE 14.1
Sample Goals and Objectives Map

	Goal 1: Enhance students' ability to assess technology		Goal 2: Develop and promote student teamwork		Goal 3: Involve students in their community (UTEP, city, state, civic organizations)	
	Objective: Student will learn to evaluate the development, societal, and ethical impacts of technology.	**Objective:** Student will conduct research using electronic and other media resources.	**Objective:** Student will participate and cooperate in TBL.	**Objective:** Students will apply critical thinking skills to solve problems that arise in their teams.	**Objective:** Student will explore and apply critical thinking in problem solving in regards to community resources, issues and concerns.	**Objective:** Student will participate in community outreach.
Consumption Assignment: We have looked at consumption and consumerism and their relationship. Keep track of your trash for a week. You don't have to weigh it, but keep track of how many bags of trash and recyclables you produce. Do some research on the Internet to see what the average production per household is. Are you below or above average? What is the impact of trash production on the landfills in El Paso? Write a blog about your trash tracking and provide a helpful hints page to your readers.	X	X		X		

TABLE 14.1 (Continued)

	Goal 1: Enhance students' ability to assess technology		Goal 2: Develop and promote student teamwork		Goal 3: Involve students in their community (UTEP, city, state, civic organizations)	
	Objective: Student will learn to evaluate the development, societal, and ethical impacts of technology.	**Objective:** Student will conduct research using electronic and other media resources.	**Objective:** Student will participate and cooperate in TBL.	**Objective:** Students will apply critical thinking skills to solve problems that arise in their teams.	**Objective:** Student will explore and apply critical thinking in problem solving in regards to community resources, issues and concerns.	**Objective:** Student will participate in community outreach.
Take a team position: Working in teams, build a case for or against recycling. Research energy requirements for recycling, and balance energy needs versus environmental and economic impact.		X	X		X	
Final Project: In your teams, identify one or more technological problems on the U.S.–Mexico border and provide solutions to issues. Teams will present their research in a poster format to the El Paso City Council.	X	X	X	X	X	X

1) because it is so different from what they are used to in other classes. Therefore, I developed a short RAP using the syllabus of the class as the content being tested and conducted it as one of the first activities in the semester. After the iRAT and the tRAT, correct answers and scores were revealed. (I did not use the immediate feedback assessment technique [IF-AT] cards for the first implementation of TBL in this course, but in subsequent courses I have used them.) We also conducted a practice peer review right after the practice RAP to give students exposure to as many elements of TBL as possible. The peer reviews were recorded on a printed spreadsheet that was handed out to all the students in class. Students were asked to rate their team members on their preparedness and contributions to the discussions on the syllabus RAT, and they had to provide reasons for assigning grades the way they did. Because 30% of the grade was a team grade, the students quickly realized this was their way to ensure that no one in the team could hide, and they now had a say in the distribution of grades for nonperforming members. In the following class we provided each team member with her or his peer evaluation along with the comments by her or his teammates. This process not only helped get students accustomed to the idea of being personally accountable but also helped them learn how to measure the accountability of other members of the team. We also debriefed the class on the process, answered any other queries about the whys and wherefores of the process, and stressed the need for them to be honest in peer evaluations.

With the teams formed and familiarized with the process of TBL, we plunged into the course material, and I gave my first real RAP. These multiple-choice questions for the RAP were drawn from the reading material and abstract concepts I wanted the students to reason with and argue about. As a result, some of the RAP questions had a clearly correct answer, and some were deliberately written to generate strong discussions between the students about the philosophical constructs of the example (such as: "The death penalty is an example of which: constructivism, determinism, or momentum?"). Now that I am using IF-AT forms, in cases where the questions did not have an objectively correct answer, I coded the IF-AT forms to have the best answer in my view. This generated more discussion within and between teams during the appeals phase of the RAP. I found that having a discussion about the gray areas engaged the entire class and created the kind of open learning environment I wanted for my interdisciplinary course. When exactly correct answers eluded us, I encouraged team appeals and let the students provide cohesive arguments for a particular choice.

For example, when we dealt with the topic of consumption and consumerism early in the semester, I included the following question in the RAP tests:

Which of the following is *not* an example of conspicuous consumption:
  a) Having individual stereos in each room of a five-room house
  b) Going into debt to have a party
  c) Buying a luxury vehicle even when you cannot afford it because it is cool to be seen in one

Debatable questions like these generated a great deal of discussion among the teams and some very well-thought-out arguments. When members of a team could not come to a consensus, they were asked to present their arguments and rationales for open discussion to the entire class. When facilitating these discussions, I took care to link arguments the students were making to the next topic we would be covering or to an upcoming application. Truth be told, some of these questions were really just meant to generate debate and to help teams learn how to grapple with questions that had no real answers or where all of the answer choices could be considered correct for different reasons. (Note: One must be cautious when using this approach and not include too many gray-area questions so that students don't lose faith in the RAP process or run out of time writing appeals.)

With the teams formed and working very well together through the RAP process, next I had to create a series of 4-S application exercises (see Chapter 1), that would dovetail into the teams' final project. It was important for me to generate a series of activities that would contribute to and build toward the final project of the semester. For example, one semester's final assignment for the term was the following:

> Thinking about the broad definitions and categories of "technology," identify a problem on the border that is caused by technology. Identify why the problem is a technological problem and present a technological solution for the same. Identify key elements of the problem and isolate the problem well. Present specific solutions to mitigate the problem. Prepare a poster presentation to take before the City Council and bring the poster on the day of presentation.

(The astute reader will notice that the project does not conform entirely to the recommended 4-S design—a matter that will be taken up shortly.)

With that final assignment as the backdrop for the semester, one unit that preceded it focused on energy needs versus waste and what we do with our waste. In preparation for this unit on waste, students had to read a description of federal constraints and requirements for transporting hazardous waste, and the RAP questions ensured they had learned the basics of these rules and regulations. Following this RAP, the application exercises involved students' figuring out how to transport low- and intermediate-level nuclear waste from Maine to the proposed disposal site in Sierra Blanca, which is 60 miles from El Paso. Each team was then provided a map of the United States and given 30 minutes to map a route from Maine to Sierra Blanca that conformed to the federal rules. At the 30-minute mark, the teams had to post their maps on the classroom walls and hand in brief explanations for their route. The students then performed a gallery walk around the room and graded their peers by giving them one to five stars. No scores could be repeated, and teams were required to be ready to justify their choice. The team with the maximum number of stars was awarded three extra points.

While the implementation of the 4-Ss worked well with these smaller application exercises that built toward the final project, there were distinct challenges with implementing all the 4-Ss in the larger final class projects like the one previously described.

Given the broad nature of the course, it was difficult to implement the specific choice component of the 4-S activities given that each team came up with very different problems they thought were significant. Furthermore, if students don't make a specific choice, it makes simultaneous reporting difficult. We needed to find a way for teams to unveil their projects at the same time.

To address these issues, we added an extra stage to the activity: Once teams had each identified a candidate problem for the final project, they reported it to the class, and then the entire class voted to select the problem the students all felt was important enough to focus on as an entire class. All teams then worked on the same problem and were required to produce their results in the form of a poster. These posters were taped up on the classroom walls, and students did a gallery walk of all teams' work. This was useful because it allowed the entire class to work on the same problem, and the teams were able to see the variety of solutions presented by each of the other teams (reported simultaneously). Teams then again voted on the best poster, and the winning team was awarded an extra 5 points as a peer reward.

In summary, the sequence looks like this:

1. The general context and the issue are shared with teams (significant problem, same problem).
2. Teams report on specific problems they feel merit the most attention, with their justifications (specific choice).
3. All teams vote on the significance of specific problems generated by the teams; teams are given 10 minutes to discuss and make their choice.
4. All teams then work on the selected problem over the course of several class sessions (same problem).
5. Teams unveil posters at the same time on the final presentation day (simultaneous reporting).
6. Teams vote on the best poster.
7. The winning team is awarded extra points.

We found overall that the students responded quite well to this, especially on the final day when they were able to see their peers' proposed solutions to the same problem they worked on themselves. It was especially interesting that there were more discussions among teams that came up with similar solutions, which they took as validation of their beliefs.

IMPACT OF TBL IMPLEMENTATION

Honestly, my first implementation of TBL in the summer of 2004 was not very successful. The students did not understand why we were using the RAPs, and they were disconcerted by the change in the course structure, which was different from what students who had taken the course before had described. Even though their overall team scores did show a marginal improvement over individual scores in the

RATs, more than half the teams performed poorly on team cohesion tests, in which students reported their perceptions of the working relations in their team.

Data analysis and focus groups revealed the causes of the issues that were remedied in the next implementation of TBL in the fall 2004 semester. Specifically, we increased the transparency of the team formation process by using the team tools in WebCT, which was the learning management system in use on the campus at the time (though WebCT has since been bought by Blackboard; see www.blackboard .com); provided the students with some advice from successful teams we'd gathered in previous classes; and introduced the practice RAP and peer evaluation process to familiarize students with the mechanics of TBL.

These interventions led to a much more successful experience, which was reflected in team cohesion scores that showed a dramatic shift in the levels of team members' equal contributions and their functioning well together (see Table 14.2). What was interesting to note was the number of students who now thought of their team members as their friends. I feel this transformation was because of the creation of strong working teams, which taught them to respect and value the diversity in teams and the role strong teams can play in helping them learn.

One thing that was immediately noticeable after the first few weeks was that we were able to shift from the lecture and interaction model to off-loading the content to a preprep mode, which allowed class time for exploring concepts and developing a conceptual understanding of the application of the materials. When needed, we gave minilectures to further explore topics that were of interest or to clarify any misconceptions. Typically teams that performed well always volunteered to share their insights with the rest of the class. This led to a minicompetition of sorts to try to be the team called on to explain its idea, which in turn drove overall performance. There always seemed to be between two and five teams in classes of 24 to 36 teams that underperformed in every class, but even those teams did not rate the TBL process negatively.

One of the biggest differences we noticed was that discussions among and between teams led to (at times) highly vociferous discussions on various topics, but the end result was that the students performed very well in critical thinking and ethical dilemma exercises, showing a great amount of thoughtfulness in their answers. The need to prep and come to class ready to participate led to a peer learning process that helped students, individually and as teams, to make connections between the diverse elements of the course. The only problem the teaching team (instructor and two TAs) faced was the need to cut off discussions that kept going even when the timers went off. In the challenge portions of the exercise, the vaguely worded questions led to deeper discussions, which again needed to be monitored for time because at one point there were 36 teams of five members each present in the class. Some of these issues were mitigated in later sections by breaking down the class into thirds, with each member of the teaching team taking charge of a third of the teams and facilitating the discussions in those groups.

Because of the varying age and experience of teams and the interdisciplinary nature of the class, we discovered that some team members who had taken broad courses

TABLE 14.2
Aggregated Team Cohesion Performance Data

Summer 2004

Total number teams = 21, Average team size = 5, N = 107			
	All the time	Most of the time	Más o menos (More or less)	Never
Do you feel your team members are cooperative?	14	31	44	28
Do you feel your team members work well together?	17	34	42	14
Do you feel your team members contribute equally to the work?	13	32	45	17
When we don't understand topics, we try to reason it out.	17	27	49	14
I think of my team members as my friends.	17	27	37	26

Fall 2004

Total number of teams = 23, Average team size = 5, N = 114			
	All the time	Most of the time	Más o menos (More or less)	Never
Do you feel your team members are cooperative?	61	34	12	7
Do you feel your team members work well together?	73	28	12	1
Do you feel your team members contribute equally to the work?	81	22	7	4
When we don't understand topics, we try to reason it out.	68	42	3	1
I think of my team members as my friends.	65	37	5	7

tended to want to take over teams. To address these issues we added a total of three peer reviews in the class. The team members were required to provide justification for their scores for each peer along with a number. We made the comments anonymous and shared them with the team members. We found that adding these extra peer evaluations helped the aggressive team members take a step back and make attempts to function with their teams. In an attempt to promote interteam learning, we also implemented a discussion board in which the most successful teams offered their ideas on why they were successful in the hope of providing some peer guidance to other teams. This strategy was successful for future classes where we were able to share success strategies from previous high-performing teams.

The success of TBL implementation in this course can best be illustrated by three examples. A student who had previously failed the course, enrolled in this section, and passed it with a B said:

> This is the first time and I hope not the only time that I was very glad that we were required to work in teams. To see that once we negotiated how we function, we could do anything as a team was very eye opening. I have learned not only how to learn, but how to learn with a team and importantly how having different people with different attitudes is actually a benefit! I hope all classes take such strategies.

Another student said:

> I really enjoyed the RAP. I never thought taking a quiz could be fun. But knowing that I could possibly look really dumb to my friends [This student is now referring to his team members as his friends.] made me want to study before I came to class.

The last example was from a colleague who approached me about showing him what I did in the class. He was going to teach an overflow section of the course and was asked by many of the students if he would be doing the "cool" things with groups like my class. My colleague was very intrigued that a student wanted to be involved in group work when instructors typically hear just the opposite from students.

SO YOU WANT TO IMPLEMENT TBL?
THINGS TO THINK ABOUT

TBL is a powerful collaborative learning technique to use in interdisciplinary classes, but it comes with its own set of unique challenges that must be carefully addressed from the beginning.

- I do not recommend using TBL in a class you have not taught before. For me and my TAs, the burden of teaching new content and employing TBL strategies became a case of doing too much at the same time. It takes time to develop good application activities, and we found that when we made major changes to the content, it was a little easier to make modifications and include just the iRAT-tRAT process along with peer evaluations in the first run of the course and then a full TBL implementation with application exercises in the next semester.

- We found the best strategy was to use backward design and make a visual map of the course goals and objectives, and map the assessments in line with the goals and objectives. Once this is done, map topics and activities according to the assessments. This lays out the course for you and will then help you write questions for the RATs.
- Map the interdisciplinary pieces of the course, and in turn map the knowledge from the outside disciplines that students may need to understand the topics and cope with the assignments. Provide students with a cheat sheet as a reminder of the broader aspects and analysis you are looking for.
- Always tell the students why you are implementing TBL, and the exact goals and objectives.
- Vary what you do in each class. It is very easy to get stuck in the rut of giving multiple-choice quizzes and then leading discussions. It is useful to include arguments, case studies, and build-your-own-quiz kind of ideas, in which students are asked to develop an exam or assignment they feel would help them measure what their peers learned about the topic under discussion. This really made the students think deeply about a topic to formulate an assignment that would serve as a measure of knowledge. We also found that providing concept maps and at times having students generate their own concept maps as an application activity was very engaging.
- Understand there may be fatigue over the course of the semester and plan for it. I have found that keeping work in Week 8 or 9 fun and light definitely helps the mood of the class. For example, when reading theorists I have asked teams to pick a theorist, brainstorm an ideal dinner menu based on what they can ascertain about the theorist's personality, and share the menu and defend their choices.

REFERENCES

Angelo, T. A., & Cross, P. K. (1993). *Classroom assessment techniques* (2nd ed.). San Francisco, CA: Jossey-Bass.

Biggs, J. B. (1999). *Teaching for quality learning at university: What the student does.* Philadelphia, PA: Society for Research Into Higher Education and Open University Press.

Haynes, C. (1998, March). *Interdisciplinary teaching and learning across the curriculum.* Paper presented at the meeting of the Association of American Colleges and Universities and the Association for Integrative Studies, Chicago, IL.

Jacobs, H. H. (1989). *Interdisciplinary curriculum: design and implementation.* Alexandria, VA: Association for Supervision and Curriculum Development.

McKeachie, W. J. (1999). *Teaching tips: Strategies, research, and theory for college and university teachers* (10th ed.). Boston, MA: Houghton Mifflin.

Michaelsen, L. K. (2004). Getting started with Team-Based Learning. In L. K. Michaelsen, A. B. Knight, and L. D. Fink (Eds.), *Team-Based Learning: A transformative use of small groups in college teaching.* Sterling, VA: Sylus.

Michaelsen, L., Knight, A., & Fink, L. (2004). *Team-Based Learning: A transformative use of small groups in college teaching.* Sterling, VA: Stylus.

Slavin, R. E. (1989). Research on cooperative learning: An international perspective. *Scandinavian Journal of Educational Research, 33*(4), 231–243.

Wiggins, G., & McTighe, J. (2001). What is backward design? In G. Wiggins and J. McTighe, *Understanding by Design* (pp. 7–19). Upper Saddle River, NJ: Merrill/Prentice Hall.

CHAPTER 15

Using Technology to Support Team-Based Learning

Karen L. Milligan

Milligan describes many creative uses of technology in a smaller Team-Based Learning class, from using PowerPoint for studycasts (Robinson and Walker, 2008) and the Readiness Assurance Process to using wikis for application exercises and peer evaluation. Of particular value to teachers in any field is how she describes her breakthrough realization that providing teams with several examples of something to evaluate or rate is an excellent design of application activities for material that has no clear right answers. "Exploring this strategy has provided me with the opportunity to think critically again, for you must think critically if you want your students to think critically."

Even for experienced teachers, adopting a new teaching strategy is a creative process that takes time and effort. It is a little like finding new clothes. Of course, before you look for new clothes you must first decide if you need them and what you need them for, a formal dinner or a trip to the gym. The need prompts you to begin a search, and once you know your needs you try on different items until you find one that fits. Finally you wear the item and make it yours by adapting it to your needs. For me, Team-Based Learning (TBL) became the garment I needed and the one I made fit.

THE NEED FOR A NEW STRATEGY

As a middle school teacher for half my teaching career, I knew and used many active and collaborative teaching strategies with K–12 students. When I began teaching future teachers, I wanted them to see the possibility for student learning these strategies provided. I learned that for future teachers to adopt a new teaching strategy they must not only read about it, but they must experience it as a student. They must see best practices in action if they are going to be able to move beyond the teaching methods they have experienced in their own K–12 education. What I needed was a collaborative strategy that worked as well for them as my collaborative teaching strategies had worked with K–12 students. I needed a strategy, a new garment if you will, that fit this situation. TBL became a way to focus my use of collaborative strategies for my adult students. While very effective and well-researched cooperative learning strategies (Johnson, Johnson, & Holubec, 1991) worked well for me with K–12 students, I had a hard time adapting them to college students. In the K–12 classroom I saw my students every day, and the majority of learning took place during class time. With college students, a greater amount of learning takes place outside class. Even though I tried to implement cooperative learning in ways to ensure the key elements of positive interdependence and individual accountability were present, it was much harder to tell how successful my attempts were. The procedures of TBL provided a way to ensure these key elements were present.

I found that for many of my students, breaking away from the common methods of lecture and recitation was not easy. The students who want to be teachers tend to be very successful students and learn effectively with lecture and recitation methods. It was not easy to convince them that collaborative strategies are effective because of the many negative experiences they had with group work and their success in working individually. TBL was the first strategy I read about that was designed explicitly for adult learners. I saw in TBL the potential to provide my students with a researched-based strategy that could convince them of the power of social learning.

GETTING A GOOD FIT

Once I had found something I felt met my needs, I had to make sure it fit. When teachers consider a new strategy, they must examine their beliefs about teaching and make sure that strategy fits those beliefs. When I began to use cooperative learning as a K–12 teacher, I knew that implementing collaborative strategies was not easy, but I also knew the rewards were great. I knew how much more I enjoyed teaching as I came to master cooperative learning approaches. I saw in TBL the potential to have that same excitement and enjoyment again working with preservice teachers. Exploring TBL has provided me with the opportunity to think critically about teaching again, for you must think critically if you want your students to think critically.

In addition to checking the fit to one's beliefs about teaching, the teacher must check the fit of the strategy to the content. The main focus of TBL is application of content. For education this is an easy fit because education is an applied discipline. Students in education courses regularly evaluate educational resources, write and teach lessons using a variety of methods, and learn ways for managing students and communicating with parents.

MAKING THE GARMENT YOUR OWN

I began the process of adopting TBL by selecting a single course from my area of speciality in my discipline, educational technology. I teach this course every semester with multiple graduate and undergraduate sections. A challenging feature of this course is that it is required of all students seeking teacher licensure, so the course has a mixture of majors from elementary education to music, art, and physical education to secondary students in many disciplines. Unlike many of the examples of TBL I read about, my educational technology course is smaller, with only about 24 students in each section. The course is also taught in a computer lab with stationary, networked computers, which limits the possibility of moving furniture for various TBL activities.

I found that obtaining the full power of TBL requires adopting all its key elements for the whole course. It is not as effective if only parts of the TBL model are used or used in only part of the course. The whole course must be designed with this in mind. I used the significant learning course design approach (Fink, 2003) to totally redesign this course. I found Fink's taxonomy of significant learning very helpful in really thinking about what I wanted to achieve in this course and about the ways I could make learning significant for my students. I think using Fink's method was crucial in helping me clarify the goals I wanted to achieve. Having clear goals makes the implementation of TBL more successful in a shorter period of time. Another reason I selected my educational technology course to begin with TBL is my belief about the role of technology in teaching. I see great potential in the use of technology as a tool for creating, communicating, and collaborating. Technology became a way for me to more effectively adapt the TBL strategy to my course. It also provided a model of best practice for my students, which again is crucial in education courses.

In the following sections, I describe the ways I have made TBL my own method through the use of technology. While you may not teach in a lab, the technology I describe can easily be adapted to any classroom if one student in each group has some type of Web-enabled device, either a laptop, a net book, or an iPad. In the examples that follow, a single computer per team was used, or students completed part of the work outside class on their own computer. I organize these ideas by the four practical pieces that make up the framework of TBL: strategically formed permanent teams, readiness assurance, application exercises, and peer evaluation.

STRATEGICALLY FORMED PERMANENT TEAMS
Introducing TBL

The first semester I used TBL I didn't have as much success as I had wanted. At the end of the semester when I surveyed the class about their feelings about TBL, I learned the students didn't see working with a team as powerful or valuable. While some students reported that TBL was better than their other collaborative experiences, some reported little or no difference. The first time I used TBL, I formed teams the same way I had in the past with cooperative learning groups. I had students fill out information cards about their licensure area and self-assessed technology skills. I didn't tell the students why I was asking for the information, which I used to form heterogeneous teams outside class. I only talked a little about why students would be working in teams and my method for creating teams when I announced the makeup of the teams in the next class.

After my first semester using TBL, I realized I needed a better way not only to form teams but also to get my students to see the value of and buy into TBL. I decided it was important to begin the class differently from the regular introductions and syllabus overview. I now begin the course with a group activity similar to the type of application problems they will be doing later. For this activity I form tempo-rary groups of four based on where the students are seated. I then show two YouTube videos that provide different viewpoints about the use of technology in teaching. After the students watch the videos I have them discuss in their groups which one they thought best describes the role of technology and to give three reasons why they selected the video they did. I have response cards with the numbers one and two for each group. Then I ask the groups to simultaneously display their cards. This is fol-lowed by a class discussion. While this is the first day, and it's not that easy to get the discussion going, it still provides a picture to the student of what class will be like. Students get the feel of TBL on the first day of class. I also give my own rationale for deciding to use TBL. From surveys taken at the end of the second semester, I found that more students saw the value of TBL. So now, I feel that sharing my own personal rationale, which includes the value of teamwork for 21st-century learners, is crucial to getting students to buy into TBL.

Forming Teams

After the team activity, we discuss what makes a good team using a sports team analogy: a football team with only quarterbacks would surely loose. I explain that I want to form teams with a diversity of learning styles and perspectives. I ask students to consider if good friends make good teammates, and we discuss the advantages and disadvantages of having close friends on teams. I lead the students to see that some-times good friends on the same team can split the team into subgroups. This discus-sion is followed by the first assignment in which the students are directed to study the syllabus for a test and go online and take the VARK (visual, auditory, read-write, kinesthetic) styles survey outside class (Fleming & Mills, 1992). This survey, taken in less than 10 minutes, provides a score that identifies the learner as visual, auditory, read-write, kinesthetic, or multimodal, for students who don't have a strong single learning type. (The questionnaire is available at www.vark-learn.com/english/page.asp? p = questionnaire.) I emphasize that this is the student's first opportunity to make a good impression on me and on the other students as the kind of team member he or she will be. Students bring a printed copy of the results of this survey to the next class period. On the second day of class I have students write on the top of the survey the names of anyone they are good friends with and their licensure area. I then collect the forms, beginning with students whose learning style survey results designated them as being multimodal. I create four teams of six students, so these are the first members of the teams. I continue gathering the forms according to each different learning style and placing students in teams based on learning style and licensure area. While I am creating the teams, the students already assigned to teams review the syllabus and come up with a list of questions. By the end of the period the teams have been formed, students introduce themselves, and they continue their discussion of the syllabus with their newly formed team.

I am convinced there is no perfect way to form teams when you don't really know your students. I have found using the VARK survey helpful in that the team-forming process is transparent. Students have reported on several surveys at the end of the semester that they like this way of forming teams. I still have teams that don't gel, but they are far fewer since I started using this method of team formation.

Developing the Readiness Assurance Test

Now the real work of team bonding begins, and it will happen slowly. The next assignment is to prepare for a test on the course syllabus, used to introduce the Readiness Assurance Process (RAP; see Chapter 1). This test, only for practice, lets the students experience the RAP without worrying about a grade. After the test we review the results, and every time I have done this so far, the team score is always higher. This has served to increase students' positive feelings about working on a team.

The heart of the RAP for the teacher is preparing the test and determining a process for giving feedback, and the more immediate the feedback is, the better. My first challenge with preparing readiness assurance tests (RATs) was developing appropriate multiple-choice questions. While I understood the importance of assessing and providing immediate feedback on students' mastery of key concepts, I was not confident I could reliably assess students' understanding using multiple choice-questions. However, this also meant I couldn't use the immediate feedback assessment technique (IF-AT) answer sheets to provide real-time feedback on the teams' choices. Thus, in addition to using some multiple-choice questions, I decided to use other objective question types, such as fill in the blank, matching, or listing, that I was more comfortable creating. However, I realized I would need to find a way to provide the immediate feedback on the team tests to be able to capitalize on the learning and team-development benefits the IF-ATs normally produce.

Providing Immediate Feedback

Since my classes are relatively small with only four teams, my first method of providing immediate feedback was to grade the team RATs (tRATs) in class as each team finished. Teams could then review their answers and determine if they wanted to appeal any questions. This worked adequately, but I still wanted something more immediate, something that would let them know how they were doing during the team RAT (tRAT) and have more impact then just waiting for me to return a graded paper. I considered using the testing features of the course management system but found this complicated and clunky. In addition, many students have reported their dislike of taking tests online. Robinson and Walker (2008) developed a TBL technology-based testing system, and I decided on something much simpler—a PowerPoint presentation. The first time I tried it I was so surprised by the reactions I began to hear. There were claps and high fives for right answers and groans for wrong ones. I also heard much better discussions and saw much more critical thinking after each question. My process for creating and implementing this procedure to give immediate feedback is as follows:

1. I created an iRAT answer PowerPoint template presentation that I used for each module, which made creating the presentation easier. For each question there were three slides.
   a. Slide one: copy of the question. I use black for the text on this screen.
   b. Slide two: a warning slide that asks students to make sure the team answer was marked and they all agreed on it. I learned I needed to add this slide the first time I tried it when one team accidently advanced to the answer slide before its members finished discussing the question.
   c. Slide three: the answer to the question. It is important to make the text on this slide another color besides black, the color I use on the original question slide; I usually use a bright color for this text. This way as I monitor the teams, it is easy to ensure that the team is not changing an answer. If I see a slide with a color other than black, and they are writing, then I immediately know they are cheating.
2. After creating the PowerPoint presentation, I save the file as a regular PowerPoint presentation and as a PowerPoint slideshow. When a user clicks on the file saved as a PowerPoint show the file opens in full-screen presentation mode so the user doesn't see all the slides laid out in a sidebar and cannot make changes to the presentation.
3. Each team has a team folder and a team flash drive for use during class. I copied the presentations to each flash drive, which I found to be much easier than trying to e-mail or post the presentation on the course management system.
4. I gave the iRAT in class as described in the RAP. When teams were ready for the tRAT they put up their writing instruments, got a blank copy of the test and a writing instrument of an unusual color from me, and opened up the team flash drive on a single computer.
5. The team then recorded its answer on the tRAT and then checked for the correct answer on the presentation. Teams mark the answer as correct or incorrect, but I also check their work after class and assign points.

This method was very successful and well liked by the students. It allowed me the freedom to use matching, fill-in-the-blank, true/false, and listing in addition to multiple-choice questions. It also provided immediate feedback to students for each question in much the same way the IF-AT forms do. Creating the presentations for each RAP was simply a matter of copying and pasting the questions from my word processing document to the presentation template and then copying the presentations on the team flash drive. It also freed me to move around the room and listen to students' conversations during the tRAT. I knew sometimes where the major misunderstandings were even before I graded the iRATs. Of course this method, like any testing situation, has opportunities for cheating. Diligence in monitoring each team and making sure the PowerPoint slide matches where students are on the test is crucial.

The next class period after the test, I returned the graded iRATs to the team folder. As soon as class begins, actually as soon as one person from the teams was in the classroom, the students recorded the grades in a spreadsheet that was stored on the team flash drive. This spreadsheet automatically calculated the average of the individual scores. Each team recorded its score on the team test on the white board as well as the average of the individual scores. I award bonus points to the teams with the highest team score and to the teams with the highest average of individual scores. I found this little extra competition was a way to motivate teams to develop team spirit and the desire to help each other do well.

Helping Students Prepare for the RAT

Another way technology supported the RAP was in helping students prepare for the test. The majority of students who take my course are freshmen or sophomores and have become so dependent on someone telling them what is important that reading even one chapter and selecting the important ideas is a new skill for many. To help them end their dependence on a teacher-created study guide, I implemented the studycast procedure developed by Robinson and Walker (2008). In this procedure each team member prepares a four-slide PowerPoint presentation, with each slide containing one of four ideas he or she thought were the most important of the reading. Students must e-mail the presentation to their team members by 5:00 p.m. on the day before class. Each team member must read over the ideas selected by their team members. Each team member who participates by sending his or her presentation to the team receives bonus points on the iRAT. In class each team is given 10 minutes to put together a team PowerPoint presentation based on the slides submitted by each member. There is no limit to the number of slides this presentation can contain. Then each team makes its presentation to the class with the requirement that each team member must speak during the presentation. After class the teams send the team PowerPoint to all members of the class. The RAT is taken in the next class period. While this method helped, it also required a lot of class time. After the first studycast and RAT, I give each team the opportunity to develop a way to help each member of the team prepare for the test using technology in some way outside class. Some teams made study guides in the form of PowerPoint presentations and posted them on the class learning management system (Blackboard). Some teams worked out ways to outline the text and post the outlines on the team wikis (described on p. 255). When I approve the method, each participating team member receives bonus points on the iRAT, and teams whose members all participate receive bonus points on the tRAT.

APPLICATION ACTIVITIES: THE IMPORTANCE OF 4-S PROBLEMS

I think for any new user of TBL, creating effective application activities is the most challenging part of the process. Since I had used cooperative projects in the past, my first attempt was to use the projects I had already created just as they were. This failed miserably. The activities I had used in the past were team projects done outside class that involved creating some sort of complex product. Predictably, students were simply splitting up the parts of the project, and each person was doing his or her own part with little discussion within the teams and even less between the teams. Thus, the assignments tended to create discord within the teams and did nothing to help build a class community.

I went back to the TBL literature and realized I was not creating application problems that followed the 4-S model: significant problem, same problem, specific choice, and simultaneous reporting (see Chapter 1). The activities I was using were significant problems and the same problem, but they did not require a specific choice and there was no simultaneous reporting of results between the teams. I looked for a way that technology could be used as a tool to improve these two aspects of my application activities. The technologies I found were learner response systems and wikis.

I began transforming my application problems by requiring them to have a specific choice. For me, the thing that made developing specific choice problems difficult was that I assumed that specific choice meant "right answer." In educational technology, unlike other disciplines that have problems with right answers, there is no one right way to use technology to support learning. So I found it difficult to develop problems that had only one right answer. To create problems with a specific choice, I decided to have students evaluate things or rate things based on the presence of certain elements. This idea seems so simple now, but when I first discovered it, it was a great breakthrough. It made application problems that fit my content much easier to develop. I now had a kind of template or structure I could vary and use in different ways.

USING TECHNOLOGY TO SUPPORT
TEAM APPLICATION PROBLEMS
Learner Response Systems

In the first team application problem I developed using this strategy, the class watched a short video of a teacher using technology. Each team then completed a ratings sheet handout to rate the use of technology with a score of one to five for each of several elements described in the text. Each team recorded its ranking and provided a rationale supporting its choice. After all the rankings were completed, each team reported its ranking for each element by holding up a card with the ranking number. While this was much better than before, there were still a few problems. Teams finished at different times, and their reasoning was inconsistent, with some teams having very good discussions with lots of critical thinking and some with very little. The next semester when I used this problem I introduced a learner response system, or clickers. We watched the same videos as before, only this time I put up one element on the interactive white board and gave the team a limited amount of time to come to a decision on the rating. The clicker system I use can display a timer on the white board. There is something about knowing the amount of time one has that keeps discussions more on track, thereby increasing the amount of critical thought. Each team had a single clicker. On signal the teams entered their responses. We could see the average rankings and team responses immediately, and then I randomly selected one student from each team to give the team's rationale for its choice. I repeated the process with the next element for the teams to rank. As we went through the elements, the quality and quantity of between-team discussions improved. We repeated the process for another video. After watching both videos and completing the ranking exercises with the clickers, I had each team select the video teammates thought was the best example of the use of technology. This time they recorded the rationale for their ranking on a handout as well as sharing their rationale in the class discussion. This provided me with a product to use for grading.

Using Wikis

After creating one application problem that had all four elements of good application problems, I wanted to develop more sophisticated ways for teams to simultaneously report more than just a single one-word response, such as an agree or disagree card or ranking an item by holding up a number card. Technology again provided a tool for improving application problems through the use of wikis. Wikis became more than just a way for simultaneously reporting in application problems; they became a tool for real collaboration for other parts of the course, a place for students to share their individual work for peer review.

What Is a Wiki?

A wiki is a Web 2.0 tool that allows multiple users to easily create Web pages and post discussions about those Web pages. It is a way for allowing anyone who knows how to use a text editor to create a website. Users can put text, images, files, and media on a page as easily as they can in a word processing file. Each wiki can have multiple pages, and viewers can move between pages using a navigation bar and links added to the text on the page. While a user can change the physical appearance of a wiki by adding colors and images, most wikis have these common features, which appear as tabs, such as the following, on each page.

- Page (or Read): This tab shows the text on the page. In some wikis this tab allows the user to print, back up, or add tags to a page.
- Discussion: This tab will bring up a box similar to an e-mail. The user gives a title to the post and then writes a message in the discussion box. Users can then reply to the post and create a threaded discussion.
- History: This tab shows who edited the page and when it was edited. The viewer can click on an item in the history and see by means of different colored text how the page has been changed.
- Edit: This tab brings up a simple editing function and allows the user to edit the page. A wiki owner can limit who can edit the page or leave it open for anyone to edit.

The largest wiki is, of course, Wikipedia, but there are more than just Wikipedia. Several wiki servers allow users to set up an account and create wikis for free; Wikispaces, Wetpaint, PBwiki, and Google Sites are the most popular. In addition, since wiki software is open source, several universities have set up their own wiki servers for use by their own students but are viewable by anyone with Internet access. In this course I used Wikispaces. While I do teach this course in a computer lab, wikis can also be used in any classroom that has a wireless connection. Only one member per team needs to bring a laptops to class. I find that at least a fourth of my students still bring their laptops to my class even though we have class in a computer lab.

Getting Started With Wikis

The hardest part of using wikis is setting them up. Wikis are relatively easy to learn to use, and most wiki servers provide good help pages and video tutorials. Introducing wikis will take about a class period. Explaining how to use a wiki is beyond the scope of this chapter; however, each of the wiki servers I have explored have excellent help features, and one can learn to use a wiki easily. I taught myself how to use wikis from help tutorials. I take the following steps to introduce wikis.

1. Before class I create a wiki for the course. I prepare an introduction to the course on the home page of the wiki, and I also make a page I call Teams. From this page I link to each section of my course and each team and individual wiki. At this point I create the page with just team names. The links must be added later after each individual and team have created their wikis. I also add a resource page with links to interesting Web resources I use in class and that students find themselves. I put a link to the course wiki in the course management system.
2. In class I explain what a wiki is and show students the course wiki. Since I have used wikis for several semesters, I have examples of course wikis from the past I

can also use. It is important to make sure students understand that anyone can see what is posted on a wiki. I ask them to only use their first name and to provide only limited personal information.

3. I review basic terminology, making sure they know they must create a user account and a wiki. (It is possible to create a user account without creating a wiki.) I explain that permissions for the wiki need to be set so that only members can edit pages, but anyone can post a comment in a discussion. I have found it is helpful to have students complete a simple checklist where they write their user name, password, the Wikispace name, and the URL that is created from that Wikispace name. It is important students do this before they create the wikis. I combine this checklist with an instruction sheet that walks students through the process with screen shots of the Wikispace page showing correct permission settings.

4. I assign each student to create an account and Wikispace outside class. I tell them some of what is required to include on the home page. They must also make a second page with their individual goal for the course. This helps students become self-directed learners. Throughout the semester they must demonstrate what actions they have taken toward meeting their individual goal and put that information on their individual wiki.

5. The following class session, after each student has created his or her own wiki, one team member is selected to create a wiki for the team. Each user account can have multiple wikis, and each team wiki has a link to each team member's wiki and the course wiki.

Once the wikis are created, each team can easily create a new page for each team application problem. Throughout the semester each team and individual continue to build on the wiki. It is important to make sure students back up their wiki. One assignment is that they turn in a copy of the backup of their wiki to me through the course management system. After the team wiki has been created, each team creates a page for each team application problem. Each application problem uses the wiki in a different way.

Examples of Application Problems Using Wikis

Using wikis has many advantages and has made it possible to extend the team application problems outside class. For example, in one application problem each individual team member is given a specific resource to evaluate before class. Students must post their evaluation on their individual wiki before class. During class each individual shares his or her review of the assigned resource. The team then selects the best one of these for a specific teaching situation (specific choice and simultaneous reporting thus being accomplished). On the team wiki students post a link to the selected resource and give two reasons they selected this resource as the best. After all selections have been posted, we have an in-class online discussion. Each team must review the wikis of the other teams in the class. If a team selected the same resource as best, it posts a discussion on the other teams' wiki congratulating that team on making the best choice and providing another reason why the selected resource is the best. If a team selected a different resource, it tries to persuade the other team that the resource it selected was a better resource. Teams can all speak at once in a way. In a class discussion each team must take turns saying why it has reached the decision; with wikis even this can happen simultaneously. Students today are much more comfortable communicating this way because it is more like Facebook and texting, which they use daily.

There is value in face-to-face and online discussions. As we progress throughout the semester both types of discussions improve in the amount of students' critical thinking and involvement. In another application problem, I used the wikis to extend the problem outside class. After our application problem using the 4-S method is completed in class, I require students to post a comment describing how their thinking has changed and what they have learned. I then require them to reply to another team member's reflection post.

Benefits of Using Wikis

By using team wikis in these various ways I have been able to gradually increase the complexity of the team application problems throughout the semester. This has also allowed me to have students participate in collaborative projects in addition to just the application problems with a single specific choice. Teams no longer have to find a time and place where they can all meet to work on a collaborative project. Because the editing of each page is tracked in the history tab and visible to any viewer, it is easier to tell what part each team member played in the creation of the project. It builds in accountability to team projects, which was missing in other collaborative projects I had done in the past.

An example of this type of collaborative project that is made possible by the skills learned in the team application projects takes place after the final module of the course. The teams participate in a mock grant competition that requires them to use all the information we have explored during the semester. They take the roles of a team of teachers at a single school of their choice, and they prepare a grant proposal in the form of a presentation. As a part of the proposal they develop a set of learning goals for their school and describe how they would use the grant money to purchase technology to meet those goals. Teams are graded on their technology selections and their presentation. To make the experience more realistic, in addition to the grade, I ask other faculty members to serve as judges, and the teams are awarded a finite number of bonus points based on the quality of the presentations. This assignment has been very successful. By this time of the semester the teams have really learned to work together well through the use of the RAP and application problems. They have the necessary skills to work collaboratively. The quality of work on these team collaborative projects is much better than before I used TBL. Students no longer just do their part of the project and piece it together at the last minute the way they did before. The projects show much more integration of ideas from different members and are much more creative.

The wikis have also been valuable collaboration tools in other ways. Most teams use the wikis to help each other prepare for the RATs with study guides they created. After each team application problem I give students an individual problem of some type. Students post some of these assignments on their individual wikis. Individual team members then review the work of another team member and suggest improvements before the final individual project is due. Several students reported they have used the resources and ideas from their own wikis and the wikis of other students in class in developing lessons they actually teach in practicum and student teaching placements. The students develop a sense of pride in their wikis and share them with other students and cooperating teachers they work with in public schools.

PEER EVALUATION

Using Wikis to Aid Team and Peer Evaluation

Wikis also play a role in peer evaluation. Twice during the semester teams evaluate their ability to work together. The first time is about a third of the way through the semester, after the first two modules have been completed. Each team creates a page on the team wiki in which teammates make a list of the qualities of a good team member. I use these qualities to develop the peer evaluations for the class. Another thing the team does is describe one thing team members do well as a team and one thing they need to improve on, and they develop a team improvement goal. About two thirds of the way through the semester the teams review their progress toward meeting the goal and determine another area of improvement or things they still need to do to reach their first goal.

Using Other Technology to Aid Peer Evaluation

Technology is also used in the individual peer evaluations. About midway through the semester, I provide the class with the individual peer evaluation instrument I created based on the qualities of a good team member that students posted on the team wikis. Because these qualities tend to remain the same semester after semester, I usually use the same peer evaluation form with minor changes. In class students are given a chance to make any suggestions or changes to the instrument. The evaluation instrument has a place for a rating and a place for comments. I prepare a word processing document with five copies of the evaluation instrument, one for each team member. I send this to each student via e-mail, and the students complete these outside class and bring a printed copy to class. I take the printed copies, sort them, and give each student the evaluations completed about him or her by his or her team members. I do this quickly in class, usually while students are taking an iRAT, and I do not look at the comments on the evaluation sheets. Students are required to turn in the printed copies as part of an assignment, so I only check to make sure that comments have been made and award points for completing the evaluations. At the end of the semester we convert this evaluation instrument to one with points. The class decides within a range that I set how many points the peer evaluation will count. As a part of the course final each student completes this peer evaluation and I average the scores given to each individual by his or her team members to count as part of the grade for the course.

CONCLUSION

These examples represent the ways that I have adapted TBL to fit my students, my own teaching style, and the content. While the process of adopting a new teaching style is not always easy and can be time intensive at first, I have found it extremely enjoyable. The key things that have made it more effective are the immediate feedback for each question during the RATs and the 4-S model for developing the application problems, especially the specific choice and simultaneous reporting elements. Using technology has helped me accomplish this. As I continue to grow in my use of TBL I will continue to search for ways to use technology, especially the many Web 2.0 tools, as a way to model the use of collaborative learning for my students.

Using TBL has given my students positive and powerful experiences working in teams. Students have not only grown in content but they have grown in their ability to collaborate. In the final project they talk about ways they can use the wikis in their future teaching. The ability to actually develop a vision for technology use and apply what they have learned about technology is so much more important to their future teaching than in the past, when they only learned how to use specific software tools, how to do effective Web searches, and how to evaluate Web resources. They now really see ways that technology can be used in teaching beyond a PowerPoint lecture. They see more authentic ways for their students to use technology, and they have developed a vision for how technology can be used beyond rewarding students for finishing work early or typing papers. For me, this should be the outcome of any educational technology course: the ability to grasp a vision of how teachers can use technology to support the learning of all students. I believe TBL has made this outcome a reality.

REFERENCES

Fink, L. C. (2003). *Creating significant learning experiences: An integrated approach to designing college courses.* San Francisco, CA: Jossey-Bass.

Fleming, N. D., & Mills, C. (1992). Not another inventory, rather a catalyst for reflection. *To Improve the Academy, 11,* 137.

Johnson, D. W., Johnson, R. T., & Holubec, E. J. (1991). *Cooperation in the classroom.* Edina, MN: Interaction Book Company.

Robinson, D. H., & Walker, J. D. (2008). Technological alternatives to paper-based components of team-based learning. In L. Michaelsen, M. Sweet, & D. Parmelee (Eds.), *Team-Based Learning: Small group learning's next big step* (pp. 79–85). San Francisco, CA: Jossey-Bass.

CHAPTER 16

Perspectives on Using Team-Based Learning to Teach Introductory U.S. Government Courses

Jessica L. Lavariega Monforti, Adam J. McGlynn,
and Melissa R. Michelson

In this chapter, the authors document their experience implementing the same course in several settings. Among their unique contributions to the volume are their menu of options a teacher could use to organize the same course in several different ways, the detail in describing how they go about orienting their students to the novel realities of the Team-Based Learning classroom, and their insightful descriptions about how to create effective readiness assurance test questions.

Introduction to U.S. Government courses are a staple of undergraduate general education programs throughout the United States. Students may be more apt to enroll in an introductory U.S. government course than another social science course to satisfy their general education requirements, as most will have taken a previous course in U.S. government during high school. This presents a significant challenge for the instructors of these courses because they are faced with a vast number of students who are taking their courses to satisfy a general education requirement and do not have a real interest in government and politics. Therefore, we must impart knowledge, but in addition we must also create enthusiasm about the course and the themes that need to be covered therein, a far more difficult chasm to cross. For us, like most faculty, the importance of our courses goes without saying. For political scientists, the success of our democracy is dependent on an educated and informed citizenry, and we believe our role as educators helps ensure that success. However, many of the students we meet are cynical about the decisions of government, and even more are largely apathetic and ignorant of the important role government plays in their everyday lives. Therefore, the fundamental challenge we face as political science professors is to educate our students in a manner that instills an appreciation of the role of government but also does justice to the myriad concepts we must teach to provide a full introduction to government and politics in the United States.

Another challenge faced by political science professors is that students often assume they already know the material. Politics is something all individuals are exposed to through media and culture. It is the topic of news headlines, water-cooler discussions, and dinner-table debates. Thus, students in an introductory course will often assume they do not need to do the assigned reading because they already know enough to pass the class. They know who the president of the United States is, they remember the *Schoolhouse Rock!* cartoon show on television about how a bill becomes a law, and they may even be regular viewers of the *Daily Show* with Jon Stewart. Thus, particularly for students who took a strong civics course in high school, it can be a challenge to get them to do the assigned readings.

There is an ongoing discussion regarding how to teach introductory U.S. government courses. Given the breadth of what we must cover, it is easy to fall victim to the problem of such superficial coverage of the course content that students walk away from the course internalizing little to none of the material. For example, Luger and Schueurman (1993) conducted a study of student knowledge of U.S. politics and government and concluded this about the students: "Even after completing a basic one semester course in American Government and Politics, they know very little about the historical development of such significant periods as the New Deal, the Great Society, and the Reagan Revolution" (p. 751). Several innovative methods to teach political science have been proposed, including simulations (Baranowski, 2006) and alternative textbooks and materials. In a particularly unorthodox adoption, a professor adopted Jon Stewart's *America: The Book* as his textbook for his introductory American government course (Teten, 2007).

As instructors of political science, we embraced Team-Based Learning (TBL) in an effort to bridge the enthusiasm gap among our students, to engage them with the course material, and facilitate their understanding of their own views on politics and government and what role they can play in the political process. We were particularly motivated to find alternative pedagogical methods, as Texas requires all students to complete six credits in U.S. and Texas government and politics; California requires a parallel set of credits in U.S. and California politics for all students of public universities. Thus, while some students choose a U.S. government course from a selection of other social science courses, most of our students had no choice and were mandated by the state to enroll in our courses. This placed even more demand on our talents as professors to create a positive and successful learning experience for our students. Our successes and failures with this endeavor are chronicled here. We advise any political science instructor to read the first chapter of this volume or Michaelsen, Knight, and Fink (2004) or Michaelsen, Sweet, and Parmelee (2008) for a more complete understanding of TBL because it may be difficult to follow the activities we describe here without the more comprehensive explanation in these works. In this chapter we discuss our experiences using TBL, provide examples of the application exercises we conducted in our courses, and present results from a student survey of the TBL experience.

GETTING STARTED WITH TBL: THE SYLLABUS, TEAM BUILDING, AND READINESS ASSURANCE

One of the daunting tasks for TBL in an introductory U.S. government course is dividing the course into the appropriate number of modules while including content that is sufficiently interconnected to make sense to students. For the traditional U.S. government course, we suggest no more than eight modules. Given the 15-week length in general of the standard semester, this leaves just under two weeks per module, and while some modules can be completed within a week, most will need at least this much time. Another approach is to divide the course into only four or five modules and make deeper connections among the various chapters; this may also be more appropriate for quarter-based systems. We struggled with what material to include in each module, and we encourage any political science instructor attempting to use TBL for the first time to develop a structure that plays to his or her strengths and interests. Table 16.1 shows eight hypothetical modular frameworks one could adopt. For example, instructors with a personal interest in issues of race and ethnicity might choose to spend more time on the civil rights and liberties aspect of U.S. politics. Instructors with more expertise in policymaking might emphasize the material on institutions and bureaucracy. Our point here is that, while it appears as if you need to shoehorn the course into your modules, you can cover the same breadth of material you would without using TBL while making minimal sacrifices in each content area. At the same time you can still enjoy the flexibility of developing modules that emphasize your areas of expertise.

TABLE 16.1
Hypothetical Modules for Introduction to U.S. Government TBL Courses

	Example 1	Example 2	Example 3
Module 1	Principles of U.S. government and the Constitution	Principles of U.S. government and the Constitution	Foundations: Principles of U.S. government, the Constitution, and federalism
Module 2	The judiciary and federalism	The judiciary and federalism	Elections, public opinion, and the media
Module 3	Civil rights and civil liberties	Civil rights	Political parties and interest groups
Module 4	Elections, public opinion	Civil liberties	Institutions (Congress, the presidency, the judiciary)
Module 5	Political parties, interest groups, and the media	Elections, public opinion, and the media	Public policy
Module 6	Congress	Political parties and interest groups	
Module 7	The president and the bureaucracy	Congress	
Module 8	Public policy	The president and the bureaucracy	

In our experience with building teams for the course, we have found that few students possess the requisite background to create significant imbalances between each team's endowment of skills and knowledge. While it is possible to analyze student transcripts prior to going into the class and creating teams, our experience did not find that to be necessary. One good strategy is simply to divide students randomly; alternatively, one might try to balance the skill levels of the teams with some quick queries about previous U.S. government courses in high school or at other institutions. At institutions with more traditional (i.e., just out of high school) students, the random method is generally sufficient. At institutions with more returning students or with a greater diversity of life experiences (and thus prior knowledge of U.S. politics), more conscious balancing may be necessary. Generally, as with other TBL classes, teams of five to seven students are best.

Depending on the time available, you could assign an ice-breaker activity to ensure that introductions go beyond each member's simply stating his or her name and major. For example, you might have students tell the others something unusual or surprising about themselves, or assign a team-building activity such as completing a jigsaw puzzle (we favor the 100-piece U.S. presidents puzzle by Crocodile Creek) or a politically themed crossword puzzle from the *New York Times* archive, with teams competing to be the first to finish. The faculty member can then circulate around the teams, meeting students individually.

During the first week we had students complete an ungraded Readiness Assurance Process (RAP; see Chapter 1), either on TBL or on something similarly general, such as the assigned summer reading for the university (or for first-year students). The purpose here is twofold: it gets them to understand the collaborative process of TBL as well as its goals and it gives them experience completing individual and team Readiness Assurance Tests (iRATs and tRATs).

The final step in the introduction process is to allow the students to set the weights for each graded activity in the course (see the TBL Collaborative [TBLC] website for details at www.teambasedlearning.org). We found it helpful in most cases to assign a range (e.g., 10%–50%) for each component of the course, rather than allowing students complete freedom. Also, particularly when teaching first-year students, we believe it is important to help students think through the implications of their initial choices. Sure, weighting peer evaluations heavily seems like a great way to make an easy class ("We'll just promise to all give each other good evaluations."), but do they really want to have to give good evaluations to folks who don't do their fair share? Making the final exam worth very little might seem like a great way to reduce the stress of finals week, but isn't it better to get that last-minute chance to raise your course grade if you haven't done so well on the other course components? And while negotiations among the team representatives were sometimes raucous, with repeated requests by other students for those representatives to come back to the team for further discussions and instructions, this was a crucial aspect of the course that significantly increased student acceptance of TBL and created almost instant team cohesion.

We begin each module as prescribed by TBL methodology with the RAP, which includes an iRAT followed by a tRAT. We attempt to keep these assessments to 15 questions. We find that 10-question assessments for modules with a single focus, such as the judiciary, are adequate in assessing whether students read the assigned material from the textbook and ascertain the main concepts of the assigned chapters, satisfying our readiness assurance criteria. In analyzing the number of questions assigned, we recognized that student performance dropped when the iRATs and tRATs exceeded 15 questions. We strongly suggest reviewing the materials on the TBLC website regarding multiple-choice question composition. While many texts come with assessment materials, we urge you to avoid questions that are simple recall questions. For example, avoid asking questions regarding the length of a term for a senator or how old one must be to serve as president. For the tRAT to be a successful part of the RAP, questions need to provoke thought and team debate. While some may be skeptical about the ability of multiple-choice questions to do this, questions focusing on concepts and not simply dates and facts can yield a quality assessment method that creates satisfactory contemplation. Especially useful are questions that require students to apply the material they have learned. For example, you could ask what type of federalism is best demonstrated by the No Child Left Behind Act (provided, of course, their readings covered these topics). This would necessitate student discussion over the facets of each type of federalism in choosing a response. In another example, questioning which constitutional principles formed the basis of a decision in any number of Supreme Court cases we cover in our courses is an effective type of question to employ as well. If students were questioned about the constitutional principles that formed the basis of *McCulloch v. Maryland* or *Mapp v. Ohio*, it would require an understanding of the necessary and proper clause and the Fourth Amendment. Further, this type of question would require teams to discuss the meaning of each constitutional principle you provide in your answer choices and will promote greater understanding of the material rather than simple memorization of facts. This type of engagement with the material is the most beneficial aspect of the RAP.

Upon completion of the tRAT, we tried two different methods for the appeal process. In the first, students had 24 hours to appeal in writing individual questions they got wrong. In the appeal, the team members had to demonstrate they understood the concepts but missed the answer anyway because a question was ambiguous or the reading either failed to support the designated correct answer or supported an alternative correct answer. This is one instance where we observed collective action problems. There were instances where the appeals were not collaborative team efforts, and it was obvious that one or two team members took it upon themselves to appeal tRAT questions. If this problem becomes chronic, you can question the team members, but we found the peer evaluation process served to hold team members accountable in these instances. The second method required appeals to be completed in class, immediately after the tRATs were returned. This was more successful, as it often led to all members of a team simultaneously searching through their textbooks ("I know I read that somewhere!") in an attempt to successfully earn more points. Again, the collaborative process sometimes broke down, but because all team members were present, free riders were more visible and thus less common. Therefore, if time allows, we suggest adopting the in-class appeals process.

Before completing our discussion of the RAP, we want to make one more point. The substantial loss of lecturing time in TBL means that the choice of a textbook is vital to maintaining control of the course. We urge you to examine the textbooks that are available on the market and choose the one that includes the content you find most important and requires a minimum of supplementary readings. In addition, you should use a combination of materials that will also be considered more user friendly, given the reading proficiency of your student population. Because the onus is on the students as individuals and team members to prepare for the iRATs and tRATs, the textbook and other materials must be able to impart the requisite knowledge to your students in an easily accessible manner.

Upon conclusion of the RAP, we provided differing amounts of lectures based on the feedback we received about student learning from the iRATs and tRATs. We included at least a small lecture during every unit to emphasize concepts the textbook did not cover or did not discuss in sufficient depth. Students had mixed reactions to the lectures. Some students, mainly those who enjoyed TBL, felt the lectures were unnecessary and disrupted the student-centered learning process of TBL. However, other students who liked or disliked TBL appreciated the lectures. In the feedback we received, it appeared as if the lectures provided a security blanket or at least an affirmation of what the students had learned in the textbook. It also helped that the small lectures we gave were often focused on a limited number of concepts from within each course module, allowing us to use colorful examples and stories to get our point across in comparison to the traditional 50-minute-plus lectures where as professors we are fighting the clock to cover as much as possible. In sum, we believe that some lecturing, of about 15 to 30 minutes for each module, is ideal for this type of course. Again, given that our students tended to be first-year freshmen with little or no background in political science, and the complexity of some of the introductory material, this is often simply the best and most effective method. However, as the use of the RAPs increased student preparation and reading, lectures became shorter and more participatory, and thus more enjoyable and productive for all.

APPLICATION ACTIVITIES AND PEER EVALUATION

More than any other aspect of TBL, we found the application activities to be the most rewarding part of the course because they created an extremely high level of student engagement. As we discuss shortly, the negative feedback team members did receive in the peer evaluations were from team members who did not productively contribute to the tRATs; it was not for lack of participation in the application activities. In part, this is probably a result of the fact that even students who did not complete the readings learned enough from the iRAT and tRAT to make substantive contributions during application activities.

While all the application activities we use are designed to employ the 4-Ss of TBL: significant problem from real life, same problem for all the groups, specific choice to answer a very specific question, and simultaneous reporting from all the groups (see

Chapter 1), the application exercises we used can be categorized in two ways. One type of activity is based on proposing a discussion question and giving teams anywhere from two to five answer options to choose from. The teams then discuss the question and come to a consensus. As described in the TBL literature, we then require the teams to work on the same problem and simultaneously provide their team responses to ensure that peer pressure does not lead any team to change its response if their team is in the minority. We use the low-tech method of giving each team laminated letter cards (A through E) to use for a simultaneous report of their decision. Once the teams' choices have been made public, we conduct a class discussion for the teams to defend their positions. It is important to get all the teams to participate and, insofar as possible, not let them off the hook by their saying something like, "We agree with Team 3." One way to counter this tendency is to roam the classroom while the activity is going on and prod the teams to share the interesting ideas you hear while walking through the classroom.

One example of the type of activity we use involves the following questions:

Based on the reading materials, decide as a group which of these demographic categories is most important in politics. Be prepared to explain why you think your group's response is best:
   a. race and ethnicity
   b. religion
   c. gender
   d. sexual orientation
   e. family structure

Then repeat that process with the following demographic categories:
   a. education
   b. wealth and income
   c. social class
   d. age
   e. region

This activity works well in that it forces students to grapple with a key concept of politics and government—how race, ethnicity, and other demographic factors work to influence political opinions and behavior—a problem that remains a focus of many scholars in the field. Other questions we pose to students using this procedure concern the legality of same-sex marriage bans, whether term limits should be applied to the U.S. Congress, and whether states' elected political leaders should continue controlling the redistricting process. All these topics are timely and controversial and meet the significance criterion of the 4-Ss. While these questions could be posed requiring yes or no answers, we found it most fruitful to pose different policy options for each question because it forces students to discuss the merits of each proposal and the question in general in more depth. This is turn leads to a more lively discussion in which teams have to defend their choices.

The second type of activity involves having teams create a chart or diagram usually to identify causes and propose solutions to specific problems. For example, one application exercise of this type involves asking teams to identify what they believe are the three most important causes of low voter turnout in the United States and to propose three solutions that address these causes. We distributed easel paper and markers to the teams and had them create a diagram or flow chart (we encourage them to be creative) of the causes and solutions. From there, we post their creations on the walls around the classroom. The teams then conduct a gallery walk and vote for the team they feel best identified the main factors causing low voter turnout and proposed the best solutions. To make things more interesting we offer extra credit points to the team whose proposal receives the most votes. While this may sound childish for an undergraduate course, the teams are always incredibly focused and engaged in this type of application activity. We are met with giddiness from our students when they see us walk in with the easel paper and markers. This task proves worthwhile as students become well acquainted with the voter registration and election processes in the United States, and many begin to examine their own voting calculus as well as those of their families as they struggle to come up with ways to improve voter participation. The activity concluded with a spirited discussion among the teams on voting holidays, weekend voting, and casting ballots by mail or online.

Along these same lines, we try to make sure the team activities are fun as well as educational. For example, we supplement the activity about increasing voter turnout with an assignment to create a 30- or 60-second television commercial (filmed using a student's smartphone and posted on YouTube), and again students vote for the best video. In November 2010, after these videos were brought to the attention of a local community television station, one of the videos was broadcast live on the night of the election. As one might imagine, this was very exciting for the students (and much appreciated by the school administration for increasing campus visibility). It also led nicely into a discussion of similar get-out-the-vote campaigns, such as those by the Rock the Vote organization.

In another activity, we ask teams to create their own party platforms that must include a set of policy areas. We find this to be a successful activity because it demonstrates to students the inherent difficulty of coming to a resolution on the most pressing national issues. Although we offer a list of 10–15 policy areas, most groups were able to come to an agreement on only a handful of issues, and even then many of their platform planks are rather generic despite our request to be as specific as possible. Teams vote for the best platform and discuss the merits of each team's platform. Further, when creating their platforms, students are asked to choose a party mascot (like the Democratic Donkey and the Republican Elephant) and explain their choice. This invariably raises questions about why the donkey and elephant are symbols of the major political parties and leads to productive discussions of symbolism and slogans in politics.

Often, our planned activities take a detour in response to student interest. For example, when discussing public opinion and the power of the wording of questions, one group of California students was skeptical that wording could have such dramatic effects as claimed in the text. Led by the instructor, the students designed two alternative wordings of a question regarding support for a proposition on the upcoming ballot about legalizing marijuana. Then every student in the class was asked to survey 10 people, using each form of the question five times. When they brought back the responses the next week, the exercise clearly illustrated the phenomenon—the result was that students learned the material but were also empowered to take charge of their own course.

Table 16.2 provides examples of some of the team application exercises we have adopted in our courses. Many of them have proven tremendously successful in requiring students to analyze the material from their textbooks and from original documents. For example, in proposing a new constitutional amendment, the students read the Constitution and discuss its strengths and weaknesses, coalescing around one proposed amendment the team could defend. In our class debates where we ask to students to decide if the president's powers over foreign affairs and the military should be limited, students read Article II of the Constitution, and examine the War Powers Act, culminating in a position on whether there should be greater checks on the president's powers as commander in chief. The federalism activities create a vibrant discussion on the Full Faith and Credit Clause, the 14th Amendment, and the legality of same-sex marriage in general. It is often interesting to see how the

TABLE 16.2
Team Application Exercise Examples

Module/Topic	Application Activity
Constitution	Propose and defend a constitutional amendment.
Federalism	Debate the Full Faith and Credit Clause and the 14th Amendment as they apply to same-sex marriage and the Defense of Marriage Act.
The judiciary	Propose reforms to the judicial nomination process and debate life tenure for federal judges.
Political parties	Create a party platform (with party mascot).
Elections	Create a proposal to increase voter turnout in the United States (with commercial).
Civil rights/liberties	Debating de facto segregation in public schools; create a flow chart for how you would respond to being discriminated against.
Congress	Debate term limits and redistricting.
The presidency	Debate signing statements and presidential power in foreign affairs.
Public opinion/behavior	Create a diagram comparing and contrasting liberalism and conservatism; create a survey.

teams negotiate this topic based on their new knowledge of the Constitution and their personal beliefs.

Overall, we find the most successful application activities are those in which class members have to evaluate their own beliefs, political ideas, and behavior juxtaposed with the beliefs and ideas of their teammates and what they are learning in the course. In many cases, the resulting discussions highlight and dispel many of the common misconceptions about U.S. government and politics. While not all activities are able to directly address each team member's personal politics, we find the students still enjoy expressing their opinions on concepts that are more abstract to them (e.g., signing statements and redistricting). We continue to examine and test new application exercises because we feel these create more student engagement than any other element of TBL.

PROMOTING PEER ACCOUNTABILITY

At two points in the semester students complete peer evaluations of their team members. There is a variety of different evaluation formats you can adopt, and again we encourage you to do your own research on the TBLC website or by reading the peer evaluation discussions in Michaelsen et al. (2004), Michaelsen et al. (2008), or Chapter 3 of this volume. We use a peer evaluation form that requires students to identify what they appreciated about each team member's presence on the team and what they would ask each team member to do differently. We feel this avoids any negative stigma associated with adopting a request for strengths and weaknesses. On some evaluation forms, we also ask each student to divide 100 points among their team members (including themselves) based on each person's performance. We use this strategy rather than asking that each student be given a grade between 0 and 100 because we feel it promotes more thought in assigning scores, whereas a 0 to 100 score might result in students giving each team member a 95 or a 100 and not engage in any type of comparative analysis. In other courses, we use a version of the peer evaluation form that asks for ratings on 12 behaviors (e.g., was on time for class, was respectful of others' opinions), with possible rankings of never, sometimes, often, and always. We find these to be effective in preventing students from giving each other perfect peer evaluations, as it was not so clearly linked to a number (despite the simultaneous distribution of a sheet explaining how the rankings would be used to calculate grades). Regardless of which form we use, team members are able to review an anonymous version of the feedback they received and their scores so they could improve their performance for the final peer evaluation at the end of the semester.

CONCLUDING COMMENTS ON TBL IN INTRODUCTORY U.S. GOVERNMENT COURSES

Based on our observations we found that TBL appeared to increase student engagement. This is essential in a required course like Introduction to U.S. Politics or Introduction to Government, where levels of student interest and enthusiasm are often low. However, we found that TBL had a limited impact on student outcomes in terms of final grades. As expected, we found a significant difference between student performance on the iRATs and tRATs of anywhere from 10 to 20 points on average. As we mentioned in the beginning of this chapter, our highest hope in adopting TBL was to combat student apathy, and we hoped the RAP and peer evaluation process would motivate students to come to class prepared and ready to participate. While some students were positively affected by our approach, despite our efforts a number of students did not embrace the RAP. Generally, the grades had been weighted to focus more on team performance than individual RAT scores, and teams relied heavily on their better-prepared members to do well on the tRATs. Specifically, rather than engaging in a peer teaching and learning process during the tRATs, some students simply asked the strongest student in their group how he or she answered a question on the iRAT without much enthusiasm for trying to understand why a response was correct. We circulated among the groups and urged students to explain their answers as opposed to just giving an answer to correct this problem. To obtain a more concrete assessment of these observations, we surveyed two of our classes at the University of Texas-Pan American to ascertain the students' perspectives on TBL. Table 16.3 shows a series of evaluative statements of TBL students were asked to respond to with one of four options: strongly agree, agree, disagree, strongly disagree.

For the two classes we assessed, the overwhelming majority of students who responded to the survey reacted positively in their assessment of TBL. The responses from each class are also highly correlated, leading us to believe these results provide a reliable and valid assessment of TBL. The results show the students felt the tRATs and application exercises enhanced their opportunity to engage in thoughtful discussion and debate. The students also responded they felt more engaged in the course and would look forward to taking another TBL course. These results also corroborate our assessment that TBL did not yield an environment in which all students came to class prepared despite the RAP, which requires a higher level of student responsibility and preparedness than other pedagogical approaches. About 15% of those who responded did not claim to read their textbooks more than in other introductory courses, and about 25% of students did not believe the peer evaluations were effective in ensuring everyone came to class prepared. The one concern with our data is that even though students were offered extra credit for the completion of the survey, our response rates were 60% and 75% for the two classes. The surveys were distributed on the day of the final exam, so some students may have chosen not to participate because of lack of time in completing the exam or a simple desire to finish the test and go on summer vacation. Of course, the possibility remains that the students who did not participate would have negative evaluations of the course, but given the consistency of responses across the two classes, we find it unlikely that full participation in the survey would significantly alter the positive feedback we received on TBL.

In summary, we believe TBL is a worthwhile pedagogical method to employ in introductory U.S. government classes. It will not completely solve the problem of

TABLE 16.3
Percentage of Students Responding "Agree" or "Strongly Agree" in Evaluative Statements of TBL

Statement/Question	Class A*	Class B**
The usage of the tRAT assessments promoted thoughtful discussion and debate.	97.2	97.8
The iRAT assessments required me to read the course textbook more than I would in other introductory or general education courses.	85.7	84.1
The peer assessment procedure used in this course was an effective method to ensure all team members participated in tRATs and application exercises.	77.1	75.6
The application exercises enhanced my ability to learn the course material by creating interactive opportunities to discuss, analyze, and demonstrate my team's understanding of course content.	91.4	93.2
I would welcome the opportunity to take another course that used the TBL method.	94.6	95.6
Overall, I felt more engaged in this course because of TBL than in other traditional lecture courses I've taken.	91.4	97.8
I think I have learned more course content in this class because of TBL.	85.7	93.3

Note: * 60% response rate, ** 75% response rate.

student apathy, and it is not a panacea for students' coming to class unprepared, but there are significant advantages to adopting TBL. One is that having around 85% of the students complete preclass reading assignments is a vast improvement over what normally happens. In addition, most students enjoy the course, and, most importantly, a high percentage engage in thoughtful discussion and debate about the material, and many feel they learn more than they have in other introductory courses, especially those who rely mainly on the instructor lecturing. Harry and Rosemary Wong (2009), who have written extensively on teaching effectiveness, explain that in this type of traditional classroom, the teachers are doing most of the work and thus are doing most of the learning. This means that if a professor relies solely on lecturing, students are allowed to remain passive and thus will be limited in what they learn. While this statement applies largely to K–12 education, and a place and a need for lecturing in higher education remains, we believe TBL presents a unique opportunity for students to do more engaging work in U.S. government courses. If our goal is to impart to our students an appreciation of the importance of being an active citizen in our democracy, we believe the level of student engagement that comes from TBL can be a tremendous aid in this endeavor.

REFERENCES

Baranowski, M. (2006). Single session simulations: The effectiveness of short congressional simulations in introductory American government classes. *Journal of Political Science Education*, *2*(1), 33–49.

Luger, S., and Schueurman, W. (1993). Teaching American government. *PS: Political Science and Politics*, *26*(4), 749–753.

Michaelsen, L. K., Knight, A. B., & Fink, L. D. (Eds.) (2004). *Team-Based Learning: A transformative use of small groups in college teaching*. Sterling, VA: Stylus.

Michaelsen, L. K., Sweet, M., & Parmelee, D. X. (Eds.). (2008). Team-Based Learning: Small group learning's next big step. *New Directions for Teaching and Learning*, *116*, 1–99.

Teten, R. L. (2007, August). *Reaching the unreachable: Using Jon Stewart's* America: The Book *as a textbook for introductory level classes to American politics*. Panel conducted at the meeting of the American Political Science Association, Chicago, IL.

Wong, H. K., & Wong R. T. (2009). *The first days of school: how to be an effective teacher*. Mountain View, CA: Harry K. Wong Publications.

CHAPTER 17

Theatre Is a Collaborative Art

Using Team-Based Learning in Arts General Education

Ronnie Chamberlain

As discussed in the first chapter, backward design is not necessarily an easy process. It can be difficult to make the transition from thinking about content to thinking in terms of what you want your students to be able to do. In situations like this, models can be extremely helpful, and in this chapter Chamberlain presents a substantial list of specific learning goals and subgoals alongside the activities used to pursue those goals. In the social sciences and humanities, we recognize that complex activities involving people (like teaching) do not change in a digital manner: Instructional change is most often an evolution of practice in which the teacher learns at every turn. Therefore, another strength of this chapter is the activities Chamberlain describes she is still working on to evolve into best practices for student learning.

Theatre is a collaborative art; the minds of a variety of artists combine to create a production of one play, a single instance at a time.[1] Each production is an adventure with new boundaries, challenges, and team members, existing for a limited amount of time before it is deconstructed. Unlike sculpture or creative writing, theatre is not recorded or hung in a gallery. It is alive; it feeds on the interactions between actors and audience and sometimes even on the interactions among audience members: Consider the roll of contagious laugher or a crowd full of tear-filled eyes, sharing an experience lasting only a few hours.

In a production team, each artist is valued for the unique expertise he or she brings from fields such as directing, stage management, or design. Each comes to the table having done the preparation and research demanded by the show at hand. Ranging in size from a handful to a hundred, these artists must solve problems and make decisions, often challenging each other in pursuit of the best possible creation. This is the nature of working in theatre, and I believe my passion for it is rooted in the idea of partnership with other artists.

I began my teaching career in theatre as a graduate student in 2005, leading small hands-on courses like Stage Makeup and Costume Construction for theatre majors.

In these courses, I would lecture and demonstrate makeup or sewing techniques to 10–20 students, then the students would work on applying the techniques while I gave them one-on-one coaching and feedback to help develop their skills. In 2007, I took a faculty position at the University of Central Missouri (UCM) in which half my teaching course load consisted of larger general education classes, and I quickly became dissatisfied with the traditional lecture approach. In this chapter, I describe the class in which I finally admitted to that dissatisfaction, why I decided to try Team-Based Learning (TBL), and the discoveries I made in the process. Finally, I describe how I adapted some TBL practices to fit the creative nature of my discipline.

THEATRE'S PLACE IN A COLLEGIATE LIBERAL ARTS EDUCATION

Theatre by nature should be seen or done, not just read about in a book. Therefore, when Introduction to Theatre became a course students at UCM could take to satisfy a general education requirement, we reexamined it with an eye toward making it more interactive and hands on. We changed the name to Discovering Theatre and challenged ourselves as instructors to make the experience of the course more of a functional journey rather than a theoretical lecture on art. Discovering Theatre is now an introductory examination of theatre as a living and viable artistic medium. The course develops a basic understanding of theatre in many areas: the purpose of theatre; the role of the audience; dramatic literature and structure; the roles of actors, directors, designers, and technicians; and the historical perspective.

Following the best practices of backward design (as described in Chapter 1), we specified the following learning goals.

1. The student should be able to communicate and collaborate effectively in the interactive and creative process of theatre.
   a. Identify the common elements and vocabulary of theatre as well as the interaction of these elements
   b. Work effectively in a team, interacting productively with individuals from diverse areas of knowledge and skill
   c. Improve professional communication skills
2. In preparation for careers with a global society, students should demonstrate a working knowledge of the historical, cultural, and stylistic dimension of drama and theatre.
   a. Identify and describe the major theatrical development in various historical periods
   b. Relate the theatre and dramatic arts to social, political, and religious history of each theatrical period
   c. Recognize the structure, style, substance, language, and historical importance of a plays that are representative of the development of theatre and drama in world cultures

  d. Place works of theatre in historical and stylistic contexts

  e. Identify theatre as viable art form for entertainment and social value

3. Students should be able to use critical thinking skills to analyze and interpret a script for the purpose of developing a concept and systematic plan for the production of the play.

  a. State a theme and explain how the theme ties together the major events and actions of the play

  b. Analyze each character, his or her character's relationships to other characters, the plot, and the overall theme

  c. Understand and implement the process of play production on a microscale

4. Students should be able to form, communicate, and defend value judgments about the quality and aesthetics in works of theatre.

  a. Apply performance productions analysis to assess theatrical works of arts

  b. Evaluate current critical thinking about theatre and other arts

  c. Communicate clearly in written and oral form a response to observed theatrical productions

  d. Critique constructively the creative works of peers

  e. Apply development aesthetic values by attending academic and professional theatre and arts events

SEEKING CHANGE IN THE CLASSROOM DYNAMIC

Clarifying the learning goals for a course is an excellent start, but how one pursues those goals in the classroom makes all the difference. When I taught using the traditional lecture format, I looked out across the glassy eyes of my students, who were removed from the material. They listened and took notes but only as a hoop to jump through on the way toward a diploma. I found myself lecturing from the assigned reading while students furiously took notes to make up for not doing the reading themselves. Discussions are extremely difficult to facilitate when only 5 out of 40 students have read the material. I quickly tired of students begging me to post my lectures online so they wouldn't even need to take notes.

I came to the realization that lecturing from the assigned readings students were supposed to have already read was doing them no favors. As a student myself, I had often asked why I needed to come to class when all the teacher does is lecture word for word from the textbook. I can read the textbook. I had wanted something more than what I could accomplish on my own, so I became motivated to explore new teaching methods and find ways to engage my students in the context of the material. After all, I was lecturing on the creative process of performing arts, yet students had no opportunities to creatively interact with the material.

Reading about an artist's process does not have the same experiential and instructional value as attempting to live a simplified version of the process to better understand it. We can teach appreciation for the arts through study and observation, but real understanding comes when you have walked in another person shoes and moved the students' experience of the material off the page and onto the stage.

TBL IN MY CLASSROOM: SOME SPECIFICS

TBL enabled me to stop lecturing and start sharing the creative process of theatre. In this section, I briefly describe how I begin the semester with a team-building exercise in democracy, and then provide a handful of the specific application exercises I use to bring teams into full contact with the course material.

If we want students to break out of the passive learning format of the traditional lecture classroom, we have to give them some reason to get active and stimulate some sense of responsibility for what is happening in the classroom. To me, this makes the classroom a much more democratic place.

Student responsibility starts with coming to class prepared. Students are expected to have completed all the assigned reading and come to class ready to apply the material. To encourage this preparation, we begin each unit with the Readiness Assurance Process (RAP; see Chapter 1).

In every Discovering Theatre class I teach, grades are broken down into individual and team components. The individual grade is composed of individual readiness assurance tests (iRATs), exams, and written play critiques. The team grade is made up of team readiness assurance tests (tRATs), group assignments, and the final team production assignment. At the beginning of the course, I allow students to discuss, lobby, and eventually reach a consensus on how these two grade components will be weighted. I find this is a very important step in getting the entire classroom on board with TBL. This is the students' first opportunity as a team to communicate, bargain, and compromise first among themselves and then with other teams to determine the values for their weighted grade.

As a class my students can decide how much each of the components will be worth in their final grade by using a grade weight setting exercise (see Michaelsen, Knight, & Fink, 2004, pp. 242–248). Every class gets to make this decision, and sometimes it varies greatly. Now, I do set boundaries: Individual and team percentages must fall between 20% and 80%, and the total for both must equal 100%. This prevents a class from under- or overvaluing one of the two components. One might think the class would often shoot for a 50/50 split, but I find this rare. Classes on average tend to put more value on the team score and less on individual scores. With classes tending to favor higher team grade weights over that of individual grades, the groups tend to institute an unspoken commitment to the success of the team from the beginning of the course.

While the RAP may look similar across classes in any discipline, application activities are unique to the content of a course and are the most difficult part of TBL to develop. Therefore, I offer the following brief descriptions of application activities I have developed that align with the chapters and sequence of our textbook.

To Be (Art) or Not to Be (Art), That Is the Question

This group activity aligns with the first chapter in the textbook, which covers the general nature of art and performing art. It discusses the purpose of art, the qualities that all art share, and the politics of quantifying art.

In the first half of this activity, each team receives five pictures of what could be considered art. One is a red square, one is by Picasso, one is highly controversial, one is a random photograph, and one is a picture of one of my old shoes hanging from a power line. As a team, students must discuss and come to a consensus on which images are art and which are not, based on the politics, qualities, and purposes of art as described in their textbook.

The second half of the assignment focuses solely on the performing arts. I show the class five video clips of what could be considered performing art, and they are encouraged to take notes to aid them in their discussion. One piece of video is from a feature film, one is a man standing on stage picking his nose, one is street mime, one is modern dance, and one is a rock band. They return to their teams to discuss and quantify what they saw, again with the requirement that they come to consensus and be able to defend their decision on which of those five videos qualify as art. This assignment is an excellent team-building assignment for early in the semester; it allows students to get to know each other better and encourages all individuals to participate and assert their opinions while also listening to and respecting others.

Audience Etiquette

Chapter 2 deals with the role of the audience and the parameters of audience etiquette. Students attend three different performances over the course of the semester, and this assignment helps them come to an understanding of appropriate behavior as audience members without my having to lay down the law. Each team brainstorms suggestions for the rules of theatre audience etiquette at our university and must submit 15 possibilities. This allows students to discuss the chapter material while filtering it through their own experiences of being an audience member at movies or concerts.

Teams report the results of their make-a-list assignments, and as a class we discuss what they came up with and must narrow the list to 10 rules that everyone in class can agree on. I find the students are extremely tough and specific in their rule making. The final 10 rules of theatre etiquette then become exam material but are also the rules they are expected to follow while attending shows for the course. The ability to make the rules gives students a sense of ownership that impresses me: At performances, I often see students policing one another to take their feet off the seats or to put their cell phones away.

"You Can't Say That!" (Freedom of Speech)

This activity explores the role of criticism and free speech, aligning with Chapter 4 in our textbook. The first part of this assignment requires students to know the

First Amendment to the Constitution and what constitutes a reasonable exception to it. Teams must list and describe five exceptions to free speech and give three clear examples of each. This is just to prepare them for the second part of the assignment, in which they are given a set of 10 performance scenarios. They have to decide and justify which are and which are not supported by our First Amendment rights. This can lead to intense discussion as students struggle with personal morals, religious values, and various perspectives on censorship.

Directors Are Effective Storytellers

This quick team exercise deals with using body language to communicate to the audience. Each team is given a set of three related scenarios and is asked to communicate each of them without moving or talking. An example of a related scenario might be the first date, the first fight, and the breakup. The group uses body position and proximity to evoke relationships and conflict. Each team is allowed 10 minutes to craft its three scenarios and then present them to the class. Can the class comprehend the relationship and conflict? Are the participants effectively communicating the story with only their posture, position, and expression?

Mildred and Stella: An Odd Pair

This group assignment aligns with a chapter discussing theatrical designs for costumes, sets, and lights. I present the students with two characters: Mildred is an 85-year-old nurse who is very clean and orderly, while Stella is a 65-year-old volunteer at the humane society who doesn't own a vacuum and is known for her incoherent outbursts.

I ask each team member to go "shopping" on the Internet for clothing and accessories for each of their characters and bring six color pictures of their selections to class. During class, teams construct a garment for each individual from the pictures everyone brought. These outfits will be worn on stage at the same time, so it is important to show each woman's character with style and color. With some tough decisions and the help of a glue stick, this is a quick and easy assignment to illustrate character expression through costume design.

CREATIVE GROUP ACTIVITIES THAT DEVIATE FROM THE 4-S FORMAT

The 4-S format recommended by Michaelsen, Knight, and Fink (2004) is a useful and powerful design for group assignments, and most of my group work follows that format. Because I teach theatre, some activities I use require the messiness of complex creative output beyond a single specific choice. These are works in progress, and I may figure out a way to meld the creativity of these assignments with the power of the 4-S format, but for the sake of completeness, I include them here.

Ensemble: Theatre Is Teamwork

The chapter aligned with this assignment revolves around the nature of creativity, how it works, and what kinds of personality traits are required to work as a professional in a creative field. This activity takes only 15 minutes and is mostly used to give students the experience of being creative in a group. The assignment starts with each individual saying what was his or her most creative moment or the most creative object the student ever made. Many students firmly believe they are not creative in any way; for these students I attempt to find something in their skills or an interest that demonstrates their creativity. For example, some are surprised I firmly believe cooking to be a creative endeavor.

Having established a connection to their own creativity, the second half of this activity requires teams to create a piece of art as an ensemble. Each team is given a shoebox filled with "stuff"—broken crayons, scraps of colored paper, glue, scissors, fabric pieces, pages from old magazines, pipe cleaners, buttons, and other random objects. Each team member is asked to count off (1, 2, 3 and so on), and teams are told that once the exercise begins, they cannot talk.

Member #1 in the team begins creating a piece of art, but after 30 seconds must hand it to the next student (students are encouraged to think in 3-D and outside the box). Member #2 also has 30 seconds to add to the piece, and this continues until everyone in the group has had a turn. The group members struggle and quietly observe each other, and the art piece that emerges is usually strange and has little sense or order.

In round two of the activity, they can talk, share ideas, and help, but each team member can only touch the creation for 30 seconds. The art piece is handed from team member to team member in 30-second intervals until everyone in the group has worked on it, and the team has produced its piece of team creativity. This activity is a wonderful and experiential introduction to the ensemble nature of theatre.

It's Not Just a Conversation, It's a Comedy

This exercise aligns with the chapter on playwriting, script development, and acting—all of which are rooted in the understanding of character. Each team is given a manila folder containing a scenario and three pictures of characters. An example of a scenario might be speed dating, a nontraditional wedding, the security screening line at the airport, waiting in line at the supermarket, and so on. Examples of pictures include men and women of various ages and dress, aliens from outer space, chickens, whatever.

Each team is then asked to construct the characters in the scenario, giving their names, ages, economic classes, professions, their purposes in the scene, and their personal desires. Having created their characters, teams must write 45 lines of comedic dialogue for their scenarios using these characters. At the end of the assignment, each team reads its scenes to the class, giving students an excellent and enjoyable warm-up to acting and public speaking.

The Final Project: Production Team

The purpose of the Production Team assignment is for students to experience a microcosm of the theatre world and think critically about and use what they have learned over the course of the semester in a hands-on, mini production of their own. Work on the final project begins just before the midterm with six in-class rehearsals and the last three class periods solely devoted to this assignment. The final productions are expected to be formal and professional and presented during finals week.

Teams choose a 10-minute acting scene from one of the four assigned plays we read and discussed in class. After choosing a play and scene, the team then assigns the following roles among its members: director, actors, scenic designers, costume designers, and publicity staff. Every scene must have at least two actors. Some groups may choose to have more actors to decrease the number of lines any one team member needs to memorize. Teams cannot succeed with this project unless they collaborate. All members must prepare for and attend all rehearsals, read the entire play, and understand its theme and the playwright's intentions. Each member researches material for his or her assigned role and applies the knowledge and terminology covered in this course.

Each team member is responsible for his or her own materials and paperwork, and not everyone in the group necessarily receives the same grade. Successfully completing this project requires individual and team effort. The assessment of this assignment is based on effort, quality of production, completing the requirements of one's role, and peer evaluation. The requirements of the roles are the following.

Directors are responsible for arriving on time and being prepared for every rehearsal as well as arranging/running rehearsals and recording what transpires in a director's log. Directors' log entries must record

1. Goals for the rehearsal
2. Attendance and punctuality
3. Discoveries and accomplishments
4. Assignments for the next rehearsal, including but not limited to the areas or pages the actors are struggling with

Director's responsibilities also include directing stage movement of the actors, assisting actors in memorization of lines, developing characters, and coaching the actors by giving them suggestions, ideas, and motivations. During the final presentation, the director introduces the scene by reading the director's notes prepared for the program and introducing the production team.

Actors and actresses are responsible for reading and understanding the entire play, writing an analysis of their character (who the character is, how he or she fits into the play, the significance of the scene and its contribution to the play), memorizing lines assigned by the director, staying open to suggestion, and arriving on time and prepared for every rehearsal.

Actors must prepare their own bios for the program and provide it to the publicity people in a timely manner, as well as keep a detailed rehearsal journal that must record

1. What happened in rehearsal
2. What seemed to go well
3. What did not go well
4. Plans for improvement
5. Director's homework assignment for the next rehearsal

Scenic designers are responsible for creating unrealized set designs based on the discussion and visions of their team. They do not build actual sets but draw a bird's-eye view of the furniture, walls, doors, windows, and so forth, on the set, as well as a scenic rendering to the best of their ability with paint, markers, or color pencils depicting what the stage looks like for the audience. The scenic rendering must be in color and illustrate the colors/patterns/sizes of anything onstage.

Scenic designers must write their own bios for the program and provide it to the publicity people in a timely manner, arrive on time and prepared for every rehearsal, and keep a detailed journal that records

1. Research sources and a bibliography
2. Fifteen appropriate images of research

Costume designers are responsible for creating unrealized costume designs. They do not construct costumes but instead must render costumes for four characters in the play to the best of their ability with paint, markers, or color pencils, depicting what the costumes should look like. These renderings should be drawn in color and should include fabric swatches.

Costume designers must write their own bios for the program and provide it to the publicity people in a timely manner, arrive on time and prepared for every rehearsal, and keep a detailed journal that records

1. Research sources and a bibliography
2. Fifteen appropriate images of research

Publicity people are responsible for exploring and creating marketing strategies. They must write a radio commercial and create an advertising poster with color graphics and pertinent ticket sales information (where the play is, the cost of tickets, and how to purchase them). They must also create a play program for the class, including each team member's bio, his or her role in the production, and director's notes. Publicity people must write their own bios for the program, arrive on time and prepared for every rehearsal, and keep a detailed journal that records

1. Research sources and a bibliography
2. Fifteen appropriate images of research

CHALLENGES AND BENEFITS OF IMPLEMENTING TBL IN MY THEATRE CLASSROOM

Implementing TBL is a creative process, so in some ways it was perfect for me, but I did face several challenges. The first challenge was being scheduled to teach in a small room where 40 people could easily sit at tables and only look forward. Turning chairs to face one another in circles, however, was quite difficult and made it hard for me to maneuver around the groups while they were working. You can imagine the difficulty groups had trying to actually rehearse in that cramped space, so I made use of rooms in the library and even lawns outside. Bolted-down chairs or auditorium-style seating are challenges that can be overcome, but even a cavernously too-large classroom is better than being cramped in too small a space.

A classic complaint about group work is the difficulty students have finding time to get together to work outside class. Therefore, all teamwork in my class happens during class time: I schedule six days for in-class meetings and rehearsals for the final Production Team assignment. I have found that more than six days leads to misuse of class time, and fewer leads to panic and unpreparedness. Having said all that, I am fully aware that teams often decide to get together outside class, particularly to work on the final. I believe this stems from lack of time and end-of-semester anxiety. Students lack time because our last class period is on a Friday, and the final period tends to fall on Wednesday or Thursday, which leaves five to six days that the group does not meet. I find that often teams do get together during this time to add final touches and build their confidence.

Another challenge is management of paperwork and grades because TBL does require good organization and planning. Another TBL instructor shared his folder set-ups, grades sheets, and such with me, which not only saved me a load of time but more importantly showed me some excellent ways of staying efficient and organized. In the beginning, developing a system that works for you is important.

I consider the challenges small when compared to the advantages of teaching in the TBL style. TBL clearly helps students think critically and participate in theatre as an art form, but one of the main reasons I fell in love with TBL in teaching Discovering Theatre is the extent to which it develops life skills in my students that all employers find desirable, regardless of occupation. These skills include professionalism in communication and having a mature perspective on responsibility and accountability. Teaching with TBL allows students to practice these skills with a variety of individuals without the specific intent to develop them further, while naturally engaging in a common endeavor with their peers.

Practicing Professionalism and Communication Skills

Part of building professionalism in the team environment is learning to communicate and work with individuals who are different from the majority, including international, nontraditional, and developmentally or physically challenged students. The students learn to work in diversified groups with individuals of different races, nationalities, classes, age groups, and needs. Students will face this diversity in the real world when they graduate, and this is an excellent way for them to practice professionalism and build new communication skills.

There will always be students who can easily communicate their ideas to those around them and in group settings. These students tend to overpower their soft-spoken counterparts. I have observed that in the safe team environment created by TBL, even the shiest of students learns to speak up, and more aggressive students give them room to do so. I have witnessed on multiple occasions more introverted students taking the leap and volunteering to be an actor in theatre scenes. Furthermore, I have had several students tell me they do not speak to their peers in other classes and often isolate themselves. Over the first weeks in my TBL class, I see students like this open themselves to others and relax some of their personal boundaries.

Holding Oneself and One's Peers Accountable

Students often begin the semester worried about having to carry the deadweight of other students or suffer the consequences to their own grade. As the course unfolds, however, students develop a sense of ownership of their team's success, not just their own personal achievement. They read the material and come to class prepared, not because I ask them to but rather because they don't want to let their team down. They don't want to be seen as the individual dragging the team score down, and they are fully aware that every other member of the team will be required to evaluate his or her teammates' preparedness, contribution, and flexibility, which often leads some students to take more responsibility and be more careful with their time management.

I find some students struggle to evaluate their peers; they want to take the easy route and give everyone the same score. Therefore, I often contextualize the exercise using a real-world scenario: "You are the boss and, of course, you enjoy your team. But someone must be laid off because of budget cuts, so I will need you to fairly evaluate and rank everyone on your team." I do not allow my students to give any two teammates the same peer evaluation score—they must differentiate. For example:

John, 16; Amy, 19; Greg, 18; and Cindy, 14. This forces them to evaluate their peers' contribution, preparedness, and professionalism. With each numeric score the teammate is also asked to provide one sentence about an improvement the student can make and one sentence about what the student is excelling at. For example, a common improvement is "come more prepared to class" or "speak out more; you have good ideas." I take the teammates' comments and anonymously type them up and hand them back to each individual. Receiving and giving peer evaluation information give students important lessons in the professional experience of criticism and feedback.

With the TBL approach, I find students are more dynamically invested and connected to the material. Team assignments allow our reading materials and lectures to become relatable, shared experiences in critical thinking. They invest in themselves and their teams. They cultivate new relationships and ways to communicate. Every individual in the room engages in the material rather than passively watching it on a video screen. TBL allows larger general education classes to mimic the intimate environment of theatre artists, allowing them to create, evaluate, and think critically about theatre as an art form. Hopefully this cultivates an understanding, an appreciation, and a future patron of the performing arts while helping students develop much needed life skills.

FINAL COMMENTS

TBL has made a huge difference to my students and to me. They are more prepared, they retain the material better, and their attitudes are more enjoyable. They expect more out of themselves and each other. In addition, because I'm speaking with groups of seven or eight rather than a class of 40, the interactive and challenging group assignments and the intimate atmosphere of teams allow me to have more personalized time with students. As a result, TBL has changed the way I relate to my students and the way they relate to the performing arts. All of these things make teaching a joy.

NOTE

1. In the performing arts, *theatre* is considered the art, and *theater* is considered the public space or structure (e.g., a theater building).

REFERENCE

Michaelsen, L. K., Knight, A. B., and Fink, L. D. (2004). *Team-based learning: A transformative use of small groups in college teaching.* Sterling, VA: Stylus.

CHAPTER 18

I Don't Dare Teach With Inquiry-Based Teaching Methods When I Have State Testing Breathing Down My Neck

Adapting Team-Based Learning to a Seventh-Grade Life Science Classroom

Scott Kubista-Hovis

Kubista-Hovis is a pioneer as the first in the Team Based Leaning community to adapt team-based learning for a middle school classroom. In this chapter he paints an encouraging picture of how he was able to implement TBL in a predefined life science curriculum and finish the year with his students outscoring the others in life science classes at his school on standardized final exams. Readers from any discipline can benefit from this chapter as Kubista-Hovis walks us through the details of his implementation of TBL in a step-by-step manner, clearly showing us—and not just telling us—what his students experience.

Seventh graders can be merciless, but put 35 seventh graders together for 90 minutes and you have a recipe for disaster. During the six years I taught at a public middle school in northern Virginia, this was exactly what I was faced with day in and day out. The big question for my peers and I was how to ensure that 35 seventh graders were on task for 90 minutes every other day. In addition to this, I had to balance the demands of administrators who were breathing down my neck to make sure my students excelled on the Virginia State Standards of Learning tests. This was on top of my own personal obsession to ensure that whatever methods I chose were fun for me and my students, and developed their higher-order thinking skills.

In the first three years of teaching, relevance was my key focus. I tried to show students why the things they were learning were important and hoped they would want to learn. During this time I introduced a career speaker's bureau that recruited parents to speak about their professions. I helped pilot a leadership incubator that targeted at-risk youth, and I worked with my school system's business industry relations division to help my school form partnerships with various local corporations.

Though this provided meaning to my life science classes, it didn't help me develop a philosophical framework to structure my overarching curriculum. In essence, I had a substantial amount of relevant content and connections to bring the material to life, but my students didn't stay awake at night anxious about what the next big scientific breakthrough would be. Instead, students were used to teachers' engaging them through fun and games, providing little substance.

My question was how can I make my class fun and engaging while ensuring that each and every one of my students excels academically? During my second and third year of teaching, I did extensive research to find the answer. I routinely raided my school system's educational library to pick the brain of the librarian. During this time I discovered the National Science Teacher Association's book *Start With a Story*, which highlighted great teaching techniques. These techniques ranged from simple to complex, but the solutions revolved around some variation of problem-based learning. I'm a fan of problem-based learning; I think it does a great job engaging students. But there are many problems with it that need to be considered when faced with teaching students who need to learn a large amount of information and facts they will be tested on during their annual state testing regimen. Unexpectedly, one variation of problem-based learning mentioned in the book showed promise: a teaching technique called team-based learning (TBL). The authors of the chapter described how a teacher could require students to preread articles, individually and collaboratively test students on their comprehension of this basic material, and then spend most of class time having students apply the information in real-world team activities. After reading the chapter I was so excited, my heart sped up. I reread the chapter and was convinced it had merit. I found more information about the strategy via the Web.

The TBL website had a variety of videos showing how the process worked (see www.teambasedlearning.org). After reviewing the website, I decided to order *Team-Based Learning: A Transformative Use of Small Groups in College Teaching* (Michaelsen, Knight, & Fink, 2004). The book was by far the best educational book I had read. It briefly described how the process worked and why, but more importantly it walked me through step by step on how to implement TBL in my own classroom (see Chapter 1 for more details). From there, I decided to experiment. First I tried a team project that incorporated TBL's 4-S model (see Chapter 1); the team project I attempted required students to take on the role of a physician. We had already covered basic cell biology, but I wanted to see if the students really grasped what the facts meant. Their first team assignment was to examine some X-rays and patient evaluations and try to determine what was wrong with the patient. Prior to the activity, we quickly covered how to read basic doctor exam results. Since we had studied cells, I told the class the culprit was a type of bacteria. Each team was given three different cards, each with a picture of a single bacteria and its name. The students' job was to identify which of the three bacterial candidates was the problem and provide three pieces of information that supported their selection.

I was amazed at the success of this activity from the beginning. Gifted and talented and special needs students loved it. They were actively interacting with each other and looking up details about each of the three bacteria in their textbook, accompanying reading material, and various preselected websites. After my success with this activity, I was sold on the approach. I started to try other sections of the TBL process one after another, and I found it worked. Not only did my students and I more thoroughly enjoy learning, but the students were excelling academically compared to previous years. The second year after implementing TBL, my average at-risk student test score had risen by two letter grades. The environment changed from grade-focused to an environment where students wanted to learn. I would routinely hear them talk about the activities they had just completed as they were leaving the classroom. Students were so energized by the process that I had difficulty stopping them from talking about the activities and answers with classes that had yet to walk through my door. I admit this was not a terrible problem to have, yet it still represented just one of the problems I faced when initially implementing TBL. Later in this chapter, I address how I attempted to resolve this and other problems.

ADAPTING TBL TO A SEVENTH GRADE
PUBLIC SCHOOL CLASSROOM

Now that I've talked about what attracted me to TBL, let's talk about how I adapted it to a seventh grade population. The first thing I need to establish is that even though I worked in one of the wealthiest counties in the nation (as of 2010), it was so large there were schools that served extremely impoverished neighborhoods and other schools that served primarily affluent clientele. My school served a middle-of-the-road, not too rich, not too poor population. But I still had outliers: Each year at least one or two of my students lived out of their parent's car. In the same classroom, I would also have other students who were the son or daughter of an ambassador; but these were the exceptions not the rule. My school was housed in a 30-year-old building that had just gone through a major two-year renovation. Being one of three technology hubs in our school system, we had an almost unlimited amount of technology available. My school was one of three 7th–12th grade schools in the county and averaged 400 students per grade per year on the middle school side. The school was also on a rotating block schedule, which meant I would see the same students every other day for 90 minutes at a time. My school system had a predefined science curriculum I was required to teach. I had a set of four lab books with predefined life science labs running the entire length of the curriculum. I taught these required labs while providing context and additional supplemental material as needed. Fortunately, these externally imposed requirements proved perfect for TBL in that I had time to prep an experiment, do the experiment collaboratively, incorporate predefined labs, and then have individual students and the class as a whole reflect on what the results meant.

This being said, I was left with the challenge of implementing TBL throughout my life science courses while meeting the unique curricular and contextual demands of my situation. My solution was to start small, just like the physician's activity I described earlier. I tried one thing, saw what worked and what didn't work, then tweaked it and tried again. I also made sure to tell students what I was doing. The first year I tried TBL, I graded as I would normally. But the second year, when I adapted my entire curriculum to a TBL format, I graded fairly leniently. Halfway through the second year, I felt confident in my abilities. I had a canned conversation ready and available when parents would ask me what I was doing in my classroom. They usually asked one of two questions: How are you grading my son or daughter? or Why is it my child can't stop ranting and raving about your class?

To the first question, I responded 10:40:50. Ten percent of the students' grade is based on peer grading, 40% is based on homework and in-class assignments, and 50% is based on tests and quizzes. Inevitably some parents would ask what type of assignments made up each segment of grades, and I would walk them through the structure of the class and the graded activities. For the second question, all I could say was that Johnny or Kate provides great insight and passion and is a tremendous asset to his or her team. After answering question number two, most parents would usually look at me in disbelief and walk away either in a state of happiness, confusion, or disbelief.

Before I began integrating TBL into my curriculum, I sat down with my immediate supervisor and told him what I was planning to do. At first he asked many questions to which I openly admitted I didn't have the answers. But once he sat through a few classes and was able to see how it worked, he slowly started to warm up to what I was doing. My test score results were what really won him over. My school used standardized final exams for all subjects. At the end of the year, my scores were the highest of all the scores of the seventh grade life science teachers by large margins. I also meticulously went through the eighth grade science state test scores and compared them with my honors, regular, and special education students; while it wasn't as clear a victory, the pattern was there.

After four years of using TBL, I present in the next section some best practices I've found worked well in my seventh grade classroom.

PRIOR TO THE FIRST DAY OF THE UNIT

Take a unit and break it apart into five or so small chunks. The easiest way I did this was to group similar labs, which resulted in around three labs per chunk. For each chunk, identify the exact state test questions that correspond to the segment. Use these questions to create a 10-question Readiness Assurance Test (RAT; see Chapter 1 of this volume) for each chunk. The goal of this RAT (which I initially called a *prequiz* and later called a *reading quiz*) is to cover the core concepts of a single chunk.

Identify three to four prereadings per chunk, which can come from the textbook, newspapers, magazines, or online, but the main requirement is the articles need to clearly highlight the major ideas on the reading quiz. Create reading guides for each set of prereadings. For my honors students this took the form of focus questions; for my special needs students I provided them with a detailed notes page with multiple fill-in-the-blank spaces, analogies, and visualizations of the key concepts. Students were provided with the reading guides at the same time they were given the prereadings.

ON THE FIRST DAY OF THE UNIT

Students walk in and take a seat. Once the bell rings, they know they need to have their materials placed under their desks and pencils out. I would hand out what I called a *prequiz*, a term that caused problems because several parents and administrators said, "If it's a prequiz, it shouldn't count toward their grade." My initial response was to say that students had actually had an opportunity to do the prereadings before coming to class. But ultimately I found the easier solution was to change the name to reading quiz.

After all the students in a group have handed in their individual quizzes, I handed out group IF-AT (scratch-off) answer sheets along with a penny for scratching. They worked in their group of four to complete their team test, which was exactly the same as the individual test, but as teams, students could discuss their answers before scratching off their choice. During this team quiz, I let students hold on to their copy of the individual quiz so they could see their previous answers.

One modification I made was that students had to get 80% on their individual quiz to get the team's score. If students got 73% on their individual quiz, I doubled their individual score in the grade book. Whereas if students got 83%, their team score was added to their individual score. Ninety-nine percent of the time the team score was higher than the individual score. On the rare occasion where this wasn't the case, I doubled the individual score. If this was a routine occurrence, I would attempt to make future reading quizzes more challenging for that specific class.

AFTER THE READING QUIZ, THREE LABS BACK TO BACK

At this point students had done the prereadings before class, they'd taken their individual quiz, and they'd retaken the quiz with their team. Once the team quiz was completed, TBL methodology included a TBL activity. Instead, I interjected three county-required labs back to back. Even before the three labs, I started off with vocabulary and moved on to an introductory activity to capture their interest. These activities built on the reading quiz concepts. Then students completed one lab, and individually and collaboratively reported on this lab. Students repeated this process two more times for the two remaining labs, and finally we moved on to a TBL activity.

THE REAL-WORLD TEAM ACTIVITY

The most important word of advice I can give about the TBL activity is to follow Michaelsen, Knight, and Fink's (2004) 4-Ss to a tee. I have found through trial and error that when I retrofitted everything according to this 4-S framework, I was much more effective at teaching and engaging my students. This is not to say you can't have fun when designing your class activities. Instead, I saw it more as a challenge to ensure that activities were different enough to be interesting but similar enough to allow students to find their comfort levels. Another benefit of using the 4-S framework repeatedly was that students understood how activities were structured, which allowed them to focus less on the structure and more on expanding their skills and knowledge base.

I have found that four to five students is the ideal number for middle school teams; groups of five to seven typically recommended by college-level TBL instructors proved to be too large. Middle school groups of six to seven dramatically decreased group productivity because of limited group accountability and students' short attention spans.

My adaptation of an activity called "Oh Deer" to the TBL format illustrates how one can leverage existing instructional materials and structure the students' experience of them in keeping with TBL principles. This activity comes directly from Project Wild by the Council for Environmental Education (see www.projectwild.org). In the "Oh Deer" activity, a student's goal is to understand how fluctuations in food, water, and shelter affect the survival of a deer. Briefly, some students take the role of the deer, and others are food, water, and shelter. Starting out, one fourth of the population is deer and three fourths are food, water, or shelter. The deer stand on one side of a field or room, while the rest of the students stand on the other side. At first the students playing food, water, and shelter are allowed to randomly pick which one they want to be. Then on the count of three, they indicate with hand gestures which of the three resources they represent. At the same time, the deer randomly choose a resource they are interested in obtaining. The only difference is that if the deer don't obtain their chosen resource, they die and get recycled into resources for other deer. If they do find resources, the resources get turned into deer for the next round. The deer attempt to pair up with a student who is pretending to be food, water, or shelter.

After the first few rounds, there are lots of deer and few resources, which is where it gets interesting. After the first few rounds the resources become rare, and deer are not able to match up as easily with their required resource and more and more deer die. Later in the game, resources are told there is a drought and no one can be water, which results in the death of many deer. Ultimately, this causes huge fluctuations in the deer population. This is a typical game you might already be playing with your students; the only difference is that I retrofitted it to match the TBL activity format. Before the game, teams are given a set of questions to focus on during the game. After every round, the class counts the number of deer and plots the change in their population.

After the activity, teams are given the role of forest ranger and have to decide if they should allow hunting in a national forest. Teams can choose to not allow hunting at all, allow hunting during limited periods, or allow a select number of deer to be hunted each year. In addition to their choice, they need to come up with their team's top three reasons for their choice. After about 20 minutes of team discussion, teams are called on to simultaneously hold up in the air a small dry erase board upon which they've written their answer. This allows all the teams to see everyone's answer, and the class launches into a discussion of about 15 minutes on why the teams chose their answer.

WRAP UP ONE CHUNK AND BEGIN THE NEXT CHUNK

Throughout this entire process, students have an expansive outline they fill in with reading quiz and lab concepts, and now they add the final details to this outline during this TBL activity. The outline started out with fill-in-the-blank, visual descriptions, and analogy questions, along with compare and contrast, short answer, and essay.

Students were told the entire reading quiz for this chunk of content would come directly from this outline. In the last 20 minutes of a class period, students are allowed to fill in any holes in their outline as a team and then ask me any questions they have about the material. The next class period, students take an individual quiz that comes directly from their outline.

REPEAT, REPEAT, THEN TAKE A TEST

Students repeat this cycle five times for every unit. After finishing the fifth unit, students have five outlines to use for some type of test preparation during class. One of my favorite activities is to have students write test questions. Each team is assigned different topics to write about. All team members get one bonus point for every question that is selected to be on the test, with each class contributing an equal number of questions to the test. All test questions are typed up and distributed to students. Depending on whether I feel they need more time to review, we either play a review game or take the test during the next class. (Remember, students had my class every other day.)

QUARTERLY TEAM GRADING

Another major component of TBL is peer evaluations. While the idea of allowing seventh grade students to grade each other might sound scary, in reality it was one of the most important components of TBL. It ensures peer-to-peer accountability. At the beginning of the year, students were told their peers would be grading them, and this grade would be 10% of their quarter grade. Many TBL instructors recommend having students grade each other twice a year, once every semester. With seventh graders, I found their attention spans were much shorter than that of college students and thus needed an opportunity to grade their peers quarterly. Not only was this effective in reminding them of the importance of working well with each other, it also fit perfectly with the quarterly grading system used by my school district.

I used a toned-down version of the peer grading form (see Appendix C in Michaelsen et al., 2004). Each team member was responsible for assigning 100 points and could give these points to anyone on their team except themselves. Students drew a three-column table on a sheet of paper. In the first column, they put their teammates' names, in the second column they put the total number of points out of 100 they wanted to give each team member, and in the third column they had to provide their justification for the number of points they gave their teammates. They had to give at least one team member an above average score and one team member a below average score. Each team then stapled all their sheets together and handed it directly to me. I compiled the total number of points for each student and entered it in the grade book. If any student's team score was below a certain threshold, the student knew he or she would be working alone in the next unit.

Based on experience I modified this process so that students could appeal their team score. If "Paul" got 40% on his team score, he could appeal it. I would review his team members' comments and ask him how he thought the unit had gone. Generally, I would interject some of his peer's comments to get his response. If the student seemed to have a strong case, I would go back to his or her team and ask some clarifying questions. Based on this discussion I would decide if the student's peer participation score would be completely waived from the records for this quarter. If the score was waived, the student knew if it happened again next quarter I would not be as lenient. In this situation, a student's grade would be determined by his or her quizzes, tests, and individual performance.

FORMING ORIGINAL TEAMS

Forming balanced teams was extremely important with TBL. I used the basic TBL approach but with a twist. The first day of class, while they were still in a haze of excitement, I had students line up by their favorite course, with English first, history second, science next, and math last. Students then counted off by eight and remained in these groups for the first unit. After the first unit, I assigned groups based on grades and personality types. I grouped students by grade point average, and then I randomly assigned the top students to different groups. I repeated the process as I went deeper and deeper down the list. Finally, I scanned the teams for personality conflicts and reassigned students accordingly. Typically I liked to have a high achiever and a low achiever as table buddies. This duo would be partners any time I had students participate in two-person activities. This same process would be repeated the second and third quarter. If I trusted my class, I typically let them self-select their groups during the fourth quarter, with the understanding that I could reassign individuals and groups for any reason and at any time.

REFORMING TEAMS

One year I had a student who was shunned by 90% of the class. This was because he would get angry and made inflammatory statements to his peers. This experience enabled me to perfect my technique, identifying what to do when teammates could not work well with each other.

To remedy the situation, I differentiated between a student who couldn't get along well with a team and a student who is disengaged from the team. For the first situation, I set team member expectations. They were allowed cooling-off periods where they worked with another team for a while. If it was a personality conflict, I used an activity called "Put Yourself in the Other Person's Shoes," in which students try to explain the situation from the other person's perspective. If the situation was excessive, I'd send the students one by one to the school counselor. All in all, this seemed to resolve 95% of the situations. If it didn't, a last resort was to reassign team members, but once again this was with the understanding that if their next team had problems with them as well, I'd impose much harsher consequences in response to their behavior.

KEEPING STUDENTS ON TRACK AND DEALING WITH NONPARTICIPATORY STUDENTS

I not only used quarterly peer feedback to gauge student participation, but I also had a comments box for students' anonymous complaints and compliments about their peers. If I received a complaint about a student, I usually started to focus more on that student during class. If it appeared there was some merit to the complaint, I called the student out on his or her behavior. Another way students were labeled nonparticipatory was when I directly observed excessive off-track behavior. With seventh graders, it is my belief that some off-track behavior is to be expected, especially if a large segment of the curriculum is structured to promote collaboration. To make sure students were productive I used three techniques. First I started every class by stating that day's class objectives. Second, at the beginning of the year, I meticulously held the students to a strict regimen. When I felt the ball was rolling, I gradually eased up. If the class or a group didn't achieve a class objective, I would apply some more pressure. Finally, if an individual or a part of a group didn't meet class objectives, I used individual team targets, which involved my breaking up the daily objectives into segmented objectives. If the individual or team couldn't meet the segmented objectives within a corresponding period of time, the individual(s) had to work on a silent alternate assignment alone in a corner of the room. After successfully completing this assignment, the student could come back and join his or her team. But if this happened two times in a unit, the student would work alone for the rest of the unit.

SHARING TBL WITH OTHER TEACHERS

Sharing TBL was quite easy; my students were my biggest advocates. They would tell teacher after teacher how much fun they had in my classroom. Next, I made sure to showcase my test scores with my peers and my administrators, and because my middle school test scores were some of the highest in the school, it was an easy sell. The biggest challenge was that teachers perceived TBL to be radically different from what they were currently doing. When my experienced peers would say, "Peer grading?" "Team quizzes?" and "Pretest?" I knew they were at risk of automatically shutting down. It was only through mentoring new teachers, forming a book reading group, and working with the administration to host information sessions that the format was able to gain any traction.

ADVICE TO K–12 EDUCATORS JUST STARTING TO EXPLORE THE POWER OF TBL

My biggest piece of advice is to start small. If this is your first year as a teacher, many of the things I've described will greatly improve your ability to focus and motivate your students. But because my first year of teaching was one of the worst experiences of my life, I recommend starting slow. Find an experienced teacher for a mentor, and do what that teacher does. When you feel somewhat comfortable, try incorporating some TBL activities. Remember, these can be exactly the same activities your peers are doing, all you need to do is figure out how you can reformat them to incorporate the 4-Ss. After you've got that down, try a reading quiz (individual and team RATs). I highly recommend that you talk with your administrator before you decide to count these toward students' grades. I find most administrators have no problem with reading quizzes, but when you start to talk about entering them in the grade book, be prepared to give a little. Just realize that the closer you get to the TBL ideal, the more you can push students to take ownership of their own learning and move away from force-feeding them information.

I'd recommend having a canned script you can repeat over and over again to parents. If you decide to go all out, or if some of the ideas run strongly counter to those of your school, please use your best professional judgment and adapt as much as you can while trying to remain true to the process. All in all, I guarantee that the more you implement TBL techniques in your K–12 classroom, the more fun you and your students will have, and students will be more engaged with the content and not with the grades. Ultimately, this translates into your students' acing your state's standardized tests.

REFERENCES

Michaelsen, L. K., Knight, A. B., & Fink, L. D. (2004). *Team-Based Learning: A transformative use of small groups in higher education*. Sterling, VA: Stylus.

Herreid, C. F. (2007). *Start with a story: The case study method of teaching college science*. Arlington, VA: National Science Teachers Association Press.

Contributors

ABOUT THE EDITORS

Michael Sweet is Director of Instructional Development in the Center for Teaching and Learning at the University of Texas at Austin. Michael earned a PhD in Educational Psychology from the University of Texas at Austin and an MA in Rhetoric and Communication from the University of California, Davis. Michael has worked in postsecondary instructional development since 1995, and has helped teachers in every discipline and class size fine-tune or completely reinvent their teaching. He has published and presented widely on Team-Based Learning and critical thinking, and is 2011–2013 president of the international Team-Based Learning Collaborative.

Larry K. Michaelsen is David Ross Boyd Professor Emeritus at the University of Oklahoma, a professor of management at the University of Central Missouri, a Carnegie Scholar, a three-time Fulbright Senior Scholar, and former editor of the *Journal of Management Education*. He earned his PhD in Organizational Psychology from The University of Michigan and has received numerous college, university, and national awards for his outstanding teaching and for his pioneering work in two areas. One is the development of Team-Based Learning. The other is an Integrative Business Experience program that links student learning in three core business courses to their experience in creating and a start-up business financed by real-money bank loan and then executing a hands-on community service project that is funded by the profits of the start-up business.

ABOUT THE CONTRIBUTORS

Edna C. Alfaro, PhD, is an assistant professor in the Department of Psychology and Anthropology at University of Texas–Pan American. She received her doctorate in family and human development from Arizona State University, obtained a Master's in human development and family studies from the University of Illinois at Urbana-Champaign, and completed her undergraduate studies in psychology at St. Mary's University in San Antonio. Edna utilizes the ecological and academic resilience frameworks to better understand the processes by which environmental, cultural, and familial factors interact with one another and impact Latino adolescents' academic outcomes.

Ronnie Chamberlain is an assistant professor in the Department of Theatre and Dance at the University of Central Missouri. Mrs. Chamberlain teaches courses in costume Design and Technology, Stage Makeup, Design Fundamentals, and a general education course called Discovering Theatre. Discovering Theatre is part of the Humanities and Fine Arts requirement at UCM and is taught using Team-Based Learning. This is her fourth year using Team-Based Learning in the classroom and finds it complements the creative process of theater. She is the resident costume/makeup faculty for the Department of Theatre and Dance, designing six main stage productions a year. Her recent theatrical designs include *The Three Musketeers*, *Electra*, *Into the Woods*, *Oklahoma*, and *The Birds*. Mrs. Chamberlain received her Master of Fine Arts from The University of Alabama.

Kristin L. Croyle is the vice provost for undergraduate education at the University of Texas-Pan American near the U.S.–Mexico border. In this capacity, she oversees undergraduate programming and retention and supports development of instructional strategies and student services that support student and faculty success, particularly in working with Mexican American students. She previously served as interim dean and assistant dean in the College of Social and Behavioral Sciences and is a tenured faculty member in the psychology program. She is a licensed clinical psychologist and her research interests focus on emotion regulation and self-harm. Kristin earned a BS in psychology from the University of Utah and an MA and PhD in clinical psychology from the University of Montana, and completed a postdoctoral fellowship in clinical neuropsychology from the University of Washington School of Medicine.

Herbert L. Coleman, PhD is an adjunct professor of psychology and the director of Instructional Computing and Technology at Austin Community College in Austin, Texas. He received his doctoral degree from the University of Texas College of Education Instructional Technology program. His research at the University of Texas was centered on gender role personality traits and computer use. He has taught psychology at Austin Community College for 20 years, including courses in general psychology, human growth and development, and human sexuality. In his role as Director of Instructional Computing and Technology, he assists faculty in obtaining, learning, and using technology to enhance instruction. He has trained faculty in using technology such as Skype, Twitter, YouTube, social networking, lecture capture, Team-Based

Learning, and iPads in instruction. As a faculty member, Dr. Coleman uses technology from clickers and podcasts to thin clients and social networking in his classrooms. He has taught the last four years using Team-Based Learning in all of his courses.

Joël Dubois is an associate professor in the Department of Humanities and Religious Studies at California State University, Sacramento, where he teaches courses on Asian religions and cultures. He earned his doctoral degree in comparative religion from the Harvard Divinity School; formative training at the Derek Bok Center for Teaching and Learning during this time set the stage for his later pursuit of Team-Based Learning. His research and publications have focused primarily on Hindu traditions, including a book on Vedanta, *Hidden Lives of Brahman*, forthcoming from SUNY Press, and an online multimedia archive documenting the rich history of the South Indian temple town where he did most of his research for the book. He is currently Chair of the Advisory Committee for his campus's Center for Teaching and Learning, through which he serves as both a faculty mentor and workshop facilitator.

Molly Espey is a professor in the John. E. Walker Department of Economics at Clemson University, where she teaches courses in microeconomic theory, environmental economics, and natural resource economics. In addition to research in these areas of economics, Molly has also published articles on Team-Based Learning and classroom design and student attitudes toward working with peers. Prior to coming to Clemson, she taught at the University of Nevada, Reno and earned her PhD at the University of California, Davis.

Roxanne Harde is an associate professor of English and a McCalla University Professor at the University of Alberta, Augustana where she teaches courses in American literature and culture, first-year English surveys, and special topics courses, including feminist literary theory, children's literature, and Ecofeminist literature and theory. Roxanne founded the Augustana Writing Centre and uses innovative pedagogies there and in her classroom, including Team-Based Learning. Before coming to the University of Alberta, Roxanne earned her doctorate at Queen's University, Kingston, Ontario, and held a postdoctoral fellowship at Cornell. Her disciplinary research focuses on American literature and culture. She has recently published *Reading the Boss: Interdisciplinary Approaches to the Works of Bruce Springsteen*, and her essays have appeared in several journals, including *The Lion and the Unicorn, Christianity and Literature, Legacy, Jeunesse, Critique, Feminist Theology*, and *Mosaic*, and several edited collections, including *Enterprising Youth, To See the Wizard*, and *Styling Texts*. Roxanne also serves her faculty as Associate Dean, Research, and is an incoming editor of *Bookbird: A Journal of International Children's Literature*.

Erica Hunter earned her PhD in sociology from the University at Albany, SUNY in 2011 where she is an instructor. Her teaching and research interests include marriage as institution, relationship processes, the social organization of sexualities, and methodology. Her interests in adapting Team-Based Learning in 2008 stemmed from a desire to challenge her students and to create a more engaged classroom environment.

Scott Kubista-Hovis has served as an adult training and development consultant for a variety of public, private, and non-profit entities. His main interest is in helping people and organizations learn faster by leveraging Team-Based Learning or other advanced instructional approaches.

Karla Kubitz received her PhD in exercise science from Arizona State University. Her dissertation examined the effects of exercise training on EEG activity during stress and was awarded the *Outstanding Dissertation Award from Division 47 of the American Psychological Association* and the *NASPE Sport Psychology Academy Dissertation of the Year*. Dr. Kubitz is currently an associate professor of kinesiology at Towson University. She teaches classes in sport psychology, exercise psychology, applied sport psychology, and the psychology of sport injury. She has a strong interest in Team-Based Learning, is a member of the Team-Based Learning Collaborative, and has published a chapter on the topic in *Team-Based Learning for Health Professions Education* (2008). Her current research focuses on the psychophysiology of sport and exercise. She has published on the relationship between EEG and sport performance, on the effects of exercise training on EEG laterality, as well as on the effects of exercise on EEG activity and vigilance performance. She has been awarded summer research fellowships with the Army; NASA; and, most recently, the Navy. Dr. Kubitz is a fellow of the American College of Sports Medicine and a member of the North American Society for the Psychology of Sport and Physical Activity.

Derek R. Lane is an associate professor in the Department of Communication and former associate dean for Graduate Programs in Communication in the College of Communications and Information Studies at the University of Kentucky (2005–2009). Derek's research can be classified in the broad area of face-to-face and mediated message reception and processing to affect attitude and behavior change in instructional, organizational, and health contexts. In addition to research in these areas of communication research, Derek has also published articles on Team-Based Learning related to faculty facilitation skills and peer feedback. His research has been funded by the U.S. Department of Education, the National Institute of Drug Abuse, the National Institute of Mental Health, and the National Science Foundation. It has appeared in *Communication Monographs, Communication Education, Media Psychology, Communication Research Reports, Health Promotion Practice, American Journal of Communication,* the *Journal of Engineering Education* and the *Journal of Experimental Education.* He teaches graduate seminars in instructional communication, theory construction, advanced survey research methods, and interpersonal communication. Dr. Lane is an endowed professor in the UK College of Engineering and is the recipient of several prestigious teaching and research awards.

Jessica L. Lavariega Monforti is an associate professor of political science and senior faculty research associate at the Center for Survey Research at the University of Texas-Pan American. She specializes in public policy analysis, race and politics, and survey research. While much of her research focuses on the differential impact of public policy according to race, gender, and ethnicity, she is specifically interested in the political incorporation and representation of Latinos, immigrants, and women. Her latest research project is a survey of the political attitudes and behaviors of Latinos and other minority groups. Recent publications include articles in *Social Science Quarterly*, the *Social Science Journal*, *PS: Political Science & Politics*, the *Latino/a Research Review*, and the *Journal of Women, Politics & Policy*. She also edited a book with William E. Nelson, Jr. entitled *Black and Latino/a Politics: Issues in Political Development in the United States*. Dr. Lavariega Monforti has been a recipient of awards for her teaching and research.

Robin Lightner is codirector of the Learning and Teaching Center at Blue Ash College, University of Cincinnati. She teaches psychology, including introductory psychology, social psychology, personality, and research methods. She earned her PhD in psychology from the University of Kentucky. At UC she facilitates a number of faculty learning communities, offers a number of workshops for faculty, and consults faculty about teaching and classroom-based research. Her own research topics include faculty development, transfer of learning, and self-regulated learning. She serves a consultant-evaluator for the Higher Learning Commission. She has been inducted into her university's Academy of Fellows for Teaching and Learning and was awarded the Blue Ash College Distinguished Teaching Award.

Sarah J. Mahler is an associate professor of anthropology in the Department of Global & Sociocultural Studies at Florida International University in Miami. Her research and publications have focused primarily on Latin American and Caribbean migration to the United States and the development of transnational ties between migrants and their home communities. Recently, she has been shifting her focus to writing about the nature of culture by emphasizing how people acquire culture and how this understanding can shift our view of culture from what we have to what we do. This perspective along with some of its implications will be published as *Culture as Comfort* in 2012.

Adam J. McGlynn is an assistant professor of political science at East Stroudsburg University where he teaches courses in American Government, Public Policy, State and Local Government, and Political Behavior. He earned a BA in Political Science from SUNY-Plattsburgh and received his MA and PhD in Political Science from Stony Brook University. Prior to his appointment at East Stroudsburg University, he served as assistant professor of political science at The University of Texas-Pan American. His research interests focus on education policy, Latino/a political behavior, and urban government. He has recently published articles in the *American Journal of*

Political Science, PS: Political Science and Politics, State and Local Government Review, The Social Science Journal, and *Urban Education.*

Karen L. Milligan, PhD is an associate professor in the School of Education at Carson-Newman College in Jefferson City, Tennessee where she teaches courses in educational technology, elementary social studies methods, and secondary planning and classroom management. She began her teaching career as a special education and middle grades teacher in the public schools. After teaching for 14 years in K–12 schools, she earned a PhD in educational technology from the University of Tennessee. She is interested in supporting pre-service and current teachers at both the K–12 and university level in their quest to find new ways to integrate technology into teaching and learning. Past research has focused on analyzing teachers' decision-making process when integrating technology and adapting the Lesson Study Model of professional development for use with pre-service teachers. She has been using the Team-Based Learning model since 2008.

Sunay Palsole is the director of instructional support at the University of Texas at El Paso. A geophysicist by academic training, he has been involved in instructional technology for over 15 years. Sunay has taught courses in the Entering Student Program, Health Sciences, Sciences, and the School of Business. He adopted Team-Based Learning as a way to increase learning efficiency and student engagement in his classes—both traditional and face to face. His current work is focused on using Team-Based Learning strategies in science classes, mainly introductory courses in geology and geophysics.

Christine Reimers earned her PhD from the University of North Carolina in 1999 and has been a university teacher in settings ranging from large Research I institutions to small colleges, including international appointments in France and Japan, as well as institutions in multiple regions in the United States. Her 20 years of classroom experience, overlapping with 15 years in faculty development, have helped her build a thorough understanding of the strategies best suited for faculty advancement, faculty mentoring, leadership development, and effective student learning in higher education. After positions in faculty development at UNC-Chapel Hill and Indiana University, she went on to direct the Center for Effective Teaching and Learning at UT-El Paso for six years before serving as founding Executive Director of the NSF ADVANCE Center at Cornell University. She now serves as Special Assistant to the Provost for Faculty and Program Development at the University at Albany where she develops programs for faculty retention and leadership development, and facilitates the assessment of student learning outcomes. Christine has worked with faculty from all disciplines, presenting programs designed to help faculty from all ranks to reflect on and integrate the varied strands of their professional and personal lives, and to find a sense of community in their academic institutions.

Penne Restad is a distinguished senior lecturer in the Department of History, University of Texas at Austin. She holds a Master's in history, and a PhD in American studies. Most recently she received the Regents' Outstanding Teacher Award. In addition to research and teaching related to late 19th and early 20th century social history, she teaches an American history survey. This course, structured on Team-Based Learning, is being developed as part of the UT System's "Transforming Undergraduate Education Initiative." Based on this experience, she currently serves as facilitator for UT's Faculty Learning Circle for Team-Based Learning.

Bill Roberson earned his PhD from University of North Carolina at Chapel Hill in 1989 and has since been in pursuit of teaching excellence—for individual faculty members, for academic programs, for institutions, and for himself. He has worked as a faculty member, instructor or a faculty development professional at 11 different institutions of higher education. His primary area of interest is the design of courses, activities, and assignments that ensure intellectual engagement of students and the development of their ability to think critically. To do this, he draws on examples from science, humanities, social science, and professional fields, to show the transferability and universality of key cognitive structures and processes that shape learning and teaching. Foremost, he is an advocate for transforming the way we define and structure learning experiences for novices in our disciplines. His public workshops and seminars ask participants to assume the role of learners in unfamiliar contexts, and experience the excitement of challenges that foster an authentic engagement with new ideas. Bill's career in university faculty development programs includes earlier positions at UNC-Chapel Hill and Indiana University. More recently he served as Director of the Center for Effective Teaching and Learning at the University of Texas-El Paso, where he was also founding executive director of that university's division of Instructional Support Services for instructional technology, classroom design, digital media production and distance learning. He came to New York in 2006 to create the Institute for Teaching, Learning, and Academic Leadership at the University at Albany, State University of New York.

Bryan K. Robinson is an assistant professor of sociology and criminal justice at Russell Sage College in Troy, New York. He has a BA in philosophy and a MA in sociology from Auburn University and is currently completing his PhD in sociology at the State University of New York, Albany. Bryan has been using Team-Based Learning in his sociology classes for the past five years.

Jim Sibley is director of the Centre for Instructional Support at the Faculty of Applied Science at the University of British Columbia in Vancouver, Canada. The Centre for Instructional Support provides pedagogical and technology support to over 200 faculty in the 10 engineering programs, a School of Architecture, and a School of Nursing. As a faculty developer, he has led a seven-year implementation of Team-Based Learning in engineering and nursing at UBC with a focus on large classroom facilitation. At UBC, he has been a tireless advocate for Team-Based Learning, giving over 20 workshops to over 250 faculty at the university. Jim has over 28 years' experience in faculty support and training, facilitation, web design, and managing software development at UBC. He also has developed and led a new faculty campus orientations series, intensive course design seminars and series, and led the development of the *iPeer* online peer evaluation software (open source with over 7,000 downloads). He is an active member of the Team-Based Learning Collaborative serving on the board, membership committee, and web strategy committee (as a member of the web strategy committee he serves as the webmaster for www.team-basedlearning.org). He continues his work as a mentor in the Team-Based Learning Center's Train the Trainer program. He is an international Team-Based Learning consultant, having worked with schools in Australia, Korea, Pakistan, the United States, and Canada to develop Team-Based Learning programs.

Index

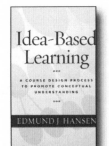

Idea-Based Learning
A Course Design Process to Promote Conceptual Understanding
Edmund J. Hansen

Hansen has the blueprint we all need to follow if we are to put together courses that will produce meaningful and long-lasting learning for our students."—*Terry Doyle is the Chief Instructor for Faculty Development, and Coordinator of the New Faculty Transition Program, Faculty Center for Teaching & Learning, Ferris State University*

Synthesizing the best current thinking about learning, course design, and promoting student achievement, this is a guide to developing college instruction that has clear purpose, is well integrated into the curriculum, and improves student learning in predictable and measurable ways.

The process involves developing a transparent course blueprint, focused on a limited number of key concepts and ideas, related tasks, and corresponding performance criteria; as well as on frequent practice opportunities, and early identification of potential learning barriers.

Idea-based Learning takes as its point of departure the big conceptual ideas of a discipline that give structure and unity to a course and even to the curriculum, as opposed to a focus on content that can lead to teaching sequences of loosely-related topics; and aligns with notions of student-centered and outcomes-based learning environments.

Adopting a backwards design model, it begins with three parallel processes: first, identifying the material that is crucial for conceptual understanding; second, articulating a clear rationale for how to choose learning outcomes based on student needs and intellectual readiness; and finally, aligning the learning outcomes with the instructional requirements of the authentic performance tasks.

Sty/us

22883 Quicksilver Drive
Sterling, VA 20166-2102   Subscribe to our e-mail alerts: www.Styluspub.com

Also available from Stylus

Team-Based Learning
A Transformative Use of Small Groups in College Teaching
Edited by Larry K. Michaelsen, Arletta Bauman Knight, and L. Dee Fink

This book is a complete guide to implementing TBL in a way that will promote the deep learning all teachers strive for. This is a teaching strategy that promotes critical thinking, collaboration, mastery of discipline knowledge, and the ability to apply it.

Part I covers the basics, beginning with an analysis of the relative merits and limitations of small groups and teams. It then sets out the processes, with much practical advice, for transforming small groups into cohesive teams, for creating effective assignments and thinking through the implications of team-based learning.

In Part II teachers from disciplines as varied as accounting, biology, business, ecology, chemistry, health education and law describe their use of team-based learning. They also demonstrate how this teaching strategy can be applied equally effectively in environments such as large classes, mixed traditional and on-line classes, and with highly diverse student populations.

Part III offers a synopsis of the major lessons to be learned from the experiences of the teachers who have used TBL, as described in Part II. For teachers contemplating the use of TBL, this section provides answers to key questions, e.g., whether to use team-based learning, what it takes to make it work effectively, and what benefits one can expect from it–for the teacher as well as for the learners.

Team-Based Learning for Health Professions Education
A Guide to Using Small Groups for Improving Learning
Edited by Larry K. Michaelsen, Dean X. Parmelee, Kathryn K. McMahon
and Ruth E. Levine
Foreword by Diane M. Billings

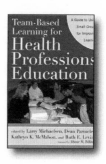

Education in the health professions is placing greater emphasis on "active" learning–learning that requires applying knowledge to authentic problems; and that teaches students to engage in the kind of collaboration that is expected in today's clinical practice.

Team-Based Learning (TBL) is a strategy that accomplishes these goals. It transforms passive, lecture-based coursework into an environment that promotes more self-directed learning and teamwork, and makes the classroom come "alive".

This book is an introduction to TBL for health profession educators. It outlines the theory, structure, and process of TBL, explains how TBL promotes problem solving and critical thinking skills, aligns with the goals of science and health courses, improves knowledge retention and application, and develops students as professional practitioners. The book provides readers with models and guidance on everything they need to know about team formation and maintenance; peer feedback and evaluation processes, and facilitation; and includes a directory of tools and resources.

The book includes chapters in which instructors describe how they apply TBL in their courses. The examples range across undergraduate science courses, basic and clinical sciences courses in medical, sports medicine and nursing education, residencies, and graduate nursing programs. The book concludes with a review and critique of the current scholarship on TBL in the health professions, and charts the needs for future research.